THE PLAIN MAN'S PATHWAYS TO HEAVEN

The Plain Man's Pathways to Heaven

Kinds of Christianity in Post-Reformation England, 1570–1640

CHRISTOPHER HAIGH

OXFORD
UNIVERSITY PRESS

OXFORD

UNIVERSITY PRESS

Great Clarendon Street, Oxford OX2 6DP

Oxford University Press is a department of the University of Oxford.
It furthers the University's objective of excellence in research, scholarship,
and education by publishing worldwide in

Oxford New York

Auckland Cape Town Dar es Salaam Hong Kong Karachi
Kuala Lumpur Madrid Melbourne Mexico City Nairobi
New Delhi Shanghai Taipei Toronto

With offices in

Argentina Austria Brazil Chile Czech Republic France Greece
Guatemala Hungary Italy Japan Poland Portugal Singapore
South Korea Switzerland Thailand Turkey Ukraine Vietnam

Oxford is a registered trade mark of Oxford University Press
in the UK and in certain other countries

Published in the United States
by Oxford University Press Inc., New York

British Library Cataloguing in Publication Data

Data available

Library of Congress Cataloging-in-Publication Data

Haigh, Christopher.
The plain man's pathways to heaven : kinds of Christianity in post-
Reformation England, 1570-1640 / Christopher Haigh.
p. cm.
Includes bibliographical references and index.
ISBN 978-0-19-921650-5 (alk. paper)
1. England—Church history—16th century. 2. England—Church
history—17th century. 3. England—Religious life and customs. I. Title.
BR756.H25 2007
274.2'06—dc22

2007028201

Typeset by Laserwords Private Limited, Chennai, India
Printed in Great Britain
on acid-free paper by
Biddles Ltd., King's Lynn, Norfolk

ISBN 978–0–19–921650–5

1 3 5 7 9 10 8 6 4 2

Preface

This is a book I have wanted to write for a very long time. I had been collecting archive material on parish religion and parish relationships off and on for twenty years, without a very clear idea of what it could lead to. And then the invitation to give the 2005 Wiles Lectures at Queen's University, Belfast, forced me to think about what it all might mean and how I could present it. There were to be four lectures—and I thought of the four characters in Arthur Dent's *The Plain Man's Pathway to Heaven* (1601). They gave me an organizing principle that, for good or ill, I have followed—with the addition of the Papist from George Gifford's *A Dialogue between a Papist and a Protestant* (1582). Evidence drawn from three national and twelve local archives is arranged around five stereotypical characters, so that the examples can illuminate the stereotypes and, I trust, the stereotypes illuminate the examples. The aim is to see how ordinary post-Reformation Christians thought about and practised their own religion, what they thought of the religion of others, and how they all got along with each other. At bottom, I suppose, the question is how much religion, and religious differences, mattered.

This is also the *kind* of book I have wanted to write for a very long time. For the first twenty-five years of my academic career I was embroiled in various controversies over the causes, nature, and consequences of Reformation (or Reformations) in England. It was my own fault, and I enjoyed it at the time. I didn't see myself as another Geoffrey Elton, but as I had been taught and much influenced by him it seemed obvious to tackle the job of writing as he did. And then Conrad Russell persuaded me that the horse I was still flogging was well and truly dead, and Patrick Collinson called me 'a middle-aged Turk': I realized I'd have to grow up. This is meant to be a grown-up book, a book focused firmly on the evidence, not on interpretations I wish to contest. Much of what I have to say here *is* controversial, and it relates to a number of current disputes, but I have approached them obliquely and without confrontation. I have not engaged directly with other interpretations, but left readers to situate my views and draw their conclusions—or not, as they wish.

I have also wanted to write a book that was archive-based and archive-driven. This book is packed with quotations from court books and visitation returns: I hope we hear the authentic, often earthy, voices of ordinary people talking about their religion and that of others. Of course, I know that churchwardens, witnesses, and scribes may not have recorded what was actually said. Of course, I know that I have chosen useful examples from the 700 and more court books consulted. I have not always explicitly stated an argument, but yes there is one, and my many quotations are cited to support it. But I have honestly tried to follow the

Eltonian precept: work through the archive, and then see what it means. I had done much of the research, collected many of the cases, before I ever thought of using the 'plain men', and the material was emphatically not selected to illustrate them—though I later found that it often did. The archives I have used are spread across southern and central England, not only because I could drive to them from Oxford, but mainly because I wanted to eschew the northern evidence I had often used before. It was said by some that my view of the Reformation was a product of the archives at Chester and York: well, not this time. I have not cited northern material even when it was apposite, except for one document concerning papists in York. I am grateful to the staffs of the local record offices I have worked at: Buckinghamshire, Essex, Gloucestershire, Hampshire, Leicestershire, Lichfield, Lincolnshire, Northamptonshire, Oxfordshire, Somerset, West Sussex, and Wiltshire. It will be obvious from the list of sources to whom I owe most.

I have chosen to show that evidence from across much of southern England shows some of the same things, and I have piled up examples from various jurisdictions. I have not done much to seek out the background to particular cases, even if (as I doubt) it could be done for more than a tiny number of them. This is a broad-brush approach, using what was to hand, and there are other ways of tackling religion and relationships. I might have done a series of local studies, and tried to establish the particular circumstances that produced parish conflict or cooperation. But then I would not have worked through so many archives, or found so many examples of the same sorts of things. Each case I cite, each quotation I use, was certainly the product of specific local situations and in itself was unique—but over so many cases, so many quotations, the biases are surely cancelled out, the oddities submerged in the general. This was the way I wanted to do it, and readers will see if it works.

I am grateful to the Wiles Trustees, and especially Ian Kershaw, for the invitation to give the lectures and sound advice on how to proceed. 'Write the book first,' Ian said, and I did (well, most of it). That invitation forced me to work out what to do with the material I had got, and prompted a final six-month blitz on additional archives. The Wiles Lectures are an excellent institution. Not only does one lecture to an attentive and responsive audience, but the Trustees ship in a band of friends and critics to discuss each lecture after dinner. Four successive evenings in May 2005 were among the most stimulating times of my academic life. It was like reading the reviews before finishing the book, and in some places the text has been changed to meet suggestions made then. I do not think I would have written Chapter 10 at all, nor the Conclusion as I have done, had I not been pressed at Queen's University to say what I thought about long-term change and the background to the Civil War. I tried to stay out of trouble, but my colleagues wouldn't let me. I am grateful to all those who joined me in Belfast and discussed the lectures, especially John Bossy, Eamon Duffy, Ian Green, Felicity Heal, Ian Kershaw, Chris Marsh, Peter Marshall, Anthony Milton, Bill Sheils, and Alex Walsham.

I thank the Governing Body of Christ Church, the Oxford History Faculty, and the Arts and Humanities Research Board (as it then was) for periods of leave. This book was possible only because these bodies gave me time for research and writing—and also because some record offices, notably Essex and Hampshire, open on Saturdays. The long early morning drives along the M40, M25, and A12 to Essex were tedious, but they were worth it. With me on Saturdays was my wife, Alison Wall, usually working on her JPs. But in those panic six months of final research before writing, she generously gave up her own research to help me out almost every day at Chelmsford, Northampton, and Taunton. Maddeningly, it was sometimes Alison who found the most interesting cases. I thank her for this support, and for her constant interest in what I was trying to achieve.

C.A.H.

Contents

List of Abbreviations   xi
Conventions   xii
    Introduction: The Plain Man in Characters and Court Books   1

I. 'THEOLOGUS, A DIVINE': THE PREACHER AND HIS PEOPLE

1. The Preacher and his People   17
2. Theologus: Pastor of a Flock   36

II. 'ASUNETUS, AN IGNORANT MAN': KNOWLEDGE AND NEGLECT

3. Asunetus: Ignorance is Bliss   59
4. Asunetus: Why All the Fuss?   79

III. 'PHILAGATHUS, AN HONEST MAN': THE PROFESSORS AND THE PROFANE

5. Philagathus: Godly Living   101
6. Philagathus: The Godly and the Rest   122

IV. 'ANTILEGON, A CAVILLER': LIBERTY AND LAUGHTER

7. Antilegon: Attitudes to Authority   145
8. Antilegon: Scoffing at the Sacred   165

V. POPERY AND OTHER ENEMIES

9. The Papist: Outside the Church, Inside the Community   183
10. Enemies of the Godly   202

Conclusion: Pathways to Heaven   218

Notes   229
List of Manuscript Sources   251
Index   255

List of Abbreviations

BL	British Library, London
BLO	Bodleian Library, Oxford
BRO	Buckinghamshire Record Office, Aylesbury
ERO	Essex Record Office, Chelmsford
GRO	Gloucestershire Record Office, Gloucester
HRO	Hampshire Record Office, Winchester
LA	Lincolnshire Archives, Lincoln
Leics. RO	Leicestershire Record Office, Wigston Magna
Lichfield RO	Lichfield Record Office, Lichfield
NRO	Northamptonshire Record Office, Northampton
ORO	Oxfordshire Record Office, Oxford
PMP	A. Dent, *The Plaine Mans Path-way to Heauen* (1601)
PRO	The National Archives (Public Record Office), Kew
SRO	Somerset Record Office, Taunton
WRO	Wiltshire and Swindon Record Office, Chippenham, formerly Trowbridge
WSRO	West Sussex Record Office, Chichester

Conventions

Dating is Old Style, taking the year to begin on 1 January.

In quotations, spelling and punctuation have been modernized and contractions silently expanded.; the spelling of book-titles has been modernized in the text, but is as in the originals in notes. Where proper names were given in variant forms, they have been standardized in a modern spelling.

Examples are usually given in chronological order, to show range over time. To show geographical range, place names are given with their county, archdeaconry, or diocese, using early modern boundaries. To avoid unnecessary repetition, if consecutive examples fall within the same county the county name is not repeated.

Introduction: The Plain Man in Characters and Court Books

The Plain Man's Pathway to Heaven was published in 1601 by Arthur Dent, who was then rector of South Shoebury on the Thames estuary. It was a lively dialogue between four characters, who discuss how to live on earth and how to get to heaven. What makes it striking is that it is a real, often acrimonious, debate, with the godly characters put on the spot—though, of course, Dent makes sure they win the arguments. It was an instant hit, and became one of the biggest sellers of the early seventeenth century. This popularity suggests it has something to tell us about the nature of English religion in the years after the Reformation. Arthur Dent was a godly preacher, with quite a reputation in Essex. His friend Ezekiel Culverwell described him as a minister 'whose diligence, yea extreme and unwearied pains in his ministry, publicly and privately, at home and abroad for four and twenty years at least, all our country can testify'. His parish seems to have been peaceful and well run, and some of his people left him generous bequests. He was also a highly successful author, and eight of his works were best-sellers or steady sellers. His first published work was *A Sermon of Repentance*, which had been preached in the nearby parish of Leigh in 1582—it had been reprinted fifteen times by 1601. Its message was stern, but its style was energetic: 'We preach the law to drive you to Christ; we preach judgement to make you to seek mercy; we preach damnation to bring you to salvation.' It was the success of this *Sermon*, said Dent, that encouraged him to publish *The Plain Man's Pathway*, 'being the second fruit of my labour'.[1] Dent died in 1603, leaving behind him *The Ruin of Rome*—an exposition of the book of Revelation, finally published in 1607. It is hard to be sure what else Dent wrote, since his popularity led to his name being used to sell spurious works after his death.

Arthur Dent was a publishing phenomenon: *The Plain Man's Pathway* had been through twenty-five editions by 1640. It soon spawned children and imitations. Samuel Hieron's *The Preacher's Plea, or, A Treatise in the Form of a Plain Dialogue* was printed in 1604, and tackled some of the issues Dent had dealt with. What purported to be *Pathway II*, a sequel, was published in 1609: it was said to have been found in draft after Dent's death, but it was a prosaic catechism and if Dent wrote it he had lost his touch. It was reprinted only once. In it, two of Dent's earlier characters, Theologus and Philagathus, plod through basic Christian issues in a question-and-answer session, with no real discussion and not much interest. But the market for Dent and pseudo-Dent was not ruined. Thomas Tuke published *The Highway to Heaven* in 1609, Samuel Gardiner *The Way to Heaven* in 1611, Thomas Playfere *The Pathway to Perfection* in 1611, and Robert Hill *The Pathway to Prayer and Piety* in 1613. Thomas Turvill's *The Poor Man's Pathway to Heaven* came out in 1616. Turvill not only ripped off Dent's title, he stole his subtitle too: Dent's 'Wherein every man may clearly see whether he shall be saved or damned' became Turvill's 'Wherein each one may clearly see whether he be in the state of salvation or damnation'. Dent's title page had explained that his book was 'Set forth dialogue-wise, for the better understanding of the simple': Turvill's text was 'Set forth dialogue-wise, for the easy understanding of the simple'. Here indeed was the best form of flattery, a straight imitation. It is, however, quite a good imitation, in a lively style and with just those earthy interjections that Dent's less-godly characters make. The running head on the pages of Turvill's book is 'Spiritual Lime and Sand', and probably that was to have been the title until it was decided to sail under Dent's famous colours.

Dent himself was a bit of a plagiarist too. At least, he did not think up for himself the idea of a down-to-earth debate on living a Christian life, in which the godly spokesman has to answer real objections. It was George Gifford who did that. Gifford's *A Brief Discourse of Certain Points of the Religion which is among the Common Sort of Christians, which may be termed the Country Divinity* was first published in 1581—when Gifford was a curate at Maldon, and Dent was curate four miles away at Danbury. The only thing wrong with Gifford's book was its tedious title: otherwise it is a racy debate, in which godly Zelotes knocks down godless Atheos's populist objections to preaching and predestinarian Protestantism. Gifford thought the dialogue form worked, and published *A Dialogue between a Papist and a Protestant* in 1582, and *A Dialogue Concerning Witches and Witchcrafts* in 1593. John Bate's *The Portraiture of Hypocrisy, lively and pithily pictured in her colours* (1589) was also a dialogue, between Philoxenus, described as 'a Christian', and Autophilus, 'an atheist', and it is also a believable encounter. Philoxenus tries to expose the merely external religion of Autophilus as hypocrisy: 'say thou art a Protestant, renounce the pope, yet except thou lovest the preaching of the word ... thou dost walk in the sins of corruptible men'.[2] And then came Dent's *Plain Man's Pathway*—a bit more ponderous than Gifford's or Bate's dialogues, but a more comprehensive guide to the Christian life. It provides simple checklists of dos and don'ts for the journey to heaven: 'the eight signs of salvation', eight 'manifest signs of damnation', nine 'signs of a man's condemnation', nine 'foresigns of wrath', 'nine signs of a sound soul', 'seven infallible signs of salvation', and 'nine gates into hell'—together with 'six remedies for adultery', four for swearing, four for lying, four for drunkenness, four for idleness, five for oppression, and 'nine things much to be thought of'. Dent's listings were soon to be copied in Lewis Bayley's *The Practice of Piety*, another classic textbook for godly living—and another early seventeenth-century best-seller.

Dent's dialogue is between four stereotypical characters: Theologus (in Greek, a speaker of God) 'a divine'; Philagathus (a lover of the good), described as 'an honest man'; Asunetus (or witless fool) 'an ignorant man'; and Antilegon (a denyer) 'a caviller'. Prompted by Philagathus, Theologus carefully explains the misery of man, the iniquity of the times, the marks of the elect and the reprobate, the few who will be saved, the ignorance of worldly men, and the promises of the gospel for salvation. Asunetus interjects with the commonsensical queries of the uninformed, and Antilegon objects that it is all too demanding and unrealistic. The debate is sometimes rancorous. Theologus condemns the sceptical Antilegon as 'a notable infidel': 'You are one of the rankest atheists that ever I talked withall.' Antilegon dislikes the godly Philagathus as arrogant and censorious: 'you do plainly show yourself to be one of these folk of God, which know their seats in heaven'. Philagathus despises the blundering Asunetus—'I had never thought any man had been so ignorant as I now perceive this man is.' And Asunetus is deferential towards Theologus, but thinks him harsh and unbending towards ordinary Christians: 'You go too far, you judge too hardly of them.' At the end of the argument, Asunetus is convinced that he is ignorant and sinful, and is persuaded to reform himself: 'I can never be thankful enough for all the good instructions and comforts which I have heard from you this day.' Antilegon is unmoved, and falls out with the new Asunetus—'Nay, if you be of that mind, I have done with you.'[3]

Some later dialogues deal with similar issues in a similar way, though the exchanges are less spirited. In Hieron's *Preacher's Plea*, Epaphras, 'a minister', answers questions raised by Nymphas, 'a private man': 'What need all this preaching?' and 'Who knoweth what to believe among these preachers?' Turvill's copycat *Poor Man's Pathway* has three 'speakers: Timothy, a professor; Ananias, an atheist; Aquila, a civilian'—but Aquila has little to say for himself and the main argument is between Timothy and Ananias. Timothy attacks the vanities and vices of the worldly, and supplies eight notes of election; Ananias protests against too much preaching and strict Sabbath observance. Timothy wins the contest, and the others go off 'praising God for the comfort you have ministered unto us'. Thomas Granger's dialogue was published in 1616 as *Paul's Crown of Rejoicing, or, The Manner How to Hear the Word with Profit*. Here the debate is between a zealous Eulalus (in Greek, a convincing speaker) and a worldly Mataologus (a worthless speaker), 'in which two persons you may easily behold the estate and conditions of these times, and see the common carnal Protestant set forth in his colours'. Mataologus complains that the preachers cause trouble and ask too much, but Eulalus says that just shows a rebellious spirit and a lack of true religion. Other religious dialogues are very different, more obviously didactic. In John Hart's *The Burning Bush Not Consumed* (1616), Scholar is full of doubts, and questions Minister on election and assurance, and in *The Righteous Man's*

Evidences for Heaven by Timothy Rogers (enlarged edition, 1627), Minister invites Convert to demonstrate that he has a true, justifying faith. So the dialogues that have real debate between the men of zeal and the men of the world are six: Gifford's *Country Divinity*, Bate's, Dent's, Hierons, Turvill's, and Granger's. To these we might helpfully add works by Robert Bolton. He did not write dialogues, but his guides to 'walking with God' and 'comforting afflicted consciences' include pungent statements that he says represent the complaints of 'good fellows' and 'profane men'.[4]

These texts say many of the same things. The godly figures (Zelotes, Philoxenus, Theologus, Philagathus, Epaphras, Timothy, and Eulalus) have much the same message: the worldlings hate the word and its preachers; they are ignorant and unreformed; and they don't take religion seriously. The less-godly characters (Atheos, Autophilus, Asunetus, Antilegon, Nymphas, Ananias, Mataologus, and Bolton's 'good fellows') all say the same things: the preachers divide communities and make unreasonable demands; the zealous are hypocritical and presumptuous; and if God has predestined people to heaven or hell it isn't fair. This consensus is somewhat artificial, however, as Dent and Hieron borrowed from Gifford, Turvill borrowed from Dent, and Bolton probably borrowed from Gifford and Dent. We may be dealing only with recycled stereotypes, polemical fictions created to serve their authors' theological purposes. Our writers were all Calvinists, and their characters are based on conventional images of the predestined elect and the reprobates. Certainly, the worthy figures are models for the godly to follow—and the worldly figures are warnings of what to avoid. The texts are meant to reinforce the faith of the faithful, and to keep them from the ways and thoughts of the faithless. Their authors are demonstrating that ungodly views are held by ungodly men, so that the opinions that these characters attack must be the truths of God. But our writers had a broader audience in mind: they were not writing for the committed godly alone. Gifford wrote 'after the manner of ploughmen and carters', and tried to reconstruct 'the most common principles of their faith and religion' for refutation by Zelotes. Dent explained that 'I have herein specially respected the ignorant and vulgar sort, whose edification I do chiefly aim at'. Samuel Hieron's book was 'meant only for men of the plainest fashion', a dialogue 'to help the understanding of common men'.[5] Their professional experience was as preachers in the villages and small towns of some of the counties from which the evidence for this book has been drawn. Gifford served at Maldon in Essex, and his Atheos was supposed to be from Great Baddow. Dent was minister at Danbury and then South Shoebury. Turvill's book was dedicated to a woman at Ringwood in Hampshire, and two of his characters said they lived near Steeple Ashton in Wiltshire. Thomas Granger was a preacher at Butterwicke in Lincolnshire, while Robert Bolton was rector of Boughton in Northamptonshire and often preached at nearby Kettering. When they put words in the mouth of the common man, they knew what they were talking about.

The Plain Man's Pathway was not a book for scholars. 'As concerning the manner, here is no great matter of learning, wit, art, eloquence or ingenious invention'—Dent wrote primarily for 'the ignorant and vulgar sort'. Although he gives his characters Greek names, and cites a few classical and patristic authors against sin, his style is plain and accessible, with country metaphors and proverbs. He is not writing for the educated godly alone. Dent insisted that 'I am in a dialogue, not in a sermon. I write to all of all sorts; I speak not to some few of one sort.' For those already converted, the book offered reassurance and handy arguments to refute the profane. Dent wrote also for the unconverted, and asked them not to put the book down after the first few pages: he admitted they might object to 'the harshness of the beginning' (about man's sin and misery), but promised 'smoother matter' in the middle and 'most smooth' at the end (God's promises to those who truly repent). For such unconverted, the text would work best if it rang true, if they saw their own prejudices and protests answered by Theologus. If they, like Asunetus, had their ignorance and worldliness confronted; if they, like Asunetus, were crushed by the fear of damnation; then they, like Asunetus, might turn to the Lord and have some hope of eternal life. But if they, like Antilegon, cavilled and contradicted; if they, like Antilegon, would not abandon their follies; then they, like Antilegon, were lost. So Dent had to get his characters right, and he did. Everyday Christians 'are excellently laid out in their colours, and to the life, by that reverend man of God Master Dent, in his *Plain Man's Pathway to Heaven*,' said Robert Bolton at Northampton in 1629.[6]

At the beginning of *The Plain Man's Pathway*, we seem to be in a different world from ours—a world where religion is a central concern and part of everyday life. When godly Philagathus sees ignorant Asunetus and awkward Antilegon approaching, he wants to engage them in talk of religion—'It may be we shall do them some good,' he tells Theologus. More surprisingly, Asunetus and Antilegon, on their way to buy a cow, are willing to postpone their business to join a discussion with Theologus and Philagathus—'we are in no great haste, we can stay two or three hours'. So they all settle down in the shade of an oak tree, expecting to chat about God and religion for up to three hours. As we shall see, that is what men and women did: they often talked about religion, because they cared about religion and because religion was unavoidable. Life, death, and disaster were explained in religious terms: it was God who brought earthquakes, plagues, and wars, and God who brought sunshine, good harvests, and health. Adults were bound by statute law to attend their parish church on Sundays, and to pay a fine if they missed. They were also bound by the law of the Church to go to services on holy days, to receive communion three times a year, and to send their children and servants to be taught the Christian faith on Sunday afternoons. The parish's churchwardens would patrol the streets and peep into houses to make sure everyone was doing their Christian duty—and those who were not might be reported to a Church court. These courts had jurisdiction over church attendance, and behaviour in church and churchyard; over proper observance of the Sabbath; over the conduct of the clergy and the people's behaviour towards them; and over sexual morality. They enforced compulsory payments to the minister and towards the upkeep of the church, they regulated marriages and separations, they granted probate of wills, and they dealt with some sorts of slander. From the cradle to the grave, the Church helped people on their way—and got in their way.[7]

Those who did not do as the Church said they should might be called before its courts. If found guilty, they would be given a penance—usually a public apology in church to God and to the parish, with a promise not to offend again. Those who failed to appear in court, or who refused to perform the penance, would be excommunicated—banned from participation in church services and sacraments—and, for serious disobedience, shunned by neighbours. And those who would not eventually submit to the authority of the Church might be 'signified', reported to the Lord Chancellor for the issue of a writ ordering arrest by secular officers. Ignoring the Church, ignoring organized religion, was hardly a long-term option. Small numbers of deviants might try to go their own way. Some thought religion was too much trouble, but the courts and their neighbours usually brought them into line. A few Protestant separatists thought the established Church of England was contaminated with superstition, as the Church of Antichrist—and they would not attend. A few more Catholic 'recusants' (or refusers) thought the Church of England was polluted with heresy: they might turn up at services from time to time to avoid the penalties and prove their loyalty to the state, though they usually worshipped in secret with underground priests. In the end, however, at the very end, everyone wanted Christian burial—and the Church of England had the graveyards. But we should not exaggerate the differences between then and now. It was a world, certainly, in which everyone talked about religion and almost everyone practised it—but with different levels of enthusiasm. Arthur Dent wrote about 'the plain man's pathway'—singular—and Theologus and Philagathus argued there was only one way to heaven, the way of the godly zealot. But Asunetus and Antilegon argued that God had allowed for easier pathways—and the records of the Church courts suggest that many agreed with them.

This book asks how ordinary people saw and practised their own religion, and what they thought about those who saw and practised religion differently. But there is an inescapable question about how we can know what ordinary people thought—all those millions of them. Historians have tried various methods to investigate grass-roots religion. We have looked at what contemporary observers said people thought and did—but writers and preachers had their own polemical purposes, as Dent and Gifford did. We have looked at wills, to see what people said about the afterlife and to examine the charitable causes to which they left money—but many wills were phrased by professional scribes, and the poor had nothing much to give. We have looked at churchwardens' accounts, to ask what parishes spent their money on and which festivals they celebrated—but much of the expenditure was compulsory, or dictated by the village elite. We have looked at didactic texts and cheap print, to see what people were told and what authors thought they would like—but it is a big leap from what people read (and only those who could read, of course) to what they thought. And we have looked at court records of what people are supposed to have said and done. This book is based on such records, and they too have their problems.

Some of these need not worry us too much. We cannot be certain that accusations and act books record exactly what was said by ordinary parishioners—though we sometimes have the original presentments by churchwardens (and, more frequently, transcripts of them), while defendants often turned up to give their own version of events. Churchwardens may not have reported correctly, and court registrars may not have recorded correctly, but it is unlikely that there was systematic misrepresentation. What we find in the records are only individual cases, which may or may not be representative of issues always and everywhere. Allegations to the courts could result from private malice or very specific local conflicts, and every prosecution had its own particular parish context and motivations. This study is, however, based on more than 700 court books from fifteen different courts, from Somerset across to Essex and from Hampshire north to Lincolnshire, and the thousands and thousands of examples in them add up to something more than local idiosyncrasies. Much more serious are the questions of selection and typicality: how do cases in the courts relate to the ordinary doings of men and women? The courts dealt only with what had gone wrong and those who had misbehaved, so we can get a misleadingly negative impression of religion and morality. Cases get into a court record or a visitation presentment because they were reported from parishes—by churchwardens or ministers. Which offences and offenders were they most likely to report? How much did they conceal? Did their choices reflect parish opinion or merely their own concerns? Were they responding to official priorities rather than what mattered to them? How did the annual turnover of wardens affect the consistency of reporting? In short, how well did the system of detection and reporting work?

Certainly, there was concealment, corruption, and false reporting. In 1574 the churchwardens of Taynton, Gloucestershire, claimed that their curate 'hath persuaded them in the making of presentments to pass lightly over things and faults'. Elizabeth Sampford of Bicknoller in west Somerset claimed in 1609 that she had been accused of scolding only by the malice of John Slocombe, one of the sidesmen. She testified that the allegation had been included in the presentment against the wishes of the wardens and other sidesmen, and the curate endorsed her statement. Denby Wilkes, churchwarden of Thorrington, Essex, agreed the 1610 presentment with his fellow warden, but then sent in another version with certain offenders omitted. In 1618 the wardens and sworn men of Moulton, Northamptonshire, reported that

They were all agreed and consented unto some eight or seven several causes of offences committed within their parish, and had the said bill of detection made and drawn ready to be exhibited into this court, yet afterward, by the means and persuasion of Master Ellis the new minister and curate there, the former bill was concealed and another bill exhibited, which containeth but only one presentment of a fame of incontinency.

Robert Lane, vicar of Hermitage in Dorset, protested in 1619 against the negligence of Timothy Maber as churchwarden and parish constable, who 'would never take notice of those which absented themselves from the church on Sundays and holy days'—'by means whereof God is much dishonoured, his Sabbath profaned, his sanctuary neglected, the well-disposed grieved, the wicked encouraged,' said Master Lane. It was alleged by a parishioner in 1622 that one of the wardens of Orsett in south Essex was bribed not to report a drunk who had to be carried out of the service for disorderly behaviour. William Thomazine of Great Bardfield presented a number of parishioners for drunkenness and suspicion of sexual offences in 1637, and Rose, wife of William Sorrell, 'for an absolute recusant'. He also cited his fellow warden, William Sorrell, and the two sidesmen 'for not coming with him in giving his presentment, and to answer charges of perjury for omitting to present Rose Sorrell, a known recusant'.[8]

These are all cases where cheating the system failed and false reporting was exposed. Making a presentment was a consultative and investigative process, and the misconduct of any of those involved might easily be revealed. Ministers, wardens, and sidesmen complained about each other's failings. The churchwardens of Fotheringhay, Northamptonshire, consulted their vicar when preparing their presentment in 1600, but he revealed their allegations to the accused parties, causing great bitterness towards the wardens—so they reported him. In January 1607 the wardens of Towcester went to the vicar to seek his advice in preparing their quarterly report, and to ask who had not received communion the previous Easter—but were abused by the vicar's wife when he told her that they wanted to present her for absence from communion and her unmarried maid for being pregnant. After a meeting of the wardens and sidesmen of St Cuthbert's, Wells, to draw up their presentment in 1609, John Gorway leaked the proceedings, and told offenders which of the sidesmen had named them. In 1612 Robert Doddymeade of Mells in east Somerset informed John Heysham which one of the other sworn men had reported him for drunkenness and sworn that the accusation was true. There were failings, certainly, but we can see wardens conscientiously doing their job and trying to establish the truth. Henry Osborne of Everdon in Northamptonshire was cited in 1618 'for refusing to tell the churchwardens of such as he knoweth guilty of gathering of peas in the field on the Sabbath day, besides those that were presented'. Andrew Small of Aldwinkle was presented in 1621 for trying to have sex with the wife of Thomas Prentice, 'which foul abuse was confessed by the woman before our minister and her husband and us the churchwardens'. In 1633 three parishioners of Brighstone on the Isle of Wight accused the wardens of making 'an unjust presentment, contrary to their oaths taken in that behalf'. The point at issue seems to have been the non-payment of a church rate—but the wardens declared that 'they have done nothing contrary to the honour of God or service unto holy Church or commonwealth, but have done all things in sincerity of heart, having God before their eyes, without spleen and malice, and have done all things fit for churchwardens and sidesmen to do'.[9]

Sometimes churchwardens used their discretion, and decided that an offence should not be reported. Some offenders were dealt with locally—and some breaches just didn't seem important enough to have the culprits called before a court and put to penance and costs. Thomas Squeere of Coggeshall in Essex was presented in 1594 for not receiving communion, 'and also for refusing to satisfy the congregation which he offended by a wicked fart committed'. If he had made an apology, he would probably not have been reported. In 1613 the minister and one of the wardens of Burnham tried to get Anne Harris to make a public apology for her scolding behaviour, but she refused and was cited to court. The wardens of Stansted Mountfichet did not report 'divers stoolball players in time of divine service' in 1620, having settled matters to their satisfaction—'there were certain young maids of the parish, whose parents and masters they have admonished thereof and promised a reformation'. At Rayleigh in 1625, it was the minister who thought a formal presentment unnecessary: when John Howlett objected to part of a sermon by Hugh Peter in 1625, 'the said Mr Peter did of his own charity cause the said Howlett to acknowledge his fault in the church before the congregation'—though someone reported it to the archdeaconry court the following year. The churchwardens of South Stoke in Oxfordshire did not cite a parishioner who came to church drunk in 1634 and slept through the service: Lewis Frewen told the court 'he did not present the same because he thought it no great fault, being committed but once'. Henry Clarke of Layer Marney, Essex, used his own judgement in 1635 and did not report John Hodge's wife for missing the Easter communion, because she 'told him she was then at a woman's labour'—and that seemed a reasonable excuse.[10]

There was, also, deliberate concealment of breaches—especially when many parishioners had offended. The churchwardens of Great Bentley, Essex, were in trouble in 1609 for not reporting that all of the parish 'except three or four' were absent from the king's accession day service on 24 March. When John Sturgeon of Sutton was admonished by the rector in 1613 to report those who failed to send their children to be catechized, he replied 'that then he must present the whole parish, which he would not do'. Wardens had to get on with their neighbours, and to report almost everyone would make their lives difficult. The previous year's wardens of Dodford, Northamptonshire, were presented in 1616 for sending in an 'omnia bene' ('all well') return, though many parishioners had not received communion at Easter: they claimed that when the time came to make their report 'they then did forget to certify them'. The churchwardens of Broxted, Essex, admitted in 1631 that they had not reported that most of the parishioners had received the communion sitting—and Nathaniel Kirkland, their vicar, was accused of not wearing a surplice and giving communion to those who sat. The wardens of Cottesmore, Rutland, neglected to present a string of offenders in 1637, including those men who wore hats at services—they admitted their failure, and also that one of them, Ambrose Stubley, had worn his hat at a sermon. In these cases, it looks as if local custom had not followed ecclesiastical rules, and wardens put loyalty to the parish before conformity to official instructions. Local opinion mattered to local men, and wardens were most likely to cite miscreants who had annoyed their neighbours—serial offenders, badly behaved drunks, and those who disrupted a peaceful Sunday. In 1631 the wardens of Kingston, Somerset, cited Eleanor Farthing for mending bags on a Sunday 'to the disturbing of her neighbours', and the wardens of Rimpton presented Agnes Buncombe for haymaking on Sunday 'to the dislike of the neighbours'.[11] If we can draw a general conclusion, it might be that some offences were more widespread than the court record suggests, rather than that they were unusual.

Blatant failure to present offenders seems to have been more frequent at the beginning of our period than at the end. Churchwardens were especially reluctant to report casual absences from church, not sending children to be catechized, and Sunday recreations. The wardens of St Martin's, Leicester, for example, failed to report absentees and parents who did not send children to catechism in 1585, and those at Little Sampford, Essex, were not reporting absences in 1587. This suggests that these offences were even more common than they are in the record—and also that communities did not taken them very seriously. Later, attitudes changed and discipline tightened: accusations of failure to report absence from services or poor attendance at catechizings became much less common. After the new ecclesiastical code of 1604, it was harder for wardens to conceal lapses: the full sets of original presentments for the jurisdiction of the dean of Salisbury often included separate certificates by both the minister and the churchwardens, and occasionally there were letters from a minister to the court registrar with specific complaints. Some wardens remained selective, presenting only the most serious offences or the most annoying offenders—but others made very full returns, going systematically through the official lists of questions and responding fully to them—at Mere in Wiltshire in 1622 and 1638, for example; at Halstock in Dorset in 1634; and at Lyme Regis in 1634 and 1635. However, it does appear that wardens had remained reluctant to report breaches of Sabbath observance—suggesting that public opinion became much more concerned about absence from church or catechism than it was about Sunday entertainments.[12]

Of course, such presentments of offenders point two ways. When William Agwilliam of Dymock in north Gloucestershire was reported for mowing grass on a Sunday in 1591, we have an example of someone flouting the Church's rules and doing what he wanted. But we also have an example of a churchwarden deciding to make a presentment and send a neighbour to court.[13] Each case we consider shows both disobedience and a concern for obedience. Where a godly Philagathus is cited for refusing to kneel for communion, we have a case of nonconformity—but we also have a desire for conformity, perhaps a churchwarden Asunetus asking for a Philagathus to be made to conform. And where a profane Antilegon is cited for missing church on a Sunday, we have an example of a casual attitude to religious observance—but we also have an example of seriousness in religion, perhaps a warden like Philagathus wanting an Antilegon to be made more godly. Are the offenders we see in the act books only deviant minorities, and were all the others behaving themselves? We have to be sensible and sensitive—aware of the frequency of different sorts of cases, and of the language used about them. In the chapters that follow, we will see some atheists—but not very many of them, and they were described in shocked terms. We will see some papist recusants—many more than the number of atheists, but concentrated in particular places and usually described in resigned tones. There will be some godly nonconformists—many more than the papists, spread across many parishes, and some of them apparently resented for their singularity. We will see lots and lots of Sabbath-breakers—objectionable if they also disturbed a church service, and those who worked resented more than those who played football. And there were drunkards and fornicators and people who chattered too loudly in church—all were disapproved of, but the regular miscreants were disliked much more.

Most wardens—and many ministers—wanted to be sure of community support for their presentments, and concentrated their attentions on the persistent offenders and the awkward customers. They cited those of the godly who made a conspicuous point of gadding off to their favourite preachers, rather than those who slipped away quietly and made no fuss. In 1632 the minister reported the two women of Pitminster, Somerset, who deliberately would not bow on entering church, rather than those who forgot or could not be bothered. The wardens of Fering, Sussex, presented a man guilty of 'extreme sleeping' in 1613, and perhaps neglected the men and women who dozed occasionally. Surely they presented the drunks who made a racket in church or vomited during a service, rather than the ones who sat quietly and tried to conceal their state. And they certainly turned in the trouble makers—the tale-tellers and the gossip-mongers who caused friction in a community, the scolds and the loud-mouths who had no thought for their neighbours. Thomas Malson of Whissendine in Rutland was presented in 1621 'for excessive and usual drinking, quarrelling, fighting and swearing'—and when he did his penance before a small group and not the whole congregation, the wardens reported him for that too.[14] Churchwardens picked out those they could safely report, knowing the parish would back them up and there would be few recriminations. In all likelihood, it was the most notorious and unpopular who were presented—and there were many more offenders than those we find in visitation returns and court books. But how many more, and how significant were they? Arthur Dent can help us.

The Plain Man's Pathway is, in some senses, representative. It certainly represents other texts of its kind: its characters, its standpoints, and its arguments are found in other dialogues. And it is also representative of aspects of the real world—it represents arguments that could be heard in the towns and villages of England. Of course, it is a *representation*, an author's construct, in which stereotypes were manipulated to make a point and reach a planned conclusion. The voices are invented, but what they have to say is not. As we shall see, the things Dent's characters say were said by real people in a real England. This makes Dent's text useful to a historian. In the following chapters, Dent's four characters are employed as ways into an investigation of popular religious attitudes. The evidence yielded by ecclesiastical court books and visitation returns is organized around his men, and used to show how the godly and the less-godly got along together. But these characters are more than convenient organizational tools: they help us to generalize from our examples. A crucial methodological difficulty for historians interested in attitudes, beliefs, and customs is how to get beyond a fistful of individual cases: what do they prove? We may find ten or twenty examples of a particular statement—but how many do we need to show that such statements were widespread and reflect a common opinion? The problem is especially acute in a study such as this, based on materials from a dozen county archives in southern and central England and looking for what is general rather than local. Ten or twenty, or forty or fifty, examples from twelve different archives: so what? Here Dent and our other authors are useful. A generous fistful of examples of something Gifford or Dent or Bolton represents as a common opinion, very probably *is* a common opinion. If men from Wiltshire, Gloucestershire, Northamptonshire, and Leicestershire say something, and Asunetus says it too—then perhaps lots of people were saying it.

Arthur Dent, George Gifford, and the other writers who claimed to represent grass-roots opinion can help us separate the common from the exceptional. The stereotypical characters in dialogues and texts can make more sense of the thousands of cases in the court record. These characters were used because they had something to tell readers—that they should listen to Theologus, and strive to be like Philagathus and not like Asunetus or Antilegon. And they worked as models because they could be found in every village, and everyone knew people like them. The fact that Dent drew our Theologus implies that there were plenty of serious-minded ministers with high expectations of their parishioners, but not much patience with those who fell short—and there they are in the court record. Our Philagathus suggests to us that there were plenty of godly laymen striving to be proper Protestants, and with contempt for the ignorant and the ill-behaved—and we will indeed see them. The character of Asunetus hints that many ordinary Christians did not spend much time or energy on their religion—but that some could be made godly. Antilegon suggests that some resisted the intellectual and moral demands of godly Protestantism, and objected to those who tried to drive them out of the alehouse and into church. We will find lots like that. And the interaction of the characters in Dent's book shows things we will observe hereafter: that religion was a subject for general discussion and it mattered to people; that religion was a contested area, with arguments and anger; and that different people had different approaches to the divine. Some were zealous, some were conformist, some were casual, some were careless, and some were papists. Arthur Dent wrote *The Plain Man's Pathway to Heaven*, one path to be followed by all—but plain men had several pathways, and they found their own routes to God.

There were, of course, more than four ways of looking at this world and the next. I do not pretend that everyone in southern and central England between 1570 and 1640 was a Theologus, a Philagathus, an Asunetus, or an Antilegon. For a start, these characters are all men, but ordinary women had just as much to say about religion as ordinary men, and we will see some of it in what follows. And none of the four is a Catholic—so for this book I have cheated, and added a fifth character, 'the Papist', because how Protestants and Catholics got along is too interesting a problem to be ignored (even if Dent, with a different agenda, did so). Fortunately, in 1582 George Gifford wrote a dialogue between a Papist and a Protestant, and I have purloined his Catholic character. Our five characters, moreover, are fixed points, ideal types, but real men and women were mobile. As a student, Robert Bolton was an Antilegon, carping at the godly; as a young academic, he almost became a Papist; he was then converted into a Philagathus—and finally he was ordained and lived the rest of his life as a Theologus, speaking of God.[15] Real people might be hybrids, too, combining together views ascribed by Dent (or Haigh) to specific characters. Nevertheless, Dent's men (plus the Papist) are useful tools. They help us to organize a huge mass of evidence, and they may help us to understand what it means.

PART I

'THEOLOGUS, A DIVINE':
THE PREACHER AND HIS PEOPLE

1

The Preacher and his People

For it is no small matter that we have taken in hand, which is to care for the flock which Christ hath bought with his blood. Would to God therefore that we would leave striving about other matters and strive together all about this: who can pull most out of the kingdom of Satan, sin and ignorance; who can win most souls, and who can perform best service to the Church.

Arthur Dent's Theologus was a model godly minister. He knew his Bible, and cited it constantly as the revealed will of God. He knew his ancient authors and the early Fathers. He knew his duty to God, and would employ all his skills in doing it. He could be stern and he could be sympathetic. He explained God's will clearly and carefully, and used homely metaphors and comparisons. He knew that the clergy must not be proud, they must not stand on their dignity and their scholarship, they must teach the poor and ignorant as Christ had done: 'If thou lovest me, feed, feed, feed my flock,' he quoted. Forty years on, in July 1640, Thomas Clark had the same message at a visitation sermon for the Dorset clergy: 'This whole flock [w]e must take heed unto, not having respect to some few principal ones but to all together and all alike ... So we must care for all, but specially the weakest, because they are in greatest danger to be lost.'[1] But how were Christ's sheep to be fed, how were souls to be saved? Master Theologus was clear: by preaching and by catechizing.

'If we will have heaven, we must have Christ. If we will have Christ, we must have faith. If we will have faith, we must have the word preached. Then it followeth thus, if we will have heaven we must have the word preached.' The godly knew well they must hear sermons for their salvation, and find them where they could. Henry Page of Westborne in west Sussex argued in 1586 that 'all ministers which had not the gift of preaching were blind shepherds and guides'. When charged with absence from his parish church in 1598, Robert Trumell of Bosham replied 'that he goeth to church where the word is preached, and that the vicar of Bosham doth not preach'. Lawrence Bullock of Alderton, Wiltshire, went to sermons at Sherston in 1602 because his own curate was 'ignorant and such as from whom he can receive no spiritual comfort'. Roger Wingfield of Fordham in Essex attended his parish church in 1611 whenever there was a sermon, but other churches when there was not. Maurice Dix's wife of Arthingworth in Northamptonshire was going to other churches in 1620, 'saying that she would not go to a dumb dog, meaning Mr Cooper the parson'. Preaching was what God and his people expected. After complaints from his congregation, the absentee vicar of Selsey promised to come one Wednesday in 1625 to preach: all the parishioners turned up as appointed, but he did not. God would have his Word preached. In 1626 the rector of Oundle reported Robert Langley 'for saying that the judgement of God was come upon the town because I the said James Fossett did not preach upon Wednesdays, being fasting days lately appointed by the king'.[2]

However, the godly laity wanted to hear the right kind of sermons. Leonard Major of Northampton went only to visiting preachers in 1615, asserting 'that reading the word of God cannot beget faith. And as for preaching, the preachers of this town do not preach powerfully.' Edward Fisher, a servant from Chew Magna in north Somerset, admitted going to sermons at other churches in 1618, but 'he hath not done it out of any contempt of his minister but only the better to edify and instruct his conscience by hearing of the word of God preached'. Robert Smith of Hatfield Peverill in Essex was dogmatic in his defence of 'gadding' away from his home parish in 1624: 'he of absolute necessity repairs to other churches for his soul's health, for he cannot learn Jesus Christ, by whom he only hopeth to have salvation, from Mr Stable his own minister so well as from other ministers, and normally Mr Holmsted of Witham'. Robert Pratt of Bradwell missed five Sunday afternoon sermons in 1629, and confessed 'he goeth to Stisted to hear Mr Sutton, by whom he sayeth he can edify better than by Mr Normanton his own minister'. William Gaylett of Tolleshunt Darcy wanted to hear any preacher he fancied, telling the archdeacon of Colchester's court in 1630 'that he sees no reason why he should not go to what church he will, if he can be edified by one minister more than another'. There was, of course, a reason: his bishop was William Laud, and Laud (and law) expected parishioners to stay put and worship as a community. The wife of Thomas Hewes of Goldhanger was another who went where she wished: she was presented in 1638 'for that having a preaching minister she does often absent herself from his sermons (and also from divine service) that are as water spilt against the wall, she sayeth, and resorts to other places to hear preachers that are soul-saving ministers, the minister of her own parish being no soul-saving minister as she sayeth'.[3]

There were sermons that saved souls, and sermons that didn't—but which ones worked? Richard Bernard, author of a standard manual for preachers, knew—those that applied biblical texts to specific parish and individual contexts. The preacher should expound a 'doctrine', and then discuss its 'use', its application to his own congregation: 'others only inform but reform not, because they speak too generally and preach as if they meant other persons and not their present auditory'. Preach against sin, sting the consciences of the sinners, and some will be saved. Theologus used a similar method to convert ignorant Asunetus. It was not the Calvinist doctrine that Theologus taught that moved Asunetus, but the insistent probing of his conscience—forcing him to recognize his sins, filling him with the fear of damnation, and inducing an authentic (albeit fictional) conversion experience. Robert Bolton, rector of Boughton, Northamptonshire, described what it was like to be on the receiving end of such a sermon, adopting the voice of someone who heard but would not be reformed:

> For the sermons of every Sabbath came home to our consciences, singling out our reigning corruptions, beating punctually upon our bosom sins, manifesting clearly our spiritual misery and certain liableness to the extremest wrath of God and endless woe. Whereupon we were all at our wits end what to do, grew weary of our lives, wished with all our hearts that such a puritan preacher had never come amongst us, told every man almost we met that we had a fellow in our town would drive us all to despair, distraction, self-destruction or some mischief or other. That we heard nothing from him but of damnation and hell and such horrible things, etc.

Then, in some, the sermons began to work:

> For being illightened, convinced and terrified in conscience for their former sinful courses, the continued piercing of the word, the work of the spirit of bondage, keeping them upon the rack, under the dreadful sense of divine wrath and their damnable state a good while, at last they happily resolved without any more delay, diversion, by-path or plunging again into worldly pleasures, to pass on directly, by the light and guidance of the Gospel, into the holy path.

Bolton's spokesman resisted, however:

> I, and the greater part a great deal, more was the pity, hating heartily to be reformed and abhorring that precise way so much spoken against everywhere, into which we conceived such ministerial counsel would have conducted us, I say we wickedly wrested out of our vexed consciences those keen arrows of truth and terror with great indignation; we unhappily hardened our hearts and foreheads against the power of the word, which particularly pursued us every Sabbath. Nay, alas, we persecuted the very means which would sanctify us, and men which would have saved us.[4]

We will return in a later chapter to those who passed 'by the light and guidance of the Gospel, into the holy path', but now let us consider the response of Bolton's speaker and his unreformed fellows. 'We hardened our hearts against the power of the Word'—we protested against the moralizing preacher and his painful lessons.

Mataologus too hardened his heart. He was another 'plain man' character, in a 1616 dialogue on 'the manner to hear the word with profit'. He too did not want his conscience stung by the preacher: 'But here is the mischief: he is too bold and too indiscreet in his catechizings and sermons, he never keeps to his text but is always roving into town's-matters and men-manners, that he hath nought to do with'—'Wherefore we think that he is too precise and curious.' Many real churchgoers felt just the same way: some subjects were just not appropriate for the pulpit. When a preacher tackled sin, his congregation might be insulted, or sometimes disgusted. In 1567 the vicar of Herriard in Hampshire preached of his congregation 'That there be'eth whoremongers, backbiters and slanderers (and some I know), which shall hang themselves, and some of shall drown themselves within the year, and that their children shall beg their bread to the third and fourth generations'—so his people protested against him. Elizabeth Smith of Abington in Northamptonshire complained in 1588 that 'the minister preached nothing all Whitsuntide but bawdry': presumably he was against it. It was reported in 1592 that when the vicar of Sandon in Essex preached against drunkenness Zachary Some called him 'prattling fool' and said 'that he could if he had authority within a fortnight space make as good a sermon as he'. Perhaps Zachary thought he knew more about drunkenness than the parson. The churchwardens of Wellingborough, Northamptonshire, reported Anthony Roane for interrupting a sermon on 14 June 1607. The preacher 'took occasion to speak against pride and find fault with the people of this age in that they were more given to pride and to deck themselves in fine clothes than to the service of God, whereunto the said Roane answered "That is a lie, my wife and I have clothes which we have worn this four years!" ' Roane thought himself a wit:

the said preacher then and there taking upon him to repeat or speak of the fable of Aesop and of a cock therein mentioned which found a precious stone in a dunghill, alleging by the which that the said stone which the cock had so found were a pearl or precious stone, yet the said cock had rather found a corn or grain, and further added it was not a corn or grain of wheat, rice or barley, whereupon the said Roane answered deridingly 'Now that is true, for it was a corn of malt, it is as seen by his nose', or words to like effect.[5]

Parishioners may have wanted to be preached to, but some of them did not want to be preached at.

Richard Bernard wanted sermons that sinners would apply to themselves—but that was the trouble: they did so, and they didn't like it. John Whale of Wennington in south Essex, a scandalmonger and heavy drinker, was presented in 1612 'for railing at the minister's doctrine, especially at such times as he speaketh against slanderers, perjured persons and drunkards'. When Marmaduke Boulton of Middlezoy in mid Somerset tried to persuade Mary Davidge into adultery in 1621, 'she refusing to yield unto him told him that Mr Tyse their minister had delivered in a sermon the Sunday before against drunkards and whoremasters, whereupon the said Boulton replied "Mr Tyse will do worse than that himself"'. Moralizing sermons easily rebounded on the preachers. Thomasine Ratcliffe of Springfield, Essex, was reported in 1626 for 'finding fault with the life of the minister then preaching, with a loud voice to the disturbance of the minister and of the whole congregation'. She admitted finding fault but denied the loud voice: 'Mr Joyner preaching against malice and one Goodwife White speaking to her this respondent, she this respondent did said [*sic*] to the said Goodwife White with a low voice that the said Mr Joyner was as malicious as another.' Sermons on serious subjects had to be well judged. In 1631 John Boyce of Ashby St Ledgers, Northamptonshire, confessed 'that upon a Sabbath day about a month since he did smile in the church in sermon time whilst Mr Patterick, vicar of Milton, was there preaching that there were ten sorts of drunkards'. A preacher might be misunderstood or misreported, to his embarrassment. The rector of Ayston in Rutland presented Thomas White in 1631 for saying he had preached 'scurrilous and blasphemous doctrine, viz. speaking of Christian love and charity said that back to back is no love, belly to back is some love, and that belly to belly is pure love'. And, as we have seen, an accusation of hypocrisy was always a possibility. After the minister of Ridgewell in Essex had preached against wickedness at Candlemas 1633, one of the churchwardens declared before the whole congregation 'that he had spoken well, but he might say as the prophet Nathan said to King David, who said "Thou king and physician, heal thyself", and that was all he said'—but it was enough to land him in court.[6]

Generalized preaching against sin sometimes provoked anger—and it is likely that specific mentions of individual sinners always did. To a conscientious minister, such 'particular preaching' could be a tool of moral reformation—but to the recipient of his strictures it was a weapon of public humiliation or personal revenge. After his parishioners had exhibited articles in 1582 against John Smeaton, rector of Scaldwell, Northamptonshire, he was ordered 'that he shall quiet and seek peace, and Item he shall not preach of malice or private affect to the discredit of any of his parishioners'. When Gilbert Hussey of Oundle and his wife were presented as non-communicants in 1587, he told the court they had refused the sacrament partly because the rector 'called his wife Jezebel in the pulpit'. In 1588 the vicar of Twiverton, Somerset, was abused by Thomas Smallcombe after he had read the homily against adultery and then admonished Smallcombe to keep his daughter away from William Hunt. In 1591 John Gilby spoke up in defence of Mr Houghton, his master, when the rector of King's Cliffe in Northamptonshire criticized him in a sermon: the diocesan court ordered that Thomas Strickland 'do not any way inveigh against the said Mr Houghton or meddle with any of his affairs in public manner'.[7]

Some of the people of Hemingby in Lincolnshire complained about the preaching of William Hieron in 1598: 'he doth so rage against some particular parishioners against whom he hath some private grudge that he disturbeth the whole peace of the congregation'. Hieron would not reprove parishioners privately for their sins, but preached against them in public, 'wherein he is no niggard with his malice'. In 1600 Francis Browne of Little Casterton in Northamptonshire stayed away from some services because the rector's brother 'hath preached divers such railing sermons in the parish church there'. The same brother also declared in church that the village schoolmaster 'was a drunkard and a wenching fellow to satisfy his own lust, and a haunter of alehouses, and that he came spinning from Stamford'. In 1606 the vicar of Basingstoke, Hampshire, 'had nominated openly in the church there some of his parishioners upon fame for suspicion of incontinence', and he had also accused William West and others of trying to kill him with drink. It seems in this second case that the vicar had got drunk at a wedding, and was trying to shift the blame.[8]

It was often claimed that personalized preaching was used for private grudges—and in the case of Thomas Sutton, rector of Islip in Northamptonshire, it obviously was. In 1609 Sutton was presented to the diocesan court on suspicion of incontinence with Barbara Sparrow—by the churchwardens, James Freeman and Humphrey Nevill. Sutton himself was spreading a story that Nevill had a suspicious relationship with Freeman's wife Ursula, but it is unclear which allegation came first. Sutton faced down his critics in church. He preached on 1 Corinthians 6:18—'Flee fornication ... '—and came briskly to the point.

Mr Sutton taking occasion to speak in his sermon, desired us to give him leave if he speak rudely, 'for if you will not give me leave I will take leave'. Then he said the whore and the whoremaster had brought his name in question, and an honest woman's; that the worst part of her body is better than the best part of theirs. And furthermore he said that these filthy and malicious fellows hath presented me upon a fame of incontinency, which, he said, he having had conference with divers and good physicians, and they telling him that he was not a man capable to commit incontinency, and more than that, which I will not make you privy on.

Sutton's temper was up. It seems that he called James Freeman 'pernicious knave', and had him carried off to the stocks. 'Heretofore I have preached "Peace, peace", and I might have cried "Beasts, beasts!" ' Freeman was outraged at the public accusation, and declared that Sutton 'will go from one end of the town to the other and cry "Whores and whoremasters!" ' There then followed a running battle. The wardens tried to convict Sutton of nonconformity and laxity, and Sutton accused them of neglect of duty. Sutton called Freeman 'ninny and goosecap', and Sutton was reported for calling one parishioner 'old fool' in church and another 'old knave' in the churchyard. The tussle between Sutton and Freeman had polarized the parish, and the sermon had contributed to the discord.[9]

Personal preaching meant trouble, and often retaliation. In February 1613 William Stepnoth, the rector of Graffham in west Sussex, preached against sexual sins, and accused Robert Baxter by name. Baxter protested at once to the rector, 'and said that I preached every Sunday on things I had nothing to do with, as of whoredom and bastard-keepers, and that such things as these were my services and Christmas carols'. Baxter's lame defence was that Stepnoth had lied, in saying that Baxter 'lived by keeping of bastards, but he doth not so get his living'. Anne Smith of Dunkerton in Somerset clearly felt got at by the minister, Mr Agasseman. She complained to the parish clerk 'that the said Agasseman did many times preach against her in his sermons', and when she was told to kneel properly at communion at Easter 1614 she took it as a personal slight: 'Mr Agasseman findeth fault with me, and he is not without fault himself, for he hath kept company with a maid in his house half a score of years, and hath promised her marriage and yet doth not marry her.' Such personal attacks by clergy might lead to accusations in court. In 1623 William Innes, vicar of Dovercourt, Essex, faced a string of charges from his parishioners. It was said that after a drunkard had died in 1620 he preached against drunkenness, and warned the congregation 'that there was one of the parish lately gone to hell by means of it'. In another sermon in 1622 he had complained about 'some of his busy parishioners, that they met together at the church gate after sermon to prate like a company of geese'. And on one occasion, seeing a woman leave church before the service was over, he had cried out, 'Woman, woman, thou goest from God to the devil.' Innes, unsurprisingly, was not popular: in 1629 John Perke described him as 'a malicious fellow', and the parish put together a further batch of articles against him. George Saunders, vicar of Moorlinch in Somerset, preached against individual parishioners too—which led those named to boycott his sermons in 1633.[10]

Perhaps it was fitting that Richard Bernard—enthusiastic advocate of sermons to smite the conscience of the sinner—found himself in court because of his preaching methods. Bernard had been a much-troubled nonconformist vicar of Worksop, where he had written his handbook for ministers, *The Faithful Shepherd* (1607). In 1613 he moved—or was moved—to the rectory of Batcombe in Somerset, and there he had a quieter life. He published a series of didactic and controversial works (most of them dedicated to local dignitaries), and attracted the godly of east Somerset to come gadding to his sermons. Bernard seems to have got along well with most of his new congregation—'a very gentlemanly assembly and a rich people, and yet, blessed be God, very tractable, sanctifying the Sabbath with reverence', he boasted. But by 1634 he had fallen out with a section of the parish—partly because of his preaching. He was denounced to the diocesan court at Wells by James Aishe, who asserted before Bishop Pierce 'that the said Mr Bernard's method of preaching is to speak in particular against his parishioners, and especially against him the said Aishe'. Samuel Millard appeared as a witness and deposed

that it is Mr Bernard's manner to preach in particular against his parishioners. And that, in regard he this deponent refused to take part with him the said Bernard about a difference between him and others, the Sunday after his said refusal he preached the next Sunday following that some were so far from taking part in a good cause that they would rather run about for a morsel of bread and a meal's meat. And deposeth that the said Mr Bernard confessed afterwards that he meant him this deponent in his said sermon.

John Millard gave evidence 'that he hath heard Mr Bernard in his sermon deliver words whereby this deponent believeth that he did particularise the said James Aishe', and Richard Jordan swore that Bernard 'hath inveighed against this deponent, but whether he hath against the said Aishe or not he knoweth not'. The bishop ordered Bernard not to preach against individuals, but he would not be silenced.

On 31 October Bernard was again before Bishop Pierce in the consistory. It was then alleged 'That in a sermon preached 12 October 1634 at Batcombe he treated of apostasy and falling from grace, and when he came to the application he said to this effect following: that it was the minister's duty to reprove generally nations, cities, towns, then particular persons, as by the example of Nathan to David.' Bernard denied that he had broken the bishop's injunction on particular preaching:

Now the minister is said to particularise when he do not, for instance if a minister do see a man to live in some notorious sin and do privately reprove him for it, and the party offending do yet continue in his wicked course of life, then if the minister do afterwards preach against such a sin the party will be ready to say that it was spoken of him, although he were never meant, so also when a man shall come to another man when he comes out of the church, and strike him on the shoulder and say 'You have been mell withal, or spoken of today', I say it is that man that struck him on the shoulder that doth particularise, not the minister.

If the sinner's cap fits, wear it, Bernard was saying—and if a neighbour accuses you, don't blame me. But this was disingenuous. The sermon on apostasy was delivered only two days after the first court hearing, and it was clearly directed at those who had testified against Bernard—the apostates in his congregation.

There were those in Batcombe who wanted sinners smitten and reprobates reproved. On the afternoon of 12 October, after Bernard's morning sermon, Richard Britten met Samuel Millard, a witness against Bernard. 'We had a very good sermon today to advise us to take heed of apostasy. God give us grace to follow it,' said Britten provocatively. 'Amen,' replied Millard. 'Are you not ashamed of what you have done,' Britten asked, 'you that have been a professor of religion, and to fall away? Look to your conscience in what you have done.' Millard challenged him to repeat these words in court: 'Call witnesses,' cried Britten, 'I will speak the same again!' Personal preaching, moralizing preaching, did not offend everyone—it did not offend Richard Britten in this case. In 1620 some of the parishioners of South Petherton complained about the vicar's sermons, describing them as personalized invective—but the churchwardens defended him, declaring 'neither are his sermons invective, but general to break down sin'.[11] But personal preaching certainly did offend some. It offended those who were a singled out, those who felt challenged but not reformed, and those who thought the minister was prying into the lives and business of the laity. Just as some nowadays think the clergy should keep out of politics, so then some thought the clergy should keep their noses out of all secular affairs. Moralizing preaching—perhaps every kind of preaching—was divisive. Some liked it, some did not. And this was certainly true of the preaching of predestination and election—God's arbitrary selection of those who would be saved and those who would be damned.

Arthur Dent's Theologus stressed 'the great and comfortable use of this doctrine of election, both in that it ministreth strength and comfort against all temptations as also because it constraineth us to love God, and of very love to fear him and obey him.' But carping Antilegon would not be convinced: he thought predestination should never have been taught, 'for some it driveth to despair and others it maketh more secure and careless'. He simply could not see 'What reason, justice or equity is there, that sentence of death should be passed upon men before they be born, and before they have done good or evil?' And he was not alone. Some disliked the doctrine, others could not make sense of what they were told—including churchwardens. In 1585 the wardens of Aston Clinton, Buckinghamshire, presented their curate 'for uttering certain words of false doctrine as we think, with words as these, he said that he that sayeth he is assured of his election may do any evil that he will'. Presumably he had said the elect were saved whatever they did, not that they could do as they liked. The churchwardens of Mapperton in Dorset protested in 1598 that their curate, George Bowden, 'doth say the best works we do is sin and abomination and filthiness before God. Moreover, he doth say that a little child when that he is born be pointed to be damned or saved': well, of course he did, that was Calvinist orthodoxy. In 1606 the vicar of Edlington in Lincolnshire reported William Smith for denying predestination, and also saying 'that he which held justification by faith only was an heretic, a devil and worse than a devil'—though he expressed sympathy for two Catholic priests executed at Lincoln, and perhaps he was a church papist. John Ottis of Glastonbury, Somerset, was presented in 1614 because 'he saith children are justified before they are born, where they shall be saved or damned, and further he saith "I know as well where I stand, that I shall be saved"'—a cocky Calvinist, assured of his salvation. John Lock of Edington, 'being schismatically affected', was in trouble in 1620, in part for 'maintaining arguments that a man may be saved although he were never christened or did never receive the sacrament of the Lord's supper'. That was taking predestination a bit too far for the conformists, and he was reported. In the case of Joseph Tucker of Ditcheat, it was the crude expression of his view that caused offence. He had declared in 1632 'that he which put that sentence in the Common Prayer Book which beginneth "At what time soever a sinner doth repent, etc." had been as good he had be-moiled his britches or be-shitten his britches'. He meant that repentance could help only the elect, not the damned.[12]

There were those who knew the doctrine of election was a comfort to the godly, some who objected to it as dangerous, and others who couldn't understand what it was all about. There was little agreement—and doubt was certainly widespread. After all, most of the cases cited above got into the court records only because churchwardens mistakenly thought predestinarian teaching was not allowed, or because that teaching had been misinterpreted. Those who simply disliked predestination had no legal recourse—at least, not until after 1628 and the king's regulation of preaching. Calvinist clergy certainly claimed that there was much hostility to the doctrine. George Gifford's *Atheos*—a 1581 precursor of Dent's *Asunetus* and *Antilegon*—didn't like it one bit. He protested that the preachers 'be overhot and severe and preach damnation to the people. Likewise they meddle with such matters as they need not, as election and predestination; what should such matters be spoken of among the people, they make men worse?' His objections were that predestination took away the incentive to behave well, and that it made those fearful for their salvation despair—which is what Antilegon was to say twenty years later. Robert Bolton described the protests of 'profane men': 'Here is a tart, harsh and austere point indeed, here is sour, desperate and uncomfortable doctrine; a man may go so and so far, have such and such graces, and yet be a castaway, and yet be damned. God forbid! Let us have mercy, comfort and salvation preached unto us!' And these were objections that Calvinist writers and preachers knew they had to counter—so that the fears of the faithful could be assuaged, and the Antilegons in the real world answered. Many of George Gifford's published sermons explained the doctrines of election and assurance—such as his *Four Sermons upon the Seven Chief Virtues or Principal Effects of Faith and the Doctrine of Election* (1582), 'wherein every man may learn whether he be God's child or no'. Arthur Dent's own *Opening of Heaven Gates* deals with 'predestination, God's word and man's free will, to the understanding of the weakest capacity and the confirming of the more strong'. It is another dialogue, between Reason and Religion: Reason trots out common criticisms of Calvinist doctrine, and Religion answers: 'I am well content,' says Reason at the end.[13] These writers were not wasting their time, they were dealing with the real difficulties encountered by their people.

Theologus knew that preaching the Word would not always work, and that congregations must first be taught the basic 'principles of Christian religion' by a question-and-answer method of rote learning. The minister was not only a preacher, he must be a teacher—a catechist: 'we that are the ministers of Christ must be content to be abased, and to teach the poor ignorant people in most plain manner, asking them many easy questions, and often questioning with them in most plain and loving manner, till we have brought them to some taste and smack of the principles of Christian religion.' Richard Bernard said the same. In his manual for ministers, *The Faithful Shepherd*, he explained the necessity and best method of catechizing, and in 'Of Catechizing' (the first part of of *Two Twins*, 1613) he repeated the exercise at greater length: 'preaching doth little good without catechizing, therefore it is necessary, that men may profit by preaching'. Bernard produced his own much-expanded version of the Prayer Book catechism, which he first used in private houses and then in church. 'It is incredible to tell how this way both profiteth and greatly pleaseth the people, so as both young and old willingly come thereunto and very willingly learn. I speak by experience, blessed be God for evermore.' And at Batcombe Bernard's method worked—'whereby we and our children have received so much benefit', said one of his followers in 1634. Catechism-writing became a thriving domestic industry in the rectories and vicarages of England, with its own marketing strategy trumpeting the virtues of catechizing in families and congregations. In

1580 Robert Cawdrey, rector of South Luffenham in Rutland, published a guide to catechizing at home and in church and argued that the gospel had worked only 'where catechizing is diligently practised both by ministers publicly and by householders privately'. Parishioners came to recognize the importance of Christian knowledge, and therefore of catechizing—if only because they were supposed to be able to recite the catechism before they were allowed to receive communion. Clergy who failed to catechize were reported to Church authorities and pressed to be diligent. In 1602 'the most part of the parish' of Ellington in Huntingdonshire sent a representative to the vicar 'to entreat him to take pains in catechizing their youth'. Many published catechisms began life as manuscript versions used by ministers with their people—though parishes did not always approve of them. In 1618 the churchwardens of Weston Favell in Northampton complained that their minister was using his own manuscript 'and thereof his son must give out copies to the parties, price 18d a piece'. The minister explained 'that his youth being disorderly he hath therefore expanded and delated upon the Bible in his catechizings and hath given written copies to his parishioners'.[14] Learning 'the principles of Christian religion' was all very well—but not at 18*d*. a time.

The catechizing campaign was, on the whole, pretty successful: by the early seventeenth century it looks as if ignorance had become an embarrassment. But the process had not been easy, and catechizing remained a zone of contention between minister and people. It was often difficult for the clergy to get cooperation in a didactic exercise on a Sunday afternoon. In 1589 John Peacock of Abbess Roding in Essex 'disdained at the minister's catechizing, saying that he did nothing but prattle'. Margery Beckwith was not impressed by Mr Wharton's catechizing at Inworth, Essex, in 1591—'he asked them frivolous questions, as what should become of their bodies when they were in the ground, and whether all the world should be saved'. In 1592 the vicar of All Saints, Northampton, called Lewis Price forward to be examined in church, but he refused—'he would rather see the minister hauled and hanged before he would make confession of his faith to him'. Elizabeth Wilson caused a stir at the Easter communion at Aveley in Essex in 1608, saying the rector 'was and is a troublesome man, and that he makes the rest to say unto him the Lord's Prayer and the Belief for very fear, but she said he should never make her say them whilst he lived, and with many more railing and outrageous speeches she departed from the communion out of the church'. In 1611 Robert Dawson of Preston, Northamptonshire, was presented 'for not repairing to our minister to learn his duty and to be catechized and taught the catechism and prayers appointed to be learned by God's divine laws, and to understand the meaning of the holy communion before such time as he was to receive the same at Easter last'—which shows not only that Dawson would not do as he ought, but also than one pompous churchwarden knew what the catechizing effort was all about and was shocked by recalcitrance.[15]

The ministers encountered various reasons for refusal to cooperate. For Joan Strickland, a servant, it was shyness: she was willing to answer the minister privately in 1615, but not before the whole congregation 'openly to be mocked and laughed at'—which tells us something of what a public catechizing session was like. On 12 April 1617 the youth of Stow Maries in Essex were assembled in church to be questioned, and the adults were there to listen. But Anne Sammes, a servant, would not respond to the minister—'though I rehearsed the answer to the question she would not say after me'. On the first Sunday in March 1620, Katherine Smart of Maxey, Northamptonshire,

sitting in a pew in the church remote from the minister's seat, being called by the minister to come out of the said pew and stand before him as others did to be instructed in the catechism, refused so to do, making answer that if he had anything to say to her he might speak, she could hear him thither, and the minister calling her the second time, she still refusing to come before him made answer that the time was when he did her a mischief, he would not call her, and so persisting in her contrary remained and continued obstinate.

Probably Katherine did not want to be a public spectacle. Perhaps Alice Adams of Charminster, Dorset, felt the same way. She turned up to catechism in April 1620, but would not recite the texts. Richard Dike, the rector, reported what happened. When he asked her what a sacrament was and why they were ordained (the answers to which were in the Prayer Book), 'she did marvel why I did press her so much'. When he asked her what faith was she would not answer, 'notwithstanding the same questions being asked two or three Sundays before' (but the Prayer Book did not provide a response to this question). Finally Dike asked her to recite the Creed: 'her answer was whether or not I did think she could not say it, and thus with many frivolous questions she made derision of the catechizing and myself, and disturbed the whole assembly'. On 15 October 1620 two female servants at Leigh in Essex would not answer when called upon, 'but in a contemptuous manner laughed'. Alice Wells of Street, in Somerset, failed for three months to go to catechism, 'being thereunto publicly warned by the minister', and when she finally turned up in January 1623 'she did most scornfully and contemptuously demean herself, refused to answer such questions of the catechism as were asked of her and disdainfully departed away again'.[16] It is striking that so many of these refusers were young females—less likely to be literate, less used to learning things by rote, and perhaps less confident in a mixed public forum.

   In 1628 five of the young of Kingsthorpe, Northamptonshire, were presented for refusing to take part in the catechizing: four of them were female, and three of these were servants. Jane Clarke claimed that 'she hath often been at the catechizing but was this time called by a wrong name, but doth not refuse'. Mellior Mottershead was there with her father, and when the minister summoned her forward her father cried 'Call louder, she cannot hear'—but still she would not go. On 31 January 1630 Thomas Williams, curate of Coleorton in Leicestershire, called Mary Wilkinson to answer his questions, 'and the said Mary Wilkinson very obstinately refused to answer, saying unto him "You shall not teach me, but teach your own wife to know her place", and uttered these words publicly, malapertly and contemptuously, in the face of the congregation there assembled to the number of about forty persons.' Her father claimed that Williams had chosen her 'out of malice, and with an intent to pick a quarrel'—but he seemed to concede that she could not or would not answer. Not long afterwards the curate tried again, but Mary stood—or sat—her ground. He reported her once more, 'for not standing up to be catechized, but sitting unreverently on her tail'. And then, it seems, things went quiet. James Harris of Alresford in east Essex 'would not come up to be catechized when the minister called him' in 1637—but he was an awkward youth, and a public refusal to cooperate in catechism was by then very rare.[17] The ministers had cracked the resistance. It seems that everyone now realized they had to be catechized, and there was no easy escape.

But it had been a long and difficult struggle for the clergy, and it had brought ridicule as well as resistance. Though the majority of those who refused to answer were females, it was the young men who had been more disruptive of the clergy's efforts. In 1613 Samuel Greenfield of Billingshurst in Sussex was presented 'for deriding and scoffing the minister and the youth that were a-catechizing'. In 1615 Christopher Hulatt, servant, of Wellingborough, Northamptonshire, had stood in the church porch deliberately singing and whistling to disturb the catechizing, and when the minister went out to tell him to be quiet he was seized by the gown and threatened with a stone. William Pease of Great Burstead in Essex had particular difficulty with the youths of his parish in 1620. Pease tried blaming the fathers and masters, and presented a string of them for allowing such misconduct. Thomas Picke's servant had answered 'rudely and contrary to the form of the catechism set down in the Communion Book'. Nicholas Weald's son answered 'saucily when he was to be catechized, I asking him who gave him his name in baptism [the second question in the catechism, to which the correct response was godparents] he answered me his father, and asked me whether I would have him tell a lie, and whether a lie were a sin, and so catechized me'. This was obviously thought to be a great joke, and James Salmon and Christopher Martin's son replied in the same way. One of the girls joined in the fun, 'fleering and laughing in the time that I did either ask her any question or the while she heard others answer, albeit I did reprove her many times'. Poor Pease had lost control. In 1622 the whole catechizing process was mocked by John Grey of Manuden, Essex, 'saying that Godfrey's dog was gone to be catechized'—and when the minister rebuked him he said, 'If the worst came to the worst, it was but a ten groats matter and there's an end.' Richard Clement of Week St Lawrence, Somerset, would not take part in the catechizing himself, 'and kept back many of the youth from the same, promising to discharge them' in 1628. And when in 1629 the vicar asked Henry Dade of Kingsdon to recite the seventh Commandment, he walked out and bragged at what he had done, 'in scoffing manner and in derision of Mr Ralph Rixton their minister'.[18] And then, again, things went quiet. Even the boys behaved better.

'Our minister is more diligent than he need to be,' said Mataologus in Thomas Granger's 1616 dialogue—'he might take the less pains and have the more thanks.' 'There is nothing but catechizing and preaching with him; if he hold on as he hath begun, he will catechize all the good servants out of the town. He makes us all weary of him.' Well, not quite all of us. Eulalus (the convincing speaker) spoke out for the hard-working godly preacher, and wondered how Mataologus would respond if John the Baptist or St Peter came to his parish. Preaching and catechizing were not universally unpopular, far from it—but they were divisive and they did bring difficulties. Moralizing preaching set the godly against the profane, and the alehouse-haunters against the godly—and against the preacher too. Catechizing set some of the youth against the minister, and perhaps divided the literate from the illiterate—even the boys from the girls. In 1609 the churchwardens at Bicknell in Somerset reported smugly that although there was no formal teaching of the catechism 'those that are learned do know it themselves'.

By about 1610 almost all adults in southern England knew the catechism, and by 1630 the youth had given up fighting the process. But that leaves us with more than half a century of struggle, when ministers battled to teach their people simple truths—and then there was the bigger difficulty of preaching them into faith. Theologus knew what had to be done, and he knew that it was hard.

It is as we say, an endless piece of work, an infinite toil, a labour of all labours. I quake to think of it. For men are so obstinate and irrefragable, that they will be brought into no order, they will come under no yoke. They will not be ruled by God, nor bridled by his word. They will follow their own swing. They will run after their own lists and pleasures. They will kick and spurn if they be reproved. They will rage and storm if you go about to curb them and restrain them of their wills, likings and liberties. They will have their wills and follow their old fashions, say what you will and do what you will.[19]

Well, Theologus was a Calvinist, and Calvinists knew that most men were reprobates: they would not listen and they would not be saved. The preachers knew that the seed of the word would usually fall upon barren ground. But Theologus was not only expressing a platitude of divinity, he was describing the clergy's experience.

The minister had a trust from God, and he had to stand to it. He was a preacher and a teacher of God's truth—and he was also a witness to God's truth. Just as the minister should preach down popery, so he should live down popery—he must be seen to reject those things identified as popish. For some clergy and members of congregations, godliness came to be identified with nonconformity—rejection of popish survivals in the Book of Common Prayer. There were many possible objections to the words and ceremonies of the Prayer Book, but for most godly clergy the sticking points were wearing a linen surplice for services and signing children with a cross in baptism. Arthur Dent himself was in trouble in 1577 and 1584 for not wearing the surplice, and he also had difficulties over the cross. In 1593 the famous John Dod, rector of Hanwell in Oxfordshire, 'yielded to conform himself in all points specified in the said detects saving for the wearing of the surplice and crossing the child in baptism, of which points he is not yet sufficiently resolved'. When Brian Lister, incumbent of Hunston near Chichester, was ordered to conform in 1605 he responded that 'if he can have his reasons answered he would do that which he ought to do by the word of God, and for the space of these twelve years last past he hath not used to wear the surplice nor signed children with the sign of the cross'. After a series of complaints against him by the churchwardens, John Rogers, parson of Chacombe, Northamptonshire, told the diocesan court in December 1607 that he had now conformed in everything but surplice and cross, 'and for the better satisfying of himself in those two points he desireth further time to confer with some of his brethren ministers adjoining and next neighbours to him'. Six months later he was reported for not wearing a surplice or christening with a cross.[20]

The surplice was a piece of popish ceremonial and superstition. At Romsley in Shropshire it was not worn in 1581 'because the ceremonial law is abolished by Christ and the surplice is ceremonious'. At Horkstow in Lincolnshire the vicar would not wear the surplice in 1585 because it was superstitious. The curate of Farthingstone in Northamptonshire was presented for nonconformity in 1590, 'for he sayeth he cannot say service (having on the surplice) with a good conscience'. As pressure for conformity increased, some clergy conformed while signalling their disapproval. When the churchwardens of Mickleton in Gloucestershire threatened to present their vicar in 1592 for not wearing the surplice, 'he said if the court would enjoin him to wear a coxcomb he would'. In 1598 George Bowden of Mapperton, Dorset, was made to wear the surplice by the dean of Salisbury, but he declared that 'the wicked had caused him to put on the badge of superstition', and said 'he that standeth in the church in his surplice doth stand as though one did bear penance in a white sheet'. Just before Thomas Whitfield, rector of Marholm, Northamptonshire, was due to appear in court in 1620 for not wearing the surplice, he 'did wear it the contrary way, viz. one sleeve at his breast and the other hanging down his back very undecently, in disgrace of the church ornaments'. Richard Winter, vicar of Long Buckby, tried a variety of excuses after he was reported by the churchwardens in 1626. First he claimed that 'he doth wear the surplice very often', but not always 'because it is too short'. The wardens testified that he had rarely worn it, and one said he had once handed the surplice to Mr Winter and asked him to wear it but he had thrown it on the floor. The wardens also pointed out that Winter had never complained about the parish's surplice until he was cited for not wearing it. The vicar then argued that 'the reason wherefore he doth not ordinarily and usually wear the surplice was and is for that (as he believeth) the strength of the law [of] this land doth not require nor enjoin [it] to be daily and usually worn'. He admitted that 'he doth sometimes neglect to wear the surplice', and the wardens conceded that he usually wore it to celebrate the sacraments. Other ministers maintained a principled refusal, and in 1631 the curate of Newport,

Essex, told the commissary court 'that his conscience will not serve him to wear the surplice and to use some other ceremonies of the Church, and therefore he humbly submits himself and craveth all lawful favour of the court'.[21]

Some ministers refused to cross a baby at baptism, regarding it as popish idolatry—though others were more flexible. In 1576 the curate of Stowell in Gloucestershire was dismissed because 'he thinketh in conscience that crossing in baptism is superstitious'. But in 1584 the vicar of Broomfield in Essex was presented 'for not using the cross in baptism, saying sometime he will and sometime he will not'. The vicar, George Parnell, argued that 'he omitted it but once, and then because the father of the child had opinion that the child was not perfectly baptised without the cross'. Parnell thought this attitude superstitious, and was teaching the parent a lesson. William Seredge, the controversial rector of East Hanningfield near Chelmsford, was presented in 1592 'for that he doth utterly refuse to use the sign of the cross in baptism'. He admitted 'that he doth not use the sign of the cross in baptism but he saith that he doth not utterly refuse to use it, and he saith that for divers causes he doth omit the sign which he can hereafter allege'—which looks like some casuistical wriggling, though he may have thought as Parnell did. John Downe, vicar of Winford, told the Wells court in July 1603 that 'he refuseth to sign the children which he doth baptise with the sign of the cross in baptism because he taketh it to be a matter unlawful, but desireth resolution therein'. In the same year Samuel Crooke, rector of Wrington, christened one child with a cross and another without. He was called before the bishop of Bath and Wells and Dr James, the diocesan chancellor, and got into a row with them and was threatened with deprivation. When Crooke appeared at the Wells consistory in September, he resumed the argument. 'You said at Bath that you would place an honester man in my parsonage of Wrington than I am,' he reminded James, 'I am honester than any that ever you placed anywhere, as the country knoweth, for you have placed Webster and Pickering'—worse men than me. Rather than continue an unseemly public wrangle about the virtues of particular clergy, Dr James said that the case would be heard in private by the bishop. But Crooke wanted his day in court—'No, I will answer openly, for I will not have any cause heard in hugger mugger, and I love not such ending of matters in hugger mugger and smoothing them up in corners.' Either the bishop winked or Crooke blinked, for he kept his benefice and in 1612 was invited to preach to the clergy assembled at Bath. Toby Randall, curate of Stowe Maries in Essex, did not sign with the cross in 1617, and instead said, 'I baptise thee with the sign of the covenant.' In the following year the rector of Childerditch was omitting the cross, and using the formula 'I sign thee with the sign of baptism'. It was reported in 1622 that the vicar of Hornchurch 'hath sometimes not signed with the cross in baptising, although at other times he hath done it and refuseth not to do it': perhaps he was responding to the preferences of parents.[22] Clergy were in a difficult position, for some parents regarded crossing as an essential part of the sacrament, others held it was superstitious.

It is clear that liturgical nonconformity was what some parishioners expected of their clergy. In 1570 the vicar of Cowley told the Gloucester consistory that all his people objected to him wearing a surplice. In 1573 the former curate of Overstone in Northamptonshire claimed that if he had conformed to the Prayer Book the parishioners 'would not have suffered him to do it'. Nicholas Reynolds of Mucking in south Essex was presented in 1574 because 'he mocked the minister for wearing the surplice'. When John Sharpe of Hatfield Peverill saw his minister in a surplice in 1586, he declared 'the fool hath gotten on his fool's coat, and did ask the minister if he would have it to keep him warm'. The rector of South Cadbury, Somerset, admitted in 1594 he did not christen with a cross, but said 'that he hath not omitted the same for any dislike that he hath therein, but for that it hath been offensive unto certain of the parish'. Toby Walkwood, rector of Beckington, produced the same excuse: 'he hath not omitted to wear the surplice, neither to sign children in baptism for any conscience sake, but for that it hath been offensive unto certain of the parishioners there, and for that there hath been no surplice there'. In 1600 a dozen parishioners of Badby in Northamptonshire were presented by one of the churchwardens for not receiving the Easter communion: 'the cause was that they refused the same by reason the minister did put on the surplice when he went to administer the communion as it is thought'. Richard Rathbone thought the surplice was just a joke, and was reported 'for saying that if Mr Heywood do wear the surplice and hang it with bells and foxtails he would come to the church'. The minister, Ralph Heywood, was pushed into nonconformity by some of his people.[23]

But there was at least as strong a demand for conformity as there was for nonconformity—and probably a much stronger one, if we may judge from the thousands of presentments of nonconforming ministers. If some refused communion when their minister wore a surplice, others refused when he did not: William Purdie of Winchcombe told the Gloucester visitation court in 1576 that 'he will not receive as long as the sacrament is polluted, for that the curate will offer without the surplice'. People wanted things done properly. Edward Fage of Doddinghurst, Essex, asked the nonconformist Mr Cottesford to keep to the Book of Common Prayer in 1583—but Cottesford preached against him so he stopped going to church. In 1586 the churchwardens of Upton Scudamore, Wiltshire, complained that their parson, Thomas Hickman, 'commandeth the parishioners to leave their scraping at the Gospel nor stand upon our feet at the said Gospel, and we must not answer to the said Gospel "Glory be to thee O Lord"'. They were distressed by his attempt to force them into nonconformity: 'we shall not bow our knees at the name of Jesus, neither put off our hats and caps, neither to do any more reverence at that time than we do at any other time, and the said parson sayeth it is plain idolatry'. What was plain idolatry to this parson was respectful ceremony to his people. The wardens of Stoke Bruern in Northamptonshire reported in 1588 that their minister did not follow the prescribed Prayer Book services, 'but taketh it here and there where it pleaseth him', and did not read the Litany, 'but doth omit it and go to preaching'. In a long list of complaints against their nonconforming curate in 1590, the wardens of Everdon reported that 'as the women of the town affirm, he will not read the thanksgiving after childbirth'. And the 1592 presentment against Francis Foster, rector of Whiston, was even more comprehensive: 'he never readeth Common Prayer, weareth not the surplice, denyeth communion to him that kneeled, receiveth divers persons of other parishes to the communion, such as disobey their own minister, giveth not thanks after the delivery of women, buryeth not the dead, marryeth without a ring, baptiseth without any cross on the child's forehead, goeth not the perambulation, and observeth no order but his own'. The anger here is obvious. But sometimes there was humour. In 1605 Anne Vincent dressed herself up, 'with a surplice on her back and a pair of spectacles on her nose and a book in her hand', and paraded before the vicar of Haydon, Dorset, saying 'I cannot endure this papistical book'—like a nonconformist complaining about the Book of Common Prayer. Some churchwardens tried hard to get their minister to conform. Robert Salterne, rector of Stockland Bristol, Somerset, did not wear a surplice in 1612, 'and being admonished by John Tydder, one of the wardens, to wear the surplice, he answered saying "I will not wear it" and "Present it!"' And sometimes everyone was affronted. In 1630 Edward Norrington of Bradwell was reported to the archdeaconry court of Essex: 'the parishioners in general complain against him, for that he doth omit to read services upon holy days and doth very seldom wear the surplice, unless it be at the communion'.[24]

At the bishop's summer visitation of Bath and Wells diocese in 1629, Thomas Parker, vicar of Queen Camel, was presented at the Yeovil session for failure to observe the Book of Common Prayer. Among the churchwardens' specific objections were that he did not always wear a surplice, did not conduct churchings or perambulations properly, did not stand for the reading of the Gospel, and did not allow time for the congregation 'to give the glory unto God for the free passage of the Gospel, having been for many years usually accustomed in their parish'. The wardens also complained 'that strangers of other parishes do come often and commonly to our church from their own parish church'—presumably to hear Parker preach, and to take part in the sanitized services he offered. Soon after, an intriguing discussion took place at Elizabeth Combe's shop in Yeovil. Thomas Rock said 'that he marvelled that Mr Parker should do so, being that he never heard but that the said Book of Common Prayer was made and allowed of by the learned men of the kingdom', and 'that he did think Mr Parker should not deny the wearing of the surplice, being it was an ornament that was used in all churches'. 'Mr Parker should have been whipped about the town for not wearing the surplice, if he should have been his judge,' declared Rock. Susan Dennis defended Parker, for 'she had heard a reverent report of Mr Parker', and 'it was a thing very unfitting to pass such a sentence upon any man unadvisedly'. Rock then questioned Susan on her opinion of the surplice. She finally replied 'that the surplice was a thing that did not concern our faith, neither were we to build our faith upon it,' and asked him, 'What holiness he could ascribe to it?' Rock said that 'It was a thing ordained by learned wise men to distinguish them from other men.'[25]

The five who talked about nonconformity in the Yeovil shop do not make a large or scientific sample, but they do show that the issue was important and that opinions were divided. Rock, a 25-year-old linen draper who could sign his own name, was a vigorous conformist, who would have liked Parker whipped and who tried to get Susan Dennis to say something compromising. Anthony Traske was a 23-year-old mercer who could also sign: he had pulled Susan into an argument and testified against her in 1630. Francis Waters was a 19-year-old barber who appeared as a witness against Susan but said very little. And William Darby was, as far as we know, silent. Susan may have been in a minority of one, though she seems to have been the most thoughtful and she avoided Rock's efforts to trap her. Rock's outrage against Parker's behaviour is clear—as is his respect for the Prayer Book, tradition, learning, and common practice. He did not like nonconformist ministers, and he wanted them punished—and he did not like their lay followers. We cannot know how many Thomas Rocks there may have been, but the wider hostility to nonconforming clergy suggests that there were people like him in many parishes. We have seen godly ministers hitting resistance over their preaching, their catechizing, and their nonconformity. They wanted to preach the Word, they wanted to teach the ignorant, they wanted to witness for truth—but it was hard. Too many people would not listen, would not learn, and objected to nonconformity as disobedience and singularity. 'Many such are utterly void of all true knowledge of God and his word,' said Theologus wearily, 'Nay, which is more, many of them despise the word of God and hate all zealous professors of it. They esteem preachers but as prattlers and sermons as good tales; they esteem a preacher no more than a shoemaker, they regard the Scriptures no more than their old shoes. What hope is there then, I pray you, that such men should be saved?'[26]

2

Theologus: Pastor of a Flock

Let us therefore be zealous and fervent in spirit, that we may through God's grace put life into others and rouse up this dead and cold age. So shall God be glorified, his Church edified, his saints comforted, his people saved, his throne erected and the kingdom of the devil overthrown.

Theologus, the divine, thought of himself as a preacher and teacher. That was the task God had given him, to preach up the gospel and to preach down sin. He spoke for the reformed clerical profession. Ordination and visitation sermons, and manuals of advice for ministers, all had the same priority—preaching the Word, stirring consciences, that men might be brought to Christ. But is that how the parishioners saw the clergy's responsibilities? Did lay and clerical expectations and priorities coincide or clash? Did people want to be told they were desperate sinners on the edge of an abyss? In 1563 the churchwardens of Stroud in Gloucestershire admitted that some things were out of order in their parish because of the turnover of curates, 'but it shall be amended if we may have a curate to continue with us who doth follow the queen's Injunctions and please the parish well in all things'. What might 'please the parish well', and how can we historians tell? We might look at both qualities the laity valued, and defects they deplored. Of course, people did not always agree. Also in 1563 the wardens of Harnhill wanted the vicar of nearby Driffield to serve as their curate, 'for he is an honest man and learned'—but Jane Goding of Driffield had said 'that if the church men and parishioners had been men, as they were but dogs, they would have pulled the vicar out of the pulpit'.[1] But for our purposes it is not the accuracy of compliment or criticism that matters, but the choice of language as it reflects parish preferences.

There were particular characteristics that parishioners commended. In 1566 a witness from Calbourne on the Isle of Wight testified that the recently departed minister had said services 'very distinctly, orderly and reverently, according to the rites and ceremonies of the Church now established and set forth', and that the new rector 'hath served them in such form and order as is aforesaid'. In 1577 the curate of Lutton in Lincolnshire, Isaac Bennington, was described by one group of parishioners as 'upright, holy and godly'. Others said he was 'a common brawler and quarreller with his neighbours', but his supporters countered that 'he is a man both for his doctrine and honest conversation meet to serve and continue still with you'. The churchwardens of Allexton, Leicestershire, presented Christopher Carrington in 1585 for calling their minister ' "scurvy priest and scurvy knave", with other spiteful and reproachful words unmeet to be uttered against any honest, old and quiet ancient preacher as he is'. Clergy knew that lay approval mattered. In 1600 the vicar of White Waltham in Berkshire commended to his patroness a new preacher he had found for her:

A man of God (I hope) and am so by others of our calling persuaded; as well approved of both pastors and people before he did or would undertake his stipendiary lector more than thoroughly; by degree a Bachelor ready to be Master of Arts, late of Balliol College Oxford, of a very modest religious conversation as it seemeth to me, answerable to his great good report.

When, in 1606, William Ford, vicar of Thurleigh in Bedfordshire, was presented for nonconformity, a dozen of his parishioners produced a testimonial that he 'is very conformable to the laws of this realm established, and doth painfully and profitably instruct his parishioners'. In 1637 the churchwardens of Canewdon in Essex complained that a woman had abused 'our minister, whom we respect and tender'. Such commendations are rather vague, and perhaps they do not tell us very much—good conduct, reverence, and diligence seem to be the favoured attributes—and only in Ford's case is there a hint that preaching mattered to his people.[2]

Parishioners had strong ideas of what a minister of the Word should be like—what was fit, and what was not. In 1584 Gilbert Spell of West Bergholt near Colchester was telling his neighbours that Mr Kirby was unfit to be a minister. Anne Hart of Stanton St John, Oxfordshire, was cited in 1598 because 'she hath given very hard speeches unto the minister in the church upon Easter Eve last past, in saying that he was not a man of God but more like a man of the devil'. William Ansell of Ingrave, Essex, declared in 1607 'that the parson was as fit to be a parson as his dog, and that he had rather hear his dog preach than the parson'. At Alresford before morning prayer on the Sunday before Easter 1613, Widow Creed told the minister 'he was more fitter to be a bearward than a minister', and in the same year Mary Wolfe denounced the rector of Graffham, Sussex, as 'a priest of the devil and not of the Church'. In 1625 William Boddington railed at the vicar of St Sepulchre's, Northampton, 'saying he was not fit to come into a pulpit'. We can learn a lot from what parishioners did not like. We must be cautious with what they are supposed to have said, however. Almost all our relevant evidence comes from visitation presentments and court proceedings, and it may reflect the concerns of Church authorities as much as the wishes of congregations. The Stroud wardens had said in 1563 they wanted a conformist as well as someone they could get along with.[3] Perhaps they did—or perhaps they knew that was what the bishop wanted to hear. But alongside often-formulaic complaints about clerical dress and the repair of parsonages are issues that really do seem to have bothered congregations—misconduct, negligence, and disruption.

Parishioners expected dignified behaviour from their minister, and objected to drunkenness and sexual laxity. William Fry, rector of Newington Bagpath in Gloucestershire, was presented in 1576 for suspicion of incontinence: 'I am abhorred of all the people for Margery Tovie's sake,' he told a young scholar he met at Cirencester. 'I might have had in this town a widow better than she by £100 if she had not been.' At a wedding party at Overton in north Hampshire in 1580, John Denbigh praised the rector 'and his godly conversation'. Thomas Waite of nearby King's Worthy responded that 'Your parson is not so good as ours is bad, a troublesome man and a naughty parson, for he begat a bastard upon his maid and perjured himself when he had done.' In 1591 Richard Tetlow, curate of Piddington, Oxfordshire, was also suspected. It was said 'that the consciences of the inhabitants of Piddington or the most part of them are grieved and very unwilling to receive the sacraments at his hands since this evil fame and report went of him', and the parishioners petitioned the bishop 'against Mr Tetlow for his suspicion of evil life'. Undignified behaviour annoyed people almost as much. It was reported in 1597 that John Fabian, rector of Great Warley in south Essex, 'to the scandal of his calling and offence of good Christians [did] behave himself very dissolutely and wantonly in the parish of Kelvedon in taking upon himself to be a lord of misrule or Christmas lord'—though perhaps the less good Christians were not so offended. The curate of Woodham Ferrers was said in 1598 to be often drunk, 'to the grief and offence of the whole congregation', and in 1611 the vicar of Havering was presented as a drunkard 'and giveth thereby great scandal to the ministry and grievous offence to the whole congregation'. The clergy were expected to live up to their calling, and to set an example—otherwise they were hypocrites. After service at Ottery in Dorset in 1617, five men were 'talking of the conditions of ministers, and that some ministers would preach against whoredom, drunkenness and other vices, and as soon as they come forth of the pulpit they will run into the same sins themselves'. 'By God's blood,' cried a churchwarden, 'if there be any that will speak well in the place and do otherwise when they be out, I would their eyes might be pulled out of his head!'[4]

Negligence by the clergy also provoked strongly worded protests. In 1584 the churchwardens of Compton in Wiltshire complained against 'our curate Sir Thomas' for not catechizing: 'we present that we have a very bad curate and that our vicar is able to maintain a sufficient curate, that we may have our children better instructed and ourselves better served in the church, and therefore we desire to have such one as can well serve the cure and instruct our children as he ought to do'. David Jenkins, curate of Locking in north Somerset, had poor eyesight by 1605. The wardens declared that 'he is not sufficient to serve the cure as they think: having the book of Canons is not able to read the same nor cannot keep the register book nor write any man's testament in such sort as it may be legibly read'—and asked for 'a sufficient minister to perform these things and others that belong to his charge'. The wardens of Charlton-on-Otmoor, Oxfordshire, presented their rector in 1618 for negligence. George Gilder testified that 'the parishioners of Charlton aforesaid are much grieved and offended that they are thus disappointed of their prayers at church and their said minister's presence to perform the offices of churching, christening and burying, wherein he hath been much wanting'. There were similar protests against the absences of the curate of Worle in Somerset in 1625, especially that he was not there to visit the dying 'and give them instructions for their souls' health' or to bury the dead. And in 1629 Walter Ridout claimed that the rector of Folke in Dorset devoted more time to his medical practice than to his ministerial duties, even on Sundays—'there was no parish so evil served within forty miles, for most commonly the prayers never began till ten of the clock or after, by reason many strangers that came to him on the Sabbath day with urinals and pots'. The rector was, he had said, 'fitter for a piss pot than a pulpit'.[5]

Perhaps the commonest criticism was of ministers thought to be argumentative and disruptive. At the visitation of Gloucester diocese in 1576, the ministers of Morton Valence, Prestbury, and Swinden were each 'no peacemaker', the curate of Great Rissington was 'no peacemaker but rather a sower of discord', the curate of Dyrham was 'not a quiet man', the vicar of Titherington was 'a common disturber of his parishioners, a brawler and a fighter', and at Ashton Somerville there was 'none so far out of charity as the parson, a brawler and sower of disorder'. The wardens of Sherfield, Hampshire, made their allegation in 1582 more in sorrow than in anger: 'the presentment which they made was not of any malice but of such matters as credibly they were informed of, and further added that their said parson was a very troublesome and quarrelsome man among them and so hath been this four or five years, and doth not go about to reform himself as they hoped he would'. The curate of Ashendon in Buckinghamshire was presented as 'a quarreller and a very unquiet man, not fit to serve any cure' in 1585, and in 1586 a Wiltshire parish complained, 'our parson is so troublesome unto us that we cannot receive the communion in charity but once in the year'. In 1597 the wardens of Parham in Sussex cited the rector, Robert Day, saying 'that complaints have been brought against him by women and others for fighting, brawling, quarrelling and other disorders used by him'. The curate of Laindon in south Essex was denounced in 1599 'for a common brawler and a debate-maker and a sower of sedition between neighbour and neighbour' and 'a man whose tongue is full of ribaldry and filthy speeches, to the great discredit of his coat and calling'. In 1600 the rector of Little Casterton in Northamptonshire was presented 'for not living quietly amongst his neighbours and not persuading them to peace and charitable agreement', and at Welford Mary Bradley told the minister, 'Thou canst say well but thou doest as bad as anybody, thou mayest be ashamed of thy doings, I will make thee known what thou art. Thou shouldest make peace but thou setteth neighbours together by the ears.' This accusation of hypocrisy was a common one. In 1614 the aptly named John Demander told the vicar of Stondon Massey in Essex that he

was a contentious, disquiet person and that usually at every good time he took occasion to trouble and fall out with somebody to disquiet the whole parish, and added that he was fitter to have made a lawyer than a minister. Moreover he said whereas he should be a lantern of light to lead men to God he was a lantern of light to lead them to the devil, besides that on the Sunday before he had preached well but as soon as he was out of the pulpit he quarrelled with all the parish.[6]

It is clear what people expected of a minister, and what they thought was appropriate clerical conduct. They wanted him to set a good moral example, to be diligent in performing services, and to keep peace in the parish. We know that the godly demanded soul-searching preachers, and would go gadding to others churches to hear them. But this was perhaps a minority taste, and most parishioners—and their churchwardens—looked for proper conduct, proper services, and a proper concern for community. Obviously, clergy and laity could agree that a minister should behave well and fulfil his duties, but they disagreed on the importance of social harmony. In June 1598 a group of parishioners from Mapperton in Dorset petitioned the dean of Salisbury against their curate and the schoolmaster:

We humbly beseech your worship that you will give us some reformation in this cause and that the old parson may have it to his own use, procuring an honest quiet man, such a man as may settle and frame together that which these hath dispersed, for now we live a most tormentable and miserable and ungodly life, and it will never be amended so long as these continue in that place, for before these came to dwell amongst us we lived quietly in love and in charity with one another, but now we live as ungodly.

'A good pastor will guide his flock charitably, but a careless shepherd will annoy them mightily,' they concluded. A good pastor was one who didn't trouble his people. In 1602 Jacob Ball of Meare, near Wells in Somerset, gave a dinner to celebrate his wife's churching, where there was 'some talk made by some of the women there at how good and honest a man the last vicar there was and how well he used the matter amongst them'. George Calvert, the new vicar, a long-winded preacher, took offence, and declared, 'Oh, therefore he was a good man because he pleased you well!'—that is, surely he didn't make a nuisance of himself.[7]

The godly thought differently. It was the preacher's job to cause a stir, to bruise consciences, to divide the godly from the profane and set them against one another. When the Papist in one of George Gifford's dialogues complains that the preachers of the gospel bring disagreement and division, the Protestant gives the classic evangelical answer: 'Yet he saith he came not to send peace but a sword, and to set the father against the son and the mother against the daughter.' 'Will ye blame St Paul and his preaching because there was stir and hurly-burly almost wheresoever he came?' asks Zelotes in another Gifford dialogue, 'Was he to be blamed, or the wicked infidels which could not abide to have their sins reproved?'

Theologus too favours confrontation. Honest citizens who thought that God would save them had to be told that they were wrong: only the regenerate would have eternal life, and worldlings were the bond-slaves of the devil. 'You go too far, you judge too harshly of them,' says ignorant Asunetus. And, no doubt, many preachers seemed too harsh. Parishioners did not like to be told that they were on the way to hell. William Hieron of Hemingby, Lincolnshire, 'likeneth his parishioners to the thieves in goal, saying that divers of them sit before him with worse consciences than such as are going to hanging this assize'. It was alleged about 1598 that he 'divideth his auditory thus, having one or two that he thinketh assent his novelties he pointeth unto them "I speak to you regenerate", and then turning his body, countenance and hand to the rest of the parishioners he sayeth "I speak to you also" '. The vicar of Bremhill in Wiltshire denied in 1605 that he had abused his congregation, but admitted to 'some angry speeches against such of his neighbours, but not the better sort of them'. In 1606 John Rowdon of Barford St Martin said of the rector that 'as there are in our orchard divers trees that yield fair blossoms, so Mr Dr Wilks carrying a fair show yieldeth very sour and bitter fruit to his parishioners and especially to him'. In 1629 William Ridout of Folke complained to Abraham Forester, the rector,

calling to mind your last sermon of five which you made upon this text ('To serve the Lord in holiness and righteousness before him all the days of your life'), and finding by your vehement pressing the text that there were some in your parish that you took to be hypocritical, or else you would not so long had iterated that point, for you came upon them with these words, as near as I can remember them, that they were captious, proud, covetous, malicious oppressors, revengeful, contentious, hypocrites, making show of religion and of no religion, yet they would come formally to the church every Sabbath day, hear the preacher, sit right over against him, receive the communion, bear them civilly and quietly in their parish, yet lukewarm fellows whom the Lord would spew out.

Here was Theologus, preaching in rural Dorset, distinguishing between the godly and the 'cold Christians', and here was Antilegon, carping about it—'who more capricious, proud, covetous, malicious, revengeful than yourself?'[8]

The rector of North Stoke in Somerset told his people in 1631 that they were gypsies and cheats, who did not know the difference between whoremongers 'and such as hung in hell'. The rector of Scaldwell, Northamptonshire, was presented in 1634 'for not burying Edward Munck as a Christian ought to be, and saying that he was a usurer and a whoremaster and did not deserve Christian burial'. Perhaps the parson was right about Munck's morals—but the wardens and sworn men still objected. In 1636 the curate of Little Dunmow in Essex told the congregation 'that he never came amongst such a rascally people in his life', and in 1637 the curate of Heathfield, near Taunton in Somerset, said 'he would baptise or christen a sow and make as good a Christian as any in our parish'. It was, of course, the preacher's duty to reprove, and the sinner will kick against the pricks. Some preachers get carried away with their own invective, some are tactless and indiscreet. The godly might sit smugly, while the profane smarted under the preacher's lash and then complained. What else should we expect? But what matters here is not that an individual minister went too far and annoyed some (but not all) of his parish. What matters is that the aggressive preacher fitted and validated a stereotype of the harsh and unreasonable minister. 'Youth must not play on the Sabbath day between morning and evening prayer; old people must not meet together at the alehouse to make merry, as they were wont to do. A man must not do any small job, nor walk to other towns upon business, nor make bargains on the Sabbath day, and I cannot tell what a hundred such prattles,' protested gabbling Mataologus in 1616. 'If you see any at bowls or suchlike sports, though between morning and evening prayer, when there is no public meeting of the congregation, they shall hear such thundering of the judgements of God against them, as if they had murdered their parents,' said a fictional 'country parson' to 'a precise preacher', probably about 1618.[9]

If aggressive preaching annoyed some parishioners, so did excessive discipline. The parish clergy had three disciplinary weapons: public or private reproof, citation to court, and exclusion from communion. A minister was permitted to refuse communion on grounds of sin, malice, and ignorance, and it is likely that most parishioners wanted notorious offenders excluded. In 1585 the churchwardens of St Ives in Huntingdonshire complained that 'their vicar doth minister the communion to offensive persons not reconciled'. But George Gifford warned his brethren to be careful:

The minister thereof may easily offend in this case divers ways, as namely if he be carried with evil will for private respects towards any, and so aggravate their offences and make that heinous which is not; or if he do not make the matter apparent so much as he can, that the flock may see there is just cause to repel them and no injury offered, the crimes for which they are removed being notorious.

It was often alleged by those refused communion that the minister had acted out of personal malice—and sometimes it seems to have been true. In 1577 Geoffrey Cowper, rector of Paston, Northamptonshire, was presented because 'he useth to revenge his own private injuries by putting his parishioners from the communion and in applying the examinations of his parishioners to his private revengements'. The particular example cited was his examination of John Smith's maid Anne before the Easter communion. When she recited the Commandments for him, he stopped her at 'Honour thy father and thy mother' and said, 'Thou hast broken this commandment because thou hast counted me not to be an honest man.' When Anne denied his accusation, ' "Why', said he, 'thou comparest thy master's honesty to mine", and the said maid standing in her master's honesty and thereon he put the said maid from the communion saying "Maid, you shall ask me forgiveness before you receive".'[10]

The parishioners of Sherborne in Dorset protested in 1582: 'Item, that Mr Dee vicar of Sherborne hath put divers from the communion, being prepared thereunto, for not paying tithes such as he demandeth'; 'Item, that Mr Dee hath put others from the communion being thereunto prepared, for private occasions of offence between Mr Dee and the parties, although they have willingly offered reconciliation.' Thomas Grey of Coggeshall explained to the Colchester archdeaconry court in 1595 'that he tendered himself dutifully and orderly to receive the communion and that Mr Newman his minister did refuse him, and that through private grudges between him and Mr Newman it happened that he did not receive as by law he was bound'. When the curate of Bozeat, Northamptonshire, was distributing communion on Palm Sunday 1607, the vicar shouted at 'certain of the communicants, wishing them to get out of the church, for if they took the communion before they had paid him his offerings he would pluck them out by the ears'. In 1628 John Watnaby sued Joshua Sponge, curate of a chapel in Asfordby, Leicestershire, for twice refusing him and his wife communion, 'to the great disquiet and trouble of their minds, perturbance of the rest of the congregation, and to the great danger and peril of your the said curate's soul'—though Watnaby asserted he 'was before and since and at that time an honest, sober and religious Christian, and one conformable to the rites and ceremonies of the Church of England, and one of good life and conversation'. The curate claimed justification, 'the said John and Lucy his wife living in open hostility with their minister, he for his part vilifying and reviling his minister'—but there was no disguising that a personal quarrel lay behind the exclusion.[11]

Gifford had also warned against apparently arbitrary rejections. John Davey of Leigh appeared in the Essex archdeaconry court in 1592 to answer a charge of absence from communion. He said that 'he hath offered himself to Mr Negus, the parson hath put him by, but upon what cause he know not'. The godly William Negus was summoned 'to show cause why he repelled Mr Davey and his wife and John Cheshire and his wife from the communion', but he failed to appear and finally sent a message that he was sick. In 1594 it was said that Thomas Morse and five other men of Donyatt, Somerset, 'came to receive the communion at Easter last but were refused by the minister, the cause they know not'. In 1600 the curate of Sandhurst in Berkshire

forbade one Agnes Arnold from the communion table after that she was kneeled down with the rest of the company, and would not minister the communion to anyone until she was gone, he not alleging to what intent he did it. And after the communion was past her uncle demanded the minister why he forbade his kinswoman from the communion, who answered that his son-in-law Thomas James would not that she should be permitted to receive.

John Sturgeon, churchwarden of Sutton in south-east Essex, complained in 1613 that the parson had rejected him from communion but had admitted two other men who had railed at him—and in 1615 he told the court that 'he offered himself ready to receive the holy communion in his parish church with some of his neighbours upon Palm Sunday, and that Mr Aylett the parson there would not admit him'. The wardens of Lancing in Sussex protested in 1624 that Mr Robinson had admitted an unmarried mother to communion, 'and did the same time put back from the communion many of the better men's daughters and servants, having been communicants a long time, for no cause that we know but of his own humours'. In 1630 John Boad of Chigwell, Essex, said he had been repelled from communion twice, though he had offered himself 'as reverently as he could'.[12]

It is likely that mass exclusions caused particular offence. Thirty-eight were rejected from communion at Inworth in Essex in 1591, at least some of them for ignorance. The nonconforming William Seredge of East Hanningfield and William Tichborne of Romford were energetic excluders, and Seredge in particular caused much discontent in his parish by his disciplinary methods. The curate of Langford excluded a dozen in 1594, and some were angry because they had already paid their Easter offering. Some ministers in effect excluded everyone, by refusing to celebrate communion. When Mr Thomas arrived at South Stoke in Somerset, he would not hold a communion until he had personally examined the whole parish, so there was only one communion in 1593–4. For the same reason, John Downe of Winford did not celebrate between his arrival at Michaelmas 1602 and the following Easter. In 1605 the rector of Chelvey cancelled a communion because of the failings of a few: John Doggett had boxed Francis Buck's ears in Nailsea churchyard, John Lowle and his wife had committed fornication before their marriage, 'and for that divers others of the company then to receive to this deponent's knowledge were out of charity, and therefore he disappointed the ministration of the communion at that time'.[13] The ministers thought they were doing their duty: at least some, and perhaps most, of their parishioners thought they were being unreasonable.

Exclusion from communion brought shame and upset. 'Yea, Master Vicar, that ye go about to shame us before the whole people,' cried Geoffrey Soden in 1570, when he and his brother were forbidden communion at Swalcliffe in Oxfordshire. When Catherine Yates of Basingstoke, Hampshire, was turned back from the communion table in 1607, 'she then and there told Mr Webb that if he would not admit her to the communion that then he should pay her that he owed her'. On Christmas Day 1616, Robert Lane, vicar of Hermitage, Dorset, sat in the chancel as usual, taking the names of those who wanted to receive communion. He told Bartholomew Mullins that he could not admit him to the sacrament because of his negligence in attending church: Bartholomew 'presently fell to threatening the minister, that he should hear order from his betters very shortly, reproaching the minister for a malicious person, a troublesome person'. There was a repeat performance on Easter Day 1617, with Mr Lane and Thomas Mullins: Thomas approached the vicar to say he wished to receive, Lane told him he could not, and Thomas called him 'a malicious person and a troublesome [one]'. Thomas Mabbott of Stanton Prior, Somerset, went to take communion in 1618 and was refused by the parson: 'Now I see the love of a brother!' he cried, 'A wiser man than you would not have done it.' The wardens of Pensford reported in 1619 that their curate had refused communion to Elizabeth Richards, 'and hath so done two or three times, to the great grief and discomfort of the said Elizabeth Richards'. The exclusion of two churchwardens from the Christmas communion at Easton Maudit, Northamptonshire, in 1620 was a particularly dramatic event. Thomas Johnson, the vicar, told John Athy 'that unless he would forsake his vice of drunkenness he would not receive him, whereunto Athy replied, "I will not leave it" ' — or so Johnson claimed. William Douglas sent his wife to tell Johnson that he wanted to receive the sacrament, but Johnson told her 'that unless her husband would present faults presentable in the town and so clear his conscience he would not admit him to the communion'. Before the communion service, Douglas stalked up to Johnson in church and expostulated, 'Why may I not receive? I am as fit to receive as you are and you are like to smart for this.' Johnson then cited the two wardens for not reporting the leaky church roof and some missing books, and the wardens cited the vicar for refusing them communion. Thomas Johnson also fell out with other parishioners: 'We will rouse you before we have done,' warned the sexton — and Johnson, indeed, was removed from his benefice in 1623.[14]

It is hardly surprising that parish reformers and disciplinarians were criticized for their efforts. The hard-line rector of North Luffenham in Rutland, Robert Johnson, had a difficult time with his parishioners. In 1576 Elizabeth Liam told him 'The devil know thy bones and the devil rue thee!', in 1586 no men would act as churchwardens with him, and in 1592 it was alleged that three women 'did make or procure to be made a slanderous libel written in rhyme tending to the defamation of Mr Johnson'. In 1590 the arch-excluder Seredge of East Hanningfield, Essex, was called 'false prophet', and when the vicar of Hartpury in Gloucestershire tried to stop Sunday dancing in 1592 he was told to mind his own business. The minister of Cold Norton in Essex reproved three men for hedging and ditching on St Mark's Day 1605 — 'he did nothing but that which God's law gave him leave to do,' protested Lawrence Cooch, 'and took up a clod to throw at Mr Webb and called him "scurvy priest" with many opprobrious terms'. What a minister saw as his disciplinary duty, others saw as heavy-handed interference. The trouble-making vicar of Aveley criticized a parishioner for his blasphemy in 1606: 'God's blood, vicar, you are out of your text!' retorted Thomas Summings. By 1612 twenty-five parishioners of Greensted had been excommunicated. Robert Dearsley's wife thought this was absurd, and told the wardens so:

she said that if Mr Denman be so popular that he will have his parishioners excommunicated, let him say his service to the wall if he will, and if you excommunicate her she careth not a fig for it, set down what you will, and saith that it is a mad trick of Mr Denman to present so many of his parishioners.

In 1619 the vicar of North Shoebury rejected Henry Harwood from communion for insulting the village constable, whereupon Harwood's wife Venus abused 'our vicar in most base and contemptible manner, saying that she would never receive a cup of salvation at the hands of of [*sic*] so damned a priest, and by comparing him to a dog, with many other vile and contemptible terms'.[15]

The vicar of Minehead, west Somerset, presented Grace Trott in 1622 for drunkenness and railing at him:

And her malice towards me was because I rebuked her for her drunkenness, which is my part to do unless I will partake with other men's sins. As I detest in malice to trouble any poor or rich, so would I not that the ministry should be made a jesting stock by their parishioners, but that they should be respectively used for their office and function sake.

Here was the minister's dilemma. Reproving sinners was a moral responsibility of the clergy—but it could lead to abuse and mockery that undermined pastoral authority and priestly status. Whatever a minister did, someone might be offended. In 1632 Thomas Lincoln of South Ockendon in Essex got a maidservant pregnant, and the parson pressed him to marry the girl 'as being the honestest and safest course'. But Thomas's brother Robert, constable of the parish, was furious with the rector, 'saying that he would take a whore's part before an honest man's'. In 1637 the minister of Worth in Sussex tried to quieten Sarah Butler, who was causing a disturbance in the churchyard—'and being admonished by the minister to forbear, she would not, but said, in contempt of him, "Mr Whiston, I care not for our minister, what care I for Mr Whiston?", and so continued in her scolding terms'.[16] Of course, these ministers were usually doing what most of their parishioners wanted: blasphemy, drunkenness, fornication, and scolding had to be checked. But if their discipline was so rigid that it looked harsh and over-intrusive, if it was exercised without tact, their lives could be difficult and their reputations suffered.

Henry Sharrock, vicar of Long Bennington, north of Grantham in Lincolnshire, bewailed his fate to Bishop Chadderton in 1606:

I live in a town so disordered and the persons so headstrong in their disorder that if I reprove publicly I am cavilled at afterwards; if privately, scorned and reviled to my face. If I speak of their viciousness to those with whom I am familiar, if it be known I am threatened to be sued for a slander, or else complained to the bishop for so many occasions as they can possibly article, either merely new or by surmises, so that I have been advised by some my neighbour ministers to pass them over with a kind of neglect, which counsel I have followed this three or four years. And now finding the forbearing hath bred contempt in them, in that when I have threatened them with presentment they decries me because I have not performed.

Sharrock was either unusually unlucky or unusually clumsy—and the advice given by his colleagues may suggest he had been unwisely energetic. Such aggressive clergy were often classed as 'puritans', and 'busy controllers' became a cliché. 'As for reproof, it maketh men think that to be the note of a puritan.

Exhortation?—that is preciseness,' complained godly Timothy, in Thomas Turvill's 1616 dialogue. Susan Kent of Wylye in Wiltshire objected to her vicar's campaign of preaching, catechizing, and moral reform in 1624, which got in the way of dancing on Sunday afternoons. When John Lee encouraged his parishioners 'as well the old as the young' to come to the catechizing, Susan told her neighbours in church 'that she would not sit there so long, for, said she, when once he (meaning Mr Lee) takes his green book in hand we shall have such a deal of bibble babble that I am weary to hear it'. When Elizabeth Wadling and others told her to keep quiet in case the minister heard her, she answered, 'I care not if he do, for he speaks against us for our dancing, but now my father is come over [i.e. is churchwarden] and if he speak against it my father will maintain it, for the king doth allow of it.' 'We had a good parson here before but now we have a puritan,' complained Susan.[17]

This is not to suggest that all godly ministers—much less all ministers—were harsh disciplinarians and were classed as 'busy controllers'. A dialogue between 'a precise preacher' and 'a country parson', probably written in defence of the 1618 declaration on Sunday recreations, sought to establish polarized stereotypes of the rigid precisian and the sensitive pastor—but that was a simplification. Parish realities meant that sensible preachers had to be pastors—otherwise, their lives would have been intolerable and their ministry ineffective. Often clergy intervened to try to moderate the rigour—and especially the cost—of ecclesiastical discipline. In 1599 the vicar of Flitwick, Bedfordshire, wrote to the chancellor of Lincoln on behalf of Mary Pink. She had had a bastard child and been whipped by the constable and excommunicated. Ralph Porte now asked for her to be absolved so she could come to church, 'wherefore I heartily desire your worship to weigh her beggar's estate for to remit the charges due for such malefactors, and because she should not be swallowed up of sorrow, she being penitent'. The vicar of Fareham appeared in the Winchester court in 1608 on behalf of four men who had been excommunicated for failing to answer for their absence from the previous Easter communion. He explained that they 'are poor people and did not receive by reason they had not money to pay their offering', and they had not obtained absolution because 'they are so poor that they are not able to travel and pay the fees'—the vicar was given authority to absolve them. Thomas Pestell, poet-vicar of Coleorton in Leicestershire, wrote to the bishop's commissary in 1620 to ask for the case against Richard Bodell and his wife for prenuptial fornication to be dropped:

Sir, this poor fellow was something rigorously dealt withal, in that the churchwarden being a white-haired bachelor and not knowing what belongs to the main point of matrimony, would needs present him for that his wife went not full forty weeks, whereof those that kept strict account say she wanted not three and two I have heard say the law allows a maid.

Pestell pleaded that 'he be not now so long since the fault called into trouble'.

And in 1640 Florence Taylor, of West Ham, took a letter from her vicar to the archdeaconry court of Essex, stating 'that in regard the fact for which she is accused was committed is nine or ten years since done and out of this jurisdiction, being also but single fornication and she very penitent for the same, she humbly desireth her penance might be re-enjoined to be done on Ash Wednesday and not on a Sunday'.[18]

Pastoral situations were sometimes handled with tact and sensitivity. Local disputes were often sorted out by the mediation of the minister, and clergy made particular efforts to reconcile parties before the Easter communion. William Auden, curate of Lingfield in Surrey, called Anne Waston and Anne Gainsford in to try to settle their dispute before Easter 1568, but without success. 'In the end, after long and uncharitable talk between the said parties', Auden told them they could not receive communion, and the two women went off shouting insults at each other: 'Thou art a whore!' and 'If I be so then you make me your fellow!' In 1606 Dr Inckforby tried to settle a controversy between two parishioners of Standlake in Oxfordshire, calling them home to meet him. In 1620 Edward Warren of Ashby-de-la-Zouch, Leicestershire, was ordered purgation by the archdeaconry court for alleged adultery—but Thomas Pestell, vicar there too, reported later that he had investigated the case and found it to be based on an untrue rumour started by Agnes Oving. Whether such intervention was always welcome is another question. In 1623 the minister of Little Houghton in Northamptonshire tried to settle a dispute between Anne Battison and his own wife before the Christmas communion. He sent a message to Anne Battison that he would refuse her communion unless she reconciled herself to his wife—but she responded that she would come to communion and let him refuse her if her dared. She did, he did, and it all went to court.[19] Whatever their success rate in dispute-resolution, however, many ministers had moral authority and respect in their neighbourhoods.

But the clergyman was always vulnerable. He was involved in so many transactions that invited dissent and disrespect—preaching against sin, calling the young to catechism, collecting his tithe, reproving and presenting offenders, pacifying local disputes—or not. He was never safe from insult—not even in church. 'Leave your babbling!' called Thomas Isodde to the vicar of Childswickham in the diocese of Gloucester as he was reading a homily in 1575. In 1588 John Phipp of Abington, Northamptonshire, interrupted a sermon and called out, 'Have we horns in the pulpit?'—suggesting the minister was a cuckold. In August 1603 there was a lively argument in Cutcombe church, Somerset, over whether Robert Nutcomb had been absolved from excommunication, 'and then, coming towards our vicar's seat in scornful sort [Nutcomb] delivered him a certificate, uttering these words most vilely, scornfully and scoffingly, "Here is for your worship", whereby most part of the people in the church were moved with laughter and laughed to hear and see him thus deride and misuse our vicar, and this was done in the midst of prayers'. Laughing at the minister in church was not unusual. In a sermon in the same year, the unpopular Mr Austin, vicar of Aveley, Essex, said 'that he had been amongst them ten years'—whereupon John Everett hissed 'it was too long'—and this was such a good joke that Everett repeated it in 1608, when Austin unwisely 'said he had been their minister for ten or twelve years': 'too long' said Everett again. In 1608 Romford Burton of Staverton, Northamptonshire, was 'a common scoffer and doth use to laugh in scorn in time of divine service and also in time of preaching'—and he had made a rhyme in mockery of the vicar, which he sang in John Herbert's house. Two men from Shepton Mallet, Somerset, were in trouble in 1615 for laughing at the parson during his sermon; Richard Hobbes of Potterspury, Northamptonshire, was presented for laughing at the minister in 1623, and so were John Black and Joseph Miller of Luddington in 1640.[20]

These are simply particular examples of abuse and mockery of individual ministers—occasioned perhaps by personal grievances or irresistible opportunities for a joke. But, especially as the incidents took place in church, they do raise the question of the status of the clergy, and of whether they had the respect and moral authority needed if they were to convert and reform. It seems to have been acknowledged that a minister was not quite as other men. In 1576 John Smith abused the vicar of Lydney in Gloucestershire as 'shitten knave, lousy knave, beggarly knave (setting his office, meaning his priesthood, apart)'—and this was a common exclusion. John Walmesley, minister of Bleason, Somerset, told Matthew King in 1610 that he was a knave, but King claimed 'he was as good and honest a man as himself (saving his coat and calling)'. A woman might use the same argument, and in 1618 Joan Barnard of Denton in Northamptonshire told Mr Baker, 'By God's blood, I am as good a woman as thou art a man, setting thy cloth aside.' When the rector of Lillingstone Lovell in Berkshire called John Billing 'a greasy, base rascal' in 1630, Billing retorted that 'Setting your ministry aside, I am as good a man as yourself'—though the rector's brother pointed out that he was not, since their grandfather had been a knight, 'but you show your breeding'. In 1632 John Ewens of Butleigh in Somerset told the curate, 'I care not a fart for you, and I am as good a man as you are, setting aside your coat.' And in 1636 Nicholas Saunders of South Petherton 'in choleric manner said unto Mr Johnson, curate there, as followeth, viz. "Thou art a base fellow, setting aside thy coat, and I will maintain it".' Sometimes such saving clauses may have been designed to avoid prosecution for defaming the priesthood (if so, they did not work)—though they were used in the heat of argument and at that moment they were probably meant. But Henry Robbins of Locking would have none of it. In 1622 he called the vicar 'pilled priest, jackanapes priest, and woodcock accusing priest and dizardly fool, and being admonished to have respect for his calling he replied that he did not care for him, neither a fart for his calling'. Underneath his cloth or coat, a priest was still a flawed human being: 'What are you, man?' asked John Hillary in an argument with the curate of Beaminster in Dorset in 1631, 'You are but

Anthony Hartford!' 'What is Dr Martin?' queried William Puckering of Uppingham, Rutland, in 1637: 'Hawsted [the minister] is Hawsted, and Puckering is
Puckering!'[21]

'Well met, good Master Theologus,' says godly Philagathus at the beginning of
The Plain Man's Pathway—and Theologus is treated with respect for his status
by both Philagathus and Asunetus. 'But you, Master Theologus, can repeat the
statutes better than I, because you are a professed divine,' says Philagathus. 'I
pray you, Sir, under correction give me leave to speak my mind,' says Asunetus.
But perhaps Theologus was a special case, since Philagathus complains that 'now
every rascal dares scoff and scorn at the most grave and ancient fathers and pastors
of the Church, and dares flout them as they walk in the streets and as they ride by
the highways'. And so it often was. On 27 June 1620, Adam Stephenson, vicar
of Grendon in Northamptonshire, passed William White in the street, who

would not so much speak unto me or uncover his head, but most unreverently and
uncivilly turned his tail unto me, who said unto him 'You might have spoken unto me
or uncovered your head', who answered and said unto me 'Who art thou?' I answered
'I am thy minister', who mockingly said with a loud voice said [*sic*] 'Wellingborough!
Wellingborough!' after a most dreadful manner.

(Presumably this was a reference to some incident at the town.) Edward Seaman
declared at the town hall in Harwich, east Essex, in 1627 'that he would regard
his minister as he would regard a dog, and wished that he might fall down in the
street when he did any reverence to him'.[22]

   Although insults were directed at particular ministers, the vocabulary of abuse
has pronounced themes that suggest general attitudes. Some terms, such as
'scurvy priest', 'knave priest', and 'pilled' or 'polled priest' were traditional, but
many hint at areas of tension between clergy and laity. The most common
insults relate to where exactly the clergy fitted in the social hierarchy, and
challenged their status. These were variations on a very few themes. Ministers
were called (omitting obvious repetitions): 'knave and knave priest' (Surrey,
1569), 'scurvy, stinking, shitten boy' (Northamptonshire, 1575), 'stinking knave
priest' (Northamptonshire, 1576), 'varlet and villain' (Northamptonshire, 1576),
'knave, villain, rogue, runagate, lousy knave' (Gloucestershire, 1576), 'knave and
arrant knave and Irish knave' (Gloucestershire, 1579), 'knave and vile knave'
(Hampshire, 1581),'knave and plaguey knave' (Oxfordshire, 1584), 'scurvy
priest and scurvy knave' (Leicestershire, 1585), 'jack scab and knave' (Wiltshire,
1586), 'pocky knave' (Northamptonshire, 1592), 'scrub bill' (Northamptonshire,
1599), 'beggarly priest' (Somerset, 1603), 'scabbed-neck and rascal' (Northamptonshire, 1605), 'snotty-nose knave' (Essex, 1607), 'hypocritical rascal, scurvy
fellow' (Northamptonshire, 1607), 'knave, arrant knave and brazen-faced knave'
(Hampshire, 1607), 'jack sauce and Welsh rogue' and 'saucy prattler' (Oxfordshire, 1608), 'scurvy, base priest' (Northamptonshire, 1608), 'totter legged and
pilled priest' (Somerset, 1609), 'scurvy jack and scurvy companion' (Essex, 1611),

'a beggarly knave, a rascal knave and a scurvy scab' (Somerset, 1611), 'rogue, rascal, villain and devil' (Northamptonshire, 1612), 'jack priest, rascal, base knave' (Sussex, 1613), 'filthy knave' (Northamptonshire, 1617), 'Scottish jack' (Sussex, 1617), 'rascally scab, scurvy knave and prating jack' (Sussex, 1617), 'a paltry and sorry fellow' (Northamptonshire, 1621), 'shitbreech' (Sussex, 1622), 'base knave, rascal knave' (Dorset, 1626), 'a runagately rogue and a prick-eared rogue' (Lincolnshire, 1629), 'base priest and runagate priest (Somerset, 1631), and 'copper-nose priest' (Warwickshire, 1635).[23] The reiteration of the term 'priest' was probably meant as an insult in itself, suggesting that Protestant ministers were no better than the ignorant pre-Reformation clergy.

Such insults seem to relate to the rising social status of the clergy, which resulted from their education, their prosperity, and their recruitment from clerical families and even from the gentry. Some laymen wanted to keep the priests in their place, with a brisk put-down—while others thought their own ministers were not up to the new status asserted, perhaps even deserved, by clerics. The contrast between clerical claims and lay attitudes was nicely put in 1609 by Sir Ferdinand Wenham, who called the vicar of Aveley, Essex, 'proud prelate' for his aspirations, but told him, 'thou art a base priest'. Some ministers were thought unbearably arrogant. 'Shall we be ruled by him, polled, scurvy, forward, wrangling priest?' asked Nicholas Lee of Washington, Sussex, in 1614, when the vicar forbade parishioners to ring the bells, and in 1616 William Deacon of Thorp Achurch in Northamptonshire asserted 'that the pope would have men to kiss his toe, but ... Mr William Browne would have them kiss his tail'. In 1629 Walter Ridout protested against the pride of the rector of Folke, Dorset:

You look for greetings in the market-place, the chiefest places at feasts and chief seats in the assemblies; you have made your wife proud, whom I thought would never be proud, in forgetting her old neighbours and taking her place before her elders, who gives her maintenance. You have no such example from Christ, for he was lowly and meek.

Prudence Carter of Great Holland in Essex would not be intimidated by her rector in 1633: 'she should not fear him if he were ten parsons, and better than he is, and that she cared not for ever a parson in England'. Ministers were often refused the verbal respect they thought was their due. 'Thou art a covetous man,' said Rowland Bowrer to the parson of Dogmerfield in Hampshire in 1581 in an argument over tithe. ' "Dost thou 'thou' me?" said Mr Coke, "I am not thy fellow!" ' 'Go take Mother Canning by the cunt again!' snapped Bowrer. Gilbert Spode of Bergholt in Essex was presented in the same year because 'he hath abused the minister, thou'ing him to his face'. Samuel Hooke, minister at Little Billing, Northamptonshire, complained in 1616 of Samuel Manning's insubordination, in saying 'that he was as good as myself and that he would never acknowledge me to be his betters [*sic*], and in all his terms naming of me he would give me no other title but called me "Hooke" '. In 1621 Roger May of Minehead in Somerset told the vicar, ' "Thou art a knave" and sirrah'd him, and called him rascal knave'. Joshua Sponge, a Leicestershire curate, complained in 1628 that John Watnaby had called him ' "Sponge, Sponge!" without any addition of title, in contempt'. And Joseph Hattersley of Ashby-de-la-Zouch was in trouble in 1636 for calling after the vicar in the street, 'Watson! Watson!' and 'Watson, I care not a fig for you!' The clergy had a new pride in their caste, which made them both more vulnerable to criticism and more likely to resent it.[24]

A university education was one aspect of the rising status of the clergy, but this too could provoke difficulties. A minister who had a university training might have his education mocked—while one who did not might be mocked for his lack. Clergymen were variously called 'ass and fool' (Essex, 1587), 'cuckoo' (Somerset, 1603), 'dunce' (Northamptonshire, 1607), 'lousy priest and scurvy ass' (Sussex, 1610), 'blockhead knave'—'any blockhead could do as much in the church as he' (Essex, 1611), 'scurvy vicar and paltry priest, a fool, goose and coxcomb' (Sussex, 1614), 'ass and knave' (Somerset, 1627), and the compendious 'an ass, a dolt, a block, a dunce, an ignorant or silly fellow' (Leicestershire, 1633)—the last addressed to Thomas Pestell, MA, poet, published preacher, and friend of bishops and deans. Even a doctorate did not go far. In 1613 Thomas Needham of Walthamstow turned up drunk at Mrs Jacob's funeral, 'at which time he did abuse Mr Dr Grant in words to the effect following, viz. he said to him "A fart for you and a turd for you, and a fart for your doctorship", with other opprobrious and unseemly speeches'. Perhaps it was an attitude such as this that prompted Dr Robert Jenison, preacher at Newcastle, to write to Samuel Ward, master of Sidney Sussex College, in 1630:

I should desire to know of you (but that I think you mind it much less than myself) what place, whether by university statute or by heraldry, if by occasion (more than search) you have heard, a Doctor in Divinity hath, not so much with respect to other degrees of learning, in law or physic, as to *the laity*, as suppose to a justice of the peace (out of his proper place) and whether their wives (by custom at least) take that place answerably. I ask not this with any intent to make other use of it than, as occasion serves, to stop their mouths that are ready too far to debase our calling and degree.[25]

Graduate status complicated the lives of the clergy. For those with degrees, there was the question of how they fitted into the status hierarchy: they had been educated with gentlemen, and they thought of themselves as gentlemen—but would they be accepted as gentlemen? And for those without degrees, there was the question of how they could maintain their authority as ministers when they were second-class clergymen.

The third theme among the insults heaped on the clergy was their sins—usually lust, covetousness, and gluttony (in the form of drunkenness). Ministers were called 'lousy knave, roguish knave, bawdy knave' (Gloucestershire, 1576), 'thief and rob-church' (Northamptonshire, 1577), 'drunken-faced knave' (Northamptonshire, 1579), 'runagate and cozening knave' (Staffordshire, 1584), 'knave, harlot and whore-hunter, and thief' (Gloucestershire, 1594), 'a rascal knave, a whoremonger knave' (Hampshire, 1595), 'wrangler and prattler' (Essex, 1597), 'false knave' (Northamptonshire, 1605), 'covetous and a cutthroat' (Essex, 1610), 'reprobate and bloodsucker' (Oxfordshire, 1610), 'bawdy priest and bawdy knave' (Somerset, 1610), 'thief, Welsh rogue, Welsh dog' (Somerset, 1612), 'rascal, rogue and murdering villain' (Somerset, 1612), 'thou whoreson, art thou foxed?' (Somerset, 1614), 'whoremaster' and 'filthy knab' (Wiltshire, 1615), 'lying knave' (Essex, 1618), 'a drunkard and a vile man' (Northampton-shire, 1621), 'goodman woodcock and cozener' (Somerset, 1623), 'God bless me, is cutthroat here?' (Northamptonshire, 1623), 'murderer and lunatic' (Somerset, 1626), 'Judas' (Somerset, 1628), 'base companion' (Buckinghamshire, 1633), 'as honest a man as any was in bedlam' (Northamptonshire, 1635), 'runaway priest, runagate priest, and base priest' (Somerset, 1637), 'malicious man', in an argument over tithe (Lincolnshire, 1638), and 'serpent' (Northamptonshire, 1639).[26] Sometimes specific insults were appropriate—there were adulterous and drunken and tithe-grabbing clergy. But insults also related to the contem-porary situation of the ministry—married, moralizing, and prosperous. Abuse relating to the status, education, and morals of ministers may or may not have been meant literally on particular occasions, but these terms also served as stock weapons in the armoury of anticlerical abuse. And, as such, they are suggestive of lay assumptions and prejudices about the clergy in general.

We must, of course, remember that this evidence is weighted towards hostility against the clergy. It is taken from the records of the regular visitation enquiries and the proceedings of Church courts: if someone criticized a minister it might be reported and recorded; if someone else praised a minister, these sources usually would not tell us. So we get only a partial view: we are told about adversarial situations and dysfunctional parishes, not about successful and popular ministers. The biographies of godly preachers tell a different story—of charismatic preachers, caring pastors, and responsive congregations. Ezekiel Culverwell's brief characterization of Arthur Dent praised his dedication to his ministry in Essex, and quoted his dying words as a fitting epitaph: 'I have fought the good fight, I have finished my course, I have kept the faith, and now is that crown of righteousness laid up for me which the Lord, that righteous judge, shall give me in that day.' William Garrett's life of Samuel Crooke narrates his work as rector of Wrington, Somerset, from 1602 to 1649—with systematic teaching of his flock from his own catechism, three sermons preached each week, sensitive treatment of cases of conscience, and generous hospitality to 'gentlemen, ministers, strangers and the poor'. Edward Bagshawe's biography of his mentor Robert Bolton tells a similar story of preaching and catechizing at Broughton and Kettering, where 'many hundreds were either absolutely converted or mightily confirmed or singularly comforted in their grievous agonies by his ministry'. Many other such lives were later collected into several volumes by Samuel Clarke, to demonstrate the evangelical and pastoral commitment of 'eminent divines' and absolve them of responsibility for the radicalism of the 1640s and 1650s. These too are weighted sources—though Bagshawe notes briefly that Bolton had troubles: 'some of his town had not only slandered his ministry but wronged him in his tithes'.[27]

We do not have to balance puritan hagiography against court statements, or ask which source is more representative of the truth: both have something to tell us, from different standpoints—that of the godly such as Dent's Philagathus, and that of the awkward squad represented by antagonistic Antilegon. Both attitudes were there, and we will not get far by counting heads. At the least, we must recognize that many ministers faced abuse, of themselves as individuals and of the clerical caste to which they belonged. In 1570 there were several presentments from Winchester diocese for speaking contemptuously of ministers in general: John and Cecily Day of Brixton, Surrey, Sampson Rich of Calbourne on the Isle of Wight, William Booth of All Saints, Southampton, and John Robinson of Bramdean, Hampshire. Perhaps they were traditionalists, objecting to new services and new teachings. Robert Alcock of Sudborough, Northamptonshire, abused his rector in 1576, 'and besought God that the curse of God might light upon the said Mr Sadler'—and then defamed all ministers of the Word, 'calling them all knaves and their wives whores'. In the same year, Francis Pilat of Egleton in Rutland told the vicar of Oundle 'that if all covetousness were lost it would be found in you priests'. In 1579 John Spark of Kelvedon in Essex was reported to have said it was now lawful to commit adultery, since lords and ladies and preachers did it all the time, and John Lowe of Rayleigh was presented as 'a slanderer of the ministers, calling them prattling knaves'—but he was also 'a swearer, a sower of discord and a disquieter'. After this decade of discontent, however, such general abuse of the clergy seems to have become less common in our record. When William Storre was murdered in 1602 by one of his parishioners at Market Rasen in Lincolnshire, some said it was 'a just reward due not only to the party murdered but also to the most of his calling or their over-bold checking and, as they term it, domineering over their betters'. 'It was a hellish ministry,' thought John Keepe of Hawkwell in Essex in 1610. In 1612 Roger Simpson of Tansor, Northamptonshire, had been 'railing against the clergy of the land, saying "There have been no good ministers for these many years" '. Francis Bowden of Curry Rivel, Somerset, spoke 'uncharitably and unreverently' of the clergy in 1618, and when asked by John Wetherall what he thought of the Hebrew scholar Ralph Cudworth of Aller he replied, 'he is the veryest Egyptian of them all'. In 1638 William Pinson of Birmingham said of the clergy that 'none belonged to the Church but drunkards and whoremasters'—but he was a thoroughly disenchanted nonconformist.[28] These few examples suggest that the descriptions applied to the clergy as a group were much the same as the stock insults available to apply to particular ministers.

In the main, the language of abuse was pretty consistent across time and place. By the 1610s, however, the clergy were being identified as 'black-coats'—which probably tells us something about the new prevalence of a distinctive clerical dress, and their obvious differentiation from laymen. In 1616 Thomas Granger complained about the anticlerical attitudes of 'Protestant atheists and epicures': 'they hate and deride the very name of a preacher, and cannot look upon a black-coat (as these black-mouthed hell-hounds term them) with a patient eye, which shows they hate our calling and are the enemies of their own salvation'—but that was going too far. John Rowswell of South Petherton, Somerset, beat the rector of Podimore Milton with a stick in 1616 and called him 'black-coat knave', and in 1622 John Gawler of Winterborne Kingston, Dorset, called 'ministers black dogs and the Bible a book of lies'. The clergy were most definitively black in the 1630s, however. Elizabeth Adams abused the minister of Storrington, Sussex, in 1630, 'saying she cared not for never a black-coat in England, and said the devil brought him into the parish and the devil will carry him out'. Miles Blacksmith of Milton, Northamptonshire, declared in 1634 'that he had as good a conscience as any black-coat in the country and that there were as base fellows and as base livers black-coats as any be of his coat, and said that he could be a black-coat for a groat'—which sounds like a protest against clerical pretensions. William Parker branded the curate of Paston 'black devil' in 1635, and in 1638 William Brinkley of Bracebridge, Lincolnshire, called the minister 'blackamore and malicious fellow', and when asked to mow for him replied 'that his grease should rot upon the ground before he would help him'.[29] A black-coat was not like his neighbours: now he looked different, and he was different—prosperous, educated, and pretentious.

Many of the insults we have seen had been used for generations, but we are not dealing only with age-old insults and individual slurs. We are dealing here with a new situation and a more difficult problem: we are seeing the consequences of Protestant Reformation and social change. Many ministers now saw themselves as preachers of regeneration and witnesses for truth—which is exactly what some laypeople, most obviously the godly, wanted them to be. Some of the laity esteemed the clergy for their social status, their education, and their uprightness—and perhaps more of them esteemed their own minister. But there was now a significant mismatch between the clerical aspiration and self-image as crusading preachers and the often-expressed lay preference for a pastor and peacekeeper. That is not to say that the roles of preacher and pastor were incompatible, but even when the two were combined together clergy and laity might prioritize them differently. That could mean trouble, and weaken the minister's impact in his parish. Further, when laymen and women abused a minister, they drew upon a ready supply of standardized abuse fed on anticlerical prejudices—some inherited, some given a different twist, some new. No matter how agreeable an individual parish incumbent might be, he had to overcome assumptions about the clergy. They were upstarts, they were greedy, and, for all their claims, 'a ploughman is as good as a priest'—as John Elkins declared in the streets of Isham, Northamptonshire, in 1634. A minister did not automatically have the prestige that might make his parishioners listen and obey. At best, he had to earn it; at worst, he would not get it. If he tried to do his job conscientiously, his relationship with many of his people was bound to be contentious. 'Is it not a tedious and irksome thing to think upon, and would it not kill a man's heart to go about it?' asked Theologus wearily. 'For how hard a thing is it to bring such into frame as are so far out of frame.'[30]

PART II

'ASUNETUS, AN IGNORANT MAN': KNOWLEDGE AND NEGLECT

3

Asunetus: Ignorance is Bliss

Well, I cannot read, and therefore I cannot tell what Christ or St Paul may say. But this I am sure of, that God is a good man, he is merciful, and that we must be saved by our good prayers and good serving of God.

When Asunetus first appears on the scene, godly Philagathus asks Master Theologus who he is: 'Asunetus, who in very deed is a very ignorant man in God's matters,' he is told. Poor Asunetus knows his own limitations: he cannot read, and he doesn't know much about the Scriptures. Bible-reading is all very well for those who have time, he thinks, 'but we have no leisure, we must follow our business, we cannot live by the Scriptures; they are not for plain folk, they are too high for us, we will not meddle with them, they belong to preachers and ministers'. He is, however, willing to listen and to learn from Theologus—'I pray you instruct me better, then'; 'I pray you tell me how it cometh to pass that I am thus deceived'; 'I pray you, good Sir, seeing I am ignorant, give me some particular directions out of the word of God.' Asunetus speaks for 'honest men'—'good neighbours and good townsmen'—and there were many like him. 'This age is full of such carnal Protestants,' says Theologus—'carnal Protestants, vain professors, back-sliders, decliners and cold Christians.' George Gifford dubs them 'men indifferent', 'profane men', and 'very atheists'; Thomas Turvill calls them 'parliament Protestants'; and Robert Bolton 'formal professors, carnal gospellers and half-Christians'. There were lots of them around, 'especially among the common and ignorant people', wrote Bolton; 'these are a kind of people who yet live in the darkness of their natural ignorance'.[1] In Arthur Dent's dialogue, Asunetus serves an obvious polemical purpose: he is there so his ignorance can be exposed and his sin revealed, and at the end he is converted by Theologus: he becomes a proper Protestant.

When Asunetus is questioned by Theologus, he gives some old-fashioned and rather silly answers. He knows that Christ's mother was 'our blessed Lady', and has a vague idea that Pontius Pilate was bad. But he thinks the two sacraments are bread and wine, that the purpose of communion is 'To receive my maker', and the use of a sacrament is 'The body and blood of Christ'. 'What is the holy Catholic Church which you say you do believe?' asks Theologus—'The communion of saints, the forgiveness of sins' is the answer. Obviously Asunetus once learned his catechism and can rattle it off, even if he does not know what it means. For him, religion is a straightforward matter—loving God and being good:

As long as I serve God and say my prayers duly and truly, morning and evening, and have a good faith in God and put my whole trust in him, and do my true intent and have a good mind to God-ward and a good meaning, although I am not learned yet I hope it will serve the turn for my soul's health. For that God which made me must save me. It is not you that can save me, for all your learning and all your Scriptures.

We don't need to know the hard stuff: we learn the basics and we behave ourselves. Asunetus was not alone. Gifford complained in 1582 of those who asked, 'What should laymen be troubled to learn, or to seek for the knowledge of the Scriptures? Let them tend to their work and look to their occupations, and learn to be quiet and to deal honestly.' 'What tell you me of these high points, or trouble me with this new learning?' ventriloquized Robert Bolton at the Kettering lecture, 'I know as much as the preacher can tell me, though he preach out his heart: that I must love God above all and my neighbour as myself, and that I hope I do.' 'Alas,' declared Thomas Clark at Blandford in Dorset in 1631, 'we have great multitudes among us professing ignorance, as if knowledge belonged not to them but to them that are book-learned and scholars by profession.'[2]

Eventually, Asunetus and his fellows did learn their catechism. We can establish this by tracking who was excluded from communion according to the Prayer Book rubric: 'there shall none be admitted to the holy communion until such time as he can say the catechism and be confirmed'. Henry Brandon of Wendon Lofts in north-west Essex was presented in 1569: 'he cannot say the catechism, therefore never received the communion'—Henry Eve could not say it either, and Thomas Eve and John Seymour were unable to recite the Commandments. Three people who could not say the catechism were refused communion at Mundham in Sussex in 1571, six at Amberley, and four at Coldwaltham. George Russell and a servant called Joan were excluded for ignorance of the catechism at Alresford in Hampshire in 1572, and Elizabeth Miller of Merstone could not recite the Lord's Prayer or the Creed. But the clergy were not as yet very determined or systematic in their examinations and exclusions. The vicar of Battersea, Surrey, was in trouble before Bishop Horne in 1570 for admitting people who could not say the catechism to communion and as godparents. In 1576 several Gloucestershire ministers were presented for disregarding the ignorance of communicants and of couples to be married: the vicar of Elmore was ordered that 'he shall signify to the parish that he hath done otherwise than his duty in doing the same'. At this stage, then, the number of exclusions is not a good guide to the level of ignorance, but there are some helpful indicators. In 1569 the Winchester consistory court began examining many of those who appeared before it on their knowledge, and by 1572 learning the catechism was a regular part of the penance imposed on offenders. Large numbers of people were instructed to learn the catechism and certify that they had done so: on 23 May 1573 twenty-four people were due to certify, but only two did so and seven asked for more time to learn. There was a strict examination of communicants at Bishop's Waltham in Hampshire at Easter 1574, when forty were excluded for ignorance and then ordered to learn the catechism. At the metropolitan visitation of Gloucester diocese in 1576 the churchwardens were asked for the names of young people who could not say the catechism. Sadly for our purposes, very few provided them—but at Edgeworth it seems that only half of the youth were competent, and at Eastington hardly any of them.[3]

But there was progress, as more ministers were pressed into a regular routine of catechizing. In 1574 George Yorke of Thurloxton in Somerset, a 28-year-old labourer, was a witness in a slander case. When his credibility was challenged, he admitted he was 'a poor fellow and in respect thereof of small credit and reputation'—'but examined of the Lord's Prayer and Belief he perfectly rehearsed the same. The Ten Commandments he answereth he cannot say by heart, but remembreth and did rehearse the effects slenderly.' In 1576 and 1577, trickles of people from various Hampshire parishes were presented for having forgotten the catechism—if they had ever learned it. In 1578 Clement Man and two others of Little Waltham in Essex 'were rejected from the communion by Mr Lock, for that they could not say the catechism without book, but they have sithence done their endeavours and can almost say it, and they will learn it as speedily as they can'. In 1582 fourteen children and servants at Fretherne in Gloucestershire could not recite the catechism: William Dythes promised that his children would learn it, and later certified that they were doing so. George Greene of Romford in Essex had refused to be examined in 1584, and told the archdeaconry court 'he is unlearned and therefore cannot as yet say the catechism, but he mindeth to learn it'. In 1585 John Thorne of Norton, north Somerset, explained that he missed communion at Easter 'for that he came not in due time to be examined, and they examined in such points as was hard for him to answer'. And when in 1587 Sarah Unwin of Hadstock in Essex was reported as an incompetent schoolteacher, it was said that 'those that told their catechism before she had them have now forgotten it'.[4]

Cases of rejection for ignorance were less common by about 1600, and after 1610 they were quite rare. Anne Walker of Farthington, Northamptonshire, did not receive communion in 1600 'because the curate sayeth she could not say the Lord's Prayer, Ten Commandments and Belief'. Boniface Behowe, churchwarden of Normanton, was presented in 1605 because 'having two maids very ignorant, doth not send them to be taught, he being oft admonished and exhorted to send them'. When Margery Jones, a servant of Barking, Essex, appeared to answer for not receiving communion at Easter 1608 she said 'she did never receive and that she understands not', and in 1609 the minister of Widford reported of Elizabeth Hills, servant, 'that by reason of her ignorance she is not fit'. Joan Jones of Wrington, north Somerset, was refused communion in 1609 'because she was ignorant in answering the minister to such questions as he propounded unto her', and in 1610 William Wash of Broadwater, Sussex, 'hath proferred himself but our parson would not admit him then by reason of his misdemeanours and gross ignorance'. By now, it seems, ministers were emphasizing the depth of the ignorance of those they rejected—no doubt because after 1604 they were supposed to justify exclusions to the ordinary, but perhaps also because total ignorance had become unusual. John Ramsey of Shelley, Essex, was reported in 1616 for not sending his children and servants to be catechized, 'being often admonished and they notwithstanding the most ignorant in all the parish', and in 1617 the curate of Stow Maries rejected Anne Sammes because 'she was so ignorant that I durst not admit her'. The minister of Combe Bisset in Wiltshire told the dean of Salisbury's registrar about Simon Long in 1620: 'at Easter last he could not (nor at leastways would not) say perfectly the Lord's Prayer nor the Belief, being a common swearer, but promising amendment I was content to admit him to the Lord's table'—and in the same year Thomas Chapman of Upton in Somerset was presented 'for being very ignorant and yet refusing to be catechized'. In 1633 three parishioners of Donnington near Chichester were refused communion as 'somewhat ignorant in the catechism', in expectation that by the next communion 'they may be better learned and taught'. Richard Spooner, a servant at Beauchamp Roding, was less cooperative and was called before the Essex archdeaconry court in 1634: 'he being a stubborn, ignorant fellow refuseth to be instructed either publicly or privately at his minister's hands'.[5]

In time, almost all the people knew their catechism, and only a few recalcitrants would not learn. But it had been a victory against the odds, for many parents and masters would not cooperate. At the 1576 visitation of Gloucester diocese, parents in twenty-eight parishes did not send their children to be catechized on Sunday afternoons. Thereafter things improved, but there were often difficulties in particular parishes. In 1577 the rector of Wardley in Rutland admitted 'that the greatest occasion why he left teaching of the catechism [was] because he cannot make his parishioners to bring their youth to the church'. At Poling in Sussex in 1586 it was reported, 'catechizing given over in the default of parents and masters'. In 1594 the churchwardens of St Mary Magdalen, Taunton, presented that parents were 'very negligent in sending their children'—'wherein they desire they be compelled, and that they cannot deliver their several names that have offended therein'. The wardens of Hutton in Somerset admitted in 1600 that 'there is a neglect in not coming to the minister at the time appointed for catechizing, but the fault is so general that they cannot in particular present upon their oaths truly'. John Paine of Banwell thought there was too much fuss over the enforcement of catechizing. In 1605 he and nine others were reported for not sending their children, and he told the wardens, 'It is not well that thus many should be presented for an old song.' Next year he admitted he had said this 'upon choler unadvisedly, for that he thought the occasion was but small to cause so many to be presented for that matter as there were'. Some parishioners simply did not recognize the need for systematic catechizing. The wardens of Wantage in Berkshire reported in 1607 'there is some negligence in catechizing, but we cannot blame our minister because children are not usually sent unto him, but we desire time for reformation thereof because we cannot present every man faulty because some of the inhabitants have none to send'. The vicar of Winscombe in north Somerset claimed in 1615 that 'he hath been always ready to catechize, but that the youth resort not unto him'. The wardens of King's Sutton, Northamptonshire, were in a quandary by 1619: 'our minister did catechize so long as he could have any to come, and when no more came then he left, and therefore [we] desire your Worship's advice what to do herein, for if we present any we must present all the parish'. When the vicar of Raunds was presented for not catechizing in 1627, he said 'he had divers times caused the bell to be tolled but nobody came to be catechized and hath long expected them, which hath caused him of late to neglect it'. Samuel Cox, rector of St Giles in Colchester, explained in 1632 that he had not catechized because the parishioners wouldn't send their children and the wardens wouldn't do anything about it: he was powerless.[6]

Despite all the problems, however, Asunetus learned his catechism. But the godly clergy were not satisfied with that. Theologus easily demonstrates that although Asunetus can recite the Creed he does not understand it. So many ministers tried to go beyond the simple formulations of the Prayer Book catechism. At Inworth, Essex, in 1591 the minister was probing his parishioners' comprehension, and excluding those who could not answer him. Some ministers wrote their own catechisms, longer and more testing: when Richard Gawton published his in 1612, he hoped that when he next examined his parishioners at Redburne in Hertfordshire he would 'not find you so ignorant as formerly I found you and your families'. Others used well-established printed catechisms. In 1587 George Reynolds and his wife were excluded from communion at Theydon Garnon, Essex, because they could not recite Dean Nowell's catechism—though they 'can say the catechism authorised'. The vicar of St Giles, Northampton, was using his own catechizing method in church in 1618, and also catechizing in private houses with Perkins's *Six Principles*. At Whitfield in 1639 the curate was using the *Six Principles* and Josias White's catechism, and refusing communion to those who could not master them.[7] Those who had learned the Prayer Book catechism were still 'ignorant'—because the godly clergy had higher standards and expected much more.

What the godly clergy wanted was not rote learning of the Commandments, the Creed, and the Lord's Prayer—they wanted an understanding and internalization of Protestant doctrines and values. When Theologus describes Asunetus as 'a very ignorant man in God's matters', he means that Asunetus is insufficiently Protestant—not that he is a Catholic, but that he does not think as a true

Protestant would. Those like Asunetus, those who were not real Protestants, remained prey to superstition and wickedness. Richard Bernard of Batcombe warned that

It is an evil too common among the ignorant vulgars, amongst the superstitious, the popishly affected, amongst others of a vain conversation, which are Protestants at large, neutrals at heart, sensual, without the power of religion, and amongst all the generation of vain people, to think presently, when any evil betideth them, that they or theirs or their cattle are bewitched, that some man or woman hath brought this evil upon them.

'Master B', the schoolmaster in Gifford's 1593 *Dialogue Concerning Witches and Witchcrafts*, argues that it is legitimate to seek any aids available against witches, and that God had given powers to cunning folk to do good. Godly Daniel shows Master B his errors, but the women in the dialogue are not persuaded. Nor were many in the real world. James Hopkins of Hornchurch, Essex, went to Mother Pearson in 1576 to find how his master's cattle had been bewitched, and in 1582 Goodwife George of Great Tey said a prayer over cattle that were 'forespoken'—bewitched. Thomas Ward of Purleigh went to a wizard in 1599 to see if his lost cattle were bewitched—but in 1613 William Presgrave of Astwell, Northamptonshire, burned some of his pigs because they were bewitched. Richard Abbey of Daventry went to a soothsayer for advice on a lost cow in 1596, and in 1598 Thomas Morris of Beauchamp Roding, Essex, 'sought to a worker with familiar spirits for certain fishes that were away'. Henry Wortley of Whissendine in Rutland consulted a wizard at Grantham in 1614 about a stolen ewe and hog, and in 1619 John Ward of Winwick asked about stolen sheep. Lost and stolen goods brought cunning folk much of their business: enquiring for lost money to Salisbury and Oxford in 1575; for stolen clothes at Welton in 1595; stolen bacon at Newnham in 1596; for a stolen petticoat to Bankside in London in 1602. In 1614 Richard Pannell saw Sowton of Sompting in Sussex about his lost purse: 'the said Sowton did will him to go home and he should have his purse again, but he never had attained it'. Sowton was himself in court in 1617, and denied that he had any skill in finding lost property—as Richard Pannell could confirm. 'Chamberlain the sorcerer' of Leicester had a reputation in Northamptonshire: Charles Drew of Stanion asked him about stolen property in 1617, and Isabel Gillet of Blatherwyke went to him in 1618 'to know what became of certain linen that was lost'. At King's Sutton, Northamptonshire, in 1619 there were several parishioners who had consulted sorcerers, but they were not listed by name as they had threatened to run the minister out of town for reporting them. And when Matthew Rodmill of Langham in Rutland lost 30s. in 1629 he tried self-help sorcery, using the well-known shears-and-sieve method for finding things.[8]

Wizards were also consulted when people were sick or thought to be bewitched. Richard James of Peterborough asked a wise man in 1590 how his master had been bewitched, and one John Bull was blamed for it. Ellen Yeo of Hullavington, Wiltshire, went to a cunning woman when she had scurvy in 1593. On Whit Sunday 1596, Agnes Garrett and Agnes Bamford of Lamport, Northamptonshire, went off to see a wise woman and on their return they seized Foster's wife, scratched her face, and called her witch—from which we can presumably guess the wise woman's advice. Thomas Saye of Buttsby, Essex, went to a wizard for help for his sick child in 1600, and Thomas Skinner consulted the sexton of Barking about his sick wife in 1602—though he said he only went for physic and didn't know the sexton used charms. As well as such family necessities, there was much to encourage belief in the powers of wizards. In 1616 Thomas Plumer's wife of Nassington, Northamptonshire, told Alice Talman that she would never get well until she married, and accurately predicted the time of a child's death. Thomas Tyzer of Charminster, Dorset, was in trouble in 1617 for persuading women who came to him for advice 'that he cannot help them without either crossing their foreskins or lying with them'. In 1618 Valentine Fulke went to a wise woman at Aston Rowant in Oxfordshire for a love potion to gain the affection of Anne Barston—which apparently worked, and 'the said Anne did extraordinarily affect the said Valentine'. William Walford of Cold Norton, Essex, was presented in 1619 for telling any sick neighbours that they were bewitched, and 'except they will be of that belief they can hardly be holpen of their disease and sickness'. Widow Forrin of Brackley, Northamptonshire, staged an elaborate ceremony in 1623 for recovering her health. Three or four other widows knelt around her and prayed for her, and then they poured wheat grains over her veiled head. She claimed that this had worked, 'which practice of hers was a great scandal to understanding religious persons and encouraged the weak and ignorant to incline to like sorceries and superstitions'. Reputation mattered in the sorcery business. It was reported in 1629 that Andrew Ward of Rothwell was known 'for a charmer or enchanter or wizard or a good witch, falsely so called, one that taketh upon him to help such as are or thought to be bewitched'.[9]

Proper Protestants did not think like that; proper Protestants had escaped the habits and superstitions of the past and knew to trust in God's providence alone. They were new men and women, born again in Christ: they did not resort to cunning folk, nor did they take part in traditional seasonal celebrations. In Thomas Turvill's *Poor Man's Pathway*, the godly Timothy debates dancing and May celebrations with wordly Ananias, who is a fiddler. Unsurprisingly, the fiddler favours dancing as a harmless pastime, while Timothy regards games and dancing as 'heathenish vanities' that breach God's commandments and lead to fornication. This argument was replicated across England, as 'Asunetus' defended traditional festivities and 'Theologus' tried to preach them down. In 1576 the churchwardens of Sonning in Berkshire complained that they had always had a 'summer pole' in the churchyard 'to make pastime for the commodity of the church', but now their vicar had forbidden it. May and Whitsun ales and games were held despite attempts by magistrates to forbid them—at Bremmett in Hampshire in 1583, at Donhead St Mary in Wiltshire in 1584, and at Bawdrip in Somerset in 1585. The wardens of Marston St Lawrence, Northamptonshire, were presented by the vicar in 1588 'for that the Sabbath is profaned with May games and Whitsun ales and other vain exercises'. In 1603 the rector of Donyatt in south Somerset complained that the churchwardens had 'unorderly kept church ale, with rioting, dancing and drunkenness upon the Sabbath day', at which John Dyght had got so drunk that he had to sleep it off in a stable. The wardens admitted they had held an ale 'with dancing and suchlike merriment, but in good order and not in the time of service'. The morris dancers of Tinwell, Rutland, were reported in 1605 for going to church after they had danced on May Day, 'sweating and blowing in their dancing attire, viz. with their napkins, ribbons, scarves and suchlike'—Richard Wadd 'in his fool's coat and his fool's cap under his arm', and Robert Bowen 'in his lordly apparel'. The 1609 churchwardens at Lyme Regis in Dorset were worried about the Whit Sunday procession, with flags and drums and other instruments—'which we take to be a profane use contrary to the right sanctifying of the Lord's day'. It is clear that such ungodly customs were now causing division within communities. There was a row over the maypole in the churchyard at East Brent in Somerset in 1615, when John Band tried to cut it down and drew his sword to frighten off the women and children who tried to stop him. A group of parishioners from Keynsham got into trouble for Sabbath disorders in 1619—they went off to fetch a maypole from Charlton, and then marched back into the town with drums beating and guns going off.[10]

Local disputes about festivals were especially common in the 1630s, after the 1633 Book of Sports had made traditionalists more confident and the protesters more desperate. At Little Somerford in north Wiltshire, Arthur Speck sponsored Whitsun celebrations in 1633, with music and dancing and drinking during a Sunday sermon. In 1632 there were arguments at Ditcheat in east Somerset over whether the parish should have a maypole: Arthur Dorvall contended that 'a maypole was an idol', and Ralph Haines said the bishop didn't understand Scripture if he allowed maypoles—but the defenders of festivities reported them and testified in court. At Adderbury in Oxfordshire in 1634 a visiting preacher criticized Whitsun ales, and attacked the parishioners for decorating their church with garlands—so the churchwardens turned him in. There were serious disorders over May celebrations in 1634 in the church of St Peter-le-Bailey in Oxford. In April there were protests by 'puritans and factious persons' against the projected Whitsun ale and games, and a suggestion that if there were to be an ale it should at least be held away from the church. On May Day, as the youth of the parish rang the bells and carried the customary garland of flowers into the parish church, John Bolt, John Wildgoose, and others tried to disrupt proceedings—which led to 'great tumult and uproar' and a fight in the church, with the outraged traditionalists led by Edward Mitchell, a butcher.

There were disagreements at Lyme Regis in 1635 over the 'Appellation day' festivities—when there were bonfires at Mill Green 'for the christening of apples', with 'gunning, drumming and shooting'. The fun (and noise) went on through the Sunday service and sermon, and one of the town justices refused to silence the racket when asked by the rector—'what a prating ... maketh he about nothing'.[11]

Bell-ringing was another traditional jollity that focused tensions within parishes. Church authorities campaigned through the 1560s and 1570s to suppress celebratory ringing, and especially 'superstitious' ringing at All Hallows—which was still widespread in Hampshire in 1568 and Gloucestershire in 1576. When the men of Wanstrow in Somerset were forbidden to ring at All Hallows 1568, some of the women did it instead, 'for they said they were lawless' (that is, they were outside the law and could not be blamed). On All Hallows' Day 1573 there was debate among parishioners in King's Worthy church in mid Hampshire over whether to continue their traditional ringing. John Webb stood up for the bells, against the opposition of the rector—'Let us do our duties and live under a law, for our parson playeth the mock friar with us; he did sit in a surplice at morning prayer like a minister, and at evening prayer he sat without his surplice like a courtholder'. Six men of Isham in Northamptonshire were reported by the rector in 1575 for ringing the bells at night on All Saints' Day, 'and churned them altogether, and for jangling a peal, a most odious hearing'—'yet would not leave until I brought others whereby they were constrained'. In 1582 Dr Ralph Jones, vicar of Bedford, complained to the bishop of Lincoln about 'immoderate ringing without cause', on Saturdays, Sundays, and holy days and their eves. Jones had tried protesting to the mayor, Alexander Hunt, 'that there might be some mean, and no abuse used'. Hunt had replied 'that he was but the vicar, and had nothing to do with it. That he [Jones] gave nothing to the church and that therefore he himself [Hunt] would cause ringing as pleased him.' A group of men at Ilkeston in Derbyshire celebrated Whit Monday 1584 by ringing the church bells at ten or eleven at night—presumably after drinking. By now, unofficial bell-ringing was associated with juvenile and drunken excess as much as tradition. In 1589, after a group of West Ham men had been drinking at John Ward's house, they fastened a pair of horns to the curate's door and then went off to the church to ring the bells—'making merry in the night-time with a stranger of London'. When the minister of Fotheringhay, Northamptonshire, tried to curtail ringing in 1596, Nicholas Goodyer asked, 'Why should I not ring after eight a'clock as well Mr Leverton catechize after eight a'clock?' Arguments in church about bell-ringing were then common in that county: at Wotton in 1600, at Towcester in 1601, at Uppingham in 1602, and at North Luffenham in 1603.[12]

Unauthorized bell-ringing might be just youthful high spirits—but it could be a real nuisance. Once in 1611, Richard Penfold and seven others of Angmering in west Sussex rang the bells until midnight 'to the great disquietness of the parish and all the country thereabouts'. At Cottesmore in Rutland in 1618, the well-named James Bellers and five others were responsible for 'disorderly jangling and ringing of the bells many times' after services, 'suffering themselves to be locked into the church because they would not give over'—and when the rector sent George Currier to tie up the ropes to prevent the ringing, he was forcibly resisted by three others. At Graffham in Sussex five servants rang the bells through most of the night after Christmas Day 1625. There was 'disorderly ringing' on Sundays at Braybrooke, Northamptonshire, in 1626, and the wardens only encouraged it when the minister protested. When 'a company of ringers' at Kilmersdon, Somerset, had finished their Christmas ringing in 1629, they settled down to a party in the church, with food and ale on the communion table. Some of the parishioners at Deddington, Oxfordshire, complained to the bishop in 1631 that their minister and others had forbidden any ringing: Bishop Corbett decreed they should be allowed to ring after evening prayer on Sundays and 'on solemn occasions as funerals, marriages and suchlike'. Hugh Conygrave, the rector of Stoke Albany in Northamptonshire, had had quite enough of bell-ringing by 1634. He forbade the young men of the parish to ring, ordered them out of the belfry, pulled one of them out by force when he wouldn't leave, and finally cut the bell-ropes short to frustrate would-be ringers. But ringers might defend their rights. John Allgood and friends rang the bells at Great Totham in Essex after the evening service one Sunday in 1638, and when a sidesman told them to stop Allgood 'asked him what he had to do with it'.[13] For the godly, however, bell-ringing was more than a noisy nuisance: it was sheer superstition, and an affront to God.

People like Asunetus—the insufficiently Protestant—were all around: those who didn't know the Scriptures, those who went to cunning folk, and those who wanted maypoles and church ales and bells. To the godly, such people were 'ignorant', 'profane', 'ungodly'—and, often, 'atheists'. As is well known, an 'atheist' was then not a man who did not believe in God but a man who behaved as if there were no God and no divine retribution, a man without religion. But the 'ungodly' did have religion, it just wasn't the same sort of religion as the godly. Asunetus thought of himself as a religious man:

I keep my church as well as any man in the parish where I dwell, and mind my prayers as well when I am there, I thank God for it. Though I say it myself, I have been always well given, and have loved God's word with all my heart, and it doth me good to hear the Epistles and Gospels read every Sunday by our vicar.

Church attendance was important to people like him. Robert Gray of Weedon in Northamptonshire was excommunicated in 1576, 'but showeth himself disobedient still and cometh into the church to the disquieting of the parish'. He wanted to go to church, despite being excommunicated: others did not want him there, because he was excommunicated. In April 1600 the churchwardens of Kettering asked for six of their parishioners to be absolved from excommunication, because they often came to church and so the service had to be halted. Eusebius Warkworth of Ringstead also kept coming to church when excommunicate, 'so that we had no service by the space of five days, which we desire to have word how it may be reformed'. Annabella Davie, a widow from Ongar in Essex, excommunicated in 1603, 'did nevertheless presume to come into the church to divine service'. In 1619 John Hix, churchwarden of Dinder in Somerset, was excommunicate for two weeks for contempt in refusing to join in the presentment—so for two Sundays he went to services at St Andrew's in next-door Wells. When Anne Cooper of Arthingworth, Northamptonshire, was excommunicate in 1623, she sat in the church porch to hear service and sermon. Alice Launden of Brixworth stood excommunicate for five or six years when presented for fornication: it was reported in 1626 that 'she sayeth that she goeth to hear the sermon sometimes but denyeth to do her penance'. William Glover of Burton Latimer abused the churchwardens in 1634 after his daughter was presented and excommunicated, and threatened to force them to allow her into the church. There were, of course, more reasons than piety for church attendance. It was a sign of respectability, and in 1630 absences were cited to discredit a witness in a matrimonial contract case at the Oxford consistory court. Nevertheless, people went to trouble for their weekly dose of religion. When Dr Andrew did not appear to say a morning service at Beaconsfield, Buckinghamshire, in 1633, the people waited for several hours—and some of them went off to neighbouring churches for the afternoon service.[14]

Rites of passage were especially significant—and missing them mattered. At Yatton Keynell in Wiltshire an unmarried mother was not churched, but in 1584 she nevertheless 'doth resort to divine service to the great grudge of the good conscience of the same parish'. The wife of William White of Charlbury, Oxfordshire, could not be churched in 1596 because she was excommunicated: he told the diocesan court that 'this respondent (being desirous that she serve God) did say and read certain prayers unto her at home'. In 1599 the wife of Richard Archer went to be churched at Barking in Essex although she was excommunicate, and as the curate did not know her state he performed the ceremony. Thomas Garth, vicar of Charlton-on-Otmoor, Oxfordshire, was often absent in 1618—so mothers went off to other parishes to be churched. In 1627 Mary Searles of St Martin's, Colchester, was presented 'for going abroad before she was churched'. But she had tried: she told the archdeaconry court on 8 February 1628 'that she did offer herself four or five times to Mr Smith, curate there, to be churched and he would not church her, and that she did keep in thirteen weeks before she went abroad, and thus it was not her fault'.[15]

Churching was only a matter of ecclesiastical rules and social custom—but many of the less-Protestant believed baptism was crucial to salvation. After all, the Prayer Book did say that in the christening a child was made 'regenerate' by Christ. At Whitsun 1597 two babies of Folkingham in Lincolnshire were taken off to Newton to be baptized because of the absence of the rector, 'to the great grief of the parents and peril of the children, for it was feared that one of the children would have died before it was christened'. In 1602 the awkward nonconformist Anthony Armitage, vicar of Ellington, Huntingdonshire, refused to christen Francis Morley's sick child on a weekday and it died unbaptized, 'to the great grief of the parents'. Elizabeth Maunder of St Aldates, Oxford, went to Chipping Norton for the delivery of her illegitimate child in 1631. After the birth the vicar refused to christen it in case the parish became responsible for the baby's maintenance—so her brother entered into a bond with the overseers of the poor, and Elizabeth's baby was baptized. In 1632 a couple of strangers gave William Smith of Pitton, Wiltshire, 30s. to have their baby nursed and baptized: his wife nursed the child, he gave the minister 10s. for the baptism and the parish clerk 3s. 4d. to act as godfather, and kept the rest for himself. He later did penance as 'a maintainer of adultery'. Baptism had mattered to the parents, and also to William Smith—he could have kept all the money for himself. Thomas Lamb and his wife, of St Giles, Colchester, were both excommunicates, and baptized their child at home in 1638—though they may have been separatists, and had a home baptism on principle.[16]

Death too had its necessary dignities and religious accompaniments. John Moore and his wife, of St James's, Bath, were presented in 1620 'for using foul and disgraceful speeches against an honest man whom the Lord had lately taken to his mercy, as that he had lived like and rogue and died like a rogue'. The wardens protested that the deceased 'had lived as an honest man among his neighbours and died in the faith of Christ, as he testified before the minister not half an hour before his death'. On a Saturday night in October 1628, Philip Kirby was found wounded in the street in Northampton: 'My friends, my friends, good people pray for me!' were his last words. In 1629 Matthew Pippin of Clipston stabbed himself in the head. Before he died, Thomas Bull asked him 'to call upon God, and presently after the said Matthew said "Ah, flinty heart!"' As Pippin faded, Bull encouraged him, 'Good father, if you can say anything more I pray lift up your heart and hands unto the Lord'—and he raised his hand. Mistress Mound and others knelt by the bed praying, and 'at the end of the said prayers he and others perceived him to lift up his eyes, and so he departed'. Bull's evidence deliberately emphasized that Pippin had turned to God at his end—'he verily believeth that he the said Matthew was before his death very sorrowful and penitent'—to justify having buried Pippin in the churchyard. But it was important to Bull and all the others involved that Pippin should have a Christian death and a Christian burial. Others behaved less well at a death, and in 1635 the curate of Sutton in Somerset was presented for revealing what Simon Small had said to him when he 'lay very sick by way of confession of his sins'. The Prayer Book required clergy to seek deathbed confessions of sin, and they were probably common. On his deathbed in 1627 William Gooding of Martock, Somerset, confessed that both he and Thomas Gardner had had sex with Christian Jeanes. When Tiffany James of Dunster lay dying in 1638, she revealed the names of two fathers of her children, and in the same year Jane Catford of Dulverton confessed that she had committed adultery with three men—with John Corner and John Fisher for 6*d*. each, and with William Fisher for a piece of wool. Joan Webb of Farington suffered a long illness and, in 1639, 'being desirous to confess her faults and to ask forgiveness for her offences, she openly confessed that she had committed the crime of adultery, especially with John Edwards the elder'.[17]

Friends and family wished the departed to receive Christian burial—even when the law denied it. There are lots of examples of excommunicates and recusants being buried in consecrated ground. In 1597 the Peterborough diocesan court investigated the burial in churchyards of two excommunicate women. The churchwardens of Ryhall attested that six wives and Widow Cott had made a grave and buried Elizabeth Fraston, and eight wives and a maid of Northampton were examined about the burial of the nonconformist Mrs Pamphlin. In 1610 Alice Baldwin railed at the minister of St James's, Colchester, for refusing to say the service at the burial of her excommunicate husband, and John Parker of Highworth in Wiltshire abused the minister for refusing a churchyard burial to the excommunicate John Temple. The suicide Elizabeth Monck was buried in the churchyard of St Cuthbert's, Wells, in 1629 after the intervention of the foreman of the coroner's jury. When Richard Bourne asked the vicar to allow the burial, the vicar answered equivocally, 'all the leave that he could give or grant he did willingly grant'—so Bourne got the sexton to dig the grave and the burial went ahead. In 1631 Richard Holloway died excommunicate, but before he died he had wished to be absolved 'and was desirous of Christian burial'—so the Oxford court issued a licence for him to be buried in the churchyard at Combe. Also in 1631, there were strenuous efforts to get a formal funeral service and burial in church for the excommunicate Mrs Horseman of Wheatley. A servant was sent to Oxford to get a faculty from the diocesan chancellor, the vicar of Halton was pressurized, and finally she was buried at night under the communion table in Halton church. 'God's blessing on their hearts that buried the dead,' pronounced Thomas George's wife, 'it is fit the dead should be buried.'[18]

Everybody wanted their proper part in Christian rites—and it is striking how seriously people regarded the receiving of communion. As is well known, almost everyone took the sacrament at Easter—though, of course, it was an ecclesiastical offence to fail. In 1577 the churchwardens at Ilminster, Somerset, stated that 'the people are many and the parish is great', so some went to service at other churches. Nevertheless, 'at Easter last all the whole parish that were of lawful age did receive the holy communion as they think, except Thomas Tolman and John Lock'. At Evenley in Northamptonshire in 1607, the curate and wardens certified 'that all in our parish above the age of sixteen years have received the communion at Easter last according to the canons, except William Stutbury and his wife'. At Ashurst in west Sussex things were just a little less organized in 1622: 'All have received the holy communion, except some few that will receive it at Whitsuntide at the furtherest.' Excommunicates wanted their communion too. John Shelford's excommunication had been pronounced at his parish church at Exford in west Somerset, so at Easter 1573 he went to communion miles away at Congresbury. Margaret Ager of Holy Trinity, Colchester, was excommunicated early in 1581, but 'since that denunciation in contempt of the law hath received the communion at Mr Kirby's hands'. In 1588 the vicar of Winscombe in Somerset received the excommunicated troublemaker William Smith at communion, after he had claimed to be covered by a general pardon 'and promised he would live quietly and in charity with his neighbours'. For the Easter communion in 1633, Francis Page of Chilton in Buckinghamshire went to Wotton Underwood, 'pressing in amongst the communicants of Wotton and receiving the communion unawares to the minister, being excommunicate the same time'.[19]

Some took the sacrament despite having been warned or forbidden. The wife of William Robbin of Holland in east Essex was warned by the curate in 1581 to seek reconciliation with her enemies before communicating, but she 'did presume to come to the communion at Christmas'. In 1584 Richard Turland of Bloxham, Oxfordshire, 'was constrained to go to King's Sutton to communicate there, because the vicar would not suffer him to communicate in his parish except he could say the catechism without the book, which he thinketh by law he is not bound to do because he can and useth to read it'. John Sexton and his wife were refused communion at their own church of Stadhampton in 1593, so she went off to Dorchester—though it seems John didn't bother. The minister at Elmstead, Essex, had often warned his parishioners that they must not receive communion unless they had been at morning prayer—but at Easter 1610 Samuel Munt, his son, and a servant came late to church and 'thrust themselves in unto the holy communion'. In 1627 William Cricket of Winterborne Kingston, Dorset, was allowed to receive communion at Easter on his promise to give up his swearing and chiding—but he 'did amongst his fellows insult over his minister for that he had promised him to become a new man but he had no such purpose'. Richard Stevenson of Thornton Curtis in Lincolnshire was a multiple offender—'being commonly reputed to be a drunkard, a swearer, a slanderer of his minister'—and was presented for fornication. The minister warned him privately not to go to the Easter communion in 1638, but he turned up anyway and had to be prevented by the wardens. Doubtless there were all sorts of reasons why people got themselves to the communion: legal requirement, social convention, assertion of rights and status, and sometimes sheer bloody-mindedness, as well as piety. But it was a serious matter to miss communion. After Easter 1574, Henry King came to the door of Andrew Severn of Tewkesbury and asked, 'Why are you so sad?' 'Because your landlord (meaning John Downe) will not let me receive the communion,' was the reply. 'If you will be ruled by me you may receive', declared King—'If you buy his wife.'[20]

Even more striking than the push for communion is the scrupulosity with which people abstained. We must be careful, since the excuses non-communicants produced when summoned to court might be calculated to gain sympathy—but many ring true. In 1569 Robert Frogmore, of St Nicholas, Gloucester, told the court he had missed communion because 'he was not with pure conscience, because his wife had committed adultery'. On Whit Sunday 1575 morning prayer at Maisemore in Gloucestershire was interrupted when the curate was given a letter disclosing that the parish had been reported for irreverence at services—'in such sort that the whole multitude was in an uproar and [Robert Eldridge] and others that were determined to receive the communion were disquieted that in their consciences they thought it not meet so to do'. Communion needed a quiet mind and a settled conscience. In 1577 Oliver Thornton of Bozeat, Northamptonshire, was denounced because 'he hath not received the communion for the space of two years, neither can the vicar or any other man persuade with him to come and receive with his brethren as a Christian man ought to do for his soul's health'. In court, Thornton testified 'that one Thomas Estwicke hath taken his house over his head, and that at this present there is a suit betwixt them and for that cause he cannot receive the communion, being disquieted in conscience with the said Estwicke's dealings'. A strong sense of grievance was a reason for abstention. John Smith of Marston St Lawrence told the churchwardens in 1601 that he could not communicate because he had been misused by the rector of Chipping Warden, 'in such sort as flesh and blood cannot bear'. John Cadbury of Hampton Poyle in Oxfordshire did not receive at Easter 1606, apparently because he 'was and is troubled in conscience about some suits and matters in law', nor did John Fleetwood of Shorthampton as 'he could not find it in his conscience because he had received some wrongs'. Since there were disputes in the household between his master and the servants, William Filkins of All Saints, Northampton, had not prepared himself for the sacrament in 1614 and did not receive. And in 1637 Jane Parrot of Shipton-under-Wychwood, Oxfordshire, explained that 'she could not with a safe conscience receive the communion' because 'there was some difference between her and her husband, who will not allow her maintenance but liveth away from her at one William Wall's house, her next neighbour'.[21]

An unquiet conscience was a particularly scrupulous application of a more general excuse—being 'out of charity' (or in dispute), specified in the Prayer Book as a reason why a minister should refuse communion. People took the need to settle quarrels seriously, and abstained from communion if they could not. On Good Friday 1581 William Howse of North Waltham in Hampshire 'desired James Rumbold if any controversy were between them that they might be friends, and thereupon the said Rumbold answered "A knave I found thee and a knave I leave thee" '—so Howse missed the Easter communion. Thomas

Barnes of Fordham informed the Essex archdeaconry court in 1591 'that he and his neighbour Studley were at variance, and by that occasion they received not, but he is content to receive at the next communion and is so purposed, for as he sayeth, he went twice or thrice before Easter unto Studley to be reconciled and he would not accept of his reconciliation'. The Prayer Book in fact decreed that if one party to a quarrel honestly sought agreement and was rejected, he or she might still receive if penitent. In 1592 William Scott of Chigwell told the court that because of controversies with some of his neighbours 'he cannot receive the communion as yet with a good conscience and quiet mind as a Christian ought to do (and he saith) that he doth not abstain from the communion upon any contempt of the laws but only upon the occasion before alleged'. At Easter 1627 Bridget Anger of East Mersea appeared to take communion, but in fact did not. On the day before the communion she had had an argument with the vicar's wife and was not in charity—so she put her lips to the communion cup without drinking the wine, and took the communion bread home and gave it to one of her children. Her conscience was clear.[22]

A common explanation for missing communion was a dispute with the minister, or some other reason for not receiving at his hands. Wilfrid Luthy of Aveley in Essex refused to receive communion in 1591 from Mr Spencer, because of lawsuits between them. In January 1592 he asked for permission to take the sacrament at another church, because the disputes still continued—and in March he certified that he had received at St Benet Fink in London. Mary Kirby of Wonston in mid Hampshire asserted in 1594 that 'she forbeareth only by reason of some discord betwixt her and the curate there, but is willing to receive at the parson's hands'. Presumably rightly, the Winchester court concluded that she was out of charity, and ordered reconciliation before she received. Philip Wateridge of Brown Candover told the same court in 1607 that he would take the sacrament 'so that he may be tolerated to receive at the hands of some other minister, because the minister Mr Stanley is his adversary and hath given out that he will never be friends with him'—and like Mary Kirby he was told to seek agreement with the minister. Ten parishioners of Halstock in Dorset stayed away from communion at Easter 1616 'by means of some discord between our parish and Mr White our late minister, but did all of them receive the same in our church on the 14th of July last'. Nicholas Weald of Great Burstead disclosed to the archdeaconry court of Essex in 1621 'that there was dissention between him and Mr Pearce their vicar, and that he received the sacrament of the Lord's Supper yesterday last past in the parish church of St Katherine Creechurch, London'—and his choice of the godly Stephen Dennison's church may suggest his religious preferences.[23]

Refusal of communion from a particular minister may reflect the popular pre-Reformation supposition that the sacrament was worth less in the hands of an unworthy priest. It was thought in the parish of Piddington in Oxfordshire in 1591 that the curate, Richard Tetlow, had an improper relationship with

Jane Doyle. John Wright affirmed 'it doth grudge his conscience to receive the communion at Mr Tetlow's hands, unless he do mend his manners', and Thomas Stephens deposed 'that the consciences of the inhabitants of Piddington, or the most part of them, are grieved and unwilling to receive the sacraments at his hands since this evil fame and report went of him': Richard Vine and his family went to communion at Ambroseden instead. John Frith of Rainham, Essex, went to take communion from Mr Danvers at neighbouring Wennington in 1600, 'for that their minister is a lewd man and he cannot find in his heart to receive the communion at his hands', and in 1602 Richard Mount and William Lunes of Berwick St John, Wiltshire, 'did forbear to come to the communion for the badness and lewdness of life of the minister'. Joan Gibb's objection to David Owen, rector of All Saints, Northampton, was rather different. She did not take the sacrament in 1614 because 'Her master (she being but a servant) commanded her not to receive the same, wherein she did the rather obey his command for that upon the day when she should have received Mr Owen excommunicated her master, which she thought was wrongful, and therefore she could not receive with a quiet conscience.' This was not an excuse that would go down well with the court (where Owen was a surrogate judge), and was presumably true. And in 1632 Margery Benson refused to take communion at Wickham in Essex, telling others that their minister was unworthy to receive the sacrament himself or to give it to any of them. That, at least, was what she thought.[24]

Many of these reasons for absence suggest a real determination that the sacrament should be taken in the right frame of mind—with a clear conscience, at peace with the neighbours, and with respect for the minister. It might also be necessary to wear the right clothes. Samuel and Agnes Pope of Marholm, Northamptonshire, asserted in 1622 that 'they would have received the communion at Easter last, if they had had any good clothes'. The churchwardens of Stadhampton, Oxfordshire, presented John Waller in 1626 'for that he did not receive the communion at Easter last, but he is a very poor man and saith he had not clothes fit to come in company then, but now he keepeth the swine and hopeth he shall earn money, and will prepare himself to receive the next communion'. Presumably absentees would not use what the court might think a frivolous explanation—and proper dress may have been a matter of respect for the occasion as well as a matter of pride in front of the parish. The preacher 'silver-tongued' Henry Smith, however, did not think much of this excuse, complaining that 'I have known many kept from the sacrament a whole year together by their masters, for want of a new suit to set them forth with their fellows': it was the inner self, not outward appearance, that mattered. But perhaps masters did not care only about how their servants' clothes might reflect on them. In 1636 Ambrose Parr of Little Braxted, Essex, was presented for not allowing a servant to receive communion at Easter. He declared 'that his servant is a thievish and unruly boy, and unfit for the receiving of the sacrament as yet'.[25]

It seems that men and women had a strong sense of the duties owed to God, and expected them to be fulfilled. Alice White of Axbridge, Somerset, was absent from church for several weeks in 1594 when her child was sick, and she was angrily reproved by a neighbour for her negligence: 'she will serve God as well under a hedge as in the church', she retorted. When Richard Edwin, churchwarden of Leyton in Essex, was seen winnowing corn on a Sunday in 1614 as others went to church, he too was reproached by a neighbour—and 'he asked him what he had to do with it'. When Benjamin Chicke swore by God's blood in St Mary Magdalene's church in Taunton in 1621, David Dickenson rebuked him: 'God's name ought to be glorified in this place …, and not to be scarified'. An oath before God was a serious matter. In an argument between Thomas Symonds and William Cock of Coggeshall, Essex, in 1579, Symonds asked for a Bible so he could swear to the truth—and Cock refused to put his hand on the book and swear. Young Thomas Bolton of Souldern appeared as a witness in a defamation case in the Oxford consistory in 1611, and declared that 'he thinketh that if he should take an oath falsely he should damn his own soul'. John Bray and Thomas Tucker argued in Weedon Lois church, Northamptonshire, in 1625 over whether Tucker had paid his taxes: 'They took both of them the Bible into their hands and kissed it, and at the same time did swear contrary oaths upon difference which was betwixt them for two shillings'. God would punish those who took his Word in vain and flouted his laws. When Joan Stoddon of Dunster, Somerset, told a crude story in Ford's house in 1612, 'the said Ford hearing reproved her for her lewd speeches and told her if he had known she had been such a wicked woman she should not have come into his house, saying unto her "I am afraid lest God will send a plague upon my house for thy sake" .' In 1621, when Agnes Johnson of Abington, Northamptonshire, was dying of a sexually transmitted disease, she accused John Wheatley of infecting her. Her claim was not believed, and the churchwardens sent some of the older women of the parish to try to persuade her not to slander Wheatley. 'If you do, the Lord that punish you now will judge you hereafter,' they warned her. In 1637 Elizabeth Scott of Wix in Essex wanted Robert Wiffen's wife to admit her husband was not the father of her child: 'What if thou be'est punished in this world, thy punishment will be the less in the world to come.'[26]

Some sinners had a real sense of their own wickedness and the need for true repentance. In 1606 the vicar of Barford, Oxfordshire, reported on his questioning of Ann Clark, accused of fornication: 'I signify that at the time of her examination I found [her] by tears so penitent, and earnest protestings of amendment of life, hoping that God would never give her over to be so void of grace that s[he] should during life fall into the like.' The churchwardens of Chewton Mendip, Somerset, reported in 1615 that Sarah Tucker would not go to church or even hear prayers in her own house, 'but sayeth that her sins be so great that they cannot be forgotten'. It was widely believed in Middlezoy in 1622 that the ghost of Christian Godfrey 'did walk again, and said that she was in hell and could not go to heaven because she had stolen bean sheaves, and when other good people did go into heaven she was kept forth'. In 1630 Stephen Dennat and Widow Dobson met Thomas Coleman on the road from Hampton Poyle to Bletchingdon in Oxfordshire. Coleman fell on his knees and cried, 'I am undone, and my child. I have foresworn myself, the bastard is mine, the child is mine!' Edith Bailey had had a child, but Dennat told Coleman that no one had accused him—'Mine own conscience doth accuse me!' he responded. Thomas Barlow of Walthamstow, Essex, appeared in the archdeacon's court in 1638 to answer a presentment for drunkenness. He admitted 'he is sometimes overcome with drink but is sorry for the same, and intended by God's grace to amend his said fault'. It was, of course, what the court wanted to hear—but perhaps he meant it.[27]

There were sceptics and cynics, and outsiders who would not be reformed—but few wished to remain outside the Christian community forever. On her deathbed in 1607, the excommunicate Jane Butler had cried, 'Lord have mercy upon me, I have no friends that will come to the court to get me absolved, and yet I would be absolved with all my heart!' She sent for the minister, but he was away, and she died the next day. At least, that was the story her brother told the diocesan chancellor of Peterborough, who decreed that she should be regarded as absolved and buried in Oxendon churchyard. In 1617 John Wheatley of Abington's brother told the same court 'that his brother Edmund lyeth sick and in danger of death, and that he desireth absolution by him and sent him on purpose to get him absolved'. Mary Grey of Crixeth in Essex stood excommunicate for seven years after failing to answer a presentment for absence from church. But by 1622, she 'being grown very poor and old and diseased', unable to get to the court herself, her minister wrote on her behalf to the official of Colchester for 'her humble suit, that you would be pleased freely to restore her to the church. Which favour, if you should vouchsafe her, not only shall the party have cause to thank you for your charity, but she shall have such occasion with more contentment to dispose herself towards God.' Similarly, William Harrell wrote to the registrar of the court in 1640:

Mr Tillingham: the bearer hereof, Elizabeth Culpeck, a poor woman of our parish of Little Horkesley, hath been excommunicated a long time and, although she hath done amiss, yet we hope she will reform her life and become penitent for her misdoing. She now desireth that you would be pleased to deal some way with her whereby she may be absolved from the sentence of excommunication, that we may receive her again into the church.

Elizabeth appeared in the court on 16 December 1640, and was absolved and dismissed with a warning.[28]

There were all sorts of reasons why Elizabeth Culpeck might want to be absolved, and take her place in Little Horkesley church—not all of them religious. We need not assume sudden rushes of great penitence or piety in these people—but they wanted to be among Christ's flock, to pray quietly, and at last to rest peacefully with their fellow parishioners. Theologus pitied and patronized Asunetus: 'I can but pity you for your ignorance, for it is exceeding gross and palpable. Your answers are to no purpose and bewray a wonderful blindness and senselessness in matters of religion.' Asunetus did not know the things Theologus thought he should—he had not done Theologus's recommended reading, 'especially Virel's *Grounds of Religion*, and the works of the two worthy servants of God, Master Gifford and Master Perkins'. But Asunetus and his kind were religious people, in a conventional, undemanding kind of way. They were not godly, but by their own lights they were God-fearing.

For so long as I do as I would be done to, and say nobody no harm nor do nobody no harm, God will have mercy on my soul. And I doubt not but my good deeds shall weigh against my evil deeds, and that I shall make even with God at my latter end. For, I thank God for it, I have always lived in his fear and served him with a true intent. Therefore I know that so long as I keep his Commandments and live as my neighbours do, and as a Christian man ought to do, he will not damn my soul.[29]

That was not Calvinism—it wasn't much like Protestantism. But it was a religion that made men and women try to be good. It may even have saved their souls.

4

Asunetus: Why All the Fuss?

Tush, tush! What needs all this ado? If a man say his Lord's Prayer, his Ten
Commandments, and his Belief, and keep them, and say nobody no harm
nor do nobody no harm, and do as he would be done too, have a good faith
God-ward and be a man of God's belief, no doubt he shall be saved without
all this running to sermons and prattling of the Scriptures.

Asunetus was a religious man—up to a point. He learned his catechism, he said
his prayers, he went to church, he liked the Bible readings, and he tried to do
what he thought God expected of him. But he didn't think God expected very
much. Religion was all very well, but it had to be kept in proportion. Asunetus's
'Tush, tush!' was a standard response to any requirement for godly learning and
godly living. 'Can you teach me any more than to resist sin and to do good,
to love God above all things and my neighbour as myself?' asked John Bate's
self-centred Autophilus in 1589, 'Tush, there is more ado than necessary!' 'I
pray you, why are you so hot? What needs all this?' queried Robert Bolton's
conventional Christian, 'What needs so much ado, when a reasonable thing will
serve the turn?' Let's not get carried away and let religion take over our lives.
'God is always in one like a cuckoo,' complained John Virgin of Odcombe in
south Somerset in 1619—getting into everyone's nest, poking his nose into
everybody's business. Religion had to be kept in its place. And many did just
that: 'there is divers that do not pass by the word of God a whore's turd', observed
Thomas Lorkin of Rayleigh in Essex in 1577.[1]

After the birth of Jane Miner's baby in 1597, she waited a whole month before
having the child baptized—and when challenged about the delay, she said the
weather had been foul. Eventually she took herself to be churched at Barking,
and the baby to be christened,

And feasted at a tavern four or five hours in the forenoon. And afternoon came to the
church rather to be seen than upon any devotion as it seemed, for whilst the minister
was burying a corpse she went out of the church unchurched unto the tavern again. And
when she was spoken unto by the clerk to return to church again and to give God thanks
after her delivery, she answered it was a ceremony.

Alice Coles of Sulgrave in Northamptonshire was reproved for negligent attendance at church in 1607, and 'hath answered that she neither can nor will come

more often'. When Richard London of Little Wakering, Essex, was cited for absence from church in 1607, he insisted that 'he is as seldom from the church as any of the parish'—he was no worse than anyone else. Some thought there were limits to what the Church should expect of them. In 1617 Averius Blake of Little Chishall told the judge of the Colchester court 'that he will never come to the church in the afternoons upon the Sabbath days so long as he lives or breathes,' and in 1630 Robert Cooke of Feering was telling people 'that no man is bound to come to his parish church more often than once upon the Sabbath day'. In fact, although the state insisted on attendance at one Sunday service, the Church demanded two. Others thought it was necessary to go to church only once a month—perhaps because the 1581 Recusancy Act punished absence by monthly fines. George Castell of Havering observed 'that it is sufficient for him if he come to church once in a month' in 1591, and others agreed: George Keynton of Bathwick, Somerset, in 1605; Walter Mayatt of Mucking, Essex, in 1612; George Davies of Ashurst, Sussex, in 1630; and John Pope of Caundle Marsh in Dorset in 1638—'once in a month is as much as can be required'.

Going to church all the time was just too much trouble. When John Brownley was found at his father's house in Colchester, Essex, in service time in 1613, 'he said it was his pleasure to be at home'. In 1620 Robert Evans of Axbridge, Somerset, asked Thomas Morton why he did not go to church more often. 'What shall I do?' responded Morton, 'If I come thither I shall hear but a tale of a tub. I can read at home as much as I can hear at church, and if I want any points to be resolved I will repair to some great learned man to be resolved.' When the churchwardens of Prittlewell, Essex, told Nicholas Bland to go to church in 1627, 'he gave railing speeches and said afterward to the minister that the minister did but prattle'. Robert Lownie and his wife missed service at St Giles, Colchester, in 1632, 'being both of them at home in bed', and when in 1636 the churchwardens allocated Nicholas Desborough a new seat in Saffron Walden church, he walked out 'saying he would go home and sit by the fire rather than sit in the place appointed'.[2]

Some of all this is bravado, some is ill temper—but there was a constant chorus: I will come when I want to, I'd rather be doing something else just now, and what has it got to do with you? Church and state demanded attendance, God probably expected it, but men might choose when they went. In 1616 the churchwardens of St Giles, Northampton, reported that their church was in poor repair and dangerous,

insomuch that most or all of our parish will not come to our church but when themselves please, neither will they go to any other parish church in town except where themselves list, so that we can take no certain notice either of their frequenting divine service and sermons or receiving the communion, according as becomes Christians ... The most part of the parish holding opinion that because our parish church is so decayed, therefore they are not bound by law to resort thither, and because they are not united to any other church they therefore suppose that they may go to what church they list and only when they list.

The wardens asked the diocesan court to settle a church for the people of St Giles to attend 'ordinarily and orderly as becomes Christians, and not to live so loosely and licentiously as many now do'. Katherine Mills of Ilchester, Somerset, declared roundly in 1619 that 'she will not come to church but at her own pleasure'. Robert Cleare affirmed to the wardens of Great Waltham, Essex, in 1627 that 'he would not come to church but when he himself listed, and what had the churchwardens or any man else to do with him for his not coming to church?' Joseph Wood and Anne Nash, two servants of Mountnessing, were reproved by the churchwardens in 1632 for their absences, 'and they made answer that every man shall answer for his own sins'. And in 1638 Thomas Lockwood of Rayleigh argued 'he might choose whether he would go to church or no'.[3]

The law regulated churchgoing, and ministers and churchwardens were horrified that people might do as they pleased. But casual absence from services was very common. 'The whole parish slack in coming to church,' noted the wardens of Titherington, Gloucestershire, in 1576—and everyone was 'very slack in coming to evening prayer' at Little Sodbury, 'all faulty about coming to church' at Taynton, and 'they have been slack in coming to church' at Lydney. Things were not usually as bad as that, but there was a good deal of negligence. There were no popish recusants at Lyme Regis, Dorset, in 1609, 'yet are there many which do too much neglect divine service and also the holy communion, and whose names in regard of the multitude of them we crave further time to enquire'. Richard Tuggle, his wife, and twenty-eight others of St Cuthbert's, Wells, were presented in 1615 for seldom attending church: Isabel Smith said she was sometimes ill, Joan Cuffe that she sometimes had to look after her child, and Anthony Hawkins was the bishop's cook and could spare time for church only when the bishop was away. The curate of Nailsea presented the churchwardens in 1618 for absence from church one Sunday, 'causing most of the congregation to do the like, some going into the alehouse and some into the fields'. In 1619 the rector of Cottesmore in Rutland had a lot to moan about,

as namely sundry persons that usually absent themselves from church, some half-papists that come but once a month, some profane that come about to feasts and other disorderly meetings, a great number of persons of Barrow, a village belonging to the parish of Sowton who, together with themselves and families, wholly absent themselves from church ordinarily in the afternoons upon Sundays.

In the same year, an unusually punctilious churchwarden at Fordington in Dorset named eleven men for dozing in services, eight for arriving late, four for leaving early, ten for not sending children to catechism, and twenty-three for slack attendance—Edward Johnson 'taketh special notice in writing of their defaults therein and will be ready at all times hereafter if need require to depose the same against them'. In 1629 sixty-one people were reported at Wells for 'not frequenting' the parish church, with a separate presentment of the four 'popish recusants'.[4]

Many parishes had one or two regular delinquents. At Mudgley in Somerset in 1588, Walter Chappell went to the alehouse at service time, 'neither cometh to the church scarce once in a month'. It was said of Thomas Richards of Portbury in 1605 'That he very seldom cometh to church to hear divine prayer or sermons, and that he useth to be in alehouses in time of service, and being required to depart to the end they might go to church he said he would not till his humour were past'. After John Mouncke of Ashington, Sussex, was presented for his absences in 1609, he was ordered to pay for a sermon 'against neglect of God's service and the church'. In 1617 the churchwardens of Burton Latimer, Northamptonshire, went to the house of the often-absent William Glover, 'and found him at home and asked why he did not come to church and wished him to come, whereunto he answered he would come anon but he did not then come'. William Sydenham of Moorlinch in Somerset had promised the bishop of Bath and Wells himself to attend church dutifully, 'but hath not hitherto reformed but rather neglected it much more than before'—missing the royal festivals of 5 August and 5 November 1618, 'and the day of the coronation being admonished to come to church absented himself and gave the churchwardens and the minister a frivolous and contemptuous answer'. John Bowker, rector of Buckland St Mary, denounced Robert Foxwell in 1622 for coming to church only once in the past six months, 'And as the neighbours inform him the said Mr Bowker to their great grief, they, when they have and do prepare themselves like good Christians and subjects towards the church on the Lord's day they see him riding in the commons, which breeds an ill example to the whole congregation.' For some, indeed, absence from church was just a question of paying the fine—'It was but a 12d matter,' said John Burghill of Dagenham, Essex, in 1614. 'Present me if you will,' declared Samuel Westly of Hempsted in 1625, 'it is but a 16d matter.'[5]

'Many absent themselves from the church oftentimes,' wailed the wardens of Poling, Sussex, in 1579, 'but everyone hath his excuse.' But some of the excuses were pretty feeble. William Abel, Richard Alcock, and William Wordall of South Weald, Essex, were presented for absences in 1590, asserting 'that upon a necessity they sometimes are invited to their friends as to a bride-ale, and sometimes to a dinner, and sometimes are visited with sickness, so they are not able to come as they ought, otherwise they are at home and in health they come to church orderly'—we come to church when it suits us, that is. In 1602 one Hellam of Stamford Rivers was reported for absence 'but he allegeth decrepitude, albeit we are fully satisfied that he can both work and wander to the market, which is of greater distance from his dwelling house than the church'. Thomas Humphrey of Munden missed services one Sunday in 1621 because he went to visit a sick friend. John Pettit of Great Chesterford was absent from an afternoon service in 1623 because 'it was a wet, rainy day'. William Roberts of Ashdon admitted in 1626 'that sometime he is absent from church upon occasion of looking to his house, being a singleman and having divers times had his goods pilfered away when he hath been at church'. Thomas Lane of Walthamstow told the court in 1630 'that he did not hear the bells ring to evening prayer and that he did not think it had been evening prayer time'. In 1632 Alice Russell of Clevedon, Somerset, confessed 'that she doth forebear going to church upon Sabbath days, as is detected, but only by reason she wanteth clothes, her husband being an idle fellow and having sold the greatest part thereof'. Francis Burrowes of St Nicholas, Colchester, stated in 1634 that he could not get to church more than once a month 'because he cannot rise soon enough', and in 1636 Anne Beale of Tollesbury claimed she had not been able to go on one Sunday because she had washed her child's clothes. In May 1640 John Brond of Birch said he had not attended through the winter months because the church was too cold.[6]

For some people, clearly, going to church had to fit around other needs and priorities—and compulsory attendance did pose some practical difficulties. Sometimes there were emergencies. Thomas Gibson of Little Oakley in east Essex attested in 1612 that he had been absent only once, when he went to see to his sunken boat: the churchwardens certified this was true and he was dismissed. In 1621 Richard Howard of Braintree had to go to fetch a midwife for his wife, and so missed a service. Thomas Kent took a realistic view of parishioners' attendance when he was churchwarden of Wylye, Wiltshire, in 1624, 'saying they had occasion to be at home about their cattle and could not be at church all at one time, dwelling far from the church too'. Thomas Sares of East Ham, Essex, explained in 1625 'that he hath four small children and that he or his wife by reason thereof must stay at home to look to his children, and that he or his wife go to church when they have their health'. Henry Lester of Axbridge, Somerset, argued in 1629 'that he hath long been troubled with the gout, and most commonly is not able to go to the church every Sunday, and that when he is able he doth not fail'. Alice Hardwick of East Tilbury, Essex, attested in 1637 that 'she was abused and beaten, whereby she was not able to go abroad at that time', and John Nun said he could not attend because he was lame, 'nor yet can, being under the hands of the chirurgion' (i.e. the surgeon). One of the most common reasons given for prolonged absence from church was fear of having a warrant served or fear of arrest. John Edmunds of Sutton Scotney, Hampshire, said in 1582 that his absence 'was for fear of being arrested, but that he hath now compounded with his creditors and useth to the church and so hereafter will'. The churchwardens of Everley in Wiltshire reported in 1599, 'Mary Fisher cometh not to the church orderly, but they say it is for fear of process to be served on her, being otherwise an honest and religious woman.' In 1627 William Snead of Brixworth, Northamptonshire, sent his son to court to explain his nine months of negligence:

his father is in danger of the law, which is the cause of his not coming to the church, by reason of a *sub poena* for costs out of the Star Chamber for great costs against him. And that he is a man which before that time did always keep his church and did never refuse so to do, and would do so if this were not the cause.

The courts usually accepted such an explanation, and, indeed, arrests at church were not uncommon. In 1623, for example, Lewis Jones arrested William Hobbs at the service in Portishead, Somerset, and in 1635 Francis Passfield arrested William Wright during the sermon at Stratford in Essex.[7]

Those who skipped church could be doing almost anything. Thomas Drinkwater of Cold Norton, Essex, was presented in 1604 'for following his delights' instead of going to church. The most popular of the alternative delights were dancing, games, and drinking. Robert Brownes of Leyton 'had in his house certain that did dance in the service time' in 1572: he explained 'that it was a wedding day and that he could not rule the youth'. Robert Salmon of Ashingden was in trouble in 1584 'for suffering dancing to be in his house on Midsummer Day last in evening prayer time, so that there could not be any service said for the great noise'. Anne Hyndye of Hartpury, Gloucestershire, was a recidivist dancer. She was first named in 1592 'for dancing in service time on Holy Thursday, and she threw stones against the glass windows of the church'—and soon after was denounced again because 'she danceth upon the Sabbath day in the time of service and sermon, and being reprehended by Master Prior, vicar there, willed him to go home to his wench behind the door'. In 1603 Henry Gray and others of South Weald, Essex, got ready during a sermon to perform their dance, and 'they met with the bridegroom and came dancing the morris home with them'. Anne Wakeford and twenty-seven others were presented for dancing in service time on Trinity Sunday 1611 at Graffham in west Sussex—which seems to have been the dancing capital of southern England. On 13 March 1624 Hugh Deane of West Ham, Essex, had music, drinking, and dancing in his house during the Wednesday service, and when the churchwardens drove the company out they moved to the house of Nicholas Parsons and continued their jollity. There was a fiddler and dancing during the evening service at Wroughton, Wiltshire, on May Day 1637—though some of the accused claimed that although their neighbours had been dancing they themselves had not joined in until after the service.[8]

While some danced at service times, others played (or watched) games—usually football or bowls. Six men of Hardwicke, Gloucestershire, played tennis during an evening service in August 1582, and at Oddington four or five played bowls. Richard Jeffery of Asheldham, Essex, 'procured company together and played football in Hackwell of Easter Monday in evening service time' in 1592—though he claimed he did not know there was a service then. In 1598 ten men from various neighbouring parishes were presented 'for playing football at Stowey [Somerset] Sunday fortnight all evening prayer time, and so near the church that the minister was disturbed at service time'. In 1603 Thomas Hoby of Cold Norton, Essex, was certified 'to be a common violator of the Sabbath days, following riotous sports far-wide with the neglect of the church exercise'. In 1614 there was a stoolball match between teams from Potterspury and next-door Yardley Gobion, Northamptonshire. The wardens of Potterspury saw this as an opportunity to make some money for the parish, and fined everyone involved for absence from church—then promised 'to bear the parties harmless for such their 12d paid'. Twenty-two men from Sherborne in Dorset were reported in 1615 'for bowling on the Sabbath day in time of divine service'. At Cottesmore, Rutland, on Sunday, 26 July 1618, there was 'cudgel play and nine-holes' in the open street, with spectators 'whooping and hallo'ing in the churchyard' and disturbing service and sermon. At Bishopstone, Wiltshire, in 1628 the wardens named seven men 'with divers others of our parishioners whom we cannot now directly nominate, some of them for playing at football and others for looking on them on a Sunday in Lent last at the time of evening prayer'—though when called into church by the wardens 'they presently left off and came to our parish church to prayers'. Others were less amenable. In 1633 the churchwardens of Foulness, Essex, caught Nicholas Crisp 'playing with his pigs under a wall', and when they admonished him he retorted, 'Shit on the church, what care I for the church?' William Brett of Great Hallingbury was a frequent absentee in the summer of 1635, and missed both services on 2 August—'he then tending and trimming his bowling green'.[9]

Selling ale and drinking during services were pretty common, though often said to have been by chance or someone else's fault. William Barrett of Wivenhoe, Essex, had company drinking and playing cards in his alehouse at the time of service and sermon on 23 October 1575—but he said he was not there. There was 'a company of lewd persons' tippling and gaming in Christopher Fisher's alehouse at Ashton, Northamptonshire, on a Sunday in 1585, 'till the constables were sent forth of the church to keep peace'—but Fisher himself 'was not at home'. On a spring Sunday in 1602, the village constable of Frome, Somerset, left the church as usual to search the inns and alehouses for anyone who should have been at the service. He found two men playing cards in Robert Stibbs's alehouse, with his wife frying eggs for them. The constable ordered them out, and when they had finished their eggs they left—but Stibbs was not to be found. Samuel Greenway of Milton, Northamptonshire, was presented in 1614 for selling ale during a service. He said that he had been at church at the time, and before he had left his alehouse he had ordered everyone out and closed the doors—but then two strangers had arrived and insisted on a drink. His wife had told them she could not sell in service time, so she 'gave them some and did give them a pot of drink or two'. When Ralph Philbricke of Great Bardfield, Essex, was accused of selling ale in service time in 1625, he said that he had been hurt by a cart and could not go to church, but 'there came two strangers to his house and they were no sooner there but the constables followed and found them there, and went away without drinking any beer'—and he forced himself to get to church despite his injury. Robert Thaye of Rudgwick in Sussex alleged in 1629 that he was in an alehouse during prayers only 'because he was not very well but had lately taken a fall'. In 1630 Hugh Cotton of Caversham, Berkshire, was found in an alehouse at service time: he claimed he had fallen off his horse and injured himself, and 'was constrained to go to the alehouse and stay there till he could get one to catch his horse, and in the meantime he was taken there by the churchwardens'. There was drinking at William Collard's alehouse in Walthamstow, Essex, during a service in 1638—but only because a company of bell-ringers who had been ringing for a wedding were keen to quench their thirst.[10]

There were lots of interesting things to get up to while everyone else was at church: sex and stealing, for example. In 1585 Richard Dunstead of Hatfield Peverel, Essex, was found with Humphreys the sawyer's wife in her kitchen during an afternoon sermon, 'with his points untrussed and his hosen in his hand and his buttons unbuttoned'—'and then from there brought to the church in the sermon time by Walter Hare, constable of the same parish'. Very embarrassing. Roger Walker of Burton Latimer, Northamptonshire, was accused in 1613 of 'carnal copulation with Dorothy the wife of Robert Shepherd at divers times on Fridays and Sundays in prayer time'. Walker claimed he had been put up to it by William Glover, who had then reported him to the churchwardens—but Glover said he had encouraged Walker only in order to get proof of his sin. Edward Wheatley of St Giles, Northampton, was suspected of adultery with Robert Child's wife in 1617, and a churchwarden 'hath seen him come out at the back door of the said Child's in sermon time'. John Pippen of Bawdrip, Somerset, was charged in 1621 with adultery with Margaret Bacon: 'on a Sunday lately happening he was seen creeping down a ditch to come privately to her at the time of divine service, her husband being then at church'. Perhaps stealing property during services was even more common than stealing wives. In 1595 William Nightingale raided an Essex orchard when he should have been at church, 'and being espied used filthy cursing and swearing to blaspheme the name of God'. Stephen Dowse and William Lee of Billingshurst, Sussex, were observed 'gathering other men's pears in prayer time' in 1614, and in 1636 Richard Aylett of Great Warley, Essex, was seen by the wardens 'a-stealing of his neighbours' peaches' in prayer time.[11]

Unsurprisingly, working during services was quite common—everything from spreading dung at Stock in Essex in 1587 to gathering strawberries at Kelvedon in 1629. Barbers were particularly likely to ply their trade in service times, when customers were not at work—or, in some cases, not at church. Thomas Warren of Bridgwater, Somerset, admitted in 1603 'that sometimes he hath trimmed gentlemen and others at the time of divine service partly, but promiseth amendment'. John Michenor of Petworth, Sussex, was presented in 1610 'for trimming of men in the service time', and both Thomas Liddell of West Ham, Essex, and a servant of Robert Crabb, churchwarden, of Chipping Ongar were cited in 1617. It was alleged in 1618 that John Becke of Bedminster, Somerset, 'doth usually trim and barb men' in prayer time, and in 1633 Williams Comes of Aveley, Essex, was reported for visiting a barber during evening prayer—he claimed 'the barber did but cut a few hairs off his upper lip, which hanged in his mouth'. Humphrey Lancelot of Milton on the Hampshire coast was accused of selling fish in service time on Sunday 16 September 1599: he said that 'he is a poor man and hath a great charge and did one Sunday morning sell fish, but protesteth he was at home again before morning prayer'. Joanna Scarpe of Thorington, Essex, was presented in 1609 for making cakes and puddings on Sundays during evening prayer, and thus enticing others to her house instead of church. Elizabeth, wife of Thomas Cricke of Benton, Northamptonshire, was cited in 1618 'for negligent coming to church'. The wardens attested that 'being required by their minister to look into the inhabitants' houses in the time of divine service, they came on Sunday was three weeks into the house of the said Cricke and there found his wife in time of public prayer at her needle busily sewing'. In 1633 George Salmon of Stifford, Essex, was denounced for gathering fruit during the afternoon service, though he said he picked only a handful of plums for his sick daughter. Margery Wright was presented to the Peterborough diocesan court in 1637 'for spinning in the time of divine service'—but she claimed she was only quietening her baby, and 'that the course of cradle-rocking was heard like a wheel'. If that was a lie, it was a good one. Those charged with working during services were likely to offer excuses or denials—and it looks as if there was public hostility to the offence, especially if it was blatant. Blaise Haggard, a churchwarden of Weston Bampfylde, Somerset, was cited in 1619 for ploughing during the commemorative Gunpowder Plot service on 5 November, 'to the great dislike and evil example of the rest of the parishioners there', and in 1623 four butchers of Bruton were cited for selling meat during Sunday services 'to the great dislike of their neighbours'.[12]

These are examples of occasional absence from church, not hostility or indifference. At service times on Sundays most people were at church—not dancing or playing football or drinking or chasing a neighbour's wife or raiding orchards or cutting hair. Most people went to most services. But what did they do when they got there? Churchgoing was a social as well as a religious event, and people had lots to talk about. The curate of Great Holland, Essex, cited Thomas Glascock and William Samuel in 1573 as 'common talkers in the church at service time'—and Glascock missed a service at Christmas and went to the alehouse at Kirby. William Walker of Walden was a 'sermon-talker' in 1576, and in 1579 Margaret Fisher argued with Elizabeth Wellocke during evening prayer at Boxted. Edmund Smyth of Wellingborough, Northamptonshire, did 'use to talk in prayer time' in 1591. Henry Enewe of Coggeshall, Essex, was presented in 1595 'for talking in the church in the service time, and being reformed or reproved for the same by the minister and chief head-boroughs in the churchyard he bade a turd for them and cared not for them'. John Bodye and Osmond Cowde talked so loudly at St John's, Glastonbury, in 1617 that others could not hear the preacher, and when one complained of the noise Bodye responded, 'What, do your pate ache, for all you have a cap on?' In 1619 Thomas Hayes of Rothwell, Northamptonshire, was reported 'for talking and conferring ordinarily with those that sit by him', and Thomas Collin of Walden, Essex, was charged with talking during services in 1636 and again in 1637.[13]

Much of the racket in church came from children, and there was little tolerance of it. The wife of William Watts of Syresham, Northamptonshire, was ordered by the Peterborough court in 1590 to leave her children at home, because they had been disturbing the parishioners, and in 1600 the wardens of Welford were cited for 'not presenting certain women that bring their children to church and molest the minister'. The offence of Bridget Simms of Ashcott in Somerset in 1618 was 'often bringing her child to church, and there keeping of it crying and making a great noise in the time of divine service divers times, to the great offence of the congregation there'. In 1619 Elizabeth Wem of Rothersthorpe, Northamptonshire, was presented for disturbing the minister 'by the crying of her child', as was Richard Kendall of Rothwell's wife—and she refused to take the child out when ordered by the minister. Five wives of Helpston were in trouble in 1629 for disrupting the sermon by walking their children up and down, presumably to keep them quiet, and in 1630 Katherine Chapman of Cottingham was presented for disturbance 'by the immoderate noise of her children'. Nor was it only the mothers who were criticized. Thomas Hibberd of All Cannings, Wiltshire, was cited in 1633 'for suffering his children to make a noise and stir in the church in the time of divine service'. At Sherborne, Dorset, in 1638 three men were presented because of their disruptive children, including John Hellier 'for that his child did disturb the congregation in crying'.[14]

There were lots of things to do in church besides paying attention. William Skington and Lucy Allen of Dingley in northern Northamptonshire would sit kissing behind the church door in 1604, before the evening service actually began—though when John Ansley and his wife of Chipping Norton, Oxfordshire, were accused of kissing during a sermon in 1634, he claimed she had only whispered in his ear to ask him to find a Scripture text cited by the preacher. On 12 September 1613 Walter Mayatt of Mucking, Essex, 'cracked nuts all the evening prayer time in the chancel'. Edward Roberts was reading books in Kelmarsh church, Northamptonshire, in 1619, and Alice Cooke of Rayleigh, Essex, was actually making clothes at a fast day sermon in 1637, 'to the great dishonour of God and the grief and scandal of the congregation'. At Backwell church in Somerset in 1638, Thomas Shortred usually passed the time by taking out his purse and counting his money. And there was often something to laugh at. Sheep followed a parishioner into church at Kelmarsh in 1619, 'causing the most parts of the people to break out into unseemly laughter'. Richard Wright of Dodford, Northamptonshire, fell asleep in a service in 1625 'and let a very loud and beastly fart which caused laughter in the people and did disturb me then at prayer,' said the vicar. At Ardleigh in Essex in 1637 some parish jokers 'did put lice upon the backs of one another, and caused a laughter in the church'. It didn't take much to make people laugh. Thomas Heckles of Thorpe, Northamptonshire, stuck a feather in one Margery's hair during a Sunday service in 1638, 'whereby a good part of the congregation in the chapel were provoked to laughter'. In 1639 Samuel Rand, Philip Raffle, and William Root of Layer Marney, Essex, were 'laughing and prating' together through the service—though Rand claimed that 'Mr Downing in a sermon used some speeches at which he sayeth he smiled a little and so did most in the church.'[15]

Some silliness, some laughing, and some talking; no doubt there was a good deal of inattention, too. But some of it did get reported, and the more earnest or respectful parishioners probably wanted an orderly service—without crying children. In a few churches, however, it seems things were anything but orderly. John Duckett, vicar of Hambleton in Rutland, had a lengthy list of complaints against his parishioners in 1599: 'no reverent behaviour used in the church in the prayers time, but sleeping, sitting with their caps on and upon their tails in prayers time, supplications and collects reading, no reverence at all used at the name of Jesus'; 'coming in and going out in prayer time and in sermon time'; 'the windows are so broken that the birds make such a chirping in the church that the minister cannot be heard'—and 'some often away from prayers and tippling and gaming in the alehouse in service time'. Duckett was cross with the churchwardens, however, and perhaps it was not much worse at Hambleton than at other places. Nicholas King of Ogbourne St George, Wiltshire, thought his congregation was totally out of control in 1607: 'I think verily that amongst the wild Irish at this day there is not a more disordered behaviour amongst them in time of divine service than in this church, and so have been of long time, that now they are not to be reclaimed but by such punishment as is committed to my lord's jurisdiction.' But his specific complaints were only that the Ayres family came to church late, that John Ayres played with the children during the service, and that John Goddard had worn his hat—'an evil example to other inferior men, in so much that other men by his example did yesterday in time of divine service sit covered, who I never perceived (to my remembrance) so to do sithence I came to this disordered charge, an intolerable offence to my judgement'. This looks like an organized hat-wearing protest against a heavy-handed minister. Few clergy were more heavy-handed than Robert Sibthorpe. In 1616 John Nicholson, vicar of St Sepulchre's, Northampton, was unable to fulfil his duties because of illness, and Sibthorpe, vicar of St Giles, was appointed to say services there. He soon made his presence felt. After the evening service on 29 September he warned the parishioners 'to use more reverent behaviour in the church there in the time of divine service than they had done at that evening prayer and divers times before, and to see that their children use more reverence, and not to talk, prate and laugh louder than the minister read, as they did'. Richard Holman then spoke up: they were not going to obey Sibthorpe since he was not their vicar, 'neither should he rule them as a gentleman amongst them'.[16] These are not examples of truly outrageous conduct in particular churches. Probably, they are somewhat exaggerated accounts of what happened in most congregations: people did not gain instant piety and concentration as they walked through the church door—and they couldn't always make their children behave.

Nor could they always keep their eyes open. Sleeping in church services was an extremely common offence in visitation and court records—not as common as extramarital sex, but about as common as Sabbath-breaking. John Dixon of Peterborough slept during a cathedral service in 1586, and abused the town constable who rebuked him. In 1592 Thomas Pope of Normanton, Northamptonshire, was 'a common swearer and a notorious sleeper in time of divine service'. In 1600 Robert Stephens and John Whiting of Croscomb, Somerset, were guilty of 'sleeping and want of reverence in the church'—and when warned by a churchwarden they replied that 'they would appoint him his office, which was to keep dogs out of the church'. When John Hill of Foxcote was presented for sleeping in services in 1605, he admitted that 'sometimes he hath so done, but not commonly'. Edward Whithead of Bugbrooke told the Peterborough diocesan court in 1607 that 'he is a very poor man and a carrier, and is constrained oftentimes to drive most part of the night and by reason thereof hath sometimes slept in the church in service or sermon time'. In 1613 William Whittington of Fering, Sussex, was accused of 'extreme sleeping', despite warnings from the minister. Three men from Moulton, Northamptonshire, were reported for sleeping in 1616, though Richard Lyme claimed that 'he hath an impediment in his head and eyes, and by reason thereof he is constrained to hold down his head with very pain, whereby some of his neighbours did imagine that he did sleep in the church'. Perhaps! In 1619 Edward Alfield of St Osyth, Essex, was presented after talking in his sleep during a service, saying hopefully, 'There is but a penny to pay, fill the other pint of sack.' William Malin of Walden confessed in 1636 'that sometimes he hath winked in the church, being so heavy through late sitting up on the Saturday at night, but he hath strived against it'. On 19 February 1637 John Brown of Mucking slept in the service at Malden, 'letting go his water in great abundance, to the annoyance of those who sat with him in the seat'. And the churchwardens of Langley were presented in 1638 'for suffering the whole parish to sit in church with their hats on in time of service and sermon, and to sleep all the time of service and sermon'.[17]

Presumably people chatted or joked or dozed because they were bored. They did not find it easy to sit attentively for hours, twice each Sunday. Abraham Crouch told his neighbours in Foulness churchyard in 1628 that he would rather be drunk in an alehouse than be at church and hear a sermon. He was reported to the commissary court for Essex—but it would be surprising if some of the less godly hadn't quietly agreed that the alehouse was more fun than church. Sermons were usually the problem. The wardens of Minsterworth, Gloucestershire, complained in 1563 that their curate 'doth weary the parish with overlong preaching, both Epistle and Gospel', and in 1576 John George stumped out of South Cerney church 'for anger that the homilies was so long'. In 1578 John Grigg of South Hayling, Hampshire, called out while the minister was reading the homily at morning service, 'I pray you leave off now until evening prayer, for we are cold.' Witnesses from Meare in mid Somerset deposed in 1602 that George Calvert usually began morning service between 8.00 and 9.00 a.m., 'and hath in saying service and preaching held the parishioners there until twelve of the clock at high noon or after, many of the parish being old people, men and women, and dwelling some half a mile, some three-quarters of a mile and some a mile from the said church'—'to the grief and dislike of all, or the greater part, of the parishioners there'. So some at Meare liked a long sermon, but most did not. In 1604, five men left Exton church in Rutland before Mr Cuthbert was done—'but not before our minister have stand [*sic*] an hour in the pulpit at his sermon,' the churchwardens pointed out: Thomas Springthorpe went 'upon necessity', Henry Killingworth to look after his master's cattle, and Richard Collin 'home to turn the spit'. There were, of course, divided opinions about sermons. Thomas King complained to the vicar of Wylye, Wiltshire, in 1624 that his sermons were too long—but John Taylor said that Mr Lee 'is not above an hour in his sermon, which is thought well of by all the rest of the parish'. Thomas Platt interrupted a preacher at Highworth in 1627, announcing that 'he could wish him to make shorter, because there were two children to be christened'. At Beaminster in Dorset, John Hilliard complained in 1634 that the curate would preach after the afternoon catechizing for well over an hour, 'that the people are oftentimes kept in church till almost five of the clock'. When the morning service had finished at Helpston, Northamptonshire, on Advent Sunday 1636, John Wright stood up and protested that it was nearly one o'clock—although, said the wardens, the preacher 'was not above an hour in sermon, as might appear by the glass'.[18]

Some people just couldn't take sermons. Everard Knott of Oundle 'departed out of the church in sermon time contemptuously' in 1589, and in 1590 John Burden of Stanion was reported 'for commonly going out of the church at sermon time'. John Reynolds of Hockley, Essex, was cited in 1591 for leaving the sermon every Sunday—he admitted that 'he hath sometimes gone forth of the church in sermon time, but not usually every Sabbath'. Perhaps a few could not help themselves: Richard Hill of Easton, Northamptonshire, claimed in 1592 'that he being troubled with a disease is compelled to depart the church before sermon be done'. On Trinity Sunday 1605, Edward Shepherd walked out of the morning sermon at Charlcombe, Somerset, went back for a while, and finally left saying, 'Let him babble until he be weary'—'as before times he hath often done in the like manner'. Elizabeth Burden of Stanion—a relation of John, perhaps—was presented in 1612 for getting to church late 'and for stubbornly departing out of the church in sermon time, with stubborn and loud words'. At Ogbourne St Andrew, Wiltshire, six people 'went away contemptuously when the sermon began' in Whit week 1619, and at Knook Robert Shaw walked out of Mr Hewlett's sermon: when rebuked by Hewlett, he remarked, 'Well, we may give you leave to speak, but what remedy you will have for it I know not.' In 1631 John Strutt, Joseph Bridge, and two young women left the morning sermon at Burnham in Essex and went to an alehouse. There they sat, 'eating and drinking and tippling both wine and beer until evening prayer'. Strutt went to sleep it off in a field and the others went back to church—but Joan Goodman left at the sermon, and settled down outside to sleep.[19] As Abraham Crouch had said, it was better to get drunk at the alehouse than to sit through a sermon. Sermons divided the godly from the less godly: the godly went gadding for more, and the less godly did not much like the ones that they had.

The Sabbath too divided. The godly Philagathus complained that people like Asunetus and Antilegon thought they could do what they liked on a Sunday, as long as they had been to church in the morning. They might tolerate a morning sermon, 'but as for the afternoon they will hear none, then they will to bowls or tables'. Opinion was strongly in favour of a fairly relaxed approach to Sabbath observance, and against godly strictness. When John Curles of Caversham, Berkshire, was accused of arguing in church in 1606, he said it was not his fault 'because the women threatened him, for he would not have the Sabbath profaned by lewd pastimes'. William Penn of Backwell, Somerset, 'spendeth the Sabbath very profanely', stated the wardens in 1609, 'and being admonished to reform the same doth very scornfully reject the admonition so given him by the minister'. When the incumbent of King's Sutton, Northamptonshire, reported Sabbath disorders to the justices in 1611, he faced the wrath of Richard Maule, 'saying that I had done Denise Capper wrong to present her for disorders in her house on the Sundays, charging me that I had an envious and malicious heart'. In 1621 Robert Bath of Stone Easton, Somerset, was convinced that his dog observed the Sabbath better than some humans. When Thomas Carter tried to chase Bath's dog out of the church, Bath insisted, 'My dog is a holy dog, and holier than some folks are.' 'My dog, when [he] heareth the bells ring, he frisketh in and out, as if he did know that it were the Sabbath day and as if he did know that he must go to the church,' he told Carter—'I think he breaketh the Sabbath day less than some people do.'[20]

Many parishioners involved themselves in enjoyable Sunday pastimes—and saw little reason why they should not, especially if they had been to church anyway. In 1607 the vicar of Bishopstone in Wiltshire presented Thomas Brooke 'for a usual profaner of the Lord's day by playing upon a instrument commonly called a crowd, so that by this means the youth of the parish do spend the time dancing'. Brooke had told the vicar that 'it was as lawful for him to use his crowding upon the Sabbath day as it was for me to go to Chiselden to preach God's word'. Preaching was Sunday labour, just like music-making. Thomas Goosen of Barking, Essex, was presented in 1616 for organizing morris dancing on Sundays, and so 'drawing many idle and dissolute people to alehouses at unseasonable times on the Sabbath'. Richard Hunt preached at Warwick against mixed-sex dancing in 1617, with tales of young people who died of dancing. The rector of Scaldwell, Northamptonshire, preached twice against dancing in 1634, saying that 'men started up to take their queens to dance', and 'that rogues and whores and bastardly broods which came out of Bridewell [prison] dance together'. In 1635 John Workman preached at Gloucester 'that how many paces a man made in dancing, so many paces he made to hell'—but Sunday dancing could not be quelled. There was dancing in the churchyard of Dundry, Somerset, in the summer of 1621, and Richard Hulyard was cited 'for playing upon his instrument to those that usually dance'. In 1623 a fiddler from Boxgrove, Sussex, went to Yapton to play every Sunday afternoon: many of the Yapton youth danced instead of going to catechism, and thirty or forty arrived from other parishes to join in the dancing—while John Waters declared that 'the people need not to be so strict and careful in keeping the Sabbath day for it is abolished, and that every day in the week is a Christian's Sabbath'. On a summer Sunday afternoon in 1634 Thomas Coleborne played his pipe and tabor at the cross in Chipping Norton, Oxfordshire, 'and there did encourage the young people to dance before prayer'—but the churchwardens did not report it, as they did not think any of the visitation articles required them to.[21]

David Noyes, the schoolmaster of Manuden in north-west Essex, was out to enjoy himself on Sundays—presented in 1588 as 'an unruly fellow, and runneth to the football and to dancing upon the Sabbath and holy days'. In fact, football was the biggest participation and spectator sport on Sundays. Eleven men were cited in 1602 for playing at Lyndon in Rutland, and nine at North Luffenham, while in 1603 eighteen from Tansor had been 'in the presence at the football play that was betwixt Warmington and Clapton on the Sabbath day'. In 1607 the vicar of Alton, Wiltshire, was himself reported 'for going to Cheselbourne to football upon a Sabbath day and carried many of his parishioners with him, and lost evening prayer'. Francis Stradling of Madehurst, Sussex, was in trouble in 1614 for selling drink at 'a meeting for football' between the youth of Slindon and Madehurst on a Sunday, 'and many were absent from evening prayer'. At a Sunday match at Great Bedwyn, Wiltshire, in 1619 there was abuse from the crowd and violence among players and fans. Twelve 'football players' and fourteen 'beholders' were fined, and four had given 'certain boxes and blows one against another at the football play on a Sabbath day'. Hooliganism and football went together. John Hawkins was 'a football player, a boxer, and a looker-on with the rest', and Agnes Halbert 'was at the football playing, and the occasion of the boxing by her foul words and quarrelling'. These offences were compounded because several of those involved had received communion before going off to the match. There was a Sunday game at Ashurst, Sussex, in 1630, with John Hellar and George Davies selling beer to the spectators: the churchwardens tried to break up the event and get people to church for the sermon, but Edward Hasselden protested 'that Mr Salisbury preaching is but babbling'. Anthony Matthew of Burnham, Essex, admitted 'profaning of the Lord's day' in 1638—'after evening prayer he had played as others did at stoolball or football'.[22]

Playing bowls, fishing, and hunting were among the favourite Sunday pastimes. Bowls seems to have been especially popular in Somerset—and in 1585 the curate of Catcott was ordered 'to make an invective against the unlawful game of bowling'. The rector of Donyatt complained in 1603 that the churchwardens had been allowing bowling and tennis in the churchyard on Sundays. In 1620 six men of Middlezoy played Sunday bowls in the churchyard, and when the minister tried to stop the game Henry Robins 'stood contemptuously with tossing and throwing up and down in his hands'. Like other games, Sunday bowling was divisive. Robert Worsdell and two others of Hinton Charterhouse were presented in 1627 'for usually spending a great part of the Sabbath days in bowling, to the profanation of the said days and the discontent and grief of the congregation, and having been interrupted for the same they have answered that if they do it not they must do worse'. Some fun was necessary on a Sunday. In 1634 William Ewes and Arthur Durvall of Ditcheat 'fell into discourse of the Scripture': Ewes asked why they shouldn't play Sunday bowls as they used to do, but Durvall replied that 'he would maintain that it was as great a sin for a man to play bowls on a Sabbath day as it was to lie with his neighbour's wife another day'. Fishing caused fewer complaints, being a quieter, solitary sport. Thomas Church of Oakley, Essex, 'fished on the Sabbath day' in 1581, John Flint of Oundle, Northamptonshire, went 'a-fishing on the Sabbath day' in 1614, and Marmaduke Hurman of Curry Rivel, Somerset, 'doth usually fish upon Sabbath days' in 1631. Hunting was rather more public. In 1603 Thomas Cane of Elton, Northamptonshire, joined nine men from Helpston in hunting deer. Richard and Robert Creech of Charlton Mackrell, Somerset, usually went hunting with their hounds on Sundays and holy days in 1619, and in October were out killing two hares during a service. Four men of Walden, Essex, were presented in 1620 'for hunting upon the Sabbath'. A churchwarden appeared on their behalf and said the quartet 'are sorrowful for their offence and do humbly crave favour of the court to [be] dismissed for this time and do promise hereafter to observe the Sabbath day more reverently'.[23] Perhaps they did.

Sunday work was presented more often than Sunday play—probably because it was more offensive, rather than because there was more of it. A shop open on a Sunday was pretty blatant—but butchers in particular thought they were providing a necessary service. Nine shopkeepers of St Martin's, Chichester, were cited for Sunday trading in 1609: John Greenfield said he had

sold some victuals on the Sundays in the evening, being a butcher, to such poor people as are not able to buy their victual upon Saturday at night until they have received their wages, but he doth it not to the intent to profane the Sabbath day but repaireth orderly afterward to the high church both to service and sermon.

At Calne in Wiltshire in 1616 nine butchers, three shoemakers, and a tailor opened on Sundays, and in 1622 the minister 'informeth that every butcher and shopkeeper doth sell upon the Sabbath days in the morning'. Presumably the shops opened only because they had willing customers. Like Greenfield of Chichester, shopkeepers had ready defences. Thomas Richman of Walden, Essex, confessed in 1626 'that in the time of the last sickness he did sell some things for sick men in case of charity', and Edward Wickes of Rochford explained in 1627 'that sometimes some poor people have not received their wages until the Saturday late at night, and by reason thereof do come to buy meat upon the Sunday morning'. Robert Buckland and eight other butchers were selling meat on Sundays at Watlington, Oxfordshire, in 1631, and seven shoemakers were offering their wares. When Elizabeth Scarr of Witham, Essex, was accused in 1633 of 'usual selling of wares on the Sabbath', she responded 'that sometimes upon a necessity, as when a woman hath been delivered of a child, she hath sold some comfortable things for her, and in other cases of necessity'.[24]

'Necessity' was a common excuse for Sunday labour. Thomas Collimore of Thornbury, Gloucestershire, baked bread on a Sunday in 1592 'for the poor at the burial of a dead woman'. Matthew Manning of Denton, Northamptonshire, told the court in 1593 'that he carried corn on the Sabbath day but upon this occasion, that the cart was overthrown overnight, otherwise if he had not carried it it had been lost'. Bridy Bassett of Helpston had been gathering peas on a Sunday in 1604, but explained that 'she was great bellied and had a covet to them', and Helen Corbet went with her 'for company'. William Lucke, the miller of Birdham, Sussex, argued in 1614 that

he doth not usually grind upon the Sabbath day and that when he hath so ground upon the Sabbath day it was by reason of scarcity of wind which had been before, and that it was to supply the wants of the poor that could by no other means have their corn ground and must, if he should not have so done, have wanted bread.

The poor were convenient explanations for bakers and butchers and millers. The weather was often invoked too, especially by farmers. Martin Webb of Drayton, Somerset, had hired two men to divert a watercourse on a Sunday in 1618, 'a great storm of rain falling in the afternoon and thereby the water arising and being likely to drown many acres of this respondent's and his neighbours'. In 1625 William Maple of Little Thurrock, Essex, told the archdeaconry court that he just had to shear his sheep on a Sunday: 'that his sheep had been washed a fortnight before, and that by reason of the wetness of the weather he would not shear them all that time and that if he had not sheared them they would have died'. John Went of St Botolph's, Colchester, was denounced in 1633 'for bringing luggage from Ipswich fair upon the Sunday'—he stated that he could not travel on the Saturday as intended 'by reason of an extraordinary tempest', and anyway was home in time for the afternoon service on Sunday. In 1635 William Kirkham of Great Saling 'in extremity of wet weather ... did upon the Sunday after dinner and before evening prayer let out the water in a furrow to save the corn'. And if you can't blame the weather, blame the pigs. When John Cron of Dagenham was presented 'for beating down acorns on the Sabbath day' in 1639, he asserted 'that one of his hogs following him as he was going into his field on the back side of his house, he having a stick in his hand beat down a few acorns to see whether it would eat, being very sick'.[25] Some of these excuses were surely true—but the guilty still had to go to court, pay the fees, and, in most cases, make confession of the fault in church. Often, the law must have seemed an ass, or a pig.

The offences might be trivial. When George Leigh of Saintbury, Gloucestershire, was cited in 1596 for 'work upon a Sunday', he protested that 'he did but draw in a wheel that was broken'. John Newman of Glastonbury, Somerset, was presented in 1616 for plastering on a Sunday: he 'did in the morning bestow two spadefuls of mortar in daubing or plastering'. William Cocke of Manuden, Essex, claimed that 'he did only knock his hatchet against a tree after he had broken the ice withal for his cattle to drink'—after he had been accused in 1638 of 'felling a tree upon a Sunday morning'. Others had just been doing a bit of gentle Sunday gardening. Francis Howen's wife dug up a few carrots for her husband's supper in 1620, George Mercy of Stansted Mountfitchet, Essex, had been weeding in 1629, and Robert Clarke of Goldhanger sowed a few seeds in 1636. No wonder some thought regulation was too strict. When Elizabeth Waters of Norton St Philip, Somerset, was rebuked by a neighbour in 1588 for spinning on Sunday, she said she would do it again if she had to. Thomas Harding of Rettendon assured his servants in 1591 'that it was no offence to God to gather acorns on the Sunday', and in 1597 Christopher Colson of Axbridge told the Wells diocesan court that sometimes on Sunday mornings he delivered shoes that had been ordered, 'only for poverty and not in contempt for religion'. When the minister of Soberton, Hampshire, preached in 1611 that 'a woman might as well play the whore as to turn the swathes of barley upon a Sabbath day', John White refused to receive communion from him. Hilda Brewer of Hadstock, Essex, had no patience with sabbatarian strictness. When warned by the churchwardens in 1626 for washing clothes, 'she told us (with cursing us) that it [was] happy for us we had such leisure to wash on the worken days'. And in 1634, when Thomas Remington of Iffley was criticized by the archdeacon of Oxford himself for Sunday fishing, he retorted 'that he did know what belonged to the keeping of the Sabbath day, and did not desist from it'.[26]

With the obvious and important difference of mass churchgoing, it rather looks as if the English Sunday was then much the same as now—football, shopping, and gardening, with perhaps a little fishing for the loners. Virtually everyone went to church, but then many played games or caught up on their chores. But there was opposition to the most flagrant profanation of the Sabbath. John Lovell of Stockland, Somerset, racked and dried dyed cloth on Sundays in 1615, 'to the great dislike of the parish'. At Bere Regis in Dorset in 1617, some shops were open 'as if it were on any market day', and a shoemaker worked 'to the offence of the congregation'. Robert Roode of Street, Somerset, regularly did his hedging and ditching on Sundays in 1619, 'to the great dislike of his neighbours'. In 1622, Henry Selwood of Chard 'doth usually every Sabbath day set his 'prentice maidens to wash cloths while other people are at church, by means whereof they very seldom come to church, to the great dislike of the parishioners there'. Thomas Collins of Blisworth, Northamptonshire, was denounced in 1624 'for commonly setting forth with his cart towards London upon the Sabbath day, to the great offence and scandal of the congregation'. In 1631, Eleanor Farthing of Kingston near Taunton mended bags on a Sunday 'to the disturbing of her neighbours', and Agnes Buncombe of Priston near Bath made hay 'to the dislike of the neighbours'.[27] Blatant breaches of the Sabbath provoked the wrath of the parish, but those little lapses to which all but the most austere were prone did not. Little sins did not count.

Our 'ignorant' friend Asunetus knew he was a sinner, but he expected to be saved by Christ's mercy: 'Christ died for all, therefore all shall be saved' was his view. 'Many acknowledge that they have sinned and do deserve eternal damnation,' observed Henry Scudder, 'but they say God is merciful, therefore their heart is quiet without all fear of condemnation'—'dreaming of universal redemption by Christ'. In 1618 Richard Bellamy of Crewkerne in Somerset was excommunicated for failing to answer an allegation of keeping Florence Windsor in his house. Two months later, he went to the bishop's office to seek absolution and was told to come back: 'If I cannot have it now, by God's blood I will never come thither again for it,' he cried. 'I care not for the excommunication, for I have a good faith in Christ and by that I live and believe in.' William Kaye of Rayleigh in Essex was presented as a drunkard and swearer in 1635, and also because 'he sayeth to the dishonour of God that he that believeth in him shall be saved'. Men like Asunetus and Bellamy and Kaye might drink, swear, skip the occasional service, doze through a sermon, and break the Sabbath—but they still thought that they were good Christians and Christ would get them to heaven as well as the zealots. 'I am none of those that will go four or five miles to a sermon,' said John Bate's Autophilus, 'and yet I trust I shall do well enough for all that, as long as I have a good faith in God and do nobody no harm.' Thomas Turvill's Timothy tells worldly Ananias that swearers and Sabbath-breakers will not be saved, but Ananias disagrees. 'If it be all true that you say, then what shall become of the whole world? But God is merciful, and Christ hath died for us, and therefore I hope we shall be saved by Christ's death as well as the best puritan of you all.' You don't have to be one of the godly to get to heaven. And Arthur Dent's Asunetus was also confident that 'good neighbours' and 'honest men' would be saved—'for if such men be not saved, I cannot tell who shall'.[28]

PART III

'PHILAGATHUS, AN HONEST MAN': THE PROFESSORS AND THE PROFANE

5

Philagathus: Godly Living

Most men nowadays have nothing to spare for Christ, nothing for his gospel, nothing for the Church, nothing for the poor children of God and needy members of Christ. Christ is little beholden unto them, for they will do nothing for him, no, not so much as speak a good word in his cause, or the cause of his poor saints.

'Well met, Master Theologus,' says godly Philagathus at the beginning of Arthur Dent's dialogue. 'What, mine old friend Philagathus?' replies Theologus cheerfully, 'I am very glad to see you in good health.' They chat amiably about the weather, but then they see Asunetus and Antilegon approaching. Philagathus proposes they should engage the two in discussion of religion—'It may be we shall do them some good'—and Theologus suggests Philagathus should raise some questions for him to answer. This opening exchange hints at the character and role of Philagathus. He is 'an honest man'—a friend and admirer of the minister, with a condescending (or concerned) attitude towards those less godly than he. He is also a literary device, a straight man for Theologus: he raises the issues, he summarizes the answers, and he keeps the dialogue moving—'Well, sir, I think you have now spent time enough in answering the objections and cavils of Antilegon.' He has a less developed identity than the other characters, and so is less helpful as an investigative tool, but he provides a useful entry to an understanding of the godly laity. Philagathus himself is eager, earnest, and questioning. In the early stages of the discussion, he seems not always to understand what Theologus is saying—but he soon becomes the partner of Theologus in correcting Asunetus and rebuking Antilegon. Philagathus is a model of assertive godliness, hostile to Antilegon and his cavils and patronizing to Asunetus for his ignorance—'I had not thought any man had been so ignorant as I now perceive this man is.' He delights in Theologus's refutations of Antilegon's objections to godliness—'Now, I must needs say you have fully stopped his mouth, and thoroughly ferreted him out of his deep burrow.' Philagathus is not as these other men. When Antilegon calls him a disciple of Theologus, his reply is tart: 'No sir, I hope I am Christ's disciple and no man's. But assuredly I cannot hold my peace at your vile cavilling and most blasphemous speeches.'[1]

Theologus advises those who wish to follow Christ to 'Keep company with the godly, and avoid the society of the wicked.' This was the conventional counsel of godly preachers. Turvill's Timothy declared, 'it is not possible for professors to sit with profane men upon the Sabbath without being defiled by them'. Robert Bolton, as ever, put it bluntly: there must be 'an everlasting separation between the Christian and profane men'. The godly knew how to distinguish between 'us' and 'them'. Those who took communion with Master Luddington in 1585 were 'rotten members and rotten sheep', thought William Leyden of Hempsted, Essex, and in 1587 Robert Hamon of Bobbingworth declared that Master Glascock 'is a blind guide, and all that follow him shall go to the devil'. The nonconformist William Bradford of Oundle, Northamptonshire, said of his neighbours in 1587, 'there is not one man in Lilford that hath either care of God or his Saviour'. Henry Browne of Whissendine, Rutland, would not attend his own church in 1592, asserting 'that half the town be papists, slanderously'. John King of North Ockendon, Essex, had claimed in 1611 that the minister 'was a maintainer of drunkards and whoremasters, and will sooner bear with them than with good Christians', and that he would be better favoured 'if he were a drunkard, a whoremaster, a profaner of the Sabbath, as many were in the parish'. John Street from Somerset told his churchwardens in 1629 'that the parish of Stogumber is such a place as he never put his foot in the like, and that it was as odious a place to him as hell itself'—and only three wardens in the last thirty years had been honest.[2]

'We' were different: 'we' were the godly: 'we' could recognize each other and 'we' knew our enemies. Though they were too often called 'puritans', 'The name that the brethren of Christ, the children of God, do desire to be called is "the professors of the gospel".' That was the language of the godly. In 1570 the vicar of Godshill, Hampshire, was 'much suspected of papistry of the brethren there', and in 1586 the walls of a Chichester church were 'stuffed with painted images to the offence of the godly congregation'. Matthew Garewe of Bobbingworth, Essex, had declared in 1587 that 'Christ hath pronounced him to be there', and that Master Glascock (again), though a preacher, 'is a blind and naughty minister'. One Elliott of Stansted Mountfichet claimed in 1588 'that he could within half an hour's warning tell how many of the town should be saved'. William Andrews of Stoke Lane, Somerset, refused to kneel at services in 1594, and, 'further, he saith that he is a chosen vessel'. The churchwardens of Rayleigh, Essex, reported in 1600 that William Peryn was a drunkard, 'to the grief of the godly and great danger of his soul', and complained of disobedient Catholics 'never yielding themselves to the obedience of godly laws made for reformation [of] the wicked recusants, to great grief of the godly'. The godly had a large capacity for grief. In 1601 Henry Smith and Ursula Curtis of Carleton, Northamptonshire, 'by their outward appearance gave great occasion to the people of God that their life is incontinent'. John Ottyes of Glastonbury, Somerset, had offended his neighbours in 1614 by explaining predestination to them, and asserting, 'I know as well where I stand, that I shall be saved.' Richard Britten of Batcombe thought Samuel Millard should be ashamed for deserting the godly cause in 1634, 'you that have been a professor of religion, and to fall away'. And Richard Nicholls of Brompton Ralph had a mission from God in 1637: 'he sayeth he is sent to convert, and to that end doth frequent divers silly families whom he threateneth with damnation'.[3]

It was a sign of God's people that they were persecuted: 'Blessed are ye when men shall revile you and persecute you,' Christ himself had promised. In 1566 Richard Rowles of Leonard Stanley, Gloucestershire, got into a row with the bishop of Gloucester over biblical translation. He admitted he could not read or write, but 'learning doth not consist of tongues, referring himself to the second chapter of the Act of the Apostles. And further he said that they were furred gowns that persecuted Christ's prophets and apostles.' When Henry Sharp of Northampton was summoned before the bishop of Peterborough's court in 1574, he declared 'that it is a shame for my lord to send for him, and that my lord persecuteth God's Church'. John Bradford of Thurlaston in Leicestershire had been excommunicated in 1611 for refusing to kneel at communion. Next year he had his son christened 'Ichabod, which signifieth "the glory is gone", whereby it is commonly conceived that he, being a man of that factious humour, doth intend to traduce and scandalise the Church of England'. The touchy new rector interpreted Bradford as meaning that 'because the discipline of the puritans is disallowed and not used, but men compelled to be conformable, therefore "the glory is gone", and more particularly because one Mr Sherwood, late parson of the said parish of Thurlaston, was deprived for nonconformity'. Abraham Sawkin of Prittlewell, Essex, complained in 1624 'that Christians were no more respected than dogs', and it was a preacher's cliché that the godly were scorned as puritans and fanatics. 'If the world lour and look sour upon thee for thy looking towards heaven, and thy good-fellow companions abandon thee as too precise,' Robert Bolton consoled the congregation at Kettering, 'In a word, if thou walkest in the narrow way and be one of the little flock … , I say, then, thou art certainly in the highway to heaven.'[4]

The 'professors' were 'the little flock', separated from the worldlings and carnal Christians—from what Theologus had called 'the society of the wicked'. Some took this separation literally. Thomas Bradford and others of Moreton Valence in Gloucestershire were presented in 1569: 'these neither will come to the church nor eat or drink with them that come to the church'—in fact, they did attend church when there was a sermon, but they kept their distance from the rest of the parish and would not take communion with them. Others separated themselves for special occasions. On a summer Sunday in 1581 fifteen or so of the godly of Ramsey in east Essex gathered for a secret picnic in the woods, at the invitation of William Collet. They ate roast beef and a goose, and then Collet read the third chapter of St John's Gospel and expounded the text. Richard Galloway's wife had been among this 'little flock' in the wood, and 'she commended the same sermon to be a spirit sermon, and that Collet came down from heaven'. Sometimes separation was not joining in what others did, especially on the Sabbath. Robert Smith of Weeley refused in 1613 to contribute to the churchwardens' Sunday collection towards the repair of St Albans abbey church, 'saying they needed not give except they list and that it was no fit work to be done on the Sabbath day'. Richard Baxter later described how in his Shropshire village in the 1620s the parishioners would divide on a Sunday afternoon into those who went dancing and those who stayed at home to read the Bible—and any who went to hear a sermon were 'made the derision of the vulgar rabble under the odious name of "puritan"'. In 1634 in the parish of St Peter-le-Bailey in Oxford there was a clear distinction between the godly and the conformists. The godly were, as they expected, traduced as puritans. Edward Mitchell and others deposed that 'John Bolt is generally accounted in the parish to be a factious man or a puritan, and one that doth separate himself from, or at least not keep any company with those persons of the said parish who are taken to be conformable to the orders of the church of England, but with such persons as are held to be puritans or of like faction.' Ralph Oxley testified that Bolt would 'not entertain any commerce or familiarity with those of the parishioners who are conformable'.[5] The godly were distinctive: the godly made themselves known.

They identified themselves most obviously by their nonconformity, their refusal to follow the prescribed order of the official service book, the Book of Common Prayer. This is not to suggest that 'professors' were necessarily non-conformists, or even that nonconformists were necessarily godly—but that the godliness might be publicly displayed and officially recorded as nonconformity. Many of the godly regarded elements of the Prayer Book as contrary to the will and the word of God. Andrew Amye of St Giles, Colchester, had stated in 1612 'that he would to God you knew the corruption that is in the divine service'. John Trott of High Littleton in Somerset disapproved strongly of a set liturgical formula, and in 1628 'sayeth that common prayers and the reading of the Word and Homilies is worth nothing nor to be respected, and if any man do contradict him he will fall out with him, and too that he doth persuade many of the youth of the parish and entice them to follow him and say as he sayeth'. When nonconformity and the Prayer Book were discussed in a Yeovil shop in 1629, Susan Dennis had said she wished that some things in the book had been omitted. When Thomas Rock asked her for her judgement of the Prayer Book, she turned the question around and enquired of Rock

[H]ow he did like of that prayer in the Book of Common Prayer which was used for the sick, when as the minister should say that he did desire God to be merciful to this thy servant who is heartily sorry for his sin, when perhaps he is not, and it may be again when the minister hath not been with him to know whether he hath been sorrow [*sic*] or no.

Susan Dennis knew her Prayer Book—and some of it she did not like. When the churchwardens of All Saints, Maldon, in Essex, tried to persuade William Grove to attend divine service more often in 1635, Grove retorted, 'Divine service? If it were divine service it were well, but it was devised service.'[6]

Many of the godly objected to parts of the service of baptism. It was alleged in 1604 that Robert Lewgate's wife, of South Benfleet, Essex, would not allow her baby to be sprinkled with water or signed with the cross—though one churchwarden said he didn't think she was that sort of person. Sybil Chapman of Hazeleigh was presented in 1620 for condemning the use of a cross, 'and snatching the child away from the minister when he went about the use of the said ceremony'. In 1628 John Payne of Stretton, Rutland, was said to have grabbed his child as it was about to be crossed—but he claimed that the minister had agreed to omit the sign, and Master Whittacres himself confirmed this. One of the churchwardens of Chelmsford was cited in 1634 for not presenting Alexander Knight's wife for covering a child's face so it could not be crossed. The woman had a different story. As godmother to her daughter's child, on coming to the font she had privately asked the curate not to cross the child, but he had not answered. She claimed that the curate had crossed the child on the body not the face, and that she had simply wiped away the water after it had been sprinkled on the baby's face. When Richard Roper of Chelmsford was required to bring his child to be christened in 1637, he responded that 'he would if he might have it baptised according to God's ordinance'. Was crossing 'according to God's ordinance'?—some parents thought a child was not properly christened, and at risk from the devil, if it was not crossed: others thought crossing was a devilish superstition. Meredith Madye, the unpopular rector of Blagdon, Somerset, had a typically cantankerous solution in 1612: the parents who wanted the cross shouldn't have it, and those who didn't want it should.[7]

The role of godparents at baptism was also questioned by the professors: by the Prayer Book, the god parents, and not a parent, gave the child's name, and they made promises on the child's behalf. In 1583 Thomas Pamplet was to be godfather to Richard Okeman's baby, and went to Walden, Essex, for the ceremony. When the minister asked, 'Wilt thou be baptised in this faith?', Pamplet answered for himself, 'I will that this child shall be baptised,' instead of giving the prescribed response on behalf of the child, 'That is my desire.' The minister, Mr Dove, refused to proceed with the baptism, so a more compliant godfather was chosen and Dove christened the child according to the Prayer Book formulas. Thomas Bradford served as godfather at the 1612 christening of the child of Richard Makernes at St Giles, Northampton—where Robert Sibthorpe was vicar. When the vicar asked the child, 'Wilt thou obediently keep God's holy will and commandments?,' instead of responding firmly 'I will' for the child, Bradford said quietly, 'We desire it may be so.' Sibthorpe was not one to stand for such nonconformist nonsense: he reported Bradford for the offence, and the churchwardens for refusing to present it. In 1621 Aaron Elsemere of Great Burstead, Essex, acted as godfather for his own child, both naming and answering on its behalf, and John Cutfold of Funtington, Sussex, refused to allow his baby to be baptized until his wife could be present—'no such thing accustomed to be done in the parish before'.[8]

Many of the godly believed that mere ceremonies had no value—worse, that they were idolatry—and insisted on the centrality of the sermon in services. Matthew Hailes of Burham, Essex, would not allow his child to be baptized in 1587 unless a sermon was preached, nor would Thomas and Jane Oakshott of Chichester in 1598. John Nicholls, vicar of St Sepulchre's, Northampton, was at the font and about to baptize Nicholas Spooner's child in 1616, but Spooner tried to stop the ceremony on the grounds that Nicholls was not a preacher and so unworthy to baptize. When the parish clerk asked Spooner, 'How if there were no preaching minister in England, what would he do with his child, he answered that he would carry it beyond the seas, and being further asked how he would carry it he answered on his back.' In 1620 John Ward of Little Yeldham, Essex, brought in the nonconformist minister Richard Blackaby to preach at his child's christening. One way of securing the right sort of baptism was to go to the minister of another parish. In 1588 John Akers of Broughton in Northamptonshire would not have his baby baptized there by Master Randall, so he took it to be christened by the godly Master Pattinson at nearby Cransley—but Mrs Dansey of Cransley had a different preference, and sent her child to be baptized at Broughton. Robert Poole and John Horwood each refused to have a child christened at Dallington in 1607, and took it to the nonconformist Robert Catlin at All Saints, Northampton.[9]

The ceremony of 'churching' after childbirth—properly intended as a thanksgiving for a safe delivery, but sometimes called 'purification'—also had elements that offended the godly. Richard Tuckley of Little Totham in Essex would not permit the churching of his wife in 1585, nor would Richard Incly, who said 'it might be left out very well'. Three Hornchurch wives were not churched in 1590: two of them had their babies christened away at Romford, and the third, Robert Aylett's wife, was in trouble again in 1592—she had not been churched after two deliveries, and after a third 'she came to give thanks without any other women with her, to the offence of many of her neighbours'. Mrs Aylett disliked ceremony: her neighbours wanted propriety. The wife of Richard Wiggington of Oundle, Northamptonshire, told an ecclesiastical judge in 1595, 'I will choose whether I be churched or no, Mr Butler.' When he affirmed that honest women were churched, she retorted, 'I pray you may be ashamed of your doings and repent you: you say all honest women are [churched]; good is evil with you and evil is good.' Ursula Bruning and Alice Hellier of Hambledon, Hampshire, refused to have the Prayer Book ceremony in 1607, and Judith Mee of Eastney did not go for her churching. Again, there were choices and evasions. Joan Hilton of South Benfleet, Essex, went to Hadleigh to be churched in 1614, and in 1628 Mrs Cranford of Daventry, Northamptonshire, went to church but fell conveniently ill during the sermon and could not stay for the ceremony.[10]

What was wrong with churching? For some godly women it was just another unnecessary and popish ceremony. Others would not go to the pew set aside for churching—such as the wife of John Dudman of Donnington, Sussex, in 1597, and Winifred Littlewood of St Leonard's, Colchester, in 1611. There had been dispute about this at Oundle in 1596, and there was a decree from the diocesan court that only 'the uppermost seat upon the left side of the middle alley in the church' should be used for churching. But it was the old custom of wearing a veil or kerchief for the ceremony that caused most protest. Agnes Meade and four other women of Hornchurch, Essex, went to be churched 'without a decent kerchief' in 1602, and Agnes and another woman in 1607: after this occasion, Agnes promised she would wear a veil if she had any more children. Joan Whitrip of Corringham, Essex, went to be churched in her hat in 1613, and 'she said that none but whores did wear veils, and that a harlot or a whore was the inventor of it'. As more ministers insisted on a veil, trouble increased. In 1621 the chancellor of the diocese of London tried to settle the issue in Rochford deanery by ordering that women should dress for churching 'as they have anciently used'—but this just meant there would be arguments over local custom. Joan Goffe of Houghton in Hampshire would not wear a kerchief for her churching in 1621: her husband claimed she had not known it was required, and promised that 'he will do his best endeavour to get her that hereafter she submit herself according to law'. It was hard to enforce the veil where it had not been customary. The churchwardens of Newbury, Berkshire, were cited in 1631 for failing to present women who went to their churching without a veil: 'they go as they have a long time', the wardens responded, 'and therefore they did not present them'. The wardens of Herstmonceux, Sussex, admitted in 1638 that 'few are churched with such a veil upon their heads'.[11] In these parishes, it was the nonconformists who were the local conformists.

The communion was the Prayer Book service that most commonly divided the professors from the conformists—thus defeating one of the objectives of the common celebration. The requirement that the communion bread and wine should be received kneeling offended the godly, for it seemed to imply that the bread and wine were worshipped as the body and blood of Christ. Four men at Tewkesbury, Gloucestershire, received communion standing in 1595, and at Cransley, Northamptonshire two men received sitting and three standing. In 1604 the clergy were expressly forbidden to give communion to anyone who did not kneel. But in 1607 the curate of Banbury reported the preacher William Whateley 'for administering the communion to such as would not kneel', and complained of plots against himself because he would not do the same. Five Banbury people were cited 'for sitting at the communion' in 1613, and Whateley tried to prevent the accusation. At Easter 1615 the vicar of Ashby-de-la-Zouch, Leicestershire, announced that he would deny communion to any who would not kneel—and a hundred parishioners, led by the preacher Arthur Hildersham, were duly rejected. In 1617 John Cole of Weedon Beck, Northamptonshire, sought absolution after he had been excommunicated for refusing to kneel. When asked by the judges

[I]f he were absolved he would receive the communion kneeling and promise so to do? He answered 'That is a matter of conscience', and he entreated their favour for that point. And being asked if he would take his oath to obey the laws ecclesiastical, he answered that he would take his oath to be obedient to the king's laws so far as he ought by the laws of God.

Richard Hall of Chippenham, Wiltshire, affirmed in court in 1622 'that to kneel at the communion is idolatry and directly against the second Commandment' (on bowing down to a graven image). In his Christmas morning sermon at Great Waltham, Essex, in 1626 Christopher Gough preached that the method of receiving communion was not a matter of conscience, so people should not refuse to kneel—but Anne Webb just laughed at him. At dinner that day she declared, 'He did preach he could not tell what things, not to be spoken of in a pulpit,' and when reproved by her host 'she answered "What skills it how we receive the communion?"': she heard a good man once teach that leaning at the communion was best of all'.[12]

Despite Gough's argument that posture was indifferent, there were clearly strong feelings among the godly on the kneeling issue. Ministers varied in their willingness to give communion to those who insisted they would not kneel, and some refused to do so. Samuel Hoard, rector of Moreton, Essex, was cited in 1629 for giving the sacrament 'to such persons as will not kneel', and five parishioners were presented for receiving sitting: one of them, William Watson, had said 'that kneeling to the bread and wine is to worship an idol god'. The courts did have some success. Three of the Moreton five had agreed to kneel by 1630, but Watson and his wife would not. Beatty Seaton of Chelmsford told the Essex commissary court in 1632 that he was not yet resolved on the lawfulness of kneeling, and asked for time to consult divines—though perhaps that was a delaying tactic. One Trigg of Cottesmore, Rutland, declared in 1637 that 'he did once receive the holy communion standing and never but once, nor ever will he do the like again, and that [he] thinketh it very fitting and necessary to receive the communion kneeling and not standing'. In 1638 John Newton of Earl's Colne, Essex, explained that 'the reason why he doth refuse to kneel is because he hath a scrupulous conscience of the lawfulness of it, and desires time to resolve him in this particular'. But in some congregations there was substantial resistance to kneeling. In 1631 forty-three parishioners from Daventry, Northamptonshire, would not kneel and took the sacrament sitting: most of them appeared in court and were ordered to receive the Christmas communion kneeling, but the record does not show if they did. In the same year, the vicar of Boxted, Essex, was cited for administering communion to seated parishioners, and also the churchwardens 'for that the parishioners of Boxted do usually receive the communion sitting, and they have not presented them for it'.[13]

As with baptism, as well as those who objected to the ceremony there were some who objected to the celebrant. William Tuckhill of Chesham Bois, Buckinghamshire, refused communion in 1584 because the minister was not a preacher. Henry Leach of Benefield, Northamptonshire, would not take communion in 1589 from Jackson the curate, whom he called 'the beast'—and, as Leach was responsible for fetching the notorious Giles Wiggington to preach there, we may guess that the motive was religious. In 1594 Thomas Griggs of Lufton, Somerset, said 'he refused to receive the communion because that their minister then knew not what a sacrament was'. In 1596 Richard Whittle and John West of Caversham, Berkshire, would not take the sacrament there 'because the word was not preached there', and went to Reading instead, while in 1609 John Williams would not communicate at Nailsea, Somerset, for the same reason and went to nearby Wrington. Some gadding away to other parishes was to receive the sacrament from a nonconforming minister. Robert Cooke and fifteen others from Daventry went for communion in 1576 to Fawsley or Southam, then notorious centres of irregularity, and in 1585–6 one Rusbrooke of Oakham in Rutland went to receive from Robert Johnson at North Luffenham and Thomas Gibson at Ridlington. Thomas Clement would go to services at his parish church of English Combe, Somerset, in 1594 only when there was a sermon, and went for communion to the nonconforming Evan Thomas at South Stoke. A change of minister could make things difficult for the scrupulous. The professors of All Saints, Northampton, had been content to communicate with Robert Catlin, but when he was removed for nonconformity in 1614 they faced the hardliner David Owen. William Filkins told the Peterborough court that he had received the sacrament from Catlin and was still willing to do so, 'but at Mr Owen's hands he will not'—and Mary Thrift said much the same. John Nicholl refused communion from Owen because he was unhappy about his teaching, 'which he also affirmed is not agreeable to the word of God'. David Owen rapidly acquired a reputation as an enemy of the godly, and in 1616 he was denounced in the diocesan court as a sower of sedition and a friend of papists.[14]

We must be cautious, however. We cannot pile up cases of lay nonconformity and assume we have found the godly. Not everyone detected for nonconformity was a godly Philagathus: some were like ignorant Asunetus, following the crowd—and others were like awkward Antilegon, doing and thinking what suited them. There were other reasons besides godliness for failure to obey the liturgical rules of the Church. Helen Sounder of Little Laver, Essex, was presented in 1587 for sitting at communion: her husband explained that she had been pregnant, and 'received the communion sitting for her own ease and not upon contempt'—though he himself was cited for gadding away to sermons. When the wife of Collins of South Weald turned up for her churching in 1602 without a kerchief or the company of other women, she said 'that in places from whence she came the use is such, neither did she at any time otherwise'. Anne Vere of Henley-on-Thames similarly went to be churched

without a kerchief in 1637: her husband told the court that it had been her
first childbirth since coming to the parish, and she had gone to church just as
she had after her eight previous deliveries, in a parish where women had not
worn a veil or kerchief for churching. Edward Firmin's wife, of St Runwald's,
Colchester, was presented in 1640 for not going up to the communion rail
for churching in 1640: she said 'that she did come to church to give God
thanks and sat in the usual churching seat, expecting that the minister would
there church her as he had done others before and since'.[15] These women
were not necessarily principled nonconformists: they were doing what they had
always done.

Formal nonconformity was sometimes a matter of local custom—and it was
sometimes just cussedness. William Manton of Hambleton, Rutland, was 'a
despiser of the minister because he useth to wear the surplice' in 1586—but
he was also 'a common blasphemer of the word of God'. No Philagathus he.
Ralph Watson of Fingringhoe, Essex, was one of several in the parish who took
the Easter communion standing in 1611—but soon after he was also cited 'for
sleeping in the church in time of divine service and sermon upon the 10 and
17 of May last and other Sabbath days also'. Of course, even professors may
nod, but regular sleeping seems somewhat ungodly. Katherine South of St Giles,
Colchester, was presented in 1628 for gadding to other preachers, and also for
abusing and swearing. Robert Soane of Hadstock was accused in 1633 of absence
from church on holy days and carting on Lady Day. He admitted the offences,
declaring that 'for the holy days he sayeth that he ought to work six days by
the law of God and that he did absent himself from church upon divers holy
days'. Perhaps industriousness was next to godliness—but, as we have seen in a
previous chapter, those who worked on holy days normally did so for entirely
practical reasons. Christopher Craven, mercer, of Hanslope in Buckinghamshire
would not bow at the name of Jesus nor stand for the reading of the Creed in
1634, but he opened his shop on Sundays and was absent from church on various
Sundays as well as holy days. In 1638 Elizabeth Walker of Woodham Mortimer,
Essex, did not wear a veil for her churching. She said this was 'by reason she was
very young she did not know the orders of the church', but she and her husband
also had a casual attitude towards worship—'coming late to church on Sundays,
and irreverent demeanour of themselves when they are there'.[16]

We know what the godly were against—sinners and ceremonies. But what
were they *for*? Philagathus asked Theologus for advice on godly living, and was
told, 'The best counsel I can give you, if it were for my life, is to be very much
exercised in the word of God, both in the hearing, reading and meditation
thereof.' First, and most important, was hearing. We have already seen godly
reluctance to go to a baptism or communion with non-preaching clergy, for
those to whom God had not given the power of preaching were hardly God's
chosen ministers. Henry Page of Westbourne, Sussex, pronounced in 1586 that
'all ministers which have not the gift of preaching were blind shepherds and

guides'. At Westerleigh in Gloucestershire in 1594, Aaron Perriman and John Friend would go to church only when a preacher came, and Friend took his child to another parish to be christened. Three men from Stoke St Mary in Somerset were going to Taunton churches on Sundays in 1613, 'and draw many people after them, speaking scandalously of all ministers not being preachers'. Robert Brinkelow, vicar of West Wittering, Sussex, was a licensed preacher but because of a dispute with the owner of the tithes he did not preach in 1615: Thomas Hoskins 'did revile him and call him base fellow, saying he was no minister but a minisher'. The wife of Maurice Dix of Arthingworth, Northamptonshire, went to other churches in 1620, 'saying she would not go to a dumb dog, meaning Master Cooper the parson'. There was, she claimed, a sermon at Arthingworth only once every ten or twelve weeks. Charles Wells of Colchester was absent from church on six Sundays in 1630, and told one of the questmen 'that he did not come to church, nor would not come to hear a dumb dog'.[17]

The godly didn't just want sermons, they wanted the right kind of sermons. John Pickman was missing services in 1589 because 'the word of God is not truly preached in Hornchurch by Mr Lambert the minister there, and that he preached unsound doctrine, viz. he did teach them that Christ's apostles were drunk, and suchlike false doctrine'. Thomas Lathom was one of the several Hornchurch parishioners who went to sermons at Romford, 'for that the word of God is truly there preached'. When asked in 1591 if he would promise to attend at Hornchurch, he replied that he would not until it had a better preacher, 'for that Master Lambert doth not edify his conscience in his preaching'. When Christian Corless of Tolleshunt Knights was admonished in 1622 to attend services more regularly, she retorted, 'Then you must provide better doctrine,' and in 1631 Phoebe Haynes of Abingdon, Berkshire, protested that the minister at St Helen's 'had starved her soul and preached false doctrine'. Thomas Baker and other parishioners of Peakirk, Northamptonshire, were presented in 1633 for missing Master Ward's sermons in their own church and going to hear Master Greene at Clinton. Thomas Angel was one of these gadders, and he expected original sermons every Sunday and not sometimes the set Homilies. He told Master Ward that 'he would not come to church to hear an homily. Did I think he could be served with an homily? He could sit in his chair at home and read an homily.'[18]

As is clear, if those who wanted sermons could not get them in their own parish, they went gadding away to where they could. When preaching was in short supply, Church authorities might be willing to tolerate a limited degree of gadding. John Thornton and seven others of Shopland, Essex, were presented in 1587 for absence from church, and were told by the judge that whenever there was no sermon at Shopland any two of them could go elsewhere, but they were not all to be absent together. In 1590 the churchwardens of Weedon Beck, Northamptonshire, complained to the Peterborough judge that 'since you gave them leave at the visitation to go to sermons, the third part of our parish cometh not to church'—though it was not clear who went to other churches, and who stayed at home. As the number of preachers increased, and as churchmen became more concerned with ecclesiastical order than with evangelical enthusiasm, there were efforts to stamp out gadding and make people keep to their own parish church. In 1621, Richard Parker of Littlebury, Essex, preached 'a tart sermon which I made against gadders about to hear sermons, when they might hear Christ as well preached at home'—but William Taylor mocked the sermon in the alehouse, and said Parker would not dare to preach like that again. Taylor was not one of the professors, however, rather a drunkard who had been in the stocks at Audley End several times. John Buck, however, was 'a puritan' according to Master Parker. Buck had been elected churchwarden, but was refusing to serve because, said Parker, 'he would not be tied to his own church se[rvice?] in the afternoon but gad about to Arkesden or Newport'. Gadding continued, but such deliberate withdrawal from common worship was divisive. In 1632 the vicar of Pitminster, Somerset, named four parishioners for going to other churches, 'as remote, sometimes more remote from their dwellings than their own church is, unto which they flock in troops, they and their families, unto the great scandal and offence of their neighbours'. But some still claimed the right to roam. Philip James of Bicester, Oxfordshire, went to other churches in 1633, and 'sayeth that he thought there had been such an order in this court that if their own minister did not preach they might go to another church'.[19]

Gadding was not a random business, it was selective and concentrated. It was the godly preachers—very often the nonconforming ministers—who attracted people from other parishes. The nonconformist William Tichborne of Romford was highly unpopular among his own people: he excluded many from communion in 1595–6, some did not like his preaching, and he had personal conflicts with parishioners. But it was to Romford that the godly of Horncastle went to hear sermons—while some of his own flock went to Horncastle to escape him. After the famous John Dod was deprived from his benefice at Hanwell, Oxfordshire, he was a popular preacher wherever he went: at Moreton Pinkney, Northamptonshire, in 1607, at Titchmarsh in 1611, and at Seaton in Rutland in the 1630s he drew gadders from Uppingham, Barrowden, Easton, and Bisbrooke. Richard Board, Thomas Millard, and Joseph Stone of Shepton Mallet, Somerset, were going to hear Richard Bernard at Batcombe in 1614, but Bernard's neighbour Thomas Spratt at Stratton was much more of a draw. Millard and Stone also went to hear Spratt, who drew other gadders from Farringdon, Stone Aston, and Stoke Lane—where in 1615 one of the churchwardens was encouraging parishioners to go to hear Spratt. The popularity of the nonconforming Spratt was rather an embarrassment, and the Wells archdeaconry court ordered three gadders from Farringdon to declare publicly that 'the reading of divine service in the church according to the Book of Common Prayer is sufficient to beget grace and to strengthen grace, and that they have not gone abroad to hear sermons in contempt of service to be read but out of desire to receive instruction by sermons for the salvation of their souls'. Terling in Essex was another popular venue. Nine parishioners of Witham were gadding there in 1626, though Philip Pledger and Daniel Ridgewell said it was only because 'they cannot understand their own minister'. Several parishioners from White Notley went to hear Master Webb at Terling in 1631, apparently because they did not think much of Master Bickerstaffe's preaching—and when Matthew Mitchell of Terling was cited for absence from church on 24 October 1630 he said that 'he could not get into the church by reason of the crowd of people'. William Reeve of Milcombe, Oxfordshire, admitted he had missed a sermon at his own church in 1631, and explained that 'the reason then was that his brother coming to him at the same time did desire to hear Mr Whateley of Banbury preach, and entreated this respondent to accompany him'—but he also confessed that he usually went to Broughton, because the curate of Milcombe had once struck him. And in 1636 people from Little Harrowden, Wellingborough, and Wollaston, Northamptonshire, were going to Wilby to hear 'doctrine according to truth'—but they were pushing parishioners there out of their own seats.[20]

After hearing the Word, Theologus wanted Philagathus to read and meditate. Reading and meditating are more difficult to trace, but we can see them in action in private conventicles—since reading was often a group activity. Some of these meetings were led by a minister, and they were usually private catechizings or 'repetitions' of sermons—when the group went over a sermon to make sure they all had thoroughly understood it. William Seredge, rector of East Hanningfield, Essex, was unpopular in the parish for the high standards he set for admission to communion—but in 1584 a dozen or more from his congregation and some outsiders met with him after evening service each Sunday to sing psalms and pray. William Bird, vicar of St Giles, Northampton, was in trouble in 1617 for catechizing in church with his own adaptation of Perkins's *Six Principles*; when forbidden to do so, he instead held classes in private houses. By 1619, Richard Bernard had a well-established Sunday regime for the professors of Batcombe in Somerset:

Between morning and evening prayer many come to my house to have the sermon repeated, which divers write and having their notes corrected do repeat them publicly before the congregation by way of question and answer; I asking the doctrine and ground, then the proofs with reasons, and after the uses with motives; and they answer accordingly, which they do and willingly; besides the catechism questions and sometimes questions out of a chapter, and all before the second sermon in the afternoon. And yet for all this variety I avoid tediousness, which keepeth the people constant, who have greatly increased their knowledge, beyond that which I am willing to speak.

Bernard was still holding his Sunday afternoon gatherings in 1634, but by then his methods had provoked opposition in the parish and he was ordered to cease. Alexander Piggott, the curate of Chapple, Essex, was holding similar meetings after Sunday evening services in 1632, for repetition of sermons, though again there was criticism in the parish. At least three of those attending had received communion from Piggott without kneeling, so to some extent the conventicle was a gathering of the disaffected. And the nonconforming Master Devenish of Bridgwater, Somerset, had meetings for 'exercises' and psalm-singing at his house and elsewhere in 1636.[21]

Although frowned on by the authorities for their divisive tendencies and allegedly separatist implications, these gatherings were essentially parochial: conducted by a parish incumbent and attended mainly by members of his own congregation. More dangerous from the official point of view were conventicles run by laypeople—held because the parish ministry was thought to be unsatisfactory by godly standards. There was a conventicle at Cirencester, Gloucestershire, in 1576, apparently led by Thomas Bradfield. Alice Long regarded the meeting as an alternative to church, and told the visitation commissioners that 'they should not command her to any parish church, and that she would choose whether she will go'. But conventicles were usually the zealots' supplement to parish worship, rather than a replacement. In the early 1580s there was often a small gathering at John Barnard's house in Shepton Mallet, Somerset, sometimes attended by Thomas Snook, rector of Shoscombe. There were prayers morning and evening, a reading from the Bible, and sometimes an exposition of the text. Sometimes Barnard led the session, sometimes Snook, and sometimes one of Barnard's servants. There were gatherings at three houses in Westbourne, Sussex, in 1586, for 'conference together in the word of God, to the edifying one of another'—and the churchwardens queried whether they were lawful. Also in 1586 John Leach, the schoolmaster of Hornchurch, Essex, was holding meetings at his house, 'to the which catechizing great company do resort'. He argued that 'he doth usually catechize and expound psalms to his family, to the which divers others than his family do resort, not at his appointment but of their voluntary wills they do resort to his catechizing, and that he is not bound to shut his doors'. On Whit Sunday the wardens found more at Leach's meeting than at church—but that was partly because men from Romford attended too. William Hill of Stoke Gifford, Somerset, 'hath made certain exhortations in private houses' in 1587, but he said he had stopped since being told he was breaking the law. The wardens of Fordington, Dorset, reported in 1601 that Luke Bower 'doth often times draw young people unto him, and in his house doth privately interpret and expound them the Scriptures, after his own weak sense and learning'. There may have been a conventicle at Walter Rutter's house in Broughton Gifford, Wiltshire, in 1605—or there may have been just one occasion when a group of neighbours sang a few psalms after supper, as they claimed. Some of those involved also went off to sermons at Melksham, because there was no preaching at their own church.[22]

In 1616 the churchwardens of Shelley in Essex were ordered to justify their presentment of Elizabeth Ramsey and Richard Palmer for adultery, and they also cited 'the offensive behaviour of the said Elizabeth in former time'. They alleged that 'when she was first married, she using to go to conventicles in the night to Chipping Ongar, her husband being at that time fast asleep, she was ordinarily brought home by one young man or other, and had then been presented by the churchwarden but that our minister dissuaded him'. Elizabeth had lost her taste for religion by 1616, when she was also cited for not going to church when there was a sermon and always missing the afternoon service. But women did sometimes play a prominent role in conventicles. Mrs Slowe of Salisbury was said to have preached a sermon to a group at the house of Robert Catterall in 1617, probably in Bere Regis, Dorset, and in 1619 Dorothy Kennell of London addressed meetings at Wells in Somerset. The Wells gatherings were in the houses of John Burdge and Augustine Brodripp, and were attended by ten from St Cuthbert's parish 'with divers others of the country'. Dorothy, 'having made choice of certain places of the Holy Scriptures did expound and interpret the same to them, with singing of a psalm and saying of a prayer after the ending'. But most conventicles were meetings of a few parishioners with no outsiders. In 1629 certain men of Bedminster would go to afternoon sermons at Bristol or Rockley, and then meet together privately 'to repeat the sermons or lectures'. There were similar gatherings at Ringstead, Northamptonshire, in 1630, where Anthony Colston certainly reported on sermons he had heard and perhaps expounded Scripture. Likewise, parishioners of Caversham, Berkshire, met on Sundays in 1634 at Thomas Jones's house, 'where they have rehearsed so much of the day's sermons as they could particularly and severally remember, and have sung psalms and read some books'.[23]

The godly were most visible when they were in opposition—when they wouldn't do as they were told, and were called before the courts. This is why we see more of them in the reign of Charles I than before. Led by Archbishop Laud, bishops and clergy were then less tolerant of nonconformity, and more likely to proceed against delinquents; neglected ceremonies were now enforced, and new requirements were introduced. There were more things to be nonconformist about—and perhaps more people were provoked to nonconformity, to show their disapproval of the drift towards popery. There was more detected nonconformity, though not necessarily more godliness. In 1630 several members of the conventicle at Bedminster, Somerset, testified against their curate Thomas Cotter, claiming he had preached at Christmas 1628 'that the blessed Virgin Mary was without sin and that the body of our saviour Jesus Christ came from heaven'—and had failed to distinguish his doctrine from that of the papists. In about 1632, a group of Taunton tailors were chatting as they worked in William Gent's shop. When Thomas Davis passed by, he stopped to talk to them, saying he would happily give £5 towards getting the organs at St Mary Magdalene church working again. Hugh Willis did not agree: 'For what purpose shall they be set up, they are good for nothing but pigs to dance by upon the Cornhill.' The new organs were quite an issue in the diocese of Bath and Wells. William Chinnock of West

Lidford complained in 1632 'that there was nothing done at prayer time in the said church of West Lidford but tooting upon the organs, and that it delighteth him as much to hear his horse fart as to hear the said organs to go, and further said that music in churches was damnable'. John Bisse of Cheddar declared in 1637 'that he would rather hear his horse bray than to hear the organs go', and John Tillie of Wrington denounced the organ as 'music for dogs, and a May game'.[24]

There were lay protests against the king's 1633 declaration allowing Sunday recreations—but perhaps not as many as one might expect, given the significance the godly attached to Sabbath observance. In a conversation around Christmas 1633, John Wildgoose of Oxford had said 'that his opinion in that particular was that the king's laws were unlawful, and said further that they which did affect His Majesty's declaration might use the same [games] but he for his part would not'. At Witney Thomas King would not listen to the reading of the declaration, and stalked out of the church. Mrs Craddock, wife of the rector of Thistleton, Rutland, had heard 'that the sports are allowed to keep them out of the alehouse', but she roundly rejected this justification in 1634: 'But this is like the pope allows stews [brothels] to avoid fornication. And we may not do evil that good may come of it.' There was much more to get mad about than before, and Mrs Isham of Slipton, Northamptonshire, deliberately signalled her discontents. In church she would sit when she should kneel, kneel when she should stand, and turn her back at the Scripture readings. She angrily described the set prayers of the Church in 1634 as 'new toys'. John Harris and his wife, of Chelmsford, Essex, were reported in 1636 'for impugning the governance of the Church of England and speaking against the rites and ceremonies of the same': they had also refused communion from their minister and would not allow him to baptize their child. Anne Farmer of Hooe, Sussex, had had enough of the new liturgical strictness by 1637, objecting to the minister's insistence on the detail of churching—'God deliver us from such a malicious priest, but if none cared any more for him than herself they would deal well enough with him.' And Daniel Harrington disapproved of the rituals performed at Great Wakering, Essex, in 1638, going 'to other churches on Sundays and there at his opportunity tells what orders we have in our church which he likes not'.[25]

The issues that caused extra difficulty in the 1630s were not all new. The requirements to stand or kneel or bow at certain points in the service had for the most part been set out in the 1559 Prayer Book, and were codified and slightly expanded by Canon 18 of 1604. But it looks as if there had not been much effort to enforce them. Three parishioners of South Benfleet, Essex, were presented in 1587 for refusing to bow at the name of Jesus, and the wardens of Wokingham, Berkshire, admitted in 1622 'that the people have not used in our church to bow at the name of Jesus'. Standing for the Creed was being imposed in some parishes of the diocese of Peterborough by 1612. William Dodson and his wife of Rothwell were cited then, 'for which offence they have been heretofore presented, yet obstinately omit to do the same'. Two parishioners of St Giles, Northampton (where Robert Sibthorpe was vicar), were also reported for not standing at the Creed, as were two women from All Saints—but they said it was 'only upon mere ignorance'. At Storrington, Sussex, in 1622 John Johnson was cited for not standing for the Creed or Gospel, and not bowing at the name of Jesus.[26] There was, however, much more trouble about such issues in the 1630s.

Bowing on entering the church and at the name of Jesus proved difficult to enforce, and it seems clear that opposition was not confined to the godly. In some parishes there were individual objectors, but in others resistance was widespread. At Arundel, Sussex, in 1629 the churchwardens admitted that the whole parish failed to bow at the name and stand for the Creed. There were, however, different levels of disobedience: the vicar of Pitminster, Somerset, cited two wives in 1632 for not bowing, 'whom I rather present (though they be women) than others that are offensive in the same kind, because I conceive them to do it out of an high contempt of the order made and the charge given to the churchwardens by our right reverend diocesan in that particular'—negligence was one thing, perversity another. The wardens of Lutton, Northamptonshire, reported in 1633 that many parishioners did not bow, and bowing was neglected generally at Hannington in 1634 and by the most part at Weekley in 1635. In 1634 John Hillary, sidesman of Beaminster, Dorset, protested that 'neither Master Spratt nor any in the parish doth bow or use holy reverence (in time of divine service) when the blessed name of the Lord Jesus is mentioned (other than himself), therefore I pray you let me not be laughed at or had in derision because I do it and none besides myself': he named Spratt, the curate, and 105 others for their failure, though he asked for leniency towards ten of his friends. Spratt and the churchwardens made a more guarded presentment, stating that 'at the naming of Jesus there is such due and lowly reverence used as hath been accustomed, but for the bowing at the name of Jesus there are but few in the congregation that do it'—in other words, we're doing what we've always done, not what we've been told to do. It is hard to imagine that all 105 parishioners (according to Hillary, virtually everyone in the congregation) were making any calculated godly gesture, and surely most were following custom and the crowd.[27]

It was, however, usually the professors who refused to stand at the Creed, the Epistle, and the Gospel. In 1630 George Giles of Great Bentley, Essex, 'neglecteth or rather contemptuously refuseth to stand up at the time of the confession of our faith'—though when Richard Farne of Dagenham was prosecuted for the same offence in 1632 he said 'that he was newly come into the church and that he did kneel down and say his prayers and that he is hard of hearing'. Just before Christmas 1633 the rector of St Peter-le-Bailey in Oxford was suspended and William Sherborne was appointed by the bishop to serve the cure. Sherborne set about teaching the congregation to stand for the Gloria and the reading of the Gospel, and to bow at the name of Jesus. He seems to have had a good deal of success, but certainly not with John Wildgoose, who sat still in his pew when those around him stood. When Sherborne tackled Wildgoose on his 'irreverent behaviour', he was told that 'we have been used to be mildly taught and to have been otherwise instructed than you now teach us, and you must not think that though you have brought over Pidgeon [a chimney sweep] and a company of such rascals that you shall so bring over us'. Wildgoose later claimed he never knew there was any rule requiring standing or bowing, so Sherborne read Canon 18 at morning service the next Sunday—but Wildgoose took no notice, and he was not alone, as several witnesses declared in 1634. There were other 'puritans and factious persons' in the parish who would not stand or bow 'when other parishioners of the said parish who are conformable to the orders of the Church of England have used the same reverences'. In 1635 Christopher Jennings and ten others from Pensford in Somerset were presented for not standing for the Epistle and Gospel or bowing at the name. Jennings and some of the others were also members of a conventicle that met in Joseph Stone's barn in Chelwood—and Stone too refused to stand or bow. Until 1635, Thomas Gowers of Little Baddow, Essex, did not stand for the Creed 'because he was not sufficiently informed of the law in that kind', but since the rule was explained to him 'he doth duly observe that posture'—or so he claimed in 1636. In that year Thomas Sharpe of Sandon and his family were presented for refusal to stand at the Creed, or to bow at the name of Jesus, 'but do scoff at the minister and others that do'. It was asserted that 'The said Sharpe is a common depraver of the government ecclesiastical and of the rites and ceremonies of this Church, since his coming from New England; he is a common sower of discord and contention in the parish that no neighbour can live quiet by him, and threateneth the churchwardens and sidesmen that they dare not perform their office.' Perhaps Sharpe's behaviour alienated others, and his family may have been isolated within the parish. Indeed, it seems generally to have been individuals and godly groups that would not conform in this respect, though the wardens of Stoke Doyle in Northamptonshire admitted in 1637 'that their parish doth not stand up at the Creeds'.[28]

An obvious novelty in most parishes was the requirement to go up to the chancel rail before the communion table for communion and churching—a novelty because few churches had such rails before they were commanded in 1634. Going to the rail seemed like approaching a popish altar, and some people would not conform. At Rochford, Essex, in 1637 John Chandler and four others refused to go to the chancel to receive communion, 'but make the minister go about the church to see where they sit'. The curate of Chapple, the vicar of Terling, and the rectors of Layer Marney, Salcot, and Little Bentley were in trouble in 1638 for delivering the communion outside the rail to those parishioners who would not come up to it: at Terling these were 'most of the principle parishioners' and at Little Bentley the rector's wife and eight other women. Dorothy Clarke of Buttsbury refused to take communion at the rail in 1638, though she had done so before: she was described by the wardens as 'a poor woman and of low condition, and a little distracted'—though the court registrar noted, 'she is a lunatic'. George Wright and his wife of Great Chishall failed to take communion at Easter 1638, and sent a message to the Colchester archdeaconry court requesting 'that they may have liberty to resolve their consciences about the lawfulness of their coming up to the rail to receive the communion till Shrovetide next'—but their consciences proved obdurate, and they were returned again as non-communicants at Easter 1639.[29]

There were similar objections to churching at the rail. A few women had in any case been reluctant to be churched in a pew set aside for the purpose, and the rail perhaps caused more offence. Sarah Taylor of Walden, Essex, went to be churched in 1636 and was called into the chancel by the minister: she explained later in court that 'she refused so to do, it being written in one place of Scripture "Thou shalt not go up by the steps unto mine altar", because it was against her conscience'. The judge ordered her to go up to the rail and kneel for her churching, but Sarah's temper was up: 'she bade the judge excommunicate her if he durst', swore at the warden who had presented her, 'and called him shitten knave and shitten churchwarden'. Mary Dowtie of Walden had also refused to go to the rail: she would not obey the judge's order and was excommunicated in 1637. Although such determined objection to churching at the rail may have been a restricted phenomenon, the rails provoked more widespread hostile comment. When Joan Goodman saw the rails at Fiddington church in Somerset in 1636, she remarked that 'We have idle fool's baubles set up now', and in 1638 Thomas Meadopp of Rochford, Essex, thought the rails 'are good for nothing but to make the devil a queen's coop'.[30]

Church rituals were regarded by some as popish—and it was often the godly who saw things that way. When Robert Davey watched the annual Rogation procession pass through Chard, Somerset, in 1622, he asked, 'What, will this popery never be left?' Thomas Penn of Donnington, Sussex, asserted in 1623 'that the absolution in the Book of Common Prayer is a rag of popery', and two parishioners objected to the minister's explanation of the act. John Smith of St Nicholas, Colchester, called churching 'an idle, popish ceremony' in 1630, and his wife refused to be churched. And as more ceremony was enforced in the 1630s, so it seemed there was more popery. Richard Nichols of Brompton Ralph, Somerset, denounced churching as 'a rag of Rome' in 1637, and John Edgill told the vicar of Chewton that 'your bowing and bending is superstition and idolatry'. When the minister of St Osyth, Essex, asked the people to kneel for prayer at a burial, one Langley's wife protested, ' "What, will you make us kneel to the dead? Will you make us pray to the dead?" and continued so bawling a long time.'[31]

But more often the objection to ceremony was not that it was un-Protestant but that it was unusual. Nathaniel Benbow of St Peter's, Northampton, would not go to the rail for the Easter communion in 1636, but stated 'that he is willing to receive the same so that the communion table be brought down into the body of the church, as he conceiveth is required by the ancient order of this Church'. Those presented for not bowing or standing or kneeling at the right points sometimes claimed ignorance: it might be a convenient excuse, but it was plausible only when the requirements had been newly enforced. John Reynolds of Ingatestone told the Essex archdeaconry court in 1638 'that he did not know that he ought to kneel at the reading of the Commandments, and bowing at the name of Jesus'—but promised he now would. Robert Holland of Maldon admitted that 'being ignorant of these ceremonies he hath not kneeled as he ought'. John Prentice of Woodham Mortimer had scoffed at the minister for telling the congregation to bow at the name of Jesus—but he declared in court that 'He did not know the contents of the 18 Canon, but so soon as he was informed what it was and did mean he was and hath been observant in every point'. The clergy who complained about such negligence called it 'irreverence'—and sometimes it was just that. John Goodale of Little Bromley would not stand for the Creed in 1635—but he also slept through service and sermon, 'and will not be reproved, having had warning divers times'. Thomas Sorrell of Great Stambridge was presented in 1638 for not bowing and 'for his irreverent clapping him down upon his tail when he comes to the house of God'—which could be the complaint of a high-flying Laudian priest against godly defiance. But Sorrell was also charged with drunkenness, absence from church, and chiding in the church and churchyard.[32] So nonconformity is a very poor index of godliness, especially in the 1630s.

When is disobedience a gesture of Protestant protest, and when is it laziness, cussedness, or conservatism? Thomas Tirrell of St Peter's, Colchester, wore his hat in church as a matter of principle. He pronounced in 1639 that 'he knew no difference between the church and other places, and that he never knew of any house that God had but the temple in Jerusalem, and that he would be drawn in pieces with wild horses before he would keep off his hat in the church'. But was the hat always, or even often, a symbol of defiance? Although hat-wearing in church had been widespread earlier, it was forbidden in 1604 and there were very few churches in the 1630s where it was at all common—though it still was at Bridgwater, Somerset, in 1636. When Matthew Draper of Cotterstock, Northamptonshire, wore his hat through the service and did not stand for the Creed in 1633, it was said to be offensive to most of the congregation. Thomas Stanierne of Oundle wore his hat at a sermon in 1637, 'but not in contempt', and he abused the sworn men with 'evil and scandalous words'. William Duckett of Elsenham, Essex, refused to remove his hat in 1639, but he informed the court that 'he hath amended his fault and will not sit covered hereafter'. We should not imagine there were massed ranks of the stern-faced godly, sitting in church with their hats clamped firmly on their heads, grimly defiant of Archbishop Laud and his minions. There were many motives for and causes of disobedience in the 1630s, and some of them had little or nothing to do with godliness. So we cannot assume that all the nonconformists were godly—but nor should we assume that all the godly were visible nonconformists. The court record gives us outward actions and occasional excuses: only God knows the heart. 'Let all men therefore in time taken heed to themselves, and to their own souls, as they will answer it at their utmost peril at the dreadful day of judgement, when the secrets of all hearts shall be disclosed', said godly Philagathus.[33]

6

Philagathus: The Godly and the Rest

Yet for all this, it is a wonder to consider how deadly the wicked hate the righteous, and almost in everything oppose themselves against them, and that in most virulent and spiteful manner. They rail and slander, scoff and scorn, mock and mow at them, as though they were not worthy to live upon the earth. They esteem every rascal and prefer every varlet before them.

Philagathus knew well that the profane hated the godly. Theologus knew it too—'many of them despise the word of God, and hate all the zealous professors of it'. As he told Antilegon the caviller, 'if a man give himself to the word and prayer, reformeth his family and abstaineth from the gross sins of the world, you will by and by say he is an hypocrite'. At the Kettering lecture, Robert Bolton warned that the unregenerate would despise the true professors—'You see these fellows, which make such a show of forwardness and purity, what they are? none so covetous, none so uncharitable, none so unmerciful and cruel in their dealings as they.' Of course, this was a preacher's topos: by definition, 'the professors of the Gospel' had to be hated, since Christ and St Paul had said it would be so, and if they were not hated they were obviously not sufficiently godly. It was reassuring to be scorned by the worldlings: 'art thou therefore slanderously traduced with slanderous, odious nicknames of puritan, precisian, hypocrite, humourist, dissembler?' asked Bolton—well then, you are among the godly. But it was not just a pulpit cliché, it was a fact of life, the way the world was. Arthur Dent had heard it for himself, as curate of Danbury, Essex, in 1578: Gabriel Horne had told him to his face 'that there were no Protestants but pratlingstants, that do use to tell lies'.[1]

In his sermon at the Northampton assizes in 1629, Bolton complained that 'Nowadays every boisterous Nimrod, impure drunkard and self-guilty wretch is ready with great rage to fly in the face of every professor with the imputation of puritanism'—claiming to be purer than everyone else. It was true. Piety was called puritanism, and 'puritan' was an insult. In 1574 the churchwardens of Weston Favell reported that their deprived rector 'continueth in puritanism'—he said he was simply teaching what he always had. Some of the parishioners of Mapperton in Dorset petitioned in 1598 against their nonconformist curate and his supporters. They set their attack in the context of a broader plea for action against 'puritans', 'for they go about to steal away the hearts of the people by their stained reformations, and also to deprive our queen of her due obedience, backbiting their superiors and condemning their brethren, disquieting the Church and abusing the office of godly preaching'. This attempt to link their unpopular minister with presbyterian subversion was a calculated appeal to their ecclesiastical superior, the dean of Salisbury, who had himself written against presbyterians: 'Master Dean hath spoken and written against against [*sic*] the puritans before this time, but now your peculiars are full and none worse than in our own parish by Master Bowden and a schoolmaster that Master Bowden hath gotten in to our parish to keep school.' George Bowden's offences were omitting to wear the surplice, refusing to lead the Rogationtide procession, not observing holy days, criticizing various rituals, and preaching predestination—exactly what one would expect of a forthright godly minister. But the petitioners wanted to be rid of him, and have 'an honest and godly man' instead. 'Puritan' had become a useful insult for those who made nuisances of themselves, or for those who had an independent mind. When Alice Gulliver of Deddington, Oxfordshire, got into an argument in 1603 with Richard Mercer over some pigs flattening a cornfield, 'the said Richard Mercer called the said Alice Gulliver "puritan" and she answered that she was as she was and he was as he was'—so Mercer then called her 'whore'.[2]

Any display of religious zeal or moral censoriousness might lead to an accusation of puritanism. In 1607 Hugh Tucker and others of Ringwood, Hampshire, were alleged 'to be of the consort of puritans in that country', even 'sectaries'. But Tucker produced a certificate from the vicar stating that he attended services regularly and had received communion from him 'even when he hath worn the surplice'. Tucker admitted that he and his friends 'have been charged by some persons to be Anabaptists, Brownists and of the Family of Love', but he suggested two reasons for this. One was 'because they have found fault with drunkards and such disordered persons'—moral censoriousness; the other, 'for that upon the Sabbath days after dinner and upon the market days the persons nominated in the accusation meet at this examinate's house, and then some one of them read a chapter, without any manner of exposition, and then they altogether sing a psalm, and so depart' —religious zeal. Tucker denied firmly that any of them 'are of the Family of Love or any other sect'—they simply took their religion seriously, and others did not like that. There was also division at Chilworth in the same year, when the churchwardens laid complaints against half a dozen of the more godly parishioners. Richard Davy had seized the Bible from the curate, 'Sir Ralph Blimston', and Nicholas Davy had said 'that the surplice was a relic of popery'. When Cecily Hewitt had defended the wearing of the surplice, Robert Austin had asked her what holiness there was in it and 'What it would profit her to put her smock upon her other apparel?' Richard Dix and Austin had received communion sitting, and John Davy had 'charged the churchwardens to be profane men' for breaking the Sabbath. The ecclesiastical commissioners who heard the case concluded, 'there is some jarring between the parties complained on and the other parishioners, some being forward in religion and therefore termed by the other to be puritans, and they on the other side terming the other to be profane men'. The little parish of Chilworth could stand for all England, where the godly saw everyone else as 'profane' and the less-godly saw the godly as 'puritans'. The diocesan commissioners advised the parish 'to agree amongst themselves concerning these brambles between them friendly, if they can'. But such an agreement was exactly what godly preachers had counselled against. The 'professors' should not live in amity with the profane—'their society is not of God but of the devil, and they that are of this society cannot be of the holy communion of saints', William Perkins had pronounced.[3]

Should any sinner find religion and reform his life, go to sermons, read the Bible, and observe the Sabbath—'In a word, to turn Christian, oh! then he is an arrant puritan, a precisian, an humourist, an hypocrite and all that nought is,' warned Bolton. And so it was. In 1615 Lawrence Clive of Wincanton in south-east Somerset was presented for 'calling men of honest religion precisian, puritan rogues' and wishing 'that the devils should have them, and that the plague should confound them'. Richard Lovell of Glastonbury complained in 1617 that he had been named as father of a bastard by 'a filthy whore', and had purged himself—'and yet through the oppression of the damned sect of puritans I am enforced to keep the child until I can find the father'. John Lee made himself unpopular in 1624 among some of his parishioners at Wylye in Wiltshire, by a standard godly regime of preaching, catechizing, and moral reform. He most annoyed Susan Kent:

We had a good parson here before but now we have a puritan, but, said she, a plague or a pox on him that ever he did come hither, and I would we had kept our old parson for he did never dislike with them at any time, and she being further reproved said in this manner, viz. 'These proud puritans are up at the top now, but I hope they will have a time to come as fast down as ever they came up!'

Susan tried to persuade Joan Wadling to go off dancing with her on Sunday afternoon, declaring that 'she would not stay for prayers but would get her afar as she could out of the devil's clutches', and, when Joan said she hoped the devil would not come to Wylye, Susan told her he was already there—'Yes, there lies Mr Lee, the great devil in his den, and I will go afar out of his reaches as I can.' Richard Peep of Long Load in Somerset felt much the same way: godliness got in the way of a good time, and the puritans were responsible. He was one of those found 'drinkering and gamestering' in John Perrott's alehouse during evening service in 1627, and the company was presented by George Drake, the curate. Later, Peep raged at Mr Drake, 'cursing him and wishing the plague of God to be in him, and calling him puritan fool'.[4]

Robert Bolton predicted that if any turned from the alehouse to a sermon, 'their old companions' would cry, 'They are turning puritans!' And they did. On a summer Sunday in 1629, Thomas Lee and George Richards were on their way to the evening service at Handsworth in Staffordshire. As they passed Francis Norris's alehouse, he called out, 'How now, Thomas Lee, art thou turned puritan?' When Lee asked, 'What do you call a puritan?' Norris answered 'That they were such as went a-gadding to sermons as they did, and that they were knaves and thieves and no better.' When Hugh Willis of Taunton was accused of nonconformity in 1636, Thomas Davis reported his criticism of organs and described him as 'being then and yet commonly accounted in the town of Taunton to be of the puritanical faction'. But Willis was able to produce a testimonial to the bishop from William Leghman, the mayor, and others, beginning with 'greeting in our Lord God everlasting':

Whereas the bearer Hugh Willis (being cited before your Lordships this next court day) hath desired testimony of his good a-bearing and honest conversation in our [parish of] Taunton Magdalene, These are to certify that the said Hugh Willis [is] a man that hath lived in an honest deportment, free from any notorious or scandalous crime, peaceable with his neighbours, and one who frequenteth the church as orderly and usually as any other, free from faction or disturbance and carrying himself loving and kind to all men, and brings up his servants in the knowledge and fear of God to the utmost of his power and in subjection to lawful authority, not allowing them in any vice whatsoever.[5]

One man's godliness was another man's puritanism.

There was particular hostility to those who were suspected—or could be plausibly accused—of religious radicalism. Robert Welford of Earl's Barton, Northamptonshire, was presented in 1592 as 'a notable Browning, a Martin'— and in his case perhaps he was, having been associated with William Hackett, who had proclaimed the Second Coming in London. In 1594 it was alleged that Thomas Harvard of Bathford, Somerset, 'hath been factious in religion and a follower of the errors of the Martinists and Brownists in religion'—but since he was merely ordered by the bishop to conform and do penance, it seems likely that he had been no more than a strident nonconformist. At the same visitation, Martin Delarue of Bedminster was cited 'for being suspected to be a sectary, and not coming to the church above three or four times, and then contentiously to these presenters' judgement'—which may have been awry. Henry Joyce of Marston Bigot was also 'suspected to be a Martinist'—perhaps because he said it was against his conscience to take communion. Three absentees from Maldon church, Essex, were thought to be Brownists in 1602, and two of them were 'vehemently suspected' in 1604. But, as we have seen, a group at Ringwood in Hampshire in 1607, 'charged by some persons to be Anabaptists, Brownists and of the Family of Love', were merely church-attending conventiclers. In 1614 John Hartford and his wife of East Ham, Essex, were returned as 'Brownists or of some suchlike sect and faction'—especially as they had dubious visitors from London. William Launce of Norton under Hamdon, Somerset, really was an oddball—presented in 1619 'for a notable Brownist, in that he hath spoken against bishops, against the Book of Common Prayer, against the rites and ceremonies of the Church of England, as also for a Traskite, in that he openly holdeth and maintaineth that swine's flesh and the blood of beasts be in these our days altogether unlawful to be eaten, causing thereby schism and division amongst his neighbours'. He had called the rector 'false prophet, devil and murderer', and it looks as it he was pretty unpopular for his views. In 1620 John Lock of Edington was 'negligent in coming to church, being schismatically affected and maintaining arguments that a man may be saved although he were never christened or did never receive the sacrament of the Lord's Supper'—which sounds like a clumsy version of predestination, used as an excuse for laxity. Colchester, Essex, had 'a Brownist' in 1628, a couple of 'separatists' in 1630, a pair of 'absolute Brownists' in 1637 and in 1639 'a schismatical recusant that for a long time hath refused to communicate with our church in divine service and sacraments'.[6] What is notable about all these offenders (except for those at Ringwood) is that they were presented in ones, twos, and threes, isolated individuals who had drawn attention to themselves by zeal or oddity.

The zealous often had a hard time. On Advent Sunday 1590 Joan Kayes of Everdon, Northamptonshire, looked out of her doorway and mocked the godly as they went home from church. William Stuckey of Stoke, Somerset, was mocked by the minister in 1600 for taking his book of psalms to church, and told he would be better off carrying a wash-bottle. In his sermon on 10 May 1603, William Ecclestone, vicar of Stogursey, argued that the Apostles had instituted holy days. William Lawrence sprang up and called, 'You preach that you cannot prove by Scripture!', and then there was a wrangle between them—but afterwards Richard King called Lawrence 'fool and ass' in the church porch. Silvester and Agnes Presgrave of Braunston, Northamptonshire, were assertive nonconformists—and they paid for it among their neighbours. They were presented late in 1603 for a number of offences. Silvester 'spake disdainfully, disgraciously and in scorn against the wearing of the surplice', and his child was not baptized at his own church, 'to the great offence of all his neighbours and to the great danger and hazard of his child'. He would not join his fellows in communion 'to the great offence of us all', and his wife was not churched, 'contrary to the laudable custom of our Church of England'.[7]

The year 1606 was difficult for the godly of Dorset. Between June and October three anti-puritan libels circulated in Dorchester and were widely read and quoted. They were 'To all sturdy puritan knaves', 'You puritans all, wheresoever you dwell', and 'The counterfeit company and pack of puritans'. These verses repeated the standard jibes against professors—hypocrisy, presumption, censoriousness, and nonconformity—and by name and implication attacked the rector, John

White, and his followers. The 'execrable company of puritans' paraded their own godliness, but in truth were hypocritical sinners:

> For no-one's so simple that on you do look
> But knoweth that you live contrary to your book.
> You carry your Bible God's word to expound,
> And yet in all knavery you daily abound.
> For envy, hatred and malice great store
> In no creatures living I think is more.
> As daily by experience amongst us we find,
> To mischief and hatred none more inclined.
> Yea, covetousness, lechery and lying for gain
> Amongst you puritans is not counted vain.

'These counterfeit brethren elected' were arrogant, claiming to be better than their neighbours:

> Others there are I know very well
> Which for pureness of life they say they excel.
> Yea saints of heaven already chosen to be,
> To judge the good and evil of every degree.

But pride comes before a fall:

> You puritans count yourselves the greatest men of all,
> But I trust in God ere long to see all of you to fall.

They were troublesome killjoys, disloyal to the king:

> For what our king commands, that they do deny,
> Yea praying, kneeling and standing all these they defy,
> All honest recreations and merriments they blame,
> And are not these puritans, speak truly for shame.

Here are several of the themes enunciated by other enemies of the godly: disobedience, as charged at Mapperton; repression, as alleged at Wylye and Long Load; and ostentatious religiosity, disliked at Ringwood and elsewhere. And, before the fuss had died down at Dorchester, in September there was another libel circulating at nearby Lyme Regis—presumably inspired by the Dorchester texts. Richard Lamerton was accused of writing a libel 'which tends to the disgrace of such as are godly disposed within this town'.[8]

Henry Bindon of Dunster in Somerset exactly fitted the popular stereotype of the self-righteous, interfering 'puritan' who tried to push other people around. He was presented in 1626 as 'a precisian and separatist'—but it was his treatment of a dying woman that had really incensed his neighbours.

Coming into the house of one Hill of the same, where the wife of the said Hill lay very sick and weak, like to die, he undertook the office of a priest and began to examine her of sins, laid to her charge many offences and amongst the rest laid unto her charge that she had committed the crime of adultery and told her that if she would not confess the truth unto him she could not be saved, whereat she being much offended with him desired the people to put him out of the house, and about an hour later she died.

Bindon was not a peaceable citizen: in 1632 he was again cited because he had called a visiting preacher 'knave' in the churchyard, and said he preached false doctrine. Abraham Cummins also had trouble with his fellow parishioners, at Great Bentley in Essex. He was reported in 1632 because he would not stand for the Creed or kneel for prayer, but his arrogance may have been more annoying. After the morning sermon on 27 May he stood up in church and delivered his own prepared mini-sermon, 'to the offence of divers of the parishioners'—though he claimed his words 'were such as could not offend the congregation'. He was presented again in 1635 for refusing to stand for the Creed, but this time he claimed that he had stood and wanted the vicar and wardens called as witnesses.[9]

A congregation might turn on the godly if they made a nuisance of themselves. The attempt by the professors of St Peter-le-Bailey, Oxford, to block the traditional Whitsun celebrations in 1634 prompted a wholesale attack on them. John Bolt, John Wildgoose, and their friends were denounced by witness after witness in the Oxford consistory as 'puritans and factious persons': they would not stand for the Creed, Gospel, and Gloria, or bow at the name of Jesus, and they had caused fighting and uproar in church on May Day. Wildgoose 'hath been violent in defence of such puritans in his private and public discourse', and had said that those who made Hocktide collections 'did as good as pick their pockets'. John Bolt was 'a factious person or a puritan', who had shared responsibility for the May Day disorders—though one witness admitted that Bolt was 'an honest and quiet neighbour, living next door to this respondent'. St Peter's had a reputation in Oxford for its nonconformists, and Thomas Allen deposed that

It is generally observed in the parish of St Ebbe's where this deponent liveth and in other parishes within the city of Oxford that there is in the parish of St Peter's in the Bailey, *dicto civitate Oxoniensis*, a factious company of separatists, men and women that express a dislike of the rites and ceremonies used and allowed in the Church of England, and the said John Bolt hath by this deponent and many other of the city of Oxford been for this long time noted to be a principal party of the said faction and a man that hath opposed the conformity to the orders of the church.

John Bolt was honest and quiet, a churchgoer and, indeed, in 1634–5 churchwarden of St Peter's—but when he stepped out of line he was a factious separatist, and even his next-door neighbour testified against him.[10]

The generality did not speak well of the godly. Carping Antilegon thought they were hypocrites: 'They will do their neighbour a shrewd turn as soon as anybody, and therefore in mine opinion they be but a company of hypocrites and precise fools.' In 1591 Elizabeth Heckford of Elmstead, Essex, declared, 'a shame take all professors, for they are all dissemblers and liars', and in that year the mayor and jurats of Rye in Sussex complained that 'a small sect of puritans, more holy in show than in deed, is sprung up amongst us'. William Farrington of Chipping Ongar, Essex, was railing in 1599 against 'most of the inhabitants who profess religion, calling them all heretics, hypocrites, such as he hath ever and in every place detested, clowns, etc.' John Manningham collected London jibes against 'puritans'—'such hypocrites are those professors' and 'what dissembling hypocrites these puritans be'—and in 1633 William Payne of Elmstead claimed that 'the chief of the parish went to church to learn to lie'. Antilegon accused godly Philagathus of presumption: 'You think there is none good but such as yourself and such as can please your humour. You will forsooth be all pure. But by God there be a company of knaves of you.' In 1585 the wife of George Tucker of Ashendon in Buckinghamshire was 'a derider of those that profess the Gospel, and calleth them "bishops' commissaries" with other names'. The godly indeed saw themselves as 'professors of the Gospel', but that smacked of pride and suggested that others were lesser Christians. John Evans preached a mock sermon in the pulpit at Chesterblade, Somerset, in 1619, poking fun 'at the word of God ... and at the professors thereof'. Theologus had advised that 'the people of God' should hear and read his word—but gadding to sermons and brandishing the Bible brought the godly abuse. One of the Dorchester libels of 1606 had pronounced

> You carry your Bible God's word to expound,
> And yet in all knavery you daily abound.

The Bible itself came to be associated with the godly and all their ways. Lewis Houlder of Romford, Essex, railed against his godly neighbours in 1619, 'wishing them and their Bibles hanged one against the other', and in 1623 John Waters of Yapton, Sussex, claimed that 'a company of puritans had lately translated the Bible falsely, and got the king to put his hand to it'. In 1629 Francis Norris of Handsworth had declared, 'he is a puritan that follows or hawks or hunts to other churches than his own parish church, and carryeth a book under his arm and the devil in his bosom, and inventeth how to do his neighbour an ill turn'—and such a judgement had acquired proverbial status. Thomas Granger's babbler Mataologus asserted that 'they that carry books in their pockets carry the devil in their hearts', and John Manningham noted that a puritan was 'such a one as loves God with all his soul, but hates his neighbour with all his heart'.[11]

So we know what the worldlings thought of the godly: not a lot. But what did the godly think of the worldlings? Again, not a lot. They expected the profane to be sinners, for they did not have the saving grace of God that might keep them from sin. Of course, the less-godly hated sin too, and as churchwardens they too presented drunkards and fornicators and blasphemers at visitation. But sometimes one can detect what sounds like the voice of godly outrage. In 1612 the wardens of Wanstead, Essex, reported Alice Walker, who had a child out of wedlock 'to the great dishonour of Christian profession and scandal of Christian people and professors'. Joan Childs of Abington, Northamptonshire, was in 1614 presented for adultery with Edward Wheatley, 'and yet she hunteth now more openly after him than ever'—and Wheatley went to her house 'without the fear of God or to the shame of all good and godly-minded Christians'. In 1619 Richard Denham of Norton, Essex, was cited for working on the Sabbath and 'for a most fearful swearer and grievous blasphemer of the name of God, to the great grief and ill example of his neighbours'—'he is very rich, yet as wicked as rich, and therefore we humbly desire that he may be made an example to other that are lewd and vile as he is'. Grace Field of Corringham was reported in 1628 as 'a common drunkard and one that behaveth herself very disorderly, to the dishonour of God and great scandal to our parish'—though her version was that 'she is sometimes merry amongst her friends' and was just once 'somewhat overcome with drinking'. Abigail Lambert of Romsey, Hampshire, had a bastard child by her master Robert Cousin in 1629, and when the baby was taken to be baptized Richard Cole's wife interrupted the service and 'would have it named Repent-Mother'—a neat adaptation of godly naming patterns that had been fashionable forty years before. In the same year John Pittiver of Scaldwell, Northamptonshire, was named as a drunkard, 'and altogether unfit for the company of God's people'. John Newball of Navestock, Essex, continued his drinking in 1636 'notwithstanding divers friendly admonitions and warnings', and was 'a notorious enticer of others to the abominable sin of drunkenness'.[12]

Perhaps it is safer to turn to the judgements of the known godly on the profane. A substantial slice of the sermon literature of the period dealt with those who were not sufficiently good or sufficiently godly, and it is unnecessary to produce great detail here. Robert Bolton complained that men said of the godly, 'They must be the Christians and other men goodfellows, they must be the brethren and all besides profane, they only must be sincere and conscionable, and others formalists and carnal gospellers'—but that was what the godly *did* say. For William Perkins the less-than-godly were 'ignorant people', 'cup companions', 'the reprobates', 'carnal gospellers', 'the common, ignorant sort of people', the ignorant multitude', the 'wicked and profane'. To John Bate's truth-seeking Philoxenus they were 'neuters and jacks-on-both-sides', and Turvill's Timothy thought the enemies of professors were 'profane men'—atheists or covetous men or whoremongers or drunkards or swearers or Sabbath-breakers or papists. Granger wrote in 1616 of 'Protestant atheists' and 'the common hypocritical Protestants', and his Eulalus argued that it was only 'the rebellious sinner' who called a godly minister 'a puritan'. Many godly ministers elided lack of religion and lack of morals, but Theologus distinguished three different kinds of reprobates: 'all papists, atheists and heretics'; any 'swearers, drunkards, whoremongers, worldlings, deceivers, cozeners, proud men, rioters, gamesters, and all the profane multitude'; and 'carnal Protestants, vain professors, back-sliders, decliners and cold Christians'—those who believed the wrong things, those who did the wrong things, and those who did not try hard enough. Most often, the less-godly were 'profane'—precisely what the godly laymen of Chilworth had called their enemies in 1607. In this binary view of the world, there were just the professors and the profane (or the puritans and the good fellows)—in 1628 John Simons of Castletown, Dorset, came to church drunk 'and there called some of the parish rogues, some drunkards and some puritans'.[13]

Whatever the professors thought of the profane, they had no choice but to live among them—unless they went to New England. How did the godly and the worldlings coexist? Often with tension and difficulty, it seems. In some communities there was an entrenched cleavage between the professors and the profane, in others a running battle—and sometimes there was a flashpoint that illuminates local disputes for us. One such flashpoint came in the little Thames-side parish of Stanford-le-Hope, Essex, in August 1591. The rector of Stanford was Martin Clipsam, a non-preaching and somewhat negligent conformist—he had failed to provide the required monthly sermons in 1590, and in 1591 he was presented for failing to visit the sick or to provide a deputy to say service in his absence. It was asserted that he and his wife would leave the church during the sermon of any visiting preacher, 'wherefore they are suspected to favour the popish religion'—but it is probable that he just did not like others preaching in his church, and that the 1591 churchwardens were trying to cause him trouble. Opposing the rector was a group of godly parishioners: they included William Partridge and his wife, William Lewger and his wife, and Robert Bailey and his wife, who had all missed communion at Easter 1589, probably because they disapproved of Clipsam. The Partridges and the Lewgers were then excommunicated, though they went to other churches instead: Partridge claimed in 1590 that he had been absolved by the commissary, but that Clipsam was keeping the absolution secret. By 1591, the godly few had the aggressive support of Tristram Blaby, a young minister with a preaching licence from the bishop of London. Blaby was then living at Stanford, and said service in the church 'upon necessity' when Clipsam was away.[14]

On Sunday, 8 August 1591, as Parson Clipsam was nearing the end of morning service, Blaby forced himself into the pulpit and instructed the people to sing a psalm before he preached. Clipsam (it was later claimed) asked politely, 'I pray you give me leave to say forth my service, it is almost done'—but Partridge and one of the wardens, Philip Perry, wanted Blaby to be allowed to preach. Other parishioners objected to the interruption, saying, 'Why do ye trouble the parson in saying of his service?' and pointing out that if Blaby had wanted to preach he should have given notice—'and there and then they multiplied words one against another'. Clipsam went off home, and Blaby preached his sermon. He declaimed against the rector, 'Dumb dog, idle pastor, unlearned and unable minister, a murderer of their souls', and declared that 'as many as did take part with him were like unto the murmurers that did murmur against Moses and Aaron'. At evening prayer on the same day, Blaby waited in the churchyard until Clipsam had finished the service, then strode up to the pulpit and once more preached against Clipsam. On the following Sunday there were further disputes. As Clipsam was about to say morning prayer, Blaby announced that he had an order from the bishop to perform services at the church—but Clipsam would not give way unless Blaby showed him his authority. At evening prayer, Blaby, Partridge, 'and divers other parishioners and some of their faction of other parishes' entered the church in a display of strength. The rector tried a new line: 'I marvel greatly, Goodman Partridge, seeing you are excommunicated. Why do you trouble me and the parish thus every day?' Partridge denied he was then excommunicate, but Clipsam demanded to see a certificate of absolution, 'or else get you forth of the church, for so long as you are in it I will say no service'. Blaby saw his chance, saying 'If you will not say service, I will go preach,' but Clipsam argued, rightly, that they could not proceed while an excommunicate was present. Partridge cried, 'Mr Blaby, take your place!' and Blaby climbed into the pulpit and began a sermon. Clipsam cried, 'Come down prating jack, thou foamest out thine own poison,' and by now the parishioners were arguing together and Blaby could not preach above the din. So he admitted defeat, saying, 'Come, let us go hence and let the parson do now what he will'—'and so they went altogether forth of the church, as many as was of their faction, and the rest tarried in the church until evening prayer was said'.[15]

During the service, Blaby, Partridge, and their friends stood talking together in the churchyard, apparently waiting for Clipsam. When Clipsam came out of the church they surrounded him, Blaby and Partridge seized him, and they threatened to carry him before a justice of the peace—'Come and go with us, we charge you in the queen's name to the justice!' As Clipsam struggled and friends came to his aid, his two captors cried for help from the watching crowd: some asked what the parson was supposed to have done wrong, but Robert Bailey said he was a rebel 'and that he would give 6d for a halter to hang with'. Amid the melee that followed, Blaby and Partridge tried to drag Clipsam away, but Clipsam resisted and finally pulled out 'his little meat knife' and threatened to use it if they would not let him go. That seems to have quietened things down, and representatives of each side then trooped off to a local justice to have their rivals bound over to keep the peace. Blaby and Clipsam were called to appear before the archdeacon of Essex on 23 August, but neither did so. William Partridge, Philip Perry, and the other churchwarden, Lawrence Gilman, were summoned to the archdeaconry court, and also failed to turn up. Blaby, Clipsam, and Partridge then had to appear at the Michaelmas quarter sessions, when the whole story came out, and Clipsam and Blaby were indicted at the Chelmsford assizes in March 1592—Clipsam for assault and scandalous words, Blaby for assault and sedition. The two ministers were bailed, but we do not know the result of the charges against them.[16]

Thus there were heated arguments in Stanford church and churchyard on two Sundays in the middle of August 1591. What do they tell us about the professors and the profane? A few parishioners would not take communion from the rector, perhaps because he was a non-preacher, and Robert Bailey had criticized the order of service; they and others supported Tristram Blaby, an evangelical preacher and perhaps a critic of current ecclesiastical policy. These, presumably, were the godly—and their enemies called them a 'faction'. What about the rest? It is unlikely that they were fervent admirers of Martin Clipsam, for he failed on two of the issues that most excited parishioners: regular services and visiting the sick. They look like conformists: they wanted a dignified service without interruption, and they weren't too bothered if there was a sermon or not. But, above all, they did not want the godly to get their way: they did not want William Partridge and his friends to dictate when there would be a sermon, and they did not like Blaby's preaching. Two of them were bound over to keep the peace against Blaby, and others offered sureties for them. An overlapping group of nine parishioners accused Blaby of seditious preaching, alleging that he had by implication denied the royal supremacy in a sermon on 25 July. It seems unlikely that Blaby was foolish enough to have actually done this, unless he was carried away by his own rhetoric: it is more likely that the accusers were misremembering or twisting what he had said, to get him removed from the parish. How 'profane' they all were, we cannot tell—though three of the nine were known Sabbath-breakers. It seems certain that the cause of the Stanford troubles was Blaby. Neither before nor after these incidents was there disruption in the parish, as far as we can tell, and the village returned to obscurity. There clearly had been religious divisions before 1591—but it was Blaby's aggressive style that had made them matter.[17]

In 1600 there was a less dramatic dispute in the Northamptonshire parish of Badby, near Daventry. A dozen parishioners of Badby were presented by one of the churchwardens for not receiving the Easter communion: 'the cause was that they refused the same by reason the minister did put on the surplice when he went to administer the communion as it is thought, and as William Downing the other churchwarden confessed to me William Goodman'. The dozen included Downing and his wife, Richard Rathbone, and his wife, Henry Hinde, and Mary Chapman: this was the core of the godly group. Rathbone appeared in the consistory court at the end of April, saying he had not been 'quiet in mind', but promising that he would receive communion from the vicar 'either wearing or not wearing the surplice'. Next, Goodman, Downing, and the two sworn men presented Rathbone and his wife for disturbing services—Rathbone by interrupting the minister and mocking his surplice, and his wife Susanna by banging on the chancel door during a service. Social relations in the parish were now breaking down. Susanna Rathbone had argued in the churchyard with the vicar's wife. Henry Hinde had a dispute with Goodman's wife, also in the churchyard, and had declared 'that he dwelleth amongst such a damned company as he cannot tell a true tale after them'. Hinde's wife had refused to be churched in the customary pew, and Mary Chapman had mocked the women who were churched there, saying they went to 'offer to St Tancred'. Ralph Heywood, the vicar, now tried to buy peace in his parish by making concessions to the godly. He agreed to church Elizabeth Piddington in her usual seat, 'which hath not been seen anytime before in our church'—though when Gregory Leek's wife asked for the same treatment she was refused. Heywood also now declined to wear the surplice, 'although the same hath been brought to him by the churchwardens'. Disruptions continued. Richard Rathbone had a fight with John Hickman in the chancel during a service. Edward Piddington was presented for mocking Goodman, the churchwarden, about pressing Heywood to wear the surplice, and for telling one of the sworn men, 'Go and help to pluck the surplice over your fellow William Goodman his ears', and declaring 'that he would give a pint of wine that he might have the surplice to wear the next day to cock barley'. And by October 1600 Goodman and the two sworn men were obviously exasperated by their colleague Downing's conduct: 'we certify your worship that William Downing, being one of the churchwardens will not at any time come to make his presentment, neither will agree to the making of our bill, but doth wrangle with us and contradict the same'.[18]

Ralph Heywood was in an impossible position at Badby, caught between the conflicting demands of warring factions. In the nature of things, the objections of the nonconformists are the better recorded. There had been visible nonconformity at Badby before: an earlier vicar had been presented in 1576 for not wearing a surplice or baptizing in the Prayer Book form, and for making the parishioners receive communion standing, while in 1577 eleven people did not receive communion and Matthew Palmer would not allow his wife to be churched. The godly did not have things all their own way, however: Thomas Palmer refused to contribute to collections for the poor, and his 'evil example hath caused others to stay their liberality'. After 1577 there were few presentments for nonconformity, probably because the tenants wished to maintain a united front in their enclosure conflict with the godly lord of the manor, Sir Richard Knightley. This unity broke down in 1600, however, and the troubles seem to have been prompted by conformists. The conformists certainly included William Goodman, and probably Michael Coles and John Cleaver, the sworn men who joined Goodman in presenting Heywood and in his protest against William Downing. They presumably also included the women who were mocked by Mary Chapman. These were not 'professors', but they were not notably 'profane'. As at Stanford-le-Hope in 1591, the stirs at Badby in 1600 were, as far as we can now tell, an isolated outbreak. Heywood tried to bring the godly into conformity, and the troublemaking Rathbones kept quiet. Perhaps the troubles were the product of the unfortunate pairing of Goodman and Downing as churchwardens—Downing apparently one of the godly, and Goodman a stickler for conformity to the Book of Common Prayer. When their year of office passed, the professors and the profane were able to live together peaceably again.[19]

At Northampton there was a tradition of low-level lay nonconformity and, as in any town, there was a degree of casual absenteeism and Sabbath-breaking: there were the professors and the profane, and they coexisted. But between 1614 and 1618 there was an eruption of godly militancy, and much more trouble than there had been at any time since the 1570s. The arch-conformist Robert Sibthorpe had been vicar of St Giles since 1608, but he does not seem initially to have had significant problems with the godly: thirty-six parishioners missed Easter communion in 1613, but they turned up in court, made their excuses, and promised to conform—so some of this was urban slackness, not principled rejection. But when the nonconformist Robert Catlin was removed from All Saints in January 1614 and replaced with the aggressive conformist David Owen, things changed in the town. Sixty-three parishioners failed to receive communion at All Saints at Easter 1614, and some of them were certainly making a stand—Simon Wastell went off to receive at Overstone instead, and others said they would receive from Catlin but not from Owen. Things had quietened down by Easter 1615, when only Wastell and four others were presented—though Owen had to make the presentment himself, after the churchwardens had (he said) refused to cooperate. By Easter 1616, it seems that everyone was receiving—but were they doing it properly? Wastell and Matthew Gilby had been ordered to certify that they had taken communion kneeling: Wastell dodged the issue by going away on business (he said), but there was dispute over whether Gilby had been kneeling when he actually took the bread and the wine. The question came up again in 1617, when Sibthorpe (as surrogate judge) questioned Timothy Ashbrooke of All Saints, who 'confessed that he did up-kneel when it was delivered unto him, but kneeled when it was given to others at the communion'. (For those who thought that kneeling to receive implied a papist adoration of the elements, it was presumably permissible to kneel only while others received.) By then, All Saints was quiet: Owen had left the parish, and, anyway, some of the people were going to St Sepulchre instead.[20]

Meanwhile, Robert Sibthorpe was having troubles of his own in Northampton, first with Leonard and Agnes Major, and then with William Bird. Leonard Major was missing services at St Giles in 1615, and went to services in Northampton only when there was an outside preacher. He considered the sermon crucial to Christian life, declaring 'that reading the word of God cannot beget faith' and complaining that 'the preachers in this town do not preach powerfully'—an assessment that cannot have pleased Sibthorpe. In 1617 Major was presented for failure to receive communion for a whole year, including Easter, but he argued that he had received twice 'at the hands of Mr Sibthorpe, both times kneeling'. He was soon in trouble again, this time with his wife, for abusing the churchwardens and sworn men and 'calling them hellhounds and foresworn men'. In 1618 Agnes Major laughed at the Rogation procession, and condemned the king's new declaration on Sunday recreations. Elizabeth Lea, a maidservant, had told her that the king now required them to play games on the Sabbath, and if they did not they would be hanged—at which Agnes asked 'whether had'st thou the king should hang thee or the devil burn thee?' In court Agnes was asked by Dr John Lambe, the diocesan chancellor, if she thought Sunday sports were lawful, and she answered that 'For her part she doth not think it lawful, let others do what they list.' Lambe invited her to take the advice of William Bird, the new vicar of St Giles, who was present in court, and asked him for his opinion—but Bird would say only 'that the works of necessity and of mercy may be done of the Sabbath day', by implication endorsing Agnes's view. Agnes also got support in court from her husband, who called out that Sunday games 'are not lawful nor to be used'.[21]

By 1616 the vicar of St Sepulchre's was unable to serve because of ill health, and Sibthorpe was appointed to serve the cure as his deputy. Sibthorpe continued as vicar of St Giles until 1617, but after he was replaced by William Bird he still sometimes said service and preached there. Sibthorpe had some difficulty in bringing the St Sepulchre's congregation to order and stopping them chattering through the service, though he did manage to get the nonconformist Nicholas Spooner to take communion kneeling. William Bird was a bigger problem. He was presented in 1617 for not wearing a surplice, and a second time for the surplice, not saying weekday services, and not using the Prayer Book catechism. He was also trying to discredit Sibthorpe, laughing at him on several Sundays in 1618 while he was saying service and especially during his sermons. Bird seems to have maintained that he was not actually laughing at Sibthorpe, but the churchwardens insisted he had been. Significantly, the wardens and sworn men were standing up for the ultra-conformist Sibthorpe against their nonconforming new vicar, and claiming that Bird's behaviour towards Sibthorpe had offended the parishioners. After 1618, things apparently settled down again in Northampton. William Prim of St Sepulchre's was accused in 1620 of abusing Sibthorpe, 'saying he cared not a fart for him', but Sibthorpe left the parish in 1622 and went to Brackley. Seventy-seven people were presented in 1625 for missing the Easter communion: William Boddington thought the vicar 'was not fit to come into a pulpit', but others produced the usual run of excuses and it is not clear whether this was a great nonconformist rebellion. There was a conventicle meeting in All Saints' parish in 1628, and the clergy and wardens resisted railing the communion table in 1637, but there was surprisingly little trouble in the town through the 1630s. The godly ground their teeth, but they did as they were told.[22]

Northampton was never a quiet town, and there was a substantial godly presence: as John Lambe warned the king in 1621, 'The puritans go by troops from their own parish church (though there be a sermon) to hear another whom their humour better affecteth.' But the professors only really made a nuisance of themselves between 1614 and 1618, when both David Owen and Robert Sibthorpe were vicars there—and when both of them were sitting as judges in the diocesan court as deputies for Chancellor Lambe. It was the two clergymen rather than the godly who were the disruptive force, and the fuss over how exactly people knelt for communion suggests a provocative and pernickety approach to issues of conformity. At Stanford-le-Hope and at Badby there had been clashes between the professors and the profane, but at Northampton the clash was between the professors and ecclesiastical authority—two vicars and the diocesan court. The profane—the less godly—were more or less innocent bystanders. One Atkins cursed the poor when there was a collection for them in 1616, and there were several sleepers during service at St Sepulchre's. Some parishioners of St Giles skipped services under the pretence of going to other churches, and some from All Saints strolled around the streets or sat on the churchyard wall during Sunday services in 1617. Probably the wardens of St Giles who presented William Bird for nonconformity and for laughing at Sibthorpe were not among the godly, but that is the only hint of lay hostility towards godliness. As at Stanford and Badby religious confrontation was a temporary state and it soon passed, but in Northampton, unlike the other two communities, the years of tension apparently did not see any obvious breach between professors and profane.[23]

In the Sussex village of Yapton near Arundel, there are signs of a polarization of opinion in 1622–3. The minister there was Hugh Roberts, who had a history of nonconformity going back at least to 1604: he had often been presented for his refusal to baptize with the sign of the cross and other offences, though by 1617 his nonconformity had been reduced to a failure to wear an academic hood—and he promised to get one 'as soon as he can conveniently send to Oxford'. There were, however, no signs of assertive godliness until 1622, when nine parishioners (including the minister's wife) 'and many others, strangers whose names I know not' were reported for receiving communion sitting, and four for refusing to stand for the Creed or kneel for the Lord's Prayer. Roberts was cited again for not wearing a surplice for communion, and for giving communion to people sitting or standing. In 1623 we see a different side of the Yapton story. Every Sunday a fiddler came over from Boxgrove to play, and many of the young people of Yapton turned out to dance instead of going to the afternoon catechizing. Further, thirty or forty people each week were coming from other parishes to join in the dancing. John Waters had criticized the clergy, 'saying that our ministers preach not the word of God but other men's words and their own fantasies', and argued that strict Sabbath observance was no longer necessary (presumably thinking of the 1618 declaration on recreations). The dancing was reported again later in the year, with a query from the wardens as to whether it was lawful. It was the professors who had been complained of in 1622, and the profane in 1623: perhaps there had been profane churchwardens in the first year and godly ones in the second. The presentments reveal an interesting confrontation: there were both nonconformists and Sabbath-breakers in Yapton, while professors from other parishes came to Yapton for communion, and the profane from elsewhere came to dance. And that was that. After the dancing in 1623, Yapton almost disappears from the record. Everyone received communion in 1633 except for the wife of Francis Edwards, and by 1636 the parish had obediently erected an altar rail, though it was 'too little'. It is hard to believe that the godly stopped being godly, or that the dancers stopped dancing—but the professors and the profane stopped complaining about each other and got on with peaceful coexistence.[24]

In a town as large as Colchester, Essex, there were of course lots of examples of godliness and of profanity: the numbers simply mean that it was a big town, not necessarily that its people were unusually godly or profane. But the evidence of godliness—as indicated by cases of nonconformity—varied considerably. It is noticeable that presentments for nonconformity in the 1630s were much more numerous in the second half of the decade than in the first. In 1630, John Smith of St Nicholas's parish asserted, 'it is an idle, popish ceremony this churching of women', and his wife refused to be churched. Charles Wells of St Mary's would not attend church 'to hear a dumb dog'. And in 1635 Thomas Seaward of St Peter's would not kneel for communion or remove his hat at a service in February—'and being wished by some that sat by him to put it off he refused'. There is rather more evidence of laxity in religion in these years. The parishioners of St Giles were negligent in sending their children to be catechized in 1632, and the churchwardens did nothing about it. Francis Burrows of St Nicholas's managed to get to church only once a month in 1634, 'because he cannot rise soon enough'. There was some Sabbath-breaking, but nothing very serious: in St Botolph's parish John Went carried luggage from Ipswich on a Sunday in 1633, because he had been delayed by the weather; and in 1635 William Branch's wife was persuaded to sell beer at sermon time, because it was for a christening. Then, at the end of 1635, the Colchester parishes were ordered to set their communion table at the east end of the chancel and to rail it in—and the religious atmosphere changed.[25]

Within a few months, nine of the twelve Colchester parishes had obeyed the order, though St Botolph's reported that the parish was poor and they would have to raise a rate before starting the work. But the introduction of rails brought a steep increase in nonconformity, as parishioners refused to go up to the rail for communion. The rector of St James's was forbidden in 1636 to give communion to anyone except those who knelt at the rail, and Susan King refused to go to the rail. Samuel Burrows of St Runwald's sat still in his seat and did not receive, Thomas Batsie of St Botolph's refused to kneel, and Thomas Lamb of St Giles 'said he would be brained before he would receive the holy sacrament after this manner'. Richard Sandie of Holy Trinity refused communion and asked, 'Do you think he will receive the bread and the devil together?'—which presumably means he thought kneeling at the rail devilish. In 1637 the rector of St Leonard's was ordered not to go outside the rail to distribute communion, and his congregation was instructed to receive at the rail. Joseph Littlewood refused to go to the rail at St Peter's in 1637, and it was said that up to sixty others did the same. But that was pretty much the end of the fuss, except for the refusal by Edward Firmin's wife to be churched at the rail in St Runwald's in 1640.[26]

The trouble in Colchester was caused by the aggressive behaviour of some of the clergy (especially Thomas Newcomen, rector of Holy Trinity and St Runwald's) and the determined resistance of a few of the godly. It was Newcomen who had John Bastwick, Richard Aske, and Samuel Burrows called before the High Commission and punished—Bastwick for his criticism of the Laudian hierarchy, Aske and Burrows for nonconformity and opposing Newcomen. Aske, his wife, a servant, and Burrows were tried in High Commission in October 1636 as 'persons schismatically affected and such as dislike the Book of Common Prayer and the liturgy thereof'. Aske and Burrows were also charged with conspiracy to convict Newcomen of administering communion in a popish fashion, allegedly to prevent him from reporting nonconformists. Burrows seems to have been the leading agitator—disturbing Sunday services at three churches, and circulating a libel against the bishops. The eagerness of Newcomen and other clergy to use the courts against their parishioners made them unpopular, and a libel of 1636 denounced them as persecutors and drunkards. The rail campaign and the actions of its supporters may have driven some in Colchester to separatism, and there were a few gestures of defiance too. Thomas Lamb and his wife refused to attend church at St Giles in 1637 and would not allow a baby to be baptized—and they were presented again for the same offences in 1639. Roger Goodwin and Thomas Broome of St Leonard's were 'absolute Brownists' in 1637, and in 1639 Richard Benson of St Mary Magdalene was cited as 'a schismatical recusant' in 1639. Daniel Hewson was hosting a conventicle in St James's parish in 1637, and he and his wife and three other couples would not attend church. Thomas Haywood of Mary Magdalene wore his hat through the sermon on Whit Sunday 1637, though warned by the minister. In 1639 Nicholas Beacon refused to remove his hat when admonished by the churchwardens of St Peter's, and Thomas Tirrell said 'he would be drawn in pieces by wild horses before he would keep off his hat in the church'.[27]

Nevertheless, we must keep such signs of godly alienation in proportion. The author of the 1636 libel complained that few had refused to contribute to the church rate to pay for rails, and slackness in religion remained almost as common as nonconformity in Colchester. Samuel Crouch of Mary Magdalene was hanging out his rugs to dry on Sundays in 1636, and in 1638 Matthew Watts and Thomas Bradshaw of St Runwald's allowed their children to disturb the congregation by playing during services. Edward Barnes and his wife missed service at St Botolph's on 17 November 1639: when the churchwardens came to tell them to go to church, the wife abused them, and later in the day the husband went to the house of one of the wardens and threatened him. We do not know why Richard Crowe and his wife were excluded from communion by the rector of St Leonard's in 1637. But it is hardly surprising that William Mannock of St James's was presented in that year—'for setting six pots against the church wall for company that come to his house to piss in, he keeping an alehouse'. There is, however, little sign in Colchester of entrenched hostility between the godly and the less godly. Perhaps the godly were most keen to have Sabbath-breakers reported, and perhaps the less godly were eager to have nonconformists presented and witness against them. But in Colchester there was no running conflict between the godly and the profane, and no confrontation such as came at Stanford-le-Hope in 1591, Badby in 1600, and Yapton in 1622–3. There was, as in Northampton between 1614 and 1618, a wave of nonconformity at Colchester in 1636–7, but it was provoked by the Church authorities, worsened by some heavy-handed clergy, and led by a few militants: it did not last.[28]

Many parishes in southern and Midland England saw an occasional collision between the godly and the rest. There was an all-too-obvious split in East Hanningfield, Essex, in 1584–5, with the rector having private meetings with the godly, but excluding large numbers of others from the communion and making no effort to ensure that the less-godly came to church. The godly complained about 'slanderers and railers against preachers' and 'drunkards, swearers, seditious persons, etc.', while the others were mocking 'saints and scripture-men' and 'contemning the word of God and dispraising the professors of the same'. There were ill-tempered exchanges at Oundle, Northamptonshire, in 1588–9, with the godly complaining about slack attendance at sermons and the less-godly complaining about nonconformity, abusing the minister and wardens, and disrupting the preaching. There was division at Banbury, Oxfordshire, in 1606 over kneeling at communion, with the kneelers led by the curate William Osborne and the non-kneelers by the preacher William Whateley—and a similar split at Ashby-de-la-Zouch, Leicestershire, in 1615, with the vicar, Thomas Hacket promoting kneeling and the lecturer Arthur Hildersham leading resistance. There were arguments at Wylye in Wiltshire in 1624 over the frequency of communion, the length of sermons, and Sunday dancing. There was a row at Ditcheat in Somerset over maypoles in 1634, and at Batcombe in the same year over Richard Bernard's catechizing and personal preaching. There were several confrontations at Lyme Regis in Dorset, usually concerning Sabbath observance—over the Whitsun feasting on the Cobb in 1609, and over the 'Appellation Day' celebrations in 1635. But these disruptions seldom lasted long: intervention by a court, a change of wardens, or, as at Ashby, the arrival of a more irenic and conciliatory minister, might restore good order.[29]

All this suggests that, though the profane abused the professors and the professors slighted the profane, they usually managed to get along with each other. There was latent antagonism and name-calling, but it was only in special circumstances—often attempts to enforce conformity or stricter Sabbath observance—that conventional coexistence broke down. The godly and the profane did not have the same approach to religion, but they lived together in communities, worked together at their tasks, and worshipped together in church. A string of witnesses testified against the godly objectors to the May celebrations at St Peter-le-Bailey, Oxford, in 1634, but their depositions were almost identical and obviously coordinated. John Bolt and John Wildgoose were each described as 'a factious man or a puritan', as a member of a 'faction or sect', as consorting with other 'puritans' and separating himself from the 'conformable'. But was it really so? John Bolt was a churchwarden in 1634–5: one of the witnesses against him ran the Whitsun ale and paid the profit over to him; another sold him stone for church repairs. He received 22s. from the Hocktide collection that Wildgoose had described as theft. Before the case came to court, Thomas Bishop offered to do his best to have the charges dropped if Bolt would make some contribution to church funds—and during the suit, 'wishing the said Bolt (being his neighbour) well', he told Bolt that if Bolt would pay his costs he would try to stop the case. Bolt and Wildgoose were certainly 'puritans'—that is, they were what the profane meant by puritans. But the accusation that they were members of a faction and separated themselves from obedient Christians was simply an attempt to load the evidence against them. It shows how angry the conformists were over the godly's disruption of the 1634 Whitsun festivities, and it may show objection to their nonconformity. It suggests there were tensions and hostilities that could burst out in a crisis. But it does not demonstrate entrenched social divisions and constant religious conflict. During their long afternoon discussion of contentious issues, cantankerous Antilegon and godly Philagathus lost their tempers with each other on the subject of preaching. But Master Theologus calmed them down and the debate continued: 'We ought friendly and in love to admonish one another, for we must have a care of another's salvation.'[30]

PART IV

'ANTILEGON, A CAVILLER': LIBERTY AND LAUGHTER

7

Antilegon: Attitudes to Authority

> You make no conscience of the observation of the Sabbath; you use not the name of God with any reverence; you break out sometimes into horrible oaths and cursings; you make an ordinary matter of swearing by your oath and your troth … You are an example in your own house of all atheism and conscienceless behaviour. You are a great gamester, a rioter, a spendthrift, a drinker, a common alehouse-haunter and whore-hunter, and, to conclude, given to all vice and naughtiness. Now then, I pray you tell me, or rather let your conscience tell me, what hope you can have to be saved so long as you walk and continue in this course?

That is what Theologus thought of Antilegon, that he was sinful and godless. Certainly, Antilegon was not one of the Calvinist godly: he could not accept predestination, he thought the Scriptures were only men's inventions, and he believed 'there is no hell at all, but only the hell of a man's conscience'. Nevertheless, Antilegon expected to be saved by Christ's mercy—'Christ died for all men, and therefore for me.' He knew he was a sinner, like everyone else. He knew he could not be saved by his own merits, but must rely on Christ. But he thought he did what God expected of him. By his own lights, Antilegon was a religious man:

I thank God for it, I say my prayers every night when I am in my bed. And if good prayers will do us no good, God help us. I have always served God duly and truly, and had him in my mind. I do as I would be done to. I keep my church and tend my prayers while I am there.

But he was sure that Theologus and Philagathus went too far in their zeal, and made no allowance for living in the real world. Theologus had listed the nine signs of man's condemnation: 'Pride. Whoredom. Covetousness. Contempt of the Gospel. Swearing. Lying. Drunkenness. Idleness. Oppression'—but Antilegon thinks that a little bit of most of these is no bad thing. Contempt of the gospel?—we have to get on with our business, and there's no time for reading the Bible and going to lots of sermons. Swearing?—but surely it's all right if we swear truly? Pride?—but we must dress well to be esteemed. Lying?—well, the godly do that as much as anyone. Idleness?—the rich don't need to work, so why should they? And drunkenness, well, a bit of that is just good fellowship.[1]

'If neighbours meet together now and then at the alehouse, and play a game or two at maw for a pot of ale, meaning no hurt, I take it to be good fellowship and a good means to increase love amongst neighbours.' Many in the real world agreed: there was no harm in a bit of fun at the alehouse, and 'good fellows' would drink together. In 1599 a group of drinkers at Corringham in south Essex

did at their parting take with them into the field at the town's end, where they meant to part, four or six pots of beer and there, setting them down, did themselves upon their bare knees humbly kneel down and kissing the pots and drinking one to the other, and prayed for the health of all true and faithful drunkards, and especially for Mr Andrew Broughton, as they said the maintainer and upholder of all true and faithful drunkards, and having done they kissed each other and, for a memory of their worthy act, did every man make his mark or name upon an oaken tree that stood there by them.

But good fellowship among the less-godly was bestial sin to the godly, and the ceremony of 'good and faithful drunkards' became notorious, featuring in Samuel Ward's 1622 sermon 'Woe to Drunkards'—where Ward claimed that the participants all 'died thereof within a few weeks, some sooner, some later'. But men and women could not be kept out of the alehouse—even when they should have been at church. When in 1571 Thomas Harmer of Stonehouse, Gloucestershire, was rebuked by the minister for playing cards in the alehouse in service time, he gave him an earful of abuse and called him 'knave'. John Gay of Childerditch, Essex, was presented in 1584 for keeping evil rule in his house on a Sunday, 'in so much that the minister could not say service for the great noise of the people'. Christopher Fisher of Ashton, Northamptonshire, had a noisy crowd of drinkers in his house on Sunday in 1585, 'till the constables were sent forth of the church to keep peace'. A string of men from East Ham in Essex were in court in 1592 for drinking in Robert Brickworth's alehouse through the afternoon service on 23 April. We do not know if they were celebrating St George, but they all had some excuse. Thomas Alland said he had only gone in to break up a fight 'and then someone bid him drink'. Francis Wood said he was not drinking, but he was 'amongst those that were drinking'. William Watton claimed that 'he came by chance into the company of some that were drinking'. John Pavie and John Johnson admitted they were there, but also were not actually drinking. And Henry Keys explained that 'the cause why he was there was for that it rained and there went in and sat down in the house, but he saith he did not drink at all there'. Poor Robert Brickworth: all those potential customers, and they piously would not drink.[2]

Drink and religion were often in contention. In 1593 three men of Dorchester, Oxfordshire, were playing bowls at Robert Ford's alehouse. The church bell rang for the afternoon service, and they went into the alehouse for another quick drink—'and there they stayed until half evening prayer was done and there the churchwardens came and found them and then they went to church'. At Mere in Wiltshire in 1610, Richard Joy sold his ale, 'drawing thereby a great concourse and multitude of people together in the time of divine prayer and making such noise and crying out in prayer time that the whole congregation was thereby much disturbed and disquieted'. On Sunday, 28 July 1611, John Gibbs of Lancing, Sussex, had 'in his house above forty or fifty persons at the least all the time of divine service, drinking, blousing and occupying themselves in their lewd actions to the great abuse and profaning of the Sabbath day'. Thomas and Griselda Cooper of Dagenham, Essex, were in court in 1614 for allowing disorder in their alehouse on Sundays, 'hiding and concealing persons in their house when the churchwardens have come to enquire and search for them in those times of holy exercises, and having some being drunk lie sleeping in the foresaid hours'. Half a dozen men of Walgrave, Northamptonshire, organized a lottery in Ralph Dexter's alehouse on Christmas Day 1620, with prizes and forfeits: any player drawing a card under ten was to drink a glass of beer; drawing a ten or knave brought two crowns and two glasses; the prize for a queen was a warming pan, and drinking three glasses; and a king brought 'the basin and ewer, and he that had him to drink four glasses'. George Wheatley of Aveley in Essex was cited in 1623 for allowing drinking in his alehouse during a service, 'and that the company did swagger and keep a great noise': he claimed that he was away at market that day, 'and that if his people did suffer any to drink in his house the same day in time of divine service he is sorry for it'—but he was in trouble again six months later for the same offence. The churchwardens of Ashby-de-la-Zouch, Leicestershire, reported that Lawrence Child had Sunday drinkers at service time in his alehouse in 1630, 'the which company could not be known because they, the said churchwardens, coming to the said house to see what disorders were then and there, the said company ran away and were not discerned by the said churchwardens as that they might know them'. That is what you did when the churchwardens came: run. Jeremiah Porter was caught by the wardens of Dagenham, Essex, at Richard Boughtill's alehouse during a Sunday service in 1631, but he was unlucky: others escaped through the shovelboard room and got away. For an alehouse-keeper, the wardens were just nuisances, patrolling the parish to see who was not at church. When William Ely was confronted by the wardens of West Tilbury in 1639, he asked, 'Wherefore do I keep such a house, but to suffer men as long as they have a penny in their purse?'[3]

Antilegon did not think a bit of sex was such a bad thing either: 'Tush, whoredom is but a trick of youth, and we see all men have their imperfections.' We are used to expecting harsh attitudes towards fornication, if only because of the costs of bastards to parishes—and harshness is certainly there. Katherine Fawcett of Hill Farrance, Somerset, had a second bastard in 1588 after having done penance for the first, 'which she cared little for, wherefore we pray you that you or our justice will appoint some punishment by whipping'. In 1602 the wardens of Calne, Wiltshire, presented nine women for having illegitimate babies:

These all we humbly beseech you to see punished, that it may be a terrifying to others to fall into the like vice; we already are overpressed with too many poor bastard children, and indeed we fear of a greater like burden, for by them (being unpunished) others are encouraged to run into many vices, hoping to escape free and unpunished as others have done before them.

But there were other responses. In 1615 James and Ellen Newman of Pilton, Somerset, were presented for harbouring a pregnant woman and allowing her to leave the parish without examination, 'by means whereof the delinquents are concealed and the execution of justice hindered'. They had brought in the midwife, looked after the mother and child, and arranged for a christening (with Ellen as godmother): the child was called John, and his mother admitted that was the father's name, but she would reveal no more about the father—'It is no matter what he is, for the goodness of him.' The woman's father took her away a month after her delivery and paid for the costs, leaving little John with the Newmans. James Newman entered into a bond with the parish to bear the costs of the child—but he and Ellen had to perform a full public penance, each wearing a white sheet and holding a wand. In 1628 Lucy Tomkins of Braunston, Northamptonshire, was cited for sending her daughter away before she did penance for bastardy—as were Richard Tomkins for helping her; a couple for nursing the baby; and three men for taking the child off to its mother. Seven people had helped Mary Tomkins evade punishment. It is not surprising that a mother stood by her pregnant daughter. At West Bradley, near Glastonbury in Somerset, the parishioners were talking after service one Sunday in 1629 about how they could avoid the costs of Eleanor Easton's bastard child: Eleanor's mother lost her temper, 'saying to some present after an angry manner that they should look to their own children'. But there was sympathy from strangers too. In 1630 Robert Brand, overseer of the poor at Munden in Essex, helped a poor woman whose child was delivered in the parish, and his wife was godmother, 'whereat some of the parishioners were offended with him'—but he angrily defended his kindness. Rachel Knuckles had her baby at the house of Alice Knight of Tolleshunt Knights in 1633 and went away unpunished: Alice explained that Rachel had been 'very ill and sick, whereupon she being moved in pity and charity took her into her house'.[4]

All this was Christian charity rather than tolerance of sexual delinquents, but some were less shocked by illicit sex than others, and joked about it. In 1578 William Mayles of Cheltenham, Gloucestershire, organized a 'quest of cuckolds', where a dozen men were called to appear to explain their situations, 'whereby great dissension hath grown between man and wife'. When a woman was doing her penance for adultery at West Ham church in Essex in 1594, Richard Thornton encouraged her 'to go forward and to return again to her former folly the morrow after, as fresh as ever she did'. John Bennett of Alton Pancras, Dorset, was bragging in 1609 'that he hath lyen with as many women as be white sheep in Barcombe, and there are eight hundred kept'—and he swore that he would make William Vincent a cuckold whenever he married. This is, no doubt, just men being silly boys—but it does suggest a less po-faced attitude to sex than one might expect. And it wasn't only men. When Alice Godsave of Blackmore, Essex, had an illegitimate son in 1610, she called him 'Francis come by chance', and jeered 'Who knows whether she be forward with another or not?'—'we desire that she may have punishment,' declared the wardens, 'or let us no longer be officers!' William Wortley of Whissendine, Rutland, held in 1614 'that women have no souls but their shoe soles, and that whoredom is but a light and trysting crime'—as Antilegon himself had said. Of course, we know of these examples only because someone didn't like what was said—but there certainly was a good deal of lewd and loose talk. William Tibbut came out of Portishead church in Somerset in mid May 1615 and 'holding his privy member in his hand swore "Gog's wounds, Gog's wounds, what shall I do for a wench?" Some standing by said, "Hast thou not a wife at home?" "Yes, Gog's wounds", quod he, "that I have, for I have a cunt in syrup at home!"' When a churchwarden at West Pennard asked Alice Cornish in 1618 where her husband had last worked, Edward Slade 'answered in the church that the said Cornish last wrought betwixt her legs, as he thought'. In 1638 John Legge of Wells told others that he had had sex with a handsome wench he had met in a bedchamber, and when he was rebuked he answered 'that he was bound by the laws of God to feed the hungry and clothe the naked'. And in 1639, when they were chosen churchwardens of Publow, Edward Maggs proposed to his colleague, 'Thou art a baker and I am a brewer, and thou keep a bear and I will keep a bull, and we will keep a church ale'—but they were to take the profit themselves and spend it on a whore.[5]

There was lewd behaviour too—sometimes even in church. After a morning service at Helpston, Northamptonshire, early in 1609, Thomas Greenhall 'called the congregation into the chancel there, and told them they shall see a play, such a one as they never saw, called "England's Lie"'. When they were all assembled, 'he the said Greenhall did in the presence of them all strip himself stark naked (saving he had his stockings on) and did then walk once or twice about the communion table in the said chancel, in most brutish and unseemly manner'. In court, he explained he had done it 'That so they might see whether he had the pox or no.' Toby Hiscox of Salisbury got drunk on a Sunday morning in 1611 and 'did the same morning put down his breeches and show his tail in Milford Street to many people that were there in most unseemly manner, and we desire that he may be well punished for the same according to the quality of the offence'. Surely, for all that were shocked there were others who laughed, even on a Sunday—and lewdness for some was fun to others. While William More and others were drinking at Mark Morris's house in South Petherton, Somerset, on an August Sunday in 1612, Mark passed out, and the others took turns to go into the kitchen with Mark's wife Eleanor—'And the rest of the company which stayed without the whiles whooped and cried with a very shrill and loud voice, saying "We hunt the hare, we hunt the whore!", reiterating the same divers and sundry times.' There were, unsurprisingly, many individual sins of indecent exposure and unwanted groping—and there was communal voyeurism too. At a late-night party at Chard just before Christmas 1617, Richard Bond propositioned Thomasine Simms: 'Thomasine, I will give thee four shillings to let me see thy cunt whilst I can tell ten.' At first she refused, but John Drake offered another shilling if he could join in and 'all the residue of the said company persuaded her so to do, asking her where she could get so much money in so short a space'. So she sat in a corner, they pulled up her clothes, and Robert Warrye got a candle and did the count to ten—very, very slowly. Thomasine thought it took half an hour, others said nearly an hour. This was not just youthful skylarking—it happened at the house of Thomasine's master, John Carswell, and he and his wife were present throughout. And there was youthful skylarking, of course. On a Sunday evening at Christmas 1629 at Ashby-de-la-Zouch in Leicestershire, four friends 'made naked and bare the privy members and secret parts of the body of one Thomas Pierce, a young man of about twenty years of age, and tied a string or packthread to the said privy member and fastened the other end of the said string to his arm or side, in a most abominable and detestable manner'. Pierce had drunk too much and fallen asleep, leaving himself vulnerable to Christmas jesting and humiliation.[6]

Cross-dressing was not quite in the same league as stalking around the chancel naked or gawping at Thomasine Simms—but it was still pretty shocking. And some people did it—for a laugh. There may have been secret cross-dressers, who got a thrill out of jumping gender—but others just wanted to put on a show. They paraded about in public in clothes they should not have worn, and pretended to be handsome boys or sexy girls. It was all about sexuality and laughter, and it was usually done in the seasons of jollity—Christmas time and the summer. William Peacock of Singleton, Sussex, 'came disguised in women's apparel into the church in time of divine service' in the early summer of 1611. Lawrence Hedge of Wootton, Northamptonshire, was presented in January 1613 'for disguising himself in woman's apparel on Sunday at night, the 29th of November, using himself very immodestly in the house of one Widow Styles'. And in 1628 William Canning went to church at Berwick Bassett, Wiltshire, dressed as a woman. These look like examples of public performance rather than deliberate disguise. The case of Thomas Salmon of Great Tew, Oxfordshire, seems to have been different, however. Salmon dressed up in women's clothes in 1633 so he could go to the women's celebration after the delivery of Ellen Rywell's baby. He hoped not to be spotted, and posed as Mrs Garrett's maid to join the party. Interestingly, he was dressed in her clothes by his mistress, Elizabeth Fletcher, who took him along with her, 'intending only merriment thereby'—but her mother-in-law recognized the clothes and threw Salmon out. When women dressed as men, they did it for fun too. Joan Towlor of Downham, Essex, went to church 'in man's apparel' in 1596, and Catherine Banks of Grays

Thurrock did the same in August 1607, staying throughout the service, 'to the contempt of religion, thereby discontenting God and disturbing the minister and the congregation'—which presumably was the whole idea. Joan Taylor of Yardley Hastings, Northamptonshire, paraded 'disguised in man's apparel, viz. with doublet and breeches', through the village just before the evening service one Sunday in August 1612, 'where she behaved herself most immodestly, as it had been a lascivious young man'. It was thought the event had been organized by her mistress, Sarah White. And at Mears Ashby in 1634, Margery Merton went about in men's clothes and Thomas Harris in women's: we don't know if they did it together and walked arm in arm, but it would have added to the fun. Such behaviour was not transgressive or subversive, and it received light punishment—usually penance in ordinary clothes, sometimes only a court rebuke. It shows a light-hearted approach to sex and sexuality. 'Oh sir,' said Antilegon, 'you must bear with youth. Youth you know is frail and youth will be youthful, when you have said all that you can.'[7]

Antilegon thought that Theologus and the godly made too much fuss about drunkenness and whoredom—and also about covetousness: 'that which you call covetousness, it is but good husbandry,' he told Theologus. 'For it is an hard world, and goods are not easy to come by. Therefore men must ply their business, or else they may go beg or starve.' Antilegon himself did not discuss Sunday working, but many found the Church's prohibition unreasonable and would regularly 'ply their business' on the Sabbath—especially the millers and shopkeepers. At Sherborne in Dorset, seven millers were presented 'for grinding on the Sabbath day' in 1602; seven shops and three barbers were busy on Sundays in 1616; and in 1622 twenty-nine tradesmen 'doth work, buy and sell' on Sundays and holy days. Nine butchers and seven shoemakers from Watlington, Oxfordshire, were cited for Sunday trading in 1631, seventeen butchers from Frome in Somerset in 1636, and eleven Peterborough shopkeepers in 1637. Others found it convenient to make their deliveries on Sundays. One Daniel of Kingscote, Gloucestershire, delivered bread on Sundays in 1598, as did Henry Jones of Mells in Somerset in 1616. Robert Mountford was absent from services at Navestock, Essex, for almost a whole year in 1621, 'spending the Sunday in carrying shoes about to divers towns', and Robert Fryer, a tailor from Ingrave, admitted in 1624 'that sometimes he carryeth home a suit of apparel to a customer on a Sabbath day in the morning'. These are not examples of occasional laxity, but of habitual flouting of Sunday prohibitions. Anne Belcher of Brigstock, Northamptonshire, was presented in 1591 'for usually baking of the Sabbath day a long season, and being admonished yet continueth in her sin', and in 1599 a tailor from Woodham Mortimer, Essex, was cited as 'a continual worker on the Sabbath day and other holy days'. John Morgan of Axbridge, Somerset, regularly worked at his limekiln on Sundays in 1619, and when two millers of Easton Maudit, Northamptonshire, were presented 'for incorrigible breakers of the Sabbath day' in 1624, they told the vicar and wardens 'that now we have done our worst they will grind in spite of us'. Joshua Smith of Walthamstow, Essex, worked his leather mill on Sundays in 1633, 'And as we are credibly informed it is their ordinary course, making no difference of the Sabbath day from the other days of the week.' Sunday was Sunday, but business was business: Thomas King of Brightlingsea ferried passengers on Sundays in 1629, 'affirming that he got more that day than he did upon the working days'.[8]

Antilegon did not like being told what to do, and complained about the censoriousness of Philagathus and his kind: 'There be a company of such controllers as he in the world, that none can be quiet for them.' It seems that many found the discipline exercised by the Church equally irksome and oppressive—and it is striking to see how much contempt there could be for ecclesiastical authority. In 1581 Julia Goodson of Marston Magna, Somerset, thought that 'Wells law is naughty law', and 'that my lord bishop's court was but a poultering court'. In 1589 John Badcock of Rayleigh, Essex, and his friends made a joke of the whole detection system. At Mother Larking's alehouse, Badcock acted the part of 'Master Parson', another was the churchwarden, a third the sworn man, another 'the honest men of the parish', and Thomas England was the apparitor—'thus sitting abusing themselves like drunken sots'. Joan Stoddon of Dunster, Somerset, was cruder in 1612: 'Last night I had in my privy part (naming it grossly) three or four fleas which did leap about it that I was not able to sleep for them. And, quod she, it is pity that they were not called to the court for it: if something should go into that place they should be called into the court for it and punished too.' Thomas Gascoigne of Rothwell, Northamptonshire, told Presgrave the apparitor in 1619 'that he had a beauty for him, that is he had a bitch went fault and that all the dogs in the town followed her and that she would prove herself a whore, and wished Presgrave to summon her to Dr Lambe's court'. It seems that Mary Wieff of Basingstoke, Hampshire, took a more solemn approach in 1621. When accused of 'praying against the spiritual courts', she claimed she was led astray by Anthony Speering, and 'did kneel down with him in the market house of Basingstoke, and then hearing him say certain prayers, good as she thought, this respondent said along with him'. Or perhaps it was just mockery.[9]

Some people said they just did not care about Church courts and discipline—though it was often in the heat of the moment. When Stephen Belly of Haselbury, Somerset, was rebuked by Roger Chappell in 1605 for playing skittles in the churchyard, he pushed him into a bed of nettles—and when Chappell threatened to have him cited to Wells he responded, 'I care not a turd for the doctor nor any of the rest.' Richard Everson of Colchester was threatened with presentment in 1609, 'and did abuse the court and said shit of the spiritual court, and it was all they could do to put him to the court and he weighed it not a turd'. The churchwardens of Wilton, Somerset, were criticized by a parishioner in 1612 for not reporting bowling on the Sabbath: they 'said they bowled before Dr James [the chancellor] was born, and therefore they will not present it'. When William Wytcher of Sidlesham, Sussex, was to be cited for adultery in 1616, he pronounced 'that he cared not a turd for my lord nor the office nor any of them, for he was now in the city of Chichester without their reaches'. At Welford, Northamptonshire, in 1617 the parish constable declared 'that these players should play that night in despite of Dr Lambe', and when Thomas Dobbs of Bozeat was forbidden to block the perambulation route in 1629 'he cared not a fig for the minister and not for any presentment, for the chancellor had nothing to do with it'. Petronella Pollet of Preston Plucknett, Somerset, had a bastard child in 1631, and was called a base wench by Thomas Gaylord. She said she was now an honest woman, for she had got absolution from the court and done her penance—so Gaylord asked her 'whether she had been with the pope for a pardon to make her honest?' Petronella took the law and her absolution seriously, but for others ecclesiastical offences were small beer. To Richard Linley of Barking, Essex, railing at a churchwarden in 1596 'was but half a crown matter'. Edward Ford of Rayleigh didn't care if he were presented for disturbing the service in 1608 because, he said, he would be discharged for 16*d*., and Matthew Shepherd of Aveley thought 'the worst was but spending sixteen pence' for working on St Matthew's Day. John Burghill told the Dagenham wardens in 1614 that missing church 'was but a twelve-penny matter', and if John Dawes of Northampton was presented in 1616 for swearing in church 'it was but eleven groats charges'. Francis Derrick told the wardens of Steeple, Essex, in 1620 'that he cares not for our presentment, for it is but paying a little money, as four groats or the like, and then "God be with you"'. It was not the offence that mattered, but the cost—and that wasn't much: 'If the worst came to the worst it was but a ten groats matter and there's an end' (Essex, 1622), or 'but a twelve-penny mulct to answer it' (Sussex, 1622), or 'but a sixteen-penny matter' (Essex, 1625), or 'it should cost him but twelve pence' (Sussex, 1632), or 'but paying of an eleven groats' (Rutland, 1635).[10]

We have learned that the Church courts were useful and well used, after the Reformation as well as before. Their party-to-party instance business boomed, as their customers used them to resolve disputes. And the volume of office prosecutions seems to show parish elites resorting to the courts to enforce norms of behaviour on local deviants. We tend to see the courts from the point of view of Theologus and godly Philagathus, rather than of Antilegon—the sort of person the controllers were trying to control. Despite the utility of the courts, disrespect for them and their officers was widespread. A Church court was 'the bawdy court'—the courts of Gloucester diocese (1578), the archdeaconry of Essex (1596), Peterborough diocese (1608), the archdeaconry of Colchester (1613), the commissary of Essex (1616), the diocese of Oxford (1631), the archdeaconry of Buckingham (1634), and doubtless others were all called that, and those who used the term were given penances. The court at Wells was 'the bum court' in 1622, 'a bawdy court and a bum court' in 1623, and 'a bawdy and bum court' in 1628. One Sunday evening in 1612 some of the drinkers at Widow Dinghurst's alehouse at East Brent in Somerset were 'deriding and scoffing at ecclesiastical authority and especially against the consistory court', holding a mock court—'and the next morning they did the like, and called one by the name of Dr James [the chancellor], another Mr Methwin [vicar of Frome and a surrogate judge], another Mr Huish [the registrar], and another Mr Maycock [a proctor] and another Chipper [an apparitor]'. The charade was reported by Thomas Mathew, who had 'refused to be a partaker of their folly'. At Goodwife Pentall's alehouse at Brightlingsea, Essex, in 1619 there was a similar performance, with the fake ecclesiastical judge excommunicating 'some that should not drink up a whole pot'. At Calne in Wiltshire in 1622 another group of drinkers staged a mock prebendal court—but it seems there was a lot to mock, for Collet the registrar had been drunk at a court session in July 1621, and had gone around Highworth clasping his codpiece and saying, 'My lord of Canterbury shall see whether he were sufficient or not, whether he were a man or a maid.'[11]

Ecclesiastical judges were often mocked in their own courts. John Lavor of Butleigh, Somerset, abused the court at Wells in 1582, 'and bade them do what they dare': they did not dare much, and made him pay a shilling to the poor. When John Masters was given penance by Dr James in a session at an inn at Bridgwater in 1603, he retorted, 'Do so if you will, but I think it is more than you can do,' and when James foolishly asked, 'Do you know where you are?' he replied, 'Yes, I know where I am, I am in Bridgwater, I am in The Ship.' In 1606 John Ivy of Romford was in the archdeaconry of Essex court for adultery, drunkenness, and swearing, and told the surrogate, Dr Repent Savage, he was too young to be a judge. David Owen, a Peterborough deputy judge, was accused in court in 1616 by John Berry of Denton as 'a sower of sedition, and one that sups and dines with papists and bears with papists that come not to church'. As Joan Dolling was being examined by Dr Duck, chancellor of Wells in 1620, her husband interrupted the proceedings, saying, 'Here, you have called my wife into court for nothing and you have had money already. I would have it again but I think that is gone already *ad diabolo*, meaning to the devil.' Edward Launden of Pitsford, Northamptonshire, warned a judge in 1628 that 'there was a parliament coming shortly, and then better men than the judge (being Mr Wade) would sit there, and if that the said judge would not absolve Richard Launden *in forma pauperis* [without the usual fees] he would set him a-work, do the judge what he could'. William Bottomley of Isley Walton said in the Leicester archdeaconry court in 1633 'that the court did send many souls to hell, and that the judge and all the court would come there at last'. And when Thomas Carpenter was ordered by the Oxford consistory in 1633 to repair his section of the churchyard fence at Hardwick, he refused 'and the said Carpenter in a jeering and derisive manner departed the court, clapping on his hat'.[12]

The cost of dealing with the court system led to accusations of greed and corruption. In 1578 William Ridley of Witcombe told the chancellor of

Gloucester that if his wife had had more money 'she should have more justice than she hath'—and as the chancellor was the corrupt Thomas Powell, he may have been right. William Daggle of Marston said of the Wells court in 1581 'that a man should have what he would in this court for money', and in 1588 William Thraske of Mells said, 'the judge judgeth for rewards and beareth with obstinate sinners, besides other contemptuous and reprobous words openly in the court'. When Dorothy Haddon of Walthamstow appeared in the Essex archdeaconry court for absolution in 1588, she declared, 'This law is the pope's law, and a man or woman may be bought forth for money, and said that the judge should have a rope afore they had any money of her.' John Bailey of Compton in Somerset told a crowd in 1598 'that it were better for a man to have his purse taken at a hedge corner than to spend his money in Wells court', and when Joan Pike was cited in 1614 she asked, 'Doth the Wells court lack money? With a pox to them, they shall all be hanged before they shall get any penny of me.' Wells does seem to have had more than its share of criticism over the years, and in 1632 Thomas Pitney of Brewham pronounced 'that the ecclesiastical courts at Wells were roguish courts'. But the Essex courts were damned too. When Petronella Foukes was examined in the Colchester court on a charge of incontinence in 1635, Robert Man of West Mersea said 'that she was a simple fool for him to get money by', and Richard Street of Colchester said in court that 'their blood was sucked and their means were taken away by being called into this court'. William Jackson of North Ockendon asserted in 1636 that the commissary court of Essex 'was as greedy as dogs, for they would not discharge a woman in his parish but would first tear her clothes off her back'.[13]

The court apparitors were vulnerable targets as they collected information or delivered citations. 'What authority hast thou?' asked the wife of William Poore of Winchester in 1567, 'I will not go to sermons for any man, do what thou canst'—and she called the apparitor 'knave, and wished a pestilence on him'. Nicholas Wright of Walden called the Colchester apparitor who had cited him in 1587 'shitten summoner and knave'. Again, it was the Wells apparitors that got much of the stick. Matthew Leave of Spaxton told Edward Wallander in 1618, 'Thou art the devil's officer, and thou dost perform the office of the devil'—'the devil is the accuser of his brethren, and so art thou!' When John Martin served process on Thomas Lavor of Martock in 1623, Lavor 'wished that his son might be hanged if he [did] not bang him wellfavourably, and called him arrant knave and rogue, and [said] with a good will I would strike thee off thy horse myself, and so bid him cite me if thou darest'. Nicholas Humphrey of Horndon-on-the-Hill declared to an Essex apparitor in 1623 that 'he would have the carnal knowledge [of] his sister or any other women even in the marketplace, in despite of the apparitor or any such officer'. When a Wells apparitor came to serve process at George Hitchcock's house at Wellington in 1626, he was told by Hitchcock 'that he came to poll and cozen his mother, and that the court was a polling court and that they were all deceivers that did belong unto it'—and when Henry Coleman was warned by the constable of Wellington that the bishop's apparitor could hear their lewd talk, he said, 'I care not a turd for my lord's apparitor, let my lord kiss my arse.' At Axbridge in 1627, Thomas Bulgin called an apparitor 'knave, rogue and rascal, and said that they are all knaves that belong unto that ecclesiastical court'. In 1632 three men from Brewham waylaid an apparitor on his way to the parish and beat him, 'and said they would make him not able to come to Brewham to execute any processes there'. Indeed, 'apparitor' was almost a term of abuse, and in 1633 Richard Cole of Wittering, Northamptonshire, called a churchwarden 'the devil's apparitor and the devil's pedlar'.[14]

It was the minister and churchwardens who were at the sharp end of ecclesiastical discipline—and they got most of the invective. If a minister rebuked a parishioner, he often got a lively reply. The parson of Wexham, Buckinghamshire, reproved Thomas Mascall for negligent attendance at church in 1585, and 'he used the parson with ill terms and unseemly contempt'. When in 1588 the rector of Priston, in Somerset, tried to stop some of his own people and some from other parishes building a summer bower in the churchyard as a sermon was due, he got abuse from five of the men and two of the women. Robert Taylor of Great Oakley, Essex, mocked all the parish leaders in 1593, 'calling Simon Dyas Spaniard, Spanish knave, rascal, and calling John Paine to be a hollow-hearted knave, John Hele the constable to be a Smooth Boots, Anthony Wick to be Dry Boots, Master Parson and Jeffrey Sadler to be Double Dealer, Thomas Sadler to be Dry Basket, Humphrey Hedge to be Dry Leather'—he was also 'a riotous person by day and night, and a breaker and tosser of pots'. Richard Walker of Kelvedon blamed the minister for his troubles in 1597, 'saying that he put him in the court and that he was in the fault and that it cost him four shillings'. When in 1607 William Garrett of Colchester was 'admonished by our minister to conform himself to good orders he raileth upon him and call him snotty-nose knave and other vile words'—and when Richard Estgate of Nuthurst, Sussex, was reproved by the minister for arguing in the churchyard in 1610, he declared, 'I will learn no wit at thy hands, go hang thyself!' Samuel Silvester of Great Wakering, Essex, was cited in 1611 'for abusing the minister and for saying he cared not for the spiritual court nor what the minister could do in the same court'. In 1614 Elizabeth Tabor of Widford told her minister 'that he might hold his tongue, when he rebuked her for her misdemeanours', and when in 1616 William Ford of West Ham was reproved by Master Holbrooke for disorderly behaviour on a Sunday he 'bid him kiss his tail'. 'I care not a fart for thee!' responded George Nash of Walcot, Somerset, when the minister criticized his conduct in 1627—and in 1635 Lawrence Rate of Cottingham, Northamptonshire, abused the minister when told to keep away from the alehouse on Sundays. When the minister of Witham, Essex, threatened to report Jeremiah Green in 1639 for using foul language in the churchyard, 'he replied and said he cared not a straw for our said minister Mr Wright, and bade him do what he could'.[15] Certainly, most of these examples are off-the-cuff, ill-tempered responses to personal rebukes—and, we might think, all-too-understandable responses. But there is a common theme, a refusal to accept the right of a clergyman to tell people how to behave.

If a minister was vulnerable to attack, the churchwardens and sidesmen were even more exposed—ordinary parishioners, serving for a year or two, and lacking the dignity of ordination and a uniform. Any reproof by a churchwarden, or, worse still, any presentment to a court, was likely to bring him trouble. The wardens of Preston upon Stour, Gloucestershire, protested in 1576 that 'two storm and threaten the churchwardens for presenting them, so that they are almost weary of their lives'. At the Hanneys in Berkshire in 1584, a suspected adulterer 'for presenting of the same did strike Richard Blissett, being churchwarden, with his dagger, which is to his great grief and hindrance'. Gilbert Brown of Fotheringhay, Northamptonshire, gave the wardens 'hard speeches' in 1597, 'saying that they were not fit to be churchwardens', and in 1599 Robert Mills of Castle Combe, Wiltshire, abused a warden 'and further said that if the said John House, churchwarden, had not been such a busy, brawling knave he should not have been in that office'. Thomas Heale of Clutton, Somerset, was reproved by the wardens in 1605 for being in the alehouse instead of the church, so he 'called them all fools and bade them do what they durst', and, when John Naishe was warned to turn Heale out of his house, he said 'he would keep him in despite of them, willing them to do what they durst'. Humphrey Hall of Newbury, Berkshire, was summoned to meet the wardens and sidesmen in 1611, and saw that he had been put down in their presentment as a drunkard: 'he was a rogue that wrote it,' he protested, and 'he was as honest a man as any of them'. The wardens of Bramber, Sussex, turned the drinkers out of Thomas Gardiner's house during service on Sunday, 22 May 1614: 'Sir Jack, Sir Jack!' cried Gardiner, 'what makest thou at my house? Thou art a drunken churchwarden!' Perhaps some churchwardens brought trouble on themselves, and Thomas Parmeter, warden of Widford, Essex, in 1621, seems to have been a pompous chap. When Joan Shuttleworth called him 'paltry fellow' in an argument over money, he presented her 'for using undecent and unreverent words to the disgrace of Thomas Parmeter, churchwarden, and his office'—and when Bridget Haddock reminded him that her husband paid more tax than he did, he cited her 'for speaking of undecent words in the parish church of Widford to the disgrace of the churchwardenship of the said Thomas Parmeter'.[16]

But usually the wardens were just doing their job. William Lucas of Old in Northamptonshire asked Edward Young to move to a different pew in 1621, and was told, 'A turd in thy teeth, I care not for thee, do thy worst!' After Thomas Bachelor of Oundle was presented for opening his shop on a Sunday in 1626, he called the warden responsible 'a scurvy, rascally knave'. Frances Coleman of Chacombe was reported by the wardens in 1629 'for calling us dunces and knaves and for abusing us whilst we were executing our office of churchwardenship, saying she would not leave us worth half-pence a-piece'. In 1633 Susan Massey of Rogate, Sussex, told a churchwarden he was a rogue and his wife an old witch, and called a sidesman a rogue, knave, thief, and bastard, 'telling him his time is but short for she would quickly rid him out of the way'. Thomas Burge, churchwarden of Chilcompton, Somerset, reported Susan Bakehouse at the 1634 visitation because she had threatened to break the sexton's head when he woke her from her sleep in a service. Martha Wakeham, her mistress, was furious, telling the wardens 'that they were busybodies, and that they should meddle with what they had to doing, and said that she would go to church herself and sleep there, to try whether the said sexton durst awake her, saying that if he did dare to do it she would break his head'. The wardens of Arlington, east Sussex, complained in 1637 against Thomas Stonham 'for giving to both the churchwardens evil words, vizt. That we were rogues and knaves and begged for our office'—and for saying that one of them 'did run after eleven whores so soon as his wife was dead'. Edmund Chesseldyne of Braunston, Northamptonshire, told William Burton in 1638 that he 'desired offices to trouble his neighbours, and that if he had not begged the office of churchwarden then that he should not have had it'. The motives of parish officers were distrusted, and doing the job might just bring insults. At Fryerning in Essex in 1640, George Turner, a quest-man, joined in the presentment when one of the wardens refused to act—but perhaps he later regretted it. When William Pulleston was presented he called Turner 'shits-man and rogue, and said the whole parish taketh him for no less, and bade him kiss his arse', and Toby Pulleston called him 'creep-hedgely fellow and stinking fellow and brazen-faced fellow'. Besides all the bravado and the standardized abuse about knavery and excrement, these insults tell us something about the hard realities of parish office. Little men on high horses had a difficult time. Their authority would be undermined and their motives impugned. They would be harassed and threatened and dared to do their worst. And the insults also tell us something about attitudes towards authority. A new churchwarden did not suddenly become a respected official doing a necessary job: for some, he was a jumped-up jack, pushing his neighbours around. [17]

The power exercised by the Church courts, ministers, and churchwardens depended ultimately on two crucial sanctions: excommunication and penance. Those convicted by Church courts were supposed to undergo penance, and that was a serious business—even though the most common form was a confession and apology before the minister, churchwardens, and a few witnesses. A full penance—in front of the whole congregation in church, bare-legged, in a white sheet, holding a wand, with a verbal confession, and perhaps an appropriate sermon preached—was a true humiliation. Unsurprisingly, those who could afford it sought commutation of the penance for a cash payment, usually after sexual offences. The requests for commutation usually give as reasons the social disgrace and/or the family disruption that would result from the performance of penance. The disgrace was both the shaming in the penitential process and the shame of publicizing the sexual sin. John Hacker of Shipton in Oxfordshire was assigned penance for fornication in 1622, but pleaded that he was Sir John Lacy's servant and 'if he should perform the penance enjoined him it would be the occasion of the loss of his service, to his utter undoing': he was allowed to pay 20s. for charitable causes. William Page of Bloxham and his wife had committed prenuptial fornication, and to escape penance in 1623 he argued 'that it will be a great disgrace to himself and his wife to do penance since they are married, and that he is heartily sorry for his offence': he too paid 20s. In 1636 John Everard of Fairsted, Essex, confessed to fornication with Mary Frank and was given penance, but he submitted 'that his parents are of good rank and quality, and to do the penance abovesaid would be a great disgrace to them and a hindrance to his future preferment'. Everard offered a £10 payment for himself and £5 for Mary, and it looks as if there was a sliding scale of fines according to status. In 1637 Richard Fuller of Great Rollright, Oxfordshire, admitted he was the father of Elizabeth Claydon's child, but asked for release from penance because 'he hath his time hitherto, this offence excepted, lived undetected and in good credit and repute amongst his neighbours, and to perform this public penance enjoined would be a great disgrace to him and give his neighbours occasion to deride and scoff at him'.[18]

Sexual offenders also sought to avoid a penance that would disrupt family relationships. In 1630 Mary Reynolds of Halsted, Essex, asked to avoid penance for an earlier fornication because she was now married and public penance 'would breed discord and difference between her and her husband': she was allowed to pay 20s. instead. On 22 May 1630 Thomas Gilkes of Swalcliffe, Oxfordshire, was assigned penance for adultery—but by 13 June he had decided he could not go through with it. He said 'that he is heartily sorry for this offence of his, and that it will be a great disgrace unto him and an occasion to make his wife to scorn him if he should perform the public penance enjoined him', and he had to pay £6—quite a price to avoid wifely scorn. John Breckland of Bampton paid £4 in 1631 to avoid penance for adultery, saying that

he is very sorry for his said fact and offence and is very willing to do any penance, but he is an old man and a married man and hath lived in good credit amongst his neighbours, in which regard the doing of public penance would be a great discredit unto him and breed discord between him and his wife.

In these cases, the offence (at least, the case) can hardly have been unknown to the spouse, so the 'discord' and 'scorn' would presumably come from the publicity a penance would bring. In 1633 William Newton of West Bergholt, Essex, admitted adultery with Anne Burgess, 'to which he is heartily sorry and humbly craveth pardon of Almighty God for the same'. He was ordered to do penance, but said 'that the said fault is not publicly known and therefore desireth his corporal punishment [i.e. the penance] be commuted into some pecuniary mulct'. John Lindsell of Ashdon also hoped to keep his offence secret in 1637. He had got a maidservant pregnant, but pleaded that 'he is a young man and lives under his father and has no other means to live upon but what he receives from him, and if his father should come to the knowledge of this offence of his he would turn him out of doors and utterly disinherit him, which would be his ruin and undoing'. He claimed he could not afford to pay much, but offered £2 down and another £2 later.[19]

If some people were willing to pay quite large sums to avoid the shame of penance, it is not surprising that those who could not afford to pay—or were not allowed the option—might rebel against the indignity. Henry Dell was called by the minister to do his penance at Chesham, Buckinghamshire, in 1585, but refused to perform it. Henry Enewe of Coggeshall, Essex, was a parish nuisance and a loudmouth. When rebuked by the vicar and others for talking in church in 1595, 'he bade a turd for them and cared not for them', and he later called a churchwarden 'a proved knave and a drunken knave'. He walked out of a Sunday service, and when called back said he had business to do. He was ordered to do penance for his offences, but asserted that 'he would never do penance so long as he lived, although he were quartered'—but he apparently did, after all. Agnes Haynes of Stanton Drew, Somerset, was accused of adultery in 1605. She denied the charge, and was ordered to purge herself with four witnesses: 'I will do no penance in a sheet for this whilst I live, whether I do my purgation or not,' she declared, 'I will rather lie in gaol.' Thomas Woodfield of Blakesley, Northamptonshire, was twice presented as a drunkard and in 1618 would not do his penance, 'but saith he will not do it, for he cares not for the court'. In 1621 Marmaduke Boulton and Mary Davidge of Middlezoy, mid Somerset, were suspected of adultery. Boulton appeared in court, denied the accusation, saying 'that they were knaves that presented him, and drunkards', and was put to purgation—but he failed to clear himself. He was outraged when given penance:

Whereupon he behaving himself like a madman said that it was for one that had a bastard to do that penance, 'Wherefore', quod he, 'the proudest knave of them all that did enjoin this penance shall not make me do it!', swearing by God and his holy name most blasphemously, doubling and trebling his oaths, swearing again and again by God that you shall have no money of him.[20]

There were, of course, others who simply failed to do their penance, without making such a public declaration of intent.

Some, perhaps many, of those who underwent penance were penitent. Mary Orton did her penance at Barking, Essex, on Sunday, 18 March 1576. She stood before the congregation through the service, and the curate read 'the first part of the homily against whoredom and adultery, the people there present exhorted to refrain from such wickedness, whereby they might incur the displeasure of Almighty God for violating his holy law'. William Thomas, the curate, certified that 'she did penitently in a white sheet confess her fault before the congregation'. But others were truculent, and mocked the proceedings. In 1609 Thomas Greenhall pinned his white sheet up around his middle, and wore his gown over it for his penance at Helpston. When Thomas Smith returned to his parish from the Peterborough court in 1614, he told his neighbours, 'I am now discharged of the bawdy court,' and when he did his penance in a sheet he scoffed, 'If he had his black bull's skin about him and his horns upon his head, he would then make a game and sport for the whole parish.' Agnes Potter of Warnham, Sussex, claimed that penance was nothing to her. When told in 1614 that she would have to answer to the bishop for her misdeeds, she retorted that 'she cared not a turd for him nor anything he could do, the worst was to be enjoined penance by him in a white sheet, which she cared not for'. William Hawes at first refused to perform his penance at Rockingham, Northamptonshire, in 1615, and then did so 'with many delays, speaking the words of his said penance very scornfully and contemptuously, to the great scandal of the whole parish'. Richard Cooper made a nuisance of himself at North Luffenham, Rutland, in 1618. He swore and blasphemed, and abused the churchwardens and the rector: he said that he would rather stand excommunicate for three years than listen to the rector, 'and the devil would sooner prevail with him than the minister'. Penance was no threat to him—'What did he care to do his penance before a company of coxcombs, he did not care if he did do it every day.' For some, penance just did not work. John Fuller of Wilmington in east Sussex was another parish troublemaker: he did his penance in 1637, but 'what sign of grace doth this fellow show from his late penance?' asked the churchwardens. The wardens of Morcott in Rutland presumably felt the same way about Henry Behoe. He kept a victualling house, and was given penance in 1638 for eating and drinking with an excommunicate person—but he was presented again early in 1639 'for contemptuous carriage in the performance of his penance, and for departing from the church usually and contemptuously in the time of divine service'.[21]

A penance was supposed to be a solemn and dignified occasion, when the offender apologized to God and the congregation and the congregation was reminded that sin was to be avoided. But it was often a highly contentious occasion, when friends and enemies of the penitent might speak out. When the vicar of Earl's Colne, Essex, called a woman to do her penance in 1581, William Turner 'told him that he was out of his text and that it was no part of his service'. Anthony Warren of Finedon, Northamptonshire, was given penance in 1619, for saying that some workmen would be better working in the fields than in the church. Seth Garrett encouraged him not to do it, 'saying the churchwardens were a company of fools to present Warren': he interrupted the penance, protesting that it would have been more appropriate to do it in the fields than in the church. As Thomas Poole of Heytesbury, Wiltshire, was about to do his penance in 1622 for fornication with Kimberley Hawkins, his sister cried out, 'The pox of God take the whore'—blaming the woman for her brother's fate. In 1629 Walter Sheldon interrupted the minister at Kilmersdon in east Somerset as he was reading out the court orders for penances to be done that day. The penance of William Cox of Donyatt on 30 January 1632 turned into a stand-up argument in the church. Henry Smith, the rector, sought to remind Cox (and the congregation) of the dangerous state he had been in while excommunicate, but some parishioners protested at this and said 'that his duty was to see the order performed and nothing else'. There was clearly sympathy for Cox, and anger against Smith. Several parishioners stormed into the chancel, John Evorey asserting that 'as he the said minister had done to this Cox, so he had dealt with him, and caused him also to be excommunicated for no offence at all'. Cox then declared that Smith had got him excommunicated unjustly, 'and that he laboured to cause him to stand in a white sheet, but he should never do it whilst he lived'. The congregation was in uproar, with up to forty parishioners in the chancel and a lot of support for Cox. When Eleanor Grover had completed her penance at Stony Stratford, Berkshire, in 1633, she tore off her white sheet and declared that William Hudson was the father of her child. 'God refuse me, body and soul, it is false,' he cried, 'thou art a damned whore.' And when Thomas Coppin did penance at Great Bardfield, Essex, in 1636 for allowing drinking in his alehouse during Sunday services, William Fletcher laughed at him—but was soon himself presented for the same offence.[22]

Those who would not bow to the authority of the Church courts—failing to appear in court or to perform the penance assigned—were usually excommunicated. This meant being banned from church services and, for the most obdurate (and in theory), being shunned by Christian people. We have already seen excommunicates wanting to go to church services, and them or their relations wanting to ensure Christian burial in consecrated ground. It was a sanction against which they rebelled, a sanction that in some ways mattered. But people did not always cower before it and come to heel. Some did not care about being excommunicated, at least for a while, and others thought it was up to them whether they were rightfully excommunicated or not. Thomas Daniel went to a service at Westbury in Gloucestershire in May 1571 when excommunicated, and refused to leave when requested by the curate and parishioners. When asked if he had been absolved, he 'crossed the curate and absolved him, and said he did not care for the bishop's absolution nor yours'. John Leech of Hornchurch, Essex, was going to sermons at Romford in 1590, though excommunicated in a tithe suit, 'as he thinketh he is unjustly excommunicated'. John Walters of Rayleigh thought excommunication a fine state to be in. He worked on Sundays and holy days in 1595, 'and being admonished to leave his naughty and bad dealings he saith that he by reason he is excommunicated he may lawfully do it'. Thomas Greenhall of Helpston, Northamptonshire (the man who was to take off his clothes in the chancel in 1609), was excommunicated in 1603 for failing to answer an accusation of adultery—but he didn't think it really applied to him. He went to church on Twelfth Night 1604, asserting, 'My lord might excommunicate wicked imps'—not people like me. In 1612 the wife of Robert Dearsley of Greensted, Essex, declared, 'if you excommunicate her she careth not a fig for it, set down what you will,' and in 1618 Richard Bellamy of Crewkerne, Somerset, said he would not come for absolution again—'I care not for the excommunication, for I have a good faith in Christ'.[23]

Clearly, some just refused to take excommunication seriously. Whatever the Church thought should happen, excommunicates were not ostracized by their communities. In 1607 Thomas and Andrew Stokes of Yardley Hastings, Northamptonshire, were cited for helping William Stokes to evade punishment after he had been presented for fornication, and for supporting him 'with meat, drink, lodging and other necessary supplies' after his excommunication—'to the dishonour of God, the contempt of His Majesty's laws, the scandal of the congregation and the danger of their own souls'. The rector, David Owen, was in a lather about it all and warned them 'of the danger which they did ever more seem lightly to regard and utterly to condemn', but they took no notice. The churchwardens of Exton in Rutland were reported in 1618 for not presenting all those who continued to go to Goodwife Burgess's alehouse, though she had been excommunicated: they claimed, lamely, that they couldn't find any. Some parishes had significant numbers of excommunicates: in 1620 there were ten at Pensford in Somerset, seven at Stanton Drew, twelve at Merriott, and nine at St Mary Magdalene, Taunton. At Frome in 1629 there were thirty. At Coggeshall in Essex there were twenty-three in 1629 and thirty-two in 1630—'they have stood long excommunicate, and still are'. Alice Launden of Brixworth, Northamptonshire, had been excommunicated for five or six years by 1626, and still refused to do her penance. In 1633 Agnes Payne of St Mary Magdalene, Oxford, admitted she had been excommunicated thirteen years before, after failing to appear in court, and by 1635 Sarah Bate of Wivenhoe, Essex, had been excommunicate for five years after a presentment for fornication. These people had not been social outcasts for all that time. Perhaps excommunication was sometimes better than the alternatives. George Wells of Debden in Essex was denounced in 1636 'for saying to Francis Stubbing that he had rather be excommunicate than not'—because 'not' meant having to go to church.[24] But, sooner or later, almost everyone but the Catholics gave in and sought absolution—so they could marry or be churched or be buried, or simply so they could go to church.

Theologus called Antilegon a 'caviller against all goodness'[25]—someone who finds fault with the demands of the Church and thinks he can do as he likes. There were lots of ungodly Antilegons about. Lots spent time in the alehouse when they should have been at God's service—and more didn't share the godly hostility to 'good fellowship'. There were lots who thought that kissing and cuddling and perhaps a bit more was all right—and lots more who joked about sex. There were lots who found it convenient to work on Sundays—and lots more who thought they could if they wanted to. There were lots who objected to the Church's discipline, at least when it was applied to them—and lots more who thought the system was corrupt, a mechanism for making money for judges, registrars, and apparitors. There were lots who would swear at a minister if reproved by him—and lots more who would swear at a churchwarden over a presentment. There were lots who refused to obey court orders and submit to authority—and lots more who submitted only grudgingly, and under protest. Of course, the records of the Church courts show us the disobedient and the discontented, and so over-represents their numbers. But there were thousands and thousands of them. These Antilegons were the profane, who set themselves against the professors and their zeal for God and goodness. They were not going to be pushed around by 'puritans' and 'busy controllers'[26]—or stopped from doing what they wished by oppressive rules and an intrusive disciplinary system. They were not all drunkards and whoremongers and Sabbath-breakers all the time: they were not an underclass of constant sinners, whatever Theologus said. But the search for Antilegon and his kind shows what the godly were up against—and why Arthur Dent had to write his book.

8

Antilegon: Scoffing at the Sacred

Now is also the time wherein the world swarmeth with papists and atheists, and most men live as if there were no God. For now religion is hated, true godliness despised, zeal abhorred, sincerity scoffed at, uprightness loathed, preachers condemned, professors disdained, and almost all good men had in derision.

Preachers always say that things are bad, worse now than they have ever been, and Theologus was no exception. But he was not entirely wrong: the world was not necessarily worse than before, but from the godly point of view it was pretty bad. There really were men and women who thought zeal was zealotry, and rather a joke. There were men and women who called professors of the word 'puritans', and there were men and women who scorned preachers. Antilegon was a churchgoer, a man who said his prayers at bedtime—but he would not accept the authority of a minister. 'What authority have you to examine me?' he asked Theologus, 'Show me your commission; when I see your warrant I will answer you. In the meantime, you have nothing to do to examine me. Meddle with what you have to do withal.'[1] By such as Antilegon, ministers were mocked, their discipline was resented, and their teaching was often despised. They and their work were objects of ridicule—and humour.

The sermon was particularly easy to mock, with a situation, style, and themes that could easily be parodied. On Shrove Tuesday 1586, Joan Agar of Little Bardfield, Essex, climbed into the pulpit and delivered a mock sermon, as if she were a minister—and William Cooke egged her on, handing her a Bible to provide her text. After a supper at the house of William Andrewes at Wrington, Somerset, in February 1605, the company sang a psalm and young Jeffrey Pippett entered a makeshift pulpit. 'Hearken, I beseech you, with reverence unto the Word of God,' he declared. He read some biblical texts, and then began his sermon, to the raucous delight of his neighbours: 'You are a stiff, wicked generation, much like unto the Jews which betrayed Christ when they went unto the Pharisee's house, and so do you to entangle me.' This was surely a direct imitation of their new hectoring rector, Samuel Crooke, who had been hauled before the bishop when the churchwardens complained of his nonconformity. It was also a mockery of the godly of Wrington, with their psalm-singing and sermon-going. Five of the company were reported to the Wells consistory court, and Pippett was sent to prison. One Sunday in June 1612 Alice Rowe of Moorlinch mounted the pulpit there 'and said she would make a sermon, and there delivered these profane and obscene words, viz. all men that have wives of old age may leave their wives and lie with their maids'. John Lewis, vicar of Luxborough, preached against usury in a morning sermon in the autumn of 1617—and in the afternoon Mary Sydenham 'got other maids into her company, went with them into the church, made fast the door unto them, and then she went into the pulpit and there told her company saying "Now I will preach against usury" '. It is significant that some of these spoof sermons were delivered by women. It was even funnier if a minister were impersonated by a woman, and perhaps women especially enjoyed mocking a male authority-figure. But men did it too. John Evans preached a simulated summer sermon in the pulpit at Chesterblade in 1619, making fun of preaching and godliness. In 1620 John Berry of White Staunton gave a mock version of 'Old Mr Greenfield's sermons' in the fields after service, saying 'that he would preach, and thereupon made a scurrilous repetition'. In 1625 a group of young men from Trent in Dorset went to Mudford church in Somerset to ring the bells: while there James Hellier got into the pulpit, put a cushion on his head like a minister's hat, 'and there used many idle speeches, to the great dislike of the parishioners of Mudford'. John Baker of Cricket Malherbie preached his counterfeit sermon in 1629, standing on a stool in the house of Widow Pitts.[2]

In an alehouse in Burford, Oxfordshire, in November 1632, a minister was made to preach his own mock sermon. Lawrence Griffiths was apparently a little drunk when he called at Robert Aston's alehouse, and joined in the drinking. When it came to paying his share, he admitted he had no money. Simon Partridge pulled off the minister's coat, and offered to lend him 2*s.* on it, and William Drewett cried, 'Come you mad priest,' pulled off his boots, and said he would pawn them for a jug of ale. Edward Hall suggested that next day Griffiths could work off his debt by threshing, but it seems that Griffiths offered to preach instead—'If any man will give me a flagon of beer, I will preach.' Partridge gave him some beer, and Ashton and Drewett put him into a tub and told him to preach—which he did, 'and then for his text propounded the word "malt", spelling the same M-A-L-T'. After that the company said he must do penance: Drewett found an apron and pinned it on him like a penitent's sheet, saying, 'I have already taken and done penance, and so shalt thou now'—and then they let him go. The 'malt' sermon seems to have been a standing joke. At Christmas 1636, John Thorne of Barrington, Somerset, performed a burlesque of a drunken minister in William Strode's house. First he called for beer and tobacco, and pretended to be drunk. Then he climbed into a barrel, as his pulpit, 'chose his text to be "malt", and delivered his text to be four parts, viz. M much, A ale, L little, T thrift, and so went on making a long discourse or speech thereon to the great laughter of those present'. The simulated sermon seems to have been a particular Somerset joke. At the sheep-shearing at Worle in 1639, Thomas Cooke amused his helpers by getting a passing beggar-boy to preach a sermon for his alms—'And after the boy had ended his speech the said Cooke, or some other of his company, said "I protest he hath done as well as either Mr King or Mr Methwin could do".'[3]

Making fun of the ministry was easy—and a good laugh. Any of the functions of the clergy could be mocked, and their claims to authority, learning, rectitude, and status. In 1574 Todd the miller of Oakham in Rutland spread a false story that he had seen a minister having sex with a woman in a hedge on the way home from the Oakham preaching exercise. In 1576 Robert Clark of Bradfield, Essex, put on a square cap to mock the minister, and in 1577 William Thresher of Sampford Brett, Somerset, would laugh at the minister 'for singing of psalms'. John Phipp of Abington, Northamptonshire, derided the minister during a sermon in 1588 asking, 'Have we horns in the pulpit?'—and because the curate of West Ham, Essex, was thought to be jealous of his wife, a pair of horns was nailed to his door by a group of drinkers. After a morning sermon at East Pennard, Somerset, in 1600, Henry Stephens threw a goose into the vicar's pew, saying, 'There is your tithing goose'; it was left there until evening prayer, when Stephens held up his purse and called 'Mr Phinian, here is eight pence for your goose. Who'll give more, who'll give more?' Anne Vincent of Castleton, Dorset, dressed up as a minister in 1605, with a surplice and a pair of spectacles, and paraded with a book in her hand saying, 'I cannot endure this papistical book!' The parson of Graffham, Sussex, sent the churchwardens out from a service in 1613 to check if anyone was at Richard Wakeford's alehouse, because there was a horse tethered outside: Wakeford stood up and asked whether he wanted the horse brought to church, pointing out 'that the horse could say no prayers'. Philip Callion of Steyning, was cited in 1617 for 'acting the person of a clergyman upon Ascension day last past, in a profane morris dance, with a book and spectacles and other apish and ridiculous gestures of eyes, hands and countenance, to the public scandal of the ministry and vilifying of that sacred function'. Catherine Woodward went down the street in Great Bursted, Essex, behind Mr Harris in 1620, calling after him ' "Hey, Sir Domine" and "Come Sir Domine" ', and Robert Ragdale announced to the rector of Oundle, Northamptonshire, in 1626, 'Parson, I will stand forty foot off'—presumably suggesting the minister smelled. In 1636, Susan James of Burton Latimer, Northamptonshire, taught her young daughter a spoof catechism against the rector, Robert Sibthorpe, and Anne Dix examined her on it: 'viz. Where is your father? R. In the gaol. Q. Who sent him thither? R. Dr Sibthorpe. What said he to him? R. Out you rogue, out you rascal, etc.'[4]

Laughing at a minister was one thing—but blasphemy and mockery of Christian religion were much more serious, and they are much more striking to see. John Boyce of Stock, Essex, was presented in 1580 'for likening the Trinity to a football play'—probably he meant there were too many persons involved. Richard Barker of Romford said that he never read the Bible, and told the archdeaconry court in 1583 'that it made no matter whether he were a Jew or Christian, seeing that he do well'. Ambrose Digby of Horton in Berkshire declared in 1584, 'When I am dead set my soul on a stake and he that runneth fasteth of God or the devil take it'—and it may be significant that he was thought to have fathered a bastard. When in about 1603 Robert Hillard of Martock, Somerset, wanted fine weather to sow seed and it rained, he complained that 'God hath done as much hurt as good, for aught I see.' As the women were going into church for a christening at South Petherton in 1613, Dorothy Langford told the others, 'I am as good a woman as Lady Mary that bear Christ'—presumably in response to some provocation, but it caused much complaint. Others were more scurrilous about Mary. Peter Lock, a cooper, was working at an inn in Montacute about Whitsun 1614, and when he got hot he took off his cap and revealed his bald head. 'This fellow is a notable whoremaster,' said Thomas Prior, 'for all bald pates be notable whoremasters.' This led to some chatter about what exactly a whore was, and Lock said an adulterous woman was 'a whore in a higher degree'. Prior argued that 'no woman can be a whore with one man than with another, "Why", said he "what was Mary?"' When Lock protested, Prior said, 'If the Virgin Mary were whore, then there be whores, or else not, as I think.' 'Why,' asked Lock, 'do you think that Christ was a bastard or the Virgin Mary a whore?' ' "I think so", answered the said Prior, "or else I think there is no bastard".' Lock 'then fell out with the said Prior, calling him "atheist", and told him saying, "I have been in England, Ireland, France and Spain, and yet never heard but one such atheist as thou art!"'—so Prior tried to quieten things down, by saying that 'whore' was loosely used: 'Come, come, they be whores which spill good malt and wheat.' Richard Trott of Cricket Malherbie apparently held the same opinion in 1615, 'saying that the Virgin Mary was a whore because she was with child and not by her husband, and that her child was a bastard'—and he also said there was no resurrection of the dead. The offence was not reported for three years and Trott denied the charge, but there were three witnesses, and proofs were shown to the court. Whether he said it or not, it was a plausible allegation.[5]

Most blasphemy was just ill-tempered and loose talk. When ploughing a steep hill in 1616 'and his plough beasts being weak', John Hix of Moorlinch, Somerset, 'cursed the hills and him that made them'. John Gawler of Winterborne Kingston, Dorset, was in trouble in 1622 for 'blasphemously speaking against the word of God, as namely calling ministers black dogs and the Bible a book of lies'. In 1627 William Moore of Moorlich cursed God's weather, 'wishing his hay were in Meare pool or at Highbridge, or else it were afire in the close'. Some blasphemy was cynicism or scepticism: Robert Ashby of South Ockendon, Essex, told Francis Vere in 1628 'that the Ten Commandments were not made by God'. When the minister of Great Holland spoke in a sermon in 1630 of Adam and Eve making clothes out of fig leaves, John Sutton asked his neighbour 'where they had thread to sew them, and withal laughed'. Margaret Gimlett of Old Cleeve, Somerset, snapped in 1631 'that she did despise God and all his works, and did spit at it'. Blasphemy was often crude humour: John Craddock of Cottesbrook, Northamptonshire, reckoned in 1631 that 'John Hill was the father, Henry Litchfield the son, and Richard Kese the holy ghost'. After the Easter communion at Meare in Somerset in 1632, Dorothy Churchhouse affirmed that 'she had received God or the devil'. In 1635 Jacob Royle of Ashby-de-la-Zouch in Leicestershire wished a plague upon God and upon his own parents, and in 1638 Giles Cosbie of Yeovil, Somerset, struck his disobedient mastiff and declared, 'Thou art he that Christ died for.' And no doubt sometimes blasphemy was simply a joke: in 1639 Samuel Rand of Layer Marney, Essex, suggested that the twelve men of the parish who had been in an alehouse all Sunday afternoon were the twelve apostles.[6]

Thomas Prior—who thought that Mary was a whore and Christ a bastard—was called 'atheist' and, in a Trinitarian sense, that is what he was. We know that when the term 'atheist' was used in this period it usually meant someone who lived as if there were no God, a worldling, rather than someone who denied the existence of God. But it seems there were some real atheists around. We cannot tell what those who denied God thought they were saying. We cannot be sure that accusations were true, and we often cannot tell what a court made of them: but they are there. In January 1601 the minister of Over Compton, Dorset, complained against Ralph Byckenell, who 'affirmed and said that there was no God, and that he could prove by certain arguments'. To make matters worse, Byckenell was a churchwarden—but he may have been a sick man, 'since that he hath seen the devil with a bush of thorns at his back' and so 'denieth God but acknowledgeth the devil'. John Deryner of Great Bedwyn, Wiltshire, got into an argument with the vicar, Henry Taylor, in the summer of 1607, 'and did maintain this most heretical and damnable opinion, that there was no God and no resurrection, and that men died a death like beasts'—and, to make this example worse too, he said it in the church and in front of Taylor's young pupils. It was alleged in 1626 that Thomas Tuck of Stoford, Somerset, had tried to persuade his brother Anthony to murder his wife, 'for that he might have another with forty pounds'. Anthony Tuck said he could not, for 'it was a wickedness before God so to do'—but Thomas argued 'that he need not fear the wrath of God for that there was no God, but that all things did come by nature or chance, and that Jesus Christ was but a carpenter's bastard'. The allegation came from the putative victim, Emma Tuck, who claimed she had overheard the conversation—and admitted she had been offered a new apron by Joan Gosney if she reported it. But even if the story was untrue, Emma or Joan or someone had thought it conceivable that there was no God and nature took its course. And Richard Sharpe of Wing in Rutland could think it too, stating in 1639 that 'there is no God, and that he hath no soul to save'.[7]

Atheists in the post-Reformation sense—men and women who seemed to have turned their back on God and religion—were much more common. In 1574, Andrew Severn of Tewkesbury, Gloucestershire, was enticed to buy John Downe's wife. Severn met Downe and his wife, and Downe indeed offered, 'Buy my wife and give me what you will for her,' for 'he loved her not better than a toad.' He tried to persuade Severn there was nothing unusual about the proposition: 'he might buy her, for others that he named so did well enough'. At first Severn refused to purchase, but agreed he would buy and marry her if the Downes could be properly divorced. John Somerset of Edington, Somerset, saw organized religion as a waste of time, declaring in 1587 'that christendom is nothing worth, and he careth not if he had never been christened'. When Richard Cowper of Goldhanger in Essex was rebuked in 1591 for hindering those who wanted to hear preachers, 'he answered contemptuously that he cared not for the word of God'—but if that is what he actually said, he perhaps meant he didn't much like sermons. At Calne in Wiltshire in 1603, Richard Hannold and Richard Taylor were noted for absence from communion for four or five years, 'not for religion but for want of religion'. It was reported in 1609 that John Neverd of Ardleigh in Essex rarely went to church, 'and giveth himself up to drunkenness and atheism'. John Keepe of Hawkwell didn't much like church services, asserting in 1610 that 'it was as good to hear a dog howl as to hear divine service read' and 'he would not spend the Sabbath day so idly'—and William Hullan of Blackmore thought much the same in 1612, 'wilfully contemning coming to the church and despising of the worship of God'. Thomas Smith of Backwell, Somerset, regarded overmuch praying as rather a joke, telling Richard Hiscox in 1619, 'I will buy thee a fool's coat and write the Paternoster in the back.' John Orlibeare of Wellingborough, Northamptonshire, refused to pay his church rate in 1620, 'wishing rather never to come to there than otherwise, for he cared not for the church'—though that is presumably what he said in anger when the churchwardens called for their money. 'Shit on the church, what care I for the church?' said Nicholas Crisp of Foulness, Essex, in 1633, when called to the church by a churchwarden. John Frogg of Great Sampford was uncharitable as well as ungodly, declaring at the visitation in 1634, 'God bless our friends, but the devil take our kindred.'[8] A joke or a heartfelt cry?—but Frogg was taken to court anyway.

Some people seem to have had no sense of the church as a sacred space. In a few cases, this was a godly principle—to be asserted by keeping a hat on in church, for example. It was claimed that John Jenkinson of Barrowden, Rutland, had said in 1634 'that his own dwelling house is as good and holy a place as the church, and that divine prayers would be as well accepted in his house as in the church'—which looks like a defence of separatism or conventicling. He covered himself by a denial, 'But if such words were uttered he is heartily sorry for the same.' In other cases there is a casual crudity of behaviour that was simply thoughtless sacrilege—and makes one suspect that the Laudians had a point about enforcing proper respect for the church. Thomas Neale set up a cockpit in the chancel of Finedon church in Northamptonshire in 1588—though many chancels had been unused and allowed to fall into ruin by then. John and Clement Smith played 'at tennis ball' in Hambleton church in the same year, and abused the vicar when he protested. In 1612 Thomas Coole of Great Bromley, Essex, amused himself during a service by spitting onto the seats of those around him when they knelt forward to pray. Hugh Gray of Oakham, Rutland, was presented in 1618 because 'he hath pissed in the church porch in boys' shoes', and in 1619 James White of Rothwell, Northamptonshire, admitted 'pissing in the church'. There were many, many examples of drunks going to church and vomiting in the service, or falling asleep and urinating—though these were involuntary acts. But Margaret Simons and Richard Way of Woolavington, Somerset, deliberately organized a cockfight in the church on 20 February 1626, 'drawing thither a great company of people'. During an afternoon sermon in 1627, John Kibbit of Leigh, Essex, 'did piss in the church into the hat of one that sat by him'—though perhaps it was a very long sermon. In 1628 William Ward urinated into the font at Exton church in Rutland—no doubt he was taken short, but he might have made it to the church door. Susanna Cooke hung her washing out to dry in the church of Little Baddow in Essex in 1636, and, when rebuked, told the minister that 'she might hang her rags there as well as the surplice'—and, because of what he had said, her daughter Anne suggested 'it were a good turn if he were hanged up there'. In 1638 John Beard of Fryerning was charged with 'pissing out of the steeple upon some of the parishioners' heads'—and admitted 'that being in the steeple singing amongst many others, he did make water which fell on some of the parishioners'.[9] We must avoid anachronism here, for churches had been used for all sorts of secular purposes and people then were not so squeamish as now about physical acts—but these cases were all in the courts because someone had objected.

One specific example of this casual attitude towards what others saw as sacred space is the intentional defiling of the church and churchyard—not deliberately to pollute the space, but to foul those who came to it. In 1596 John Southend of Great Warley, Essex, 'beastly and lewdly did defile a stile leading to the church on New Year day at night'—to catch people going to church. He was a butcher, so who knows what he used? This seems to have been a rather poor but not uncommon New Year's joke. Just before New Year of 1615 Richard Baker of Weston Zoyland, Somerset, '[did] besmear and beshit the three churchyard styles of Weston aforesaid with Christian folks' dung': the wardens had heard 'that two or three women of the said parish having occasion to go into the churchyard there, and that their clothes were defiled therewith'. At the beginning of 1616, John Howt of Dundry 'did with the excrement of his body defile the church style'—though he was a notorious drunkard, and presumably it seemed funny at the time. This trick might even be played in church. Margaret Barnwell of Wakerley, Northamptonshire, was said in 1618 to have encouraged her son

John and others 'to defile or beshit the seat or pew of Lawrence Barnwell'. She admitted 'that she wished her brother Lawrence's seat were beshitten, but saith she did not bid the boys to do it'—which was the classic Henry II defence: yes, I said it, but I didn't *mean* it. Two witnesses testified they had heard her say 'that she wished her brother Lawrence's seat were beshitten', but it was never clear whether she had given a definite instruction. There was a slightly sanitized version of this trick, and Euseby Pettit of Orton was accused of 'laying filthy ashes and dust an inch deep where a woman should sit, kneel and lean at divine service'—on 1 January 1631.[10]

Perhaps these examples suggest lack of sensibility rather than lack of religion, and perhaps the concepts of 'pollution' and 'sacrilege' were relevant only to those concerned for a High-Church 'beauty of holiness'. It might be better to think of momentary a-religion, rather than irreligion or anti-religion. But some very strange things were done in churches, and many mocked the Church and its services—or, to say the least, had a light-hearted attitude towards them. When Robert Taylor and Nicholas Ayleward of Great Oakley, Essex, were selected as godfathers in 1593, they threw dice on a gravestone to see who would chose the child's name—highest throw naming the child. In 1594 Agnes Horn and Margery Higgs of Tormarton, Gloucestershire, not far from Bristol, 'baptised a calf, calling it Eleanor'—though this may have been sentimentality rather than sacrilege. Also in 1594, Humphrey Howe and others forcibly re-baptized John Goodier, aged over forty, in the font at Uffculme church in Devon, calling him 'John A-Gaskins' (or John Breeches)—an event described by the wardens as 'odious before God and offensive to our consciences'. In May 1608 Thomas Branwood of Corringham, Essex, was also re-baptized: before evening prayer, four men dragged him to the font, one urinated and put the liquid into the font, another said 'name the child', and a third intoned, 'Hemp, halter and sick, in the name of the Father, the Son and the Holy Ghost.' In 1616 William Vigors of Portbury, Somerset, 'did piss in his hat and put it on the head of one William Jones *de eadem* [of the same place], using the words of baptism'. John Croose of Shepton Mallett went to a christening service drunk in 1619 and cried, 'My masters, whose children are these, they are none of mine are they?' When a child of John Osborne was to be baptized at Tollesbury, Essex, in 1623, he declared that 'he would have none to be witnesses to his child for the godfathers but a whoremaster, a drunkard and a cuckold, nor for the godmothers but whores, sluts and scolds'. One Sunday in August 1630, John Misson, John Carrick, John Browne, and John Emms were all drinking together and eating peas with John Higgins at his father's alehouse in Chipping Norton, Oxfordshire. Struck by the collectivity of Johns, they 'would suffer none to eat with them unless his name were John, and some coming unto them whose names were not John, they undertook to name them John, sprinkling or throwing drink in their faces and so named them John, and then suffered them to eat with them'. William Reeve was baptized by John Carrick, who said, 'I name thee John', and Ralph Walter by John Misson with the same words. And women did re-baptisms too. Instead of going to evening prayer on a Sunday in early July 1634, half a dozen women from South Cadbury, Somerset, went together up the hill to Cadbury Castle, drew water from the well, and baptized each other with obscene names—' Nine Cunts and Long Pricks and suchlike, and signed themselves with the sign of the cross'.[11] Baptism was a holy sacrament—but it could be a real joke.

Mock marriage ceremonies seem to have been less common—perhaps because of the risk of ending up with a valid marital commitment. But they happened. William Adams and Elizabeth Cosin went through a mock wedding at the house of Andrew Corpe at East Pennard, Somerset, in 1618, using the official Prayer Book words and rituals. John Richards asked the banns, and William Gryce pretended to be Elizabeth's father and gave her away. This looks like a case of summer jollity, on a Sunday evening at the end of August or the beginning of September. In the same year, Andrew Jackson of Twywell, Northamptonshire, conducted a mock marriage between George Robinson and Margery Gewyn. Jackson took Margery to Robinson's father's house, and there went through the Prayer Book form: Robinson repeated the words and tried to put a ring on Margery's finger; she apparently resisted, but Jackson forced it on. This may have been a forcible marriage rather than a spoof wedding, for Margery told the court 'that forsomuch as the said Jackson, perceiving that she could not love the said Robinson, threatened her with the spiritual court and that she should be cited thither by Mason', an apparitor. To try to get herself out of trouble, and out of Robinson's clutches, Margery, 'by reason that she would work her own peace, did leave twenty shillings in the hands of the mother of the said Andrew Jackson, to the use of the said Robinson'. Having the banns published for people who were not going to marry was an old joke—and John Pearson of Stratford, Essex, tried it again in 1629. He asked the minister to announce the banns for himself and John Colby's maidservant, without her consent—'as it were in scoffing manner, abusing the holy sacrament of marriage'. There was a funnier version of this prank at Stanton Harcourt, Oxfordshire, in 1637. Some men of the parish, 'being merry and drinking together', persuaded old Elizabeth Bullock to claim that she was pregnant by William Allen, and that he had promised to marry her. She was said to be about 100 years old, which added to the jollity. She stuffed a cushion under her petticoat and asked curate to publish the banns, and one of the churchwardens, John Wood, reported her to the diocesan court on a charge of fornication. The court was told that she took part in the charade only 'out of her weakness and dotage'—but let us hope that she enjoyed the attention.[12]

There was an elaborate mock wedding at Stamford, Lincolnshire, at Christmas 1636. It was decided that the festival's Lord of Misrule must have a wife, and Elizabeth Pitto, daughter of the town's swineherd, was selected for the honour. One of the gentlemen played the part of the minister, and put on 'a gown and a shirt or smock instead of a surplice', and with a Bible or Prayer Book in hand recited the words of the marriage service: the lord and lady held hands and exchanged vows, and the 'minister' pronounced them married. That night the company tried to get Elizabeth into bed naked with the lord, but she resisted and the revellers left the chamber with the lord and lady still in bed together. When the lord tried to have sex with her, she screamed and the company returned to rescue her. There was another mock marriage at Rettendon, Essex, in 1640. Thomas Thomson acted as the minister, and Leonard Oxley took the part of father of the bride. The young couple were John Bover and Margaret Burrows. Oxley 'asked the said John Bover whether he would take the said Mary [*sic*] to be his wife or no, and told him that if he had a mind thereunto he would give her unto him'. The fake wedding seems to have been followed by a real consummation, and Bover and Burrows were both presented for fornication. There was some sort of marriage prank in Layer Breton church in the same year, when Helen Spurgeon marched up to the minister's desk on a Sunday and asked, 'Who giveth this woman to be married to this man?' We do not know the circumstances, except that there was some scuffling and disorder in the church. Helen told the Colchester archdeaconry court that she had done it 'ignorantly, thinking no harm by it'.[13] Doubtless, that is what they all said.

The Church, of course, saw things differently. A mock marriage—or a mock baptism—was not a bit of fun, it was a profanation of a holy rite, a calculated insult to God and his Church. All those Johns of Chipping Norton did public penance at morning prayer on Sunday, 17 April 1631, each with a paper on his head saying:

I do come to do this penance for profaning the holy sacrament of baptism on the Sabbath day, together with the rest of our company in our drink and merriments, by sprinkling drink on the faces of those whose names were not John and naming them John before we could consent to admit them to eat or drink with us.[14]

They must have been pretty big pieces of paper to carry such a message—or perhaps the writing was illegibly small. One wonders how the Chipping Norton congregation reacted. Did they laugh, as we might do, to see and hear the offence described? Or were they shocked, as the Oxford diocesan court obviously expected? Or both, perhaps?—wasn't it naughty, but, oh yes, wasn't it fun? Like the examples of cross-dressing in the previous chapter, these parodies of religious ritual often took place in the periods of licensed jollity around Christmas and Shrovetide, or in the summer—embracing religion as part of the everyday, by making fun of it. But in some cases at least, the joke was not on God nor on the Church, but on the victims: those who were baptized in urine or given a silly name, and those set to marry an inappropriate partner. The Church provided a convenient script, but it was not always the intended target. Some of the mock marriages may have been a prelude to sexual activity—though it is not clear whether the 'wedding' would give some legitimacy to fornication or whether it would emphasize its illegitimacy. Probably it just added to the occasion. At the

Robinson–Gewyn marriage in 1618 there was a strong element of coercion, and the same may have been true at Stamford in 1636. But for most participants, surely, the aim was jollity rather than profanity.

Perhaps it was different when other church services were mocked in, as it might be, victimless jests. On Sunday, 2 March 1595, John Gosse and other parishioners were lounging about in the churchyard at Ramsey, Essex, at the beginning of morning prayer. The minister had started the service and got up to the Lord's Prayer, when Gosse cried ' "Our Father, which art in heaven"! By God, we must go into the church!' We cannot hear the tone, but the wardens thought he used 'other scoffing speeches', and he was later also cited 'for deriding of Mr Bland his minister'. Roger Pole of Oakham, Rutland, joked in the alehouse about the communion in 1602, telling his neighbours that 'it was more meet for our vicar to minister a whole loaf of bread at once than a piece, for that he did not know the fine stomachs of the communicants, and by the wine he spake in like manner'—in other words, we are all very hungry and need a proper feed (and a decent drop of wine). It was a jest we will see again. In 1620 Edward Jarvis of Spratton, Northamptonshire, played a cruel trick on his childless wife, announcing that she had had a baby, 'and called wives of his companions to his wife's churching … and there he caused a cat to be wrapped in clothes like a child: all this was much grief to his wife'. Hardly a victimless jest, and Jarvis deserved his day in court. At Monksilver church, Somerset, in 1621, Richard May made fun of a service by singing out the responses and a loud 'Amen!'—'hindering the congregation from their devotion and driving them to a great laughter by his folly'. When taken to task, he responded, 'Why, am I not in a cathedral church? In cathedral churches they use so to do.' In 1630 several parishioners of Weldon, Northamptonshire, were in trouble for passing around the joke that the prayer their minister said before his sermon 'is like Sellinger's Round'—presumably because he repeated it each time. Some of these quips may have been godly protests against Prayer Book formulas, but most were just irreligious jokes. A mare belonging to Anthony Bennett of Cottingham, Northamptonshire, fell sick in 1636, and his daughter asked 'why they sent not to the minister to pray for her in the church': this was thought by the wardens to be 'in scorn of the church prayers' rather than an innocent query.[15]

Some people went to church quite deliberately to make trouble—or were so thoughtless of others that trouble ensued. A village church was not a quiet place, where the eternal verities could be contemplated in earnest tranquillity. The wife of John Reynolds of Bardfield Saling, Essex, took her prayer book to church in 1585, and during service and sermon 'she readeth so loud upon her book that the people cannot understand'. Reading from a primer or other book was a favourite device of protesting Catholics, but if this were her motive the churchwardens would have said so. During a service at Carleton in Northamptonshire in 1592, four men rattled the weaponry stored in the church 'to the great terror of the people'. Henry Wise, vicar of Elsfield near Oxford, was standing in his surplice ready to begin evening prayer on Low Sunday 1604, when John Spittle called out that he would impound the vicar's mare and two colts. '"Then", said Mr Wise, "what shall I do with my fodder?" Then said John Spittle, "Eat it thyself if thou wilt", then said the said Mr Wise, "Hold your peace", whereupon John Spittle said "You will prove yourself for a fool when all is done".' He already had. Christopher Pannell went drunk to evening prayer at Bury, Sussex, on 6 March 1614, and when the minister said, 'Oh Lord, show thy mercy upon us' he called out to the congregation 'Say "And grant us thy salvation"!'—the service had to be stopped because of the laughter. Perhaps Thomas Milborne, parish clerk of East Ham, Essex, ruined the services unintentionally, but ruin them he did in 1614: 'he singeth the psalms in the church with such a jesticulous tone and altitonant voice, viz. squeaking like a gelded pig, which doth not only interrupt the other voices but is altogether dissonant and disagreeing unto any musical harmony, and he hath been required by the minister to leave it but he doth obstinately persist and continue therein'. William Palmer tied a dog to a bell-rope at West Pennard, Somerset, in 1616 and made it run around during evening prayer, 'and made a stir and a laughing in the church thereby'. Thomas Collins of Buckland St Mary took his dog to church on Palm Sunday 1621, with 'a great clog' (a block of wood) tied to it—so it clattered round the church and made such a noise that the rector had to stop the service and get Collins and his dog to leave. In 1629 Sarah Jarmyn of Asheldham, Essex, interrupted William Guthrie's sermon, 'clapping of her hands and saying that he the said William was a liar'—and in the churchyard afterwards 'reviling the said William in most godless, wicked and impudent manner'. Some surprising things happened in church—and in 1637 George Heath of Balcombe, Sussex, was presented 'for letting of his bitch to farrow in his seat in the time of divine service'. And some people were just plain contrary. Richard Peters of Farringdon, Somerset, jeered his way through services in 1638, 'and when any psalm is singing he will sing the contrary tune, by which he is a disturber of the congregation'.[16] So much for Laud's beauty of holiness.

The communion service, the solemn commemoration of the Last Supper and a memorial (or more) of the Crucifixion, was sometimes mocked or disrupted. Several wags had a laugh about the bread distributed at communion. The curate of Publow in Somerset was preparing the bread for communion at Christmas 1632 or Easter 1633, when John Parsons marched into the chancel and declared, 'I require you to cut bigger pieces of bread than you have usually cut,' and when asked why responded, 'because you should give bigger bites to the people.' Parsons claimed that it had been a polite request, 'for that some of the parishioners complained that the bread which he was wont to deliver them was so little that they could hardly taste whether it were bread or not'. In 1637 Widow Devereux of Lewes, Sussex, complained, '"Here is dry bread indeed", and withal eating a piece of cheese with it.' That really was profaning the sacrament—but was it deliberate sacrilege, or casual humour? Anyway, communion was not always the dignified occasion both the godly and the ceremonialists expected. Sometimes it was a scramble, sometimes it was a farce—and sometimes it was an occasion for dispute. It certainly raised practical difficulties—especially over how much wine to provide when the wardens did not always know how many would communicate and how much they would drink. Economical wardens tried to keep costs down. Ralph Glessom attempted to limit the quantity each person took, telling the communicants at Oakham, Rutland, in 1601 that 'If ever the one of them did drink a pennyworth of wine, the devil choke them.' When the parson of Blagdon in Somerset saw that there would not be enough wine for the eighty communicants on Palm Sunday 1612, he asked for the churchwardens to bring more—'but the wardens sent him word he should have no more until the first was spent'. At Wylye in Wiltshire in 1622, Thomas Kent bought sack from the alehouse for communion instead of muscadine from Salisbury, and wanted fewer communions: when the minister announced a communion Kent said that 'there should be no communion that day, adding that Mr Lee would make a poor parish of it if there should be a communion so oft as he would have it'. Churchwardens often erred on the side of caution, providing too little wine. In 1599 some of the parishioners of Stubbington, Hampshire, received the communion bread but then found there was insufficient wine and had to go home without. In 1637 about forty parishioners got no wine at Weston in Zoyland, Somerset: the wardens claimed it was not their fault, as the minister had asked them to supply ten quarts and they had got twelve to be sure. At Bathford the wine ran out at a morning communion in 1639, and some parishioners waited in church until 2.00 p.m. while the wardens went for more. A common resort when the wine was running out was to mix in some beer, as at Blewbury in Berkshire in 1601, Sutton in Northamptonshire in 1605, and Great Tey in Essex in 1623—though at Mistley in 1622 some people had only beer.[17]

Supplying the wine was a headache for churchwardens, especially when the authorities were pressing for greater solemnity in services. The wardens of Beaulieu, Hampshire, explained at visitation in 1607 that 'they did commonly bring for the communion sufficient bread and wine, rather too much than too little, and of the best they could get, and say they brought the wine in a glass bottle covered with leather'. In 1615 William Reade of Little Billing, Northamptonshire, kept an extra glass of wine in his pocket at the communion, and produced it when the minister needed more—which was thought unseemly by both the parishioners and the court. The wardens of Earls Barton were presented in 1622 for providing wine in a disgusting old leather bottle, and one of them kept a spare hidden under his cloak, obviously hoping it would not be needed. At Braybrooke in 1626 the rector claimed the churchwardens had kept an extra bottle under their seat, meaning to take it for themselves—and the wardens said the rector asked for more wine only so he could have the rest of the opened bottle. Who should have any leftover wine was a contentious issue. The Prayer Book rubric seemed clear—any wine left was the minister's (which is why churchwardens hid extra bottles)—but there was often argument. When the curate of Towersey, Oxfordshire, took home the leftover wine to which he was entitled in 1608, one of the churchwardens abused him. After a communion at Shapwick in mid Somerset in 1612, some of the communicants toasted one of the wardens with the residue of the consecrated wine, so he quaffed what was left, to the annoyance of the minister—and when a warden at Meare drank 'five or six spoonfuls' left in the communion cup the vicar said that 'he was a rude clown in so doing'. And in 1629 James Gilbert of Binstead, Sussex, splashed the wine left in the cup around the chancel, saying that 'the wine and bread was the parish's charge, and therefore the parishioners ought to spend it in the church'.[18] With the exception of the splashing of the wine, perhaps, these communion cases do not suggest sacrilege or deliberate profanity. But, as with other things we have seen, they show people who were not thinking about sacred space and holy things—they were thinking about eating enough bread and getting as much wine as they could. Religious ceremonies were not awesome occasions clothed in sanctity, they were among the ordinary doings of everyday life.

One might expect more mockery of baptism and marriage and the regular services of the Church than of the rituals of death and burial. But it was not so: there were jests about death and dying too. In 1600 there was a mock funeral at East Tilbury, Essex, when Richard Prentice and three women trundled William Goodwin through the churchyard on the old parish hearse, and John Jobson organized the ringing of the bells. However, most funereal jokes involved only bell-ringing. In 1586 John Copeland caused the bell at Coggeshall to be tolled for his own death, sending Ralph Reeve with a message to the parish clerk—though he was perfectly well. Richard Gay of Stroud in Gloucestershire asked in 1592 if a knell would be tolled for a dead dog—perhaps a nonconformist protest, perhaps just a joke. And in the 1620s there was a flood of cases in different parts of the country of bells being rung for people who were not dead. In 1621 one Banks of Loddington, Northamptonshire, sent John Pye to ring the bell 'because his wife was speechless'. This became a common joke: a woman who was 'speechless' must be dead or dying. John Shotbolt of Great Bursted, Essex, got home drunk in 1625 and his wife would not speak to him—so he sent his son to ask the sexton to toll the bell 'for she was speechless'. The sexton thought the woman was dying and so rang the bell, 'and so made but a mock of this ancient laudable custom'. Francis Calvert of Meare, Somerset, rang the bell on 5 July 1627, saying it was for the sister of Mrs Bysse, 'and told them that she lay speechless, whereas she was well and not sick at all'. In the same year, William Dyer and four others of Trent in Dorset rang the bells for the last constable, who they said was dead, 'making themselves merry therewith', and in 1628 John Wormell of Shepton Mallett, Somerset, had the bell tolled for Zachary Browse, who was as well as ever. The church bell was tolled at Walthamstow, Essex, in 1628 for John Powell's wife: he claimed she went black in the face and could not speak for half an hour—but the wardens said she would not speak to him after a quarrel, 'and she not answering his unkind speeches [he] reported that she was speechless and thereupon caused the bell to be tolled'. In 1629 William Boreham of Great Bardsfield had the bell rung for his wife as if she were dying, 'which thing is taken to be a mock to religion because the bell is usually tolled to put people in mind to pray for those for whom it is tolled'. And in 1633 John Growte of Walden sent a message to the sexton, and the bell was tolled for his wife, 'she being not sick, to the scandal of the Church and great offence of the parishioners'—if only because it was by then a very stale joke.[19]

Perhaps the tolling of the passing bell was rather more serious than the other religious pranks we have seen—because it prompted people to pray over a falsehood. It was not Christian religion that was mocked, however, but the 'speechless' wife or the ex-constable whom the drunkards would have liked to be dead. As with mock baptisms and spoof marriages, the victim of the lark was usually an individual, not an institution. Religious rituals and customs provided the scenario, but they were not necessarily the object of mocking exercises. We have seen men behaving badly, men something like Antilegon—and we have seen women too: blaspheming about the weather, cursing the Church when they owed it money, spreading filth on approaches to the church, and twisting religious ceremonies so they could have a good laugh. We have seen that a large number of people didn't want to go to church so often, and couldn't concentrate when they were there. There were some cases that look like genuine atheism, and more of scepticism or humour over details, so people could think outside the orthodox box. In an age of faith, some people wore their religion very lightly—and a few had cast it off altogether. But we have not seen much that was incompatible with a genuine, if shallow, Christian faith. Theologus tells Antilegon straight: you don't take religion seriously, you gamble, you swear, you drink, you chase women; 'Therefore I conclude that, for as much as your whole course is carnal, careless and dissolute, you can have no warrantable hope to be saved.' But Antilegon is unmoved and thinks he has the answer: he loves Christ, and Christ will save him. The plain man's pathway to heaven was not always by the approved godly route, but Antilegon and his kind thought they were heading in the right direction. 'I hope to be saved by Jesus Christ, as well as the best of you all,' he tells Theologus.[20]

The professors of the Word had religion at the centre of their lives, every day of the week. They were supposed to follow a testing routine of prayer, Bible-reading, psalm-singing, and family catechizing—fitted around necessary labours as best they could. The profane were not like that, and had no wish to be. Antilegon's religious habits consisted of church on Sundays and prayers at bedtime, and Theologus complained that 'You have no prayers in your family, no reading, no singing of psalms, no instructions, exhortations or admonitions, or any other Christian exercises.'[21] The difference between godly Philagathus and less-godly Antilegon might seem be that for one religion is central and constant, and for the other it is peripheral and occasional—just bedtime prayers and a Sunday service. In terms of domestic 'Christian exercises', that is certainly true—but in terms of religious awareness, it may be misleading. For God was everywhere, and could not be avoided—'God is always in one like a cuckoo,' as John Virgin had put in 1619. Religion was part of the way things were, a given, to be used and abused in all sorts of circumstances. There were jokes about religious practice, mocking a minister or aping a ceremony. When someone was to be insulted, it often took a religious form—a forced re-baptism, an improbable marriage announced, a death knell tolled. Sometimes people settled down to chat about religious matters, and ordinary conversation might turn to religion: a bald head could lead to talk of whores, the Virgin Mary, and Christ. God was blamed for the shape of hills and cursed when it rained: no doubt he was sometimes blessed when the sun shone, but that was not reported. And when Anthony Tuck was advised in 1626 to murder his wife so he could get himself a richer one, it was the wrath of God that he feared rather than the hangman.[22]

God mattered to the less-godly as well as to the godly, though he was a different sort of God. Their world was as it was because God had made it so, not because men had rebelled against him and ruined it. The ordinary ways of the world were good ways, even God's ways. So Christians should do as their neighbours did, and take the world as they found it. This was how Antilegon saw things. But that, said Theologus, was the way to perdition, and he warned of the folly of threescore years of worldliness at the risk of an eternity of suffering in the fires of hell. And poor, ignorant Asunetus was terrified: 'The laying open of these doctrines of hell-fire and the judgement to come maketh me quake and tremble,' he said, 'I am afraid I shall be damned.' Antilegon did not share that polarizing distinction between the way of the world and the way of God: a good citizen like Asunetus would go to heaven, simply by being a good citizen.

Damned, man, what speak you of damning? I am ashamed to hear you say so. For it is well known that you are an honest man, a quiet liver, a good neighbour, and as good a townsman as any in the parish where you dwell, and you have always been so reputed and taken. If you should be damned, I know not who shall be saved.[23]

Antilegon was a fictional character, but surely he spoke for many conventional Christians.

PART V

POPERY AND OTHER ENEMIES

9

The Papist: Outside the Church, Inside the Community

We are they which hold the ancient Catholic faith, yours is new doctrine. We believe as our forefathers did. If your doctrine is true, then all our forefathers were damned, for they always believed contrary to that which you believe.

There is no Papist in *The Plain Man's Pathway*, and we must look for him in another dialogue. He speaks out in a different debate—George Gifford's *A Dialogue between a Papist and a Protestant, Applied to the Capacity of the Unlearned*, published in 1582. Gifford knew how to write racy dialogues and create convincing characters. His *Country Divinity* (1581) is a lively and realistic argument between Zelotes and Atheos, in which Atheos attacks troublesome preachers and the self-righteous godly, and Zelotes defends godliness and argues that Atheos's religion is only watered-down popery. Zelotes expounds basic Protestant tenets, but Atheos stands his ground. It was a popular work, printed five times in three years. In 1593 Gifford published *A Dialogue Concerning Witches and Witchcrafts*, where godly Daniel tries to persuade Samuel, his wife, and his friends that cunning folk are servants of the devil just as much as witches. The sexist outcome is that Samuel and the schoolmaster M.B. are convinced, but Samuel's wife and 'the goodwife R.' retain their womanish superstitions and their trust in white wizards.[1]

Gifford, like Arthur Dent, was a successful Essex author and preacher, and various editions of his collected sermons were altogether reprinted twenty times. He served as a schoolmaster at Brentwood, then as curate and afterwards vicar of All Saints, Maldon. He was suspended for nonconformity and then deprived of his benefice in 1584, but he was soon appointed town preacher and served on in Maldon until his death in 1600. When Gifford wrote and preached against popery and profanity, he knew what he was talking about: he had faced them and preached them down. During his suspension, fifty-two of the leading citizens of Maldon petitioned in his favour, citing his 'godly and sincere preaching' in the town and his reform of 'the outrage of many notorious sins commonly used before his coming'. It was only 'the profane and wicked' that had conspired against him, representing him as disobedient and subversive.[2] Gifford was a tireless warrior against sin, ignorance, superstition, and popery—above all against popery and its vestiges.

Of the three Gifford debates, *A Dialogue between a Papist and a Protestant* is the least realistic discussion, an exchange of standard polemical slogans with little development of characters or real engagement between them. But there Gifford does suggest some of the reasons why his Papist is still a papist, and not a Protestant. Gifford explains that his book is meant to arm 'the simple unlearned man' against error, answering 'those points which do most commonly trouble them'—the doubts that might worry them, the arguments they might encounter if they met a papist in the street. And that his how the dialogue begins, with a chance encounter 'between a Papist and a Professor of the Gospel'. 'I am glad to see you well, sir,' says amiable Papist, 'for old acquaintance sake, which I would be content to renew again.' The Protestant is more cautious: 'I am glad also that you are in health, I saw ye not a great while before now.' Papist asks for news from London, and 'What is become of the Catholics?' His conviction that the Jesuit Edmund Campion had the better of his disputation with reformed theologians raises Protestant's suspicions: 'I perceive ye are a papist, or at the least a favourer of the papists.' When Papist declares, 'I am obedient to the laws, and do not refuse to go to the church', Protestant identifies him as 'a church papist'—'there are papists which can keep their conscience to themselves, and yet go to church'. Papist admits, 'I am a Catholic', and 'I take ye to be heretics.'[3] So the argument begins.

Papist has read the Bible and cites a few biblical examples, but admits, 'I am an unlearned man': he relies on the authority of the Pope and the Catholic Church. He can, nevertheless, argue his corner, and he offers three broad justifications for his religion. The first is tradition: 'We believe as our forefathers did.' God would not have allowed his own people to err for so long, so the traditional teaching of the Roman Church must be true. 'I will keep me to the ancient faith,' he boasts. His second explanation is catholicity, and follows from the first: 'ye be heretics and apostates, insomuch as ye have departed from the holy Catholic Church'—'ye be all damned heretics, which be out of the Church'. And his third reason is the moral decline he thinks results from Protestantism: 'ye teach all looseness and licentious liberty to the flesh'—'Oh this corrupt age, whither will it tend at the last?'[4] These are views we will see reproduced whenever real Catholics explained themselves.

In previous chapters we have examined what the ignorant, the godly, and the profane thought of each other and of the religion taught by Theologus, the preacher—using the records of the Church courts. The professors and the profane argued among themselves in the church, churchyard, street, and alehouse: sometimes their words were reported to authorities, and sometimes they spoke out in court. The ordinary papists are much harder to get at. 'Church papists', like Gifford's Papist, went to church to avoid trouble: they usually kept their heads down, and their opinions to themselves. Catholics who stayed away from church—the recusants (or 'refusers')—denied the legitimacy and authority of the Church of England, and so rarely bothered to appear before its courts. When recusants were indicted at quarter sessions or assizes, certified absence was enough to convict them, and their reasons hardly mattered. So historians have found it difficult to write about grass-roots Catholic opinion—what ordinary Catholics thought of their own religion and of the religion of Protestants. We know what Catholic leaders and writers told their people, and we know what Catholic priests were advised to teach their people. We know quite a lot about the lives of the underground priests, something of the lives of the leading Catholic gentry, and a little of the lives of the untypical lay martyrs. What, if anything, can we learn about the less heroic? What can we learn about people like our Papist?

Some of the most striking early statements from ordinary Catholics come from outside the areas of southern and central England on which we have concentrated. In November 1576 the mayor and various councillors of York interrogated 'certain persons utterly refusing to come to the church', on orders from the queen. Some of those they sought could not be found, a few were sick or pregnant, and two said they had conformed. Thirty-eight were clearly Catholics, and gave their reasons for recusancy. A dozen simply declared that their 'conscience would not serve' them to attend church, and another seven complained that Mass was not celebrated—'there is neither priest, altar nor sacrifice'. Six more cited both conscience and the absence of the Mass. Others had more to say for themselves. William Bowman, locksmith, would not attend because 'it is not the Catholic Church, for there is neither priest, altar nor sacraments'. His wife Katherine refused 'for her conscience would not serve her, because there is not the sacrament hung up, and other things as hath been beforetime, and further she sayeth that she doth not believe that such words as the priest readeth are true'. Janet Strickett, widow, 'sayeth she cometh not to the church because her conscience will not serve her, for the bread and wine is not consecrate as it hath been in time past'. Alice Lobley, wife of a tanner, 'sayeth her conscience will not serve her, for she sayeth she thinketh the baptism is not as it hath been, and sayeth she will not receive [communion] so long as she liveth'. The reiteration of 'conscience will not serve' in these responses may suggest that these York Catholics had been drilled by a priest, but several of those interrogated expressed their own concerns in their own ways. Janet Geldart, a butcher's wife, cited her conscience, but added that 'there can be no greater cause for the same than her conscience'.[5] These conscientious objectors wanted the true Church they had known before Elizabeth came to the throne, not schismatic and heretical Protestantism.

Some of the York recusants had a fierce moral objection to Protestant worship, and believed it flouted the will of God. Elizabeth Aldcorne, wife of a tiler, would not go to church 'because she sayeth she is certified in her conscience otherwise, and that she should displease God if she should do otherwise'. Margaret Tessimond, a saddler's wife, stated that if she now went to church 'she thinketh she should offend God', and Helen Booth, widow, 'sayeth if she should come to the church she should rather offend God than otherwise'. Jane West, servant, 'thinketh it is not the right church, and that if she should come there it would damn her soul', and Anne Brimley, seamstress, also feared 'she should damn her own soul'. Several declared that they would not desert the faith of their fathers and of their own baptism. Gregory Wilkinson, felt-maker, 'sayeth he cometh not to the church because his conscience will not serve him so to do, for he will remain in the faith that he was baptised in', Dorothy Vavasour said much the same, and Frances Hall 'believeth in the faith that she was baptised in'. Isabel Porter, wife of a tailor, protested that 'things are not in the church as it hath been aforetime in her forefathers' days', and Elizabeth Porter, widow, said 'the service there is not as it ought to be, nor as it hath been heretofore'.

Catholics were advised by their priests and lawyers to give explanations much like those employed at York. 'A brief advertisement how to answer unto the statute for not coming to church', a manuscript produced in response to the 1581 Act against recusancy, gave clear reasons why Catholics should not attend church, and suggested what recusants should say in their own defence. The key points were conscience and tradition. First, the Protestant service 'is not that ancient form of prayers which hath been received throughout the Church of God by the inspiration of the Holy Ghost', and 'therefore he cannot without utter damnation resort to it, for thereby he should do that act which in conscience he taketh to be to the dishonour of God and so for conscience sake damnable'. Second, if the Protestant service really was as God wished and the Catholic Mass only superstition, then 'all princes and people here in England have lived in a damnable estate of darkness and in the shadow of death, because they have lived without the true service of God, without which no faith or religion is acceptable to God'.[6] That could not be so.

These are, more or less, the things Catholics did say when challenged. In 1576 the churchwardens of Romford, Essex, complained that Widow Painter would not take communion, 'and that always when she is exhorted thereunto she will find herself aggrieved with one thing or other, and sayeth there is a thing speaketh within her and telleth her what she should do'—she thought up excuses for her absence, and then appealed to her conscience. Forty-one recusants from six Hampshire parishes were cited to appear at the Winchester consistory on 21 July 1583: seventeen turned up, and some gave reasons for their stand. John Bufford of Otterbourne admitted that 'he hath not been at church since Shrovetide last, and he repenteth that he hath come so often come [*sic*] to the church for that his conscience will not suffer him'. Lawrence Cox cited his minister's nonconformity as a reason, 'and besides his conscience will not serve him and therefore he will not come to the church yet'. Thomas Platt had last attended church about Michaelmas 1582, and also cited his conscience. Robert Lincoln of Twyford attested that he and his household had been at a sermon on Whit Monday 1583, 'but now his conscience will not suffer him to come to church', and Humphrey Rose told the court that 'He thinketh the Latin service is necessary'. Richard Wilson 'allegeth that he is under age and the law cannot compel him to come to church'—but it was noted that 'by chance he heard some part of service, and said he were as good hear a bear-baiting'. It seems that these people had abandoned churchgoing within the previous year, some only a few months before, and several used the 'conscience will not serve' formula—which may suggest the influence of a newly arrived Catholic missionary priest.[7]

In 1594 Richard Gaye of Keynsham, Somerset, was 'vehemently suspected to be a recusant'. The churchwardens reported that 'He saith that her majesty's laws are not agreeable to God's laws, and he doth not usually come to Church.' William Myles of Weeke in Hampshire confessed in 1598 that he had not been to church since Queen Mary's reign, and when asked if he would now go replied, 'God forbid that I should come to church, I am fully resolved not to [go to] church.' Alice Mills of Itchen Abbas was another forty-year absentee by 1598, and 'she cannot find in her conscience'. John Clement of St Maurice's, Winchester, had not been for sixteen years, because 'he cannot find in his conscience so to do'. Seven parishioners of St Clement's, Winchester, were asked in court in the same year 'whether they will conform themselves to their obedience in coming to the church, and they answered all with one accord that they cannot resolve themselves to come to the church and that their conscience will not serve them to conform themselves in that behalf'.[8]

Others gave more individual answers when challenged for recusancy. John Coates of Timsbury, Hampshire, admitted in 1598 that 'he hath not been at church these twenty years last past, and being demanded whether he will now conform himself or no sayeth he will not unless his father will'. Alice Kewen of Hursley explained in 1603 that recusancy had been good for her: 'her conscience would not nor will not serve her to come to church, and further sayeth that these twelve years past she hath forborne the church and sayeth that so long as she used to come to the church she could not have her health but since she hath forborne the church she hath had her health'. Alice Cooper, wife of an Andover clothier, gave several reasons in 1607 for her seven-year absence from church: 'she observed and perceived such misliving among [Protestant] ministers'; 'precise and curious courses' (i.e. nonconformity) by the minister of her previous parish; and that when she had been ill she had sworn never to attend church again—she would keep her oath 'for that her friends died in that religion and lived in the fear of God'. In 1620 William Ireland of Rochford, Essex, thought 'that the sacraments as they are ministered with us have no promise of blessing': it is just possible that he was a Protestant sectary, but on balance he sounds rather more like a Catholic, expecting blessings from a sacrament. An appeal to conscience remained the usual Catholic response, however. In 1625 Mary Slinge of Woodham Walter was presented as 'a Romish recusant': when she was admonished to attend by the minister and wardens, 'she refused, pleading her conscience'. Brian MacDonnell, an Irishman living at Woodham Mortimer in 1626, 'being often admonished and persuaded by me the minister, and being able to yield no reason of recusancy, hath notwithstanding obstinately refused to come to divine service, pretending nothing but that he cannot come'—because of his conscientious objection, presumably.[9]

To protect themselves from persecution, papists usually kept quiet: they did not often announce their loyalty to Rome or their Catholic beliefs. But some spoke out, proudly or when provoked. Thomas Green had affirmed at Burwash, Sussex, in 1574 that 'It was a merry world when there were no such presentments [for religious offences] made, and that he hoped to hear or see a mass in Burwash church within a twelve-months.' William Binkes, a tailor of Finchingfield, Essex, got into an argument about religion at William Cooke's house in 1577. He contended that when the bread and wine at communion were consecrated by a priest, it became the body and blood of Christ—' "Why", said the said Cooke, "then we are wrong taught." "Marry, so you are", quoth he, "and that I will prove by good authors, for the true religion is at Rome".' Binkes did not think much of the Church of England: 'what manner of religion we have here in England I know not, for the preachers now do preach their own inventions and fantasies, and therefore I will not believe any of them'. George Binkes, another Essex tailor, also defended Catholic worship: 'the mass is good and *Confiteor* is good and that he will believe as long as he liveth'. George Binkes was Gifford's Papist in the flesh: 'he desires and would be called by the name of the Papist'. David Browne of Moulsham near Chelmsford had told his neighbours 'that he the said David Browne was a papist, and that he would pray for the pope'—which were dangerous words on 11 August 1588, only two weeks after the Spanish Armada had sailed through the Channel, and Browne was convicted of sedition. In 1592 'Papist' George Binkes was again in trouble, allegedly declaring 'that the pope is supreme head over all Christendom, and that King Philip is right king of England'. In the same year, Ralph Duckwell, a labourer at Bradwell-on-Sea, asserted, 'it was merry in England when there was better government, and if the queen die there will be a change and all those that be of the religion now used will be pulled out'—and hit the rector over the head with his cudgel. Gabriel Painter had avoided communion at Keynsham, Somerset, for eleven years at least, and was reported in 1605 because 'he doth maintain the real presence in the sacrament of the Lord's Supper'—Catholic doctrine.[10]

It is, inevitably, the noisier papists we know most about: those who drew attention to themselves or caused a nuisance. John Turner of Irthlingborough in Northamptonshire was cited in 1577 as 'an enemy to God's word, a whisperer in old men's and women's ears, a great nuzzler up of them in Romish and corrupt religion'—and Henry Bull was one of his followers, 'a fellow of the same sect of like religion, a stout champion and a maintainer of his master'. John Bent of Blackmore, Essex, was reported in 1584 as 'suspected much of papistry, for that he counselleth divers from reading the Bible, and affirming a carnal presence in the sacrament after the word spoken'. In 1598 Robert Siers of Brigstock, Northamptonshire, was 'a recusant and is ready to hurt many'—though it is not clear whether his menace was to souls or bodies. Mary Crabb of East Tilbury, Essex, was described in 1604 as 'altogether brought up in popery; she is a seducer of others as the common fame goeth, and conference will not prevail with her, she is obstinate and yet ignorant'. James Digby of North Luffenham, Northamptonshire, had meetings of Catholics in his house in 1605—and disturbed the Protestant service by blowing his horn in the churchyard.[11]

Historians tend to think of post-Reformation Catholics as quiescent—especially after the Gunpowder Plot in 1605—but there were still militants about. William Smith of Edlington, Lincolnshire, declared in 1606 that 'he which hold justification by faith only was a heretic and worse than a devil, and further he said that a man might fulfil the Commandments before God unblameably, for God had given him free will so to do'. Smith had also denied predestination and affirmed the Catholic doctrine of transubstantiation. When two priests were executed at Lincoln in June, he pronounced that they 'died not for treason but for their conscience, and wished that he might die as they died'—and when the vicar said that 'he was no good subject because he maintaineth doctrines of popery' and had refused to go to church on the anniversary of the plot, Smith sued him. John Taylor of Skirbeck was cited in 1607 as 'a seducer (as it is thought) to draw others to his acquaintance to hold a papistical opinion, and a great favourer of that sect'. In 1609 Dorothy Smith of Finchingfield, Essex, was a recusant and 'a common seducer' to popery, and, when the minister of Aisholt in Somerset preached against popish ceremonies that year, Henry Foxwell 'said he would meet him both with word and sword'. Robert Garnett, an alehouse-keeper of Stondon Massey, Essex, was presented in 1613 as 'a papistical recusant', and also for abusing the minister and churchwardens. Henry Bird of St Cuthbert's in Wells had been a recusant for four or five years by 1616, and the churchwardens were so fed up with his doings that they wanted the Oath of Allegiance put to him: he had persuaded Joan Whiting to have a crucifix, John Morgan to become a papist, and John Skeat to go on a pilgrimage 'to the pope his holy father'. And Charles Bawles of Peterborough was another persuasive Catholic, in 1621 'attempting to his power to seduce the simple and young ones by his speeches and popish books'.[12]

Some (at least nominal) Protestants were indeed enticed to popery. Richard Cottell of Christchurch, Hampshire, admitted in 1606 that he had been a recusant for three years: he denied that anyone had persuaded him, 'but pretended that his landlord took some hard courses with him and over-pressed him with over-hard dealing, and those were the chief motives for his recusancy'. If there was anything in his story, it was presumably that a Protestant landlord's lack of charity turned him from the state religion—but perhaps that was not a compelling reason for recusancy, and Cottell had already conformed to the Church of England by the time he appeared before the ecclesiastical commissioners. Personal grievances might be a motive for Catholicism, however: George Sandford of Bowers in Essex told the Colchester archdeaconry court in 1623 'that he was wronged by some of the parishioners in the church and therefore now he is turned a Romish Catholic, and that he hath been absent from church ever since Easter last'. Servants were especially vulnerable to persuasion. The churchwardens of Fairlight, Sussex, reported in 1639 that the recusants Richard and Clare Miles had taken as an apprentice Joan Sandes, 'which cometh not to church to divine service, being seventeen years of age, whom we suspect to be seduced by her master and dame'.[13]

There were losses as well as gains for Catholics. At York in 1576, two butchers' wives who had been recusants each said that 'she now cometh to church and so she is willing to do still'—though we do not know why they had conformed. Richard Davies of Orcheston in Wiltshire had been secretly married by an old Marian priest in Oxford gaol in 1589, and his child had a Catholic baptism—but in 1592 he told the consistory court that 'albeit he hath been heretofore remiss and careless in coming to church, he is now contented and hath reformed himself in that point'. Emma Cowdrell of Dorchester did not take communion at Easter 1593 'because she is not satisfied in conscience to receive the same, and further sayeth that she hath been a recusant but now she cometh to church'. In 1605 John Horney of Clevedon, Somerset, promised to attend church and receive communion, declaring 'that by some evil counsel he hath before this time been in some dislike of the religion now established within this kingdom, but he protesteth and giveth God thanks for the same that by resorting to sermons and attending the doctrine by them preached is now otherwise resolved'. This sounds like conversion, rather than enforced conformity—but it may have been a pretence, using the words a Protestant judge wanted to hear. Robert Porter of Wells was 'suspected to be popishly inclined and doth ordinarily in his conference with her majesty's subjects use reasons and arguments tending that way'—but in 1605 he attested that he was now attending church and would do so in future. In 1606 John Bayley of Somerton, Oxfordshire, affirmed that 'he hath refused the church but now is resolved to repair to the church and thereupon desireth absolution' from excommunication—and William Beckley of Wendlebury likewise requested absolution 'for that he is resolved in his conscience to repair unto the church'.[14] Perhaps the inconvenience of excommunication was proving too much.

Clergymen of the Church of England were sometimes optimistic that they could persuade Catholics into conformity or even conversion. When Arthur

Silvester and six others of Warblington, Hampshire, were presented for missing communion at Easter 1599, the rector attested that 'the said Silvester's wife and her mother are lately fallen backward in religion, but he hopeth to reclaim them again having had conference with them'. The curate of West Hanningfield, Essex, reported in April 1613 that Anne Clovely had agreed to confer with him and other ministers 'and that he hopeth that she will shortly be contented to come to her parish church'. It took longer than expected to bring her round, but when she was firmly instructed to conform in March 1616 the curate declared that 'he verily thinketh that she will'. In 1636 the rector of Faulkbourne reported that Master John Fortescue had promised him to receive communion and his wife to answer summonses—but neither kept their word. Some recusants could not be moved, whatever anyone said. Elizabeth Harmer of Wartling, Sussex, 'will not come to our church by any persuasions', said the wardens in 1638.[15]

There seems, however, to have been a surge towards conformity by former recusants between 1612 and 1615. Those Catholics who had been convicted of recusancy in the secular courts were (in theory) subjected to a fierce regime of monthly fines, and (again in theory) the only escape was by a formal submission and promise of conformity, certified to the Exchequer by a bishop. Nearly 870 certificates of conformity were recorded at the Exchequer between 1590 and 1625, with a sharp rise in the number of new conformists in 1612–15. Some former recusants had their conformity certified to the court of King's Bench, with by far the largest numbers occurring in 1614–15. The fining system was focused primarily on those who could pay, so the gentry are over-represented among certified conformists—but others were forced to conform too. Eight new conformists from Northamptonshire were reported to King's Bench in 1614–15, including John Seeley, a miller from Culworth. There were five from Dorset (a surgeon, a yeoman, and three husbandmen), and six from Somerset, including two yeomen and William and Jane Culliford of Queen Camel, though it was said that Jane had already been receiving communion 'for divers years'. It is very likely that the unusual numbers of new conformists in these years reflects a tightening of the fining system, so that more abandoned recusancy to avoid the financial burden: whether they abandoned their Catholic religion is another question. In 1627, however, the vicar and churchwardens of Norton Disney, Lincolnshire, certified that William Disney, formerly convicted as a recusant, had now conformed for twelve or thirteen years, attending sermons and receiving communion.[16]

Papists adopted a variety of ruses to avoid or delay conviction for recusancy and the heavy fines that might result. In 1583 Lawrence Cox of Otterbourne, Hampshire, went to be seen at church, but was not present for the actual service. Elizabeth Fisher went to Martyr Worthy church from time to time—'only to save the penalty of the statute', said the churchwardens in 1586. Former recusants who decided to go to church but would not receive communion were probably

Catholics seeking to avoid fines: William Lenthall of North Leigh, Oxfordshire, admitted in 1593 that 'he hath heretofore absented himself from church but he hath reformed himself thereof, but for the receiving of the communion he is not yet satisfied in his conscience'. In 1601 someone helpfully compiled a list of answers that recusants could give churchwardens when challenged over absence from church, without actually lying—'Think you that I live like an atheist?' 'Doubt you not but I will behave myself like a good Christian, and dutiful to God and my prince.' I may have to stay at home to look after a sick person, or if I am away on business I may go to another church. 'I may go to twenty places or churches, can you swear I go to none?' In 1603 William Bassett of Cheriton, Hampshire, claimed he 'doth usually frequent the church sometime at Kilmeston, sometime at Upham, and sometime at Owslebury': perhaps he did, but nobody checked. In 1607 the churchwardens of Cogenhoe, Northamptonshire, reported John Sharp,

which was presented heretofore for a recusant and after that he came once to our church, and then not long after sent word to our minister that he was removed to another parish, and for that cause neither we nor the minister did present him for not coming to our church, but now of late we hear that he is dwelling in that ground again and therefore with the consent of our minister we do present that he hath not yet communicated with us, nor any of his family.

In 1614 two Essex couples denied they were parishioners of Wanstead and declared that was why they had not been seen at church there for some years—but Robert Stephens at least was convicted of recusancy. Maurice Lund of Wells admitted in 1626 that he had not been to church for 'a long time', claiming he was in debt 'and therefore dareth not to go abroad for fear of arresting'. When he was ordered to receive communion he responded, 'I cannot do it, for I am to ride to London very shortly.' Anne Lund had also been absent from church 'a long time', and neither she nor Maurice certified that they had received as instructed, so it is likely that they were Catholics playing the system.[17]

It is hard to know if papists' promises to conform were genuine or merely tactical. In the Wells consistory in 1624, Christian Bussie of St Cuthbert's parish admitted her recusancy and also

[T]hat she hath offended God therein and in following the Romish religion, and that she is heartily sorry for the same and acknowledgeth that the bishop or see of Rome hath not nor ought to have any power or authority over the king's most excellent majesty or within his majesty's realms or dominions, and faithfully promised that without any dissimulation or any colour or means of any dispensation from henceforth she will from time to time obey and perform his majesty's laws and statutes in repairing to the church and hearing divine service, and to do her uttermost to maintain and defend the same.

This follows the prescribed official formula for conformity, and she was ordered to make the statutory declaration publicly during a service in church—so she probably meant to conform as the law required. But in 1626 Henry Hippesley's servant Mary Hill simply told the court 'that she hath been but now is no popish recusant', and Mary Phelps of Shapwick, Somerset, 'now promiseth to be more obedient and conformable and to frequent the church and receiving the sacraments there': perhaps they meant it, perhaps they did not. In April 1629 the curate of Irthlingborough, Northamptonshire, certified that Elizabeth Bryan 'being excommunicate [for] recusancy is desirous to be absolved and [to c]ome to church', and two local gentlemen asked for her to be absolved without fees, 'she being a poor man's wife'. Other cases seem rather more suspect. Rose Sorrell of Great Bardfield, Essex, sought absolution in 1635, and 'then the said Rose being presented for a popish recusant desired a competent time to be assigned to her to resolve herself'. She was given until Easter, but failed to certify her willingness to attend church. Similarly, in 1638 John Prince of Mapledurham, Oxfordshire, confessed 'that he doth not go to church because he is in conscience not satisfied in some points of religion held by the church of England, and therefore humbly prayed that he may have a time assigned to himself and his wife to advise with some divines to conform themselves'. There is no Oxford act book to tell us whether they conformed or not. Thomas Paul of Chipping Ongar, Essex, was more decisive: when he petitioned for absolution he declared 'that he was a Romish Catholic but is now become a Protestant, and so intendeth by God's grace to continue'. This was in 1640—when it was dangerous to be a Catholic in Essex.[18]

It was never easy to be a Catholic. How difficult it would be depended on who you were, where you were, when it was—and how determined you might be. But if Catholicism was hard, so was conformity. For a Catholic it meant bending the conscience, abandoning the faith of forefathers and friends, and joining the schismatics and heretics. In the mid 1580s a manuscript libel was circulating in Essex, bewailing the destruction of true religion and the rise of heresy and wickedness:

> Weep, weep and still I weep, for who can choose but weep
> To think how England still in sin and heresy doth sleep.
> The Christian faith and Catholic is everywhere detested,
> The holy service and suchlike of all degrees neglected.
> The sacraments are taken away and holy orders all,
> Religious men do beg astray, to ground their houses fall.
> The bishops and our pastors gone, our abbots all be dead,
> Dead, alas, alive not one, nor other in their stead.
> The churches gay defaced be, our altars are thrown down,
> The walls left bare, a grief to see, that once cost many a crown.
> The monuments and life of saints are burnt and torn by violence,
> Some shed the holy sacraments. Oh Christ, thy wondrous patience.
> The memory of Christ his death is rooting out apace,
> The joys above, the pains beneath in few men's hearts have place.
> Instead of these cometh tumbling in a gospel full of heresies,
> Wived goats their life of sin, their mouth of blasphemies.

Next, farewell virginity, let Venus have a place,
Come Bacchus, banish modesty, say Epicurus' grace.
For sacraments, a loaf of bread, good baker make it fine,
And tapster with thy drunken head, take heed we want no wine.
Now favour hindreth equity, and riches rule the roost,
In vain the poor cry 'Charity', 'God help you' say the most.
Now pride doth fit the fashion, and flattery can thrive,
Now truth doth miss the cushion, one fox can cozen five.
Oh time of times that ever have been, the wickedest I fear,
For less good fruits no age hath seen, nor more sins I dare swear.

And so on. This doggerel repeats the gist of Gifford's Papist's complaint to the Protestant: traditional religion is destroyed, the new religion is rank heresy, and Protestantism leads to licentiousness. The York recusants of 1576 would not attend church because the old worship had gone and the new was damnable; the Binkes brothers and William Smith declared that Protestantism was heretical; and Richard Cottell and George Sandford associated the state religion with lack of charity. In 1603 Henry Glascock of High Easter, Essex, was indicted for a comprehensive attack on Protestantism and 'professing knaves', arguing

[T]hat the pope of Rome is as good a Christian as any bishop in England, and he would join himself with him and his religion and with the Catholics before he would with the Protestants, and that bishops, ministers and priests lived lewdly in lechery, and that their marriage is unlawful and their children bastards, and he hoped to see the day when all the professors, these priests and protestantly slaves shall be trodden down, and when that day cometh I will not be the last but one of the first that shall cut the throats of them, and if I might have the blood of one of these priests I think it would be the means whereby I should enjoy heaven.[19]

Whatever some Catholics may have thought, whatever some may have said in anger or frustration, they had to coexist with the Protestants. Papist had to live alongside Asunetus, Antilegon, and Philagathus—though he probably tried to avoid Theologus as much as possible. Catholics too were part of the parish community, and church and churchyard might feature in their lives too. In 1630 Anne Allum of St Michael's, Oxford, was 'presented for a recusant'. She told the consistory 'that she hath always been brought up in the Romish religion and came not to church to hear divine service except when she was married and when she was churched after her delivery of child'. Perhaps rites of passage were public celebrations, not heretical services. There were sound legal reasons why marriage in church was more secure, but it is striking that Anne was churched before she went out among her neighbours. The secret burial of Catholics in church or churchyard is much more often recorded. The vicar and wardens of Desborough, Northamptonshire, reported in 1607 that Dorothy Weston 'died the 11th of April, being a popish recusant this three years, but we know not where she was buried; the grave was made in the churchyard, but we cannot of a certainty say she was buried there'. In 1611 a number of parishioners of Tisbury, Wiltshire, papists and others, assisted in the midnight burial of an excommunicate recusant, using the parish bier to carry the body to the churchyard. Thomas Little, 'a papist excommunicate', was buried by his family and friends in the churchyard of Littlebury, Essex, in 1618, and in 1628 Anthony Warwick, with relations and servants, buried his recusant wife at night in Flore churchyard, Northamptonshire. In 1634 Grace Worsley, another excommunicate recusant, was buried in the churchyard at Castle Cary, Somerset, apparently with the agreement of the churchwardens.[20]

Burials of Catholics inside now-Protestant churches is more surprising: recusants who would not go to a church when alive were put there by their relatives when dead. Mrs Haselrigg was buried at night in the chancel of Arthingworth, Northamptonshire, in 1600, and Master Hasper sent two of his servants along to help. In 1607 the wife of Robert Syres of Isham was buried in the chancel, 'she being a popish recusant and excommunicate': Robert swore that 'he doth not know whether she be buried there or no, but he sayeth he thinketh she is'. It seems that Catholic corpses were usually left where they had been buried, but not always. Just before Christmas 1620 the body of Nicholas Estmond, another excommunicate recusant, was secretly buried at night in Chardstock church, Dorset: after consulting local justices and 'chiefest divines of our country adjoining', the vicar and wardens had the coffin removed 'and have placed it in a remote place of our churchyard, without the bounds of Christian burial'. Here the minister and churchwardens were deliberately denying what Estmond's family or friends had wanted: that he should rest with fellow Christians in consecrated ground—but they nevertheless allowed the body to remain within the bounds of the churchyard. In 1625, the wardens of Little Sampford, Essex, said they did not know who had buried Mrs Greene, 'a papist excommunicate', in their church, and that seems to have been that. As far as we know, Mrs Greene stayed where she had been put.[21]

When the excommunicated Mistress Horseman of Wheatley, Oxfordshire, died on New Year's Eve 1630, her servants, neighbours, and friends tried to give her the customary send-off. The bells of Holton church were rung, there was a supper in her honour, and permission was sought from the rector of Holton and the chancellor of the diocese for her burial in the church. When permission was refused, Mrs Horseman was secretly buried under the communion table on Twelfth Night—and, in the face of an exhaustive investigation by Church authorities, there was a conspiracy of silence to cover those who had done it. Not only had the Catholic woman wished for burial in Holton church, but her neighbours made sure she got it and then protected those who had done the deed.[22] Certainly desire for a body to rest in consecrated ground was a key consideration in these cases, but it seems likely that membership of the community was an issue too—papists or not. Lesser Catholics should be buried in the churchyard, those of higher status in church or chancel as befitted their rank—and Mistress Horseman under the communion table. That was what

Catholics wanted, and, at least in some places, enough non-Catholics wanted them to have it too.

In Gifford's 1582 dialogue, the Protestant spokesman complains that many people don't take the Catholic threat seriously enough: 'Some will say, wherefore should we eschew them, being honest?'—why can't we just get along with the good papists? In William Redman's bakery at Lyde in Somerset in 1605, there was a discussion about papists and especially Henry Foxwell. Some of the customers said they didn't like him because he would not go to church with the rest, but Redman stood up for him—'I think in my conscience he liveth a better life than we do.' When asked why he thought so, Redman replied, 'Marry, ... because he keepeth every fasting day and holy day better than we do.' Mary Lyne was not impressed: 'He keepeth holy days and fasting days better than the Sabbath day, but he will be seen unto well enough I warrant you'—he would get his deserts, she thought, because he would not go to church. Redman pointed out that Foxwell had been in trouble about his religion before, but had always managed to escape penalties. Redman's view was the one that Gifford's Protestant objected to: there's not much wrong with a good papist; Mary Lyne shared Protestant's opinion: there's no such thing as a good papist.[23]

The importance of anti-popery as a shared ideology among English Protestants has been well established, and the 'deliverances' of 1558, 1588, 1605, and 1623 assumed mythic significance. God had showed his favour in saving England from the Marian persecution, the Spanish Armada, the Gunpowder Plot, and the Spanish Match: he had declared himself against popery and papists. There is certainly evidence of grass-roots hostility towards Catholics. By 1571 the aged, unmarried rector of Penton Mewsey, Hampshire, had had enough of it: 'I am called papist, and so hooted that I am disposed to marry'—so he proposed to wed his servant Lucy Deane, and prove he was a Protestant minister and not a celibate Catholic priest. Florence Cole of Ash Priors, Somerset, was 'suspected to be a papist' in 1577 because she had given an old man a penny to pray for her husband's soul. Seven parishioners of Clavering, Essex, were cited in 1585 for not seeking absolution after excommunication, 'whereupon we do greatly suspect that they are reconciled to the Romish religion'. Perhaps people were on the lookout for Catholics and wanted them dealt with, as Mary Lyne of Lyde did in 1605. Robert Parratt of Hanslope, Buckinghamshire, was cited in 1607 'for very negligent or seldom coming to his parish church, whereby he giveth vehement suspicion that he is inclined to popish religion'. When Thomas Morton was observed in Axminster, Somerset, to wear an ornament round his neck in 1620, it added to suspicion that he was a Catholic and he was questioned by locals on whether it was a crucifix. In 1622 the churchwardens of Winterborne Kingston, Dorset, reported William Bezant's wife 'for holding popish opinions, as the fame goeth, who (as is reported) when she received the Lord's Supper took the bread out of her mouth and would not eat it'. When the recusant Abington family moved to Rye in Sussex in 1624, the mayor and jurats asked if they could send them away—'we desire not the company of any of that religion, if possibly we may lawfully avoid them'. The wardens of Westham named sixteen Catholics who refused communion in 1639, protesting, 'We have often complained and presented the papists, but nothing is done against them.' When the Catholic Anne Freele was buried at Rye in 1641 and the minister used the Prayer Book reference to 'our dear sister', Samuel Jeake protested, 'Nay, she was an infidel for being a papist, for they deny the faith of us Christians and cleave to the covenant of works.' 'What fellowship hath righteousness with unrighteousness?' Jeake asked. But there was not always such hostility. On Ascension Day in 1612, John Wood of North Petherton, Somerset, 'led the horse of one Capper, a recusant, into the church porch, telling the said Capper saying "If thou wilt not go to the church, thy horse shall!"' Wood was, admittedly, a little drunk, and, when he stumbled at the porch threshold, he swore at the horse and the women watching. But Capper's recusancy was something to laugh about, a local oddity as much as an affront to Protestants.[24]

Bishop Chadderton of Lincoln complained in August 1605 that it was difficult to get parishioners to report recusants: 'there is no man will become an accuser of his neighbours unless he be very malicious or be charged upon his oath by authority'. The recusants were papists, yes, but they were neighbours, even friends. In some places, there was a world-weary acceptance of Catholics as an unavoidable fact of life. When Mary Wolfe of Graffham, Sussex, was presented in 1613 for abusing the rector, the churchwardens explained that 'she hath been nuzzled and brought up amongst the papists about Midhurst'—so what could you expect? Thomas Vinton of Beauchamp Roding, Essex, was furious at his neighbours' tolerance of papists in the parish. In 1634 he hoped to get the parson deprived of his benefice and a churchwarden punished for neglect of duty, saying he 'cared not though he set all the parish together by the ears for he would be gone, he could live in another country as well as here'. But he was in a minority, it seems: the rest were willing to leave the Catholics alone.[25]

For Gifford's Protestant character, Catholics were traitors: 'Let all the people of this land consider thus, and shun such filthy and abominable men.' Papists were to be spurned, sent to Coventry if not to the gallows. Others did not see things that way. In 1607 John Bonney, one of the churchwardens of Lowick, Northamptonshire, was a servant of the recusant Master John Staughton, and the rector complained that Bonney consorted with other recusants and rang the church bells on saints' days with them. The wardens of Little Oakley reported in 1612 that their minister Master Austin and his wife Anne had dined on New Year's Day at Sir Thomas Tresham's house, in company with Elizabeth Bull, an excommunicate recusant, and that Mrs Austin often visited Elizabeth. In 1619 twenty-six people from Earls Barton, Ecton, and Wellingborough were presented for attending a wedding feast in the presence of Christopher Lewis and his wife, excommunicate recusants. In 1623 the vicar of Rothwell cited Owen Harrison and sixteen other parishioners for sending their children to be taught by Richard Douse, another excommunicate recusant. Clearly, some clergy and churchwardens were reporting such breaches of ecclesiastical rules, but other parishioners thought that religious differences should not prevent normal social relationships and customary decencies. In 1631 Richard Goodyear of Wolvercote near Oxford had no difficulty in organizing the burial of his mother, an excommunicate papist. The curate performed the service, and 'all or the most part of the parishioners of Wolvercote were at the burying of his said mother'. When in 1633 Cornelius Simpkin from Hanslope in Buckinghamshire met on the road a youth who seemed to know the Digby family, he enquired if 'he was of the old religion', and they exchanged news. Even the godly Robert Woodford of Northampton managed to put up with papists. In 1638 he travelled with a Catholic and 'used what arguments I could to convince him of his error, and prayed unto the Lord in his behalf'. In 1639 he had supper at a Catholic household, and suspected that the man who sat next to him was a priest in disguise.[26]

So we have examples of marked hostility towards Catholics, and examples of a cautious tolerance of them. There are various explanations for this. Probably it was the more committed Protestants, the godly, who saw papists as enemies of God and servants of Spain: papists were idolators, traitors, and liars, who schemed to overthrow true religion and God's anointed princes. That was Gifford's Protestant's view of them, but he complained that others did not share it. Perhaps the less-godly did not have this binary vision of the world, divided between the forces of good and the forces of evil: perhaps they regarded papists as quirky individuals, men and women with a few odd ideas but essentially harmless. The more hostile and the more tolerant were probably different people. Another explanation is that while the unseen machinations of unknown papists were a threat, the papists one knew had shown themselves innocent—they were the good papists, the papists one might dine with. Only in special circumstances were the good papists and the bad papists elided: there were particular times when all papists seemed dangerous, when no chances should be taken—as during the Armada crisis, or in the months following the Gunpowder Plot. There were Catholic scares that could mobilize the wider community behind the anti-papist godly, especially, it seems, at times of political crisis or uncertainty.[27]

As a war with Spain began in the autumn of 1625, the deputy lieutenants of Buckinghamshire were worried by rumours of suspicious gatherings and stockpiling of arms at the houses of recusants, 'the country being much amazed and affrighted'. They looked back to earlier dangers, in 1588 and 1605: 'this present repair is thought to have exceeded those others which did fore-run the attempts both of the Spanish invasion and the gunpowder treason'—the Catholics were preparing for a Spanish-backed rebellion again, they feared. In April 1633, as the king prepared for his visit to Scotland, similar stories of popish plotting swept through Buckinghamshire and Northamptonshire. Two separate rumours came together. One was a tale in Buckinghamshire that a wagonload of armour had been delivered to the Catholic Lady Digby's house at Gayhurst; the other was a prediction that the papists would attempt a massacre of Protestants during the king's absence. The second originated with a story in Huntingdonshire, that when the king went to Scotland the Scots would keep him there and the English would have to fight to get him back. This turned into a fear that 'there would be much hurly-burly in England' in the king's absence—and was twisted into a scare about a Catholic uprising and carried into Buckinghamshire by a travelling mole-catcher. The mole-catcher, young Henry Sawyer, told men he met on the road near Gayhurst on 20 April 'that the king was to go into Scotland the fifth of May next and then the papists after the king's going would rise against the Protestants'. 'Suppose that men should go over their shoe tops in blood before Whitsuntide, so near as it is,' he added, and 'it was to be doubted that many Protestants and papists would lose their lives before that day.' The two tales became one, that the papists were gathering arms for a rising, and the story spread. It soon reached Northampton, where the rector of Greens Norton heard it from an attorney: he passed it on to his colleague the parson of Alderton—who took the story back to Northampton and reported it to the mayor on 26 April. By then, the rumour was everywhere around, and it was harder 'to find those who had not reported it than to produce reporters'. Local justices traced the rumour back to Henry Sawyer and tried to scotch it—but for a week there had been a major panic over a papist insurrection.[28]

There were further fears in Northamptonshire six years later. Late in March 1639 Robert Woodford of Northampton recorded, 'The times in the apprehension of all seem to be very doubtful, and many fears we have of dangerous plots by French and papists.' There was a full-scale panic at Kettering in April—when the recruitment of levies to fight the rebellious Scots was causing anxiety and local tensions. There was a rumour that a papist had hired two workmen to set fire to the town, and John Sawyer and his godly allies organized an extra watch, with eight men on duty day and night 'for fear of papists'. On Sunday, 7 April, some men went to church armed with swords and pistols, and set lookouts on the church roof and tower 'to discover any soldiers or soldier-like men or company who came towards the town'. On the next two Sundays, men again went armed to services, 'for fear lest the papists should surprise them in church'. Robert Sibthorpe, rector of nearby Burton Latimer, thought the scare was got up by Sawyer and others—but he was prone to conspiracy theories: 'I live in the midst of the faction, who are too many and too mighty for me.' Whatever the cause, however, the fear spread, and on Maundy Thursday few came to Kettering fair. It was a typical anti-Catholic panic—in a heightened political atmosphere, there was a scare that hitherto peaceful Catholics were then about to massacre the Protestants.[29]

The Scottish wars and the political instability that came with them sharpened suspicion of Catholics. Late in May 1640, three weeks after the dissolution of the

Short Parliament, there was a scare in Colchester that 'raised almost the whole town, men, women and children, and put them into a very great amazement and fright'. It was rumoured that two Irishmen were planning to fire the town, and two little girls had seen them peering into a house through a hole in the wall—which led to suspicion that they would 'throw in some wildfire'. The mayor and aldermen strengthened the watch on the gates, had the constables search the town for Irishmen, and called out forty men from the trained bands to patrol the streets. Next morning, there were stories that 'a great number of papists were assembled' at a nearby manor house (which one was not clear), and the youth of the town gathered to march off to challenge them. Early in June it was said in Oxford that papists were holding suspicious meetings at the Mitre, where the innkeeper himself was a recusant—which led to a sharp rebuke from the Privy Council to the major and aldermen for allowing such gatherings.[30]

At Rye in Sussex in mid September 1640 (after Newcastle had fallen to the Scots and the king had called a Great Council of peers to meet at York), there were further scares about armed papists. Again, there were two related stories—that another wagonload of armour had been delivered to the house of Mr Thomas Threele outside the town, and that papist musketeers had been seen drilling in Threele's fields. Three boys claimed they had seen thirty-one men 'with their muskets and bandoliers', and the mayor called out the trained band to guard the town, 'which was in a great fear'. It was then rumoured that a justice had gone to search Threele's house and been refused entry: in fact, the justice and Rye's leaders had searched the house, and found nothing unusual—a few old guns, and no more men than the household servants. The mayor and jurats tried to calm matters by issuing an explanatory testimonial for Threele, 'who, although he be a recusant convict and therefore maketh fine to his majesty, yet for that he hath always (so far as we know) carried and demeaned himself peaceably and quietly in the commonwealth, and friendly and lovingly to his majesty's subjects of all sorts that live near about him'.[31]

At Kettering the terror was of unknown papists, and at Colchester there was a suspicion of nondescript Irishmen. But there were also fears that particular local Catholics were gathering forces against true Protestants. In 1633 Buckinghamshire and Northamptonshire were afraid of Lady Digby. In 1640 Colchester was in a panic about Lady Audley and Master Barker, Oxford about Green the innkeeper, and Rye about Thomas Threele. In uncertain times, peaceable local Catholics could become dangerous enemies: the reality of the quiet neighbour was replaced by the bogey of the malignant Romanist, servant of Antichrist. Gifford's Protestant asserts that Catholics are traitors because the Pope has absolved them from obedience to the queen and they plot against her: Papist replies, 'it is one thing to commit treason against a prince which is godly, and another thing to kill an heretic which is no lawful prince'. Protestant seizes on this as an admission of popish guilt: 'Let all men see that your kingdom is not of God, which ye uphold by treasons, perjuries, lies, murders and all evil means.' So Papist and Protestant part in bad temper. 'Well, another time I will be better provided for ye,' declares Papist. 'I pray God disclose all your traitorous practices and repress your cruelty, and otherwise provide what ye can,' is the patriotic Protestant's answer. Political fears had got in the way of civil coexistence.[32]

10

Enemies of the Godly

So far in this book, we have used dialogues and other texts as tools towards an investigation of grass-roots religious attitudes in post-Reformation England. We have seen the views expressed by literary characters replicated in the real world of English parishes, and we have heard the arguments and hostilities of the texts repeated in streets, shops, and alehouses—and in churches. But we have to be very careful. The authors of our texts were not anthropologists or sociologists, trying to describe the thoughts and habits of the people around them. They were evangelists and polemicists: they wrote at particular times, in particular contexts, and for particular purposes. The books have political contexts and objectives, as well as their more obvious religious purposes—and their characters were deliberately created to serve political ends.

When George Gifford published his *Country Divinity* in 1581, he was a curate at Maldon in Essex. He had already been prosecuted in 1575 for failing to take communion at his own parish church (perhaps to avoid kneeling), and for preaching that people should follow what ministers said and not what they did. The archbishop of Canterbury had been suspended since 1577 for his defence of evangelical preaching, the queen was trying to contain what she regarded as disruptive preaching, and bishops were pressed to proceed against nonconforming clergy. Later, Gifford was again in trouble, for refusing to wear a surplice and not following the Prayer Book, and he was himself suspended from preaching. So the supply of effective preachers and the silencing of nonconformist preachers were serious worries for the godly—and Gifford wrote his book. His dedication to the earl of Warwick makes his worries clear. He blames the corruptions of Church and commonwealth on the shortage of preachers—'the want of a sincere ministry of the word'. His book is to be an illustration of the problems that have arisen in England: 'there are the most in number who, having popery taken from them and not taught thoroughly and sufficiently in the Gospel, do stand as men indifferent, so that they may quietly enjoy the world, they care not what religion come'. And there is a heavy hint that the Church of Christ cannot combat popery unless Warwick and other privy councillors set the queen right: 'She [the Church] cannot but most humbly crave his duty at the hands of those that are near about her dear nurse', Elizabeth.[1]

In *The Country Divinity*, Gifford's Atheos serves as a living proof of what happens where there is no preaching: popery survives in the mind. Atheos thinks his village curate is 'the best priest in this country': 'Sir R' reads the services carefully, he reconciles quarrelling parishioners, he sets a good example, and 'he will not stick when good fellows and honest men meet together to spend his groat in the alehouse'. But he does not preach, so he cannot promote in Atheos a saving Protestant faith. Atheos still believes he will be saved by prayers and charitable acts, as if he were a Catholic. He protests that there is too much preaching in the land, too much Bible-reading, too much division and disruption, too much discipline by 'busy controllers', too many who claim to know they are saved: 'I see that popish dung doth stick between your teeth,' retorts godly Zelotes. Atheos is outraged to be accused of popery: 'What tell ye me of the pope, I care not for him, I would both he and his dung were buried in the dunghill!' But Zelotes is not impressed: 'I know there be many which care not for the pope, but yet believe much of his doctrine.' 'All you atheists which have no knowledge of God are crammed as full of popish dross as ye can hold,' Zelotes declares later. For Gifford, the author, this is perhaps the key argument of his book: those who are not proper Protestants are as good (or rather, as bad) as papists—they have not shaken off popery, and they are still prey to popery. This was in 1581, when Catholic missionary priests were active in England, and the first Jesuits had only recently arrived. Popery had not been defeated. And in 1582 Gifford published *A Dialogue between a Papist and a Protestant, Applied to the Capacity of the Unlearned*: his dedication to the earl of Sussex argued that although Protestant scholars had refuted the papists, 'it doth not so well serve the turn of the simple unlearned man'. The dialogue opens with news of the debate in the Tower of London between Edmund Campion, one of the earliest Jesuits in England, and Protestant theologians—'I hear he behaved himself very learnedly and with great victory against all which were set upon him,' says Papist. So Gifford wants more Protestant preaching—and he wants more preaching because without it, he thinks, the people are still papists at heart.[2]

Despite his hatred for the Pope, Atheos still hankers for aspects of the popish past. 'I will follow our forefathers. Now there is no love, then they lived in friendship and made merry together; now there is no good neighbourhood, now every man for himself, and are ready to pull one another by the throat,' he complains. Zelotes asks if many others agree with him, and Atheos tells him, 'Yes, the greatest part. For I know almost none but they will affirm this matter.' Atheos did not want the Pope again, perhaps he did not want the Mass again—but he was sure that, all in all, things had been better before. And he was probably right that 'the greatest part' agreed. This nostalgia was widely shared, especially among the elderly, and Protestantism ('the new religion') was blamed for making things worse. In 1565 a preacher at St Paul's Cross complained that 'the husbandman sayeth there was never a good year since the gospel came into England', and Richard Greenham later protested against those who were still saying 'the gospel hath brought dearth, diseases and war'. In the early 1570s Robert Middlam of Burnham in Somerset was wailing, 'It was never merry in England since this new law began, and never will be so long as it doth last', and in 1577 John Howard told a bunch of servants at Bocking in Essex, 'It was never merry in England sithence the Scriptures were so commonly preached, and talked upon among such persons as they were.' 'It was never merry since men unlearned have meddled with the Scriptures,' said Atheos, and Philip Day of Ditcheat, Somerset, declared as late as 1634 'that it was not lawful nor fit for laymen to read the Bible, and that it was never well since they did read it'. 'It was a merry world when the service was used in the Latin tongue,' thought David Browne of East Tilbury, Essex, in 1581, 'and now we are in an evil way and going to the devil.' John Field caught the nostalgic mood of the older generation, and mocked it:

They say the mass is nought, but I cannot tell. Then we had a merry world, and all things plenty. Oh, since I can remember, what mirth there was in towns, in our villages and wakes, what good fellowship, when no man's wife was in safety, when few men's daughters were married virgins, and as for men's servants, they had more mirth then in a day than they have now in a hundred.

Francis Trigge complained in 1589 that it was generally held 'that our times are unhappy and miserable, and that the former days, the days of our fathers, were happy and very blessed, very calm and prosperous'. In 1610 Hugh Holland of King's Sutton in Northamptonshire was saying 'the world was never merry since priests were married'.[3]

It was a long time indeed before people got used to married clergy, and learned to be polite to their wives. Proper Protestants approved of clerical marriage, but Gifford feared there weren't enough proper Protestants around. The rector of Minstead in the New Forest complained in 1566 that 'some of the parishioners there cannot brook that he should have any wife', and about 1572 Robert Middlam, already mentioned, was saying 'that never an honest woman in England would marry with any priest or bishop'. Robert Long of Salcott, Essex, declared 'that ministers' wives were whores and their children bastards'—and had to do public penance in 1571 on two Saturdays at the market and two Sundays in church, to teach him and others better. In 1577 Richard Turvill of Newent, Gloucestershire, 'discommendeth the marriage of priests, and sayeth their children be not legitimate', and William Wood of Oxenhall was in trouble 'for misliking with priests' marriages'—'he confessed that he had said he would ride his horse forty miles to make a priest cuckold'. 'Priest's whore' was now a standard insult whenever anyone got into an argument with a minister's wife, with occasional variations into 'priest's jade' (1578), 'drab and jade' (1612), and 'blackamore jade' (1619). Perhaps these terms were losing their particular sting, but there remained a certain unease about clerical wives and offspring. In 1607 Frances Bradshaw of Rushton, Northamptonshire, was presented for 'scolding and brawling speeches, that she scorned but to be honester than any parson's wife in England'. Henry Sholeford told the wife of the rector of Exford, Somerset, in 1618, 'I am as well born as thou art, thou art but a priest's child, and I do hold a priest's child, a priest's brat, and a priest's chat to be all one, brat and chat'. In 1634 a group of women from Shiplake, Oxfordshire, were discussing their vicar's prospective bride, and Isabel Cotton said the girl 'was in a dangerous case, speaking the proverb that she that put her leg into the parson's bed did put her foot into hell'.[4]

If a few blamed the marriage of ministers for the decay of all things, many more blamed the preachers. 'It was a merry world before there was so much preaching,' said Joan Greene of Welton in Northamptonshire in 1584. 'It was never merry world since there were so many puritans and such running to sermons as there is now,' complained the Papist character in a Marprelate dialogue, and ungodly Ananias, in Thomas Turvill's later debate, agreed: 'it was never merry since there was so much preaching and so many controllers'. 'The simple sort, which can no[t] skill of doctrine, speak of the merry world when there was less preaching, and when all things were so cheap that they might have twenty eggs for a penny,' said the Protestant in Gifford's 1582 dialogue—though John Bate's Autophilus thought he could have had 'as many eggs for a penny as would serve him half a dozen meals'. Thomas Stoughton of Billericay in Essex had heard too much of this sort of thing:

> Yea, but methinks I hear one object the great plenty that was in the time of popery, when one might buy twenty-four eggs for a penny, a good cow for a noble or eight shillings, an ox for a mark, a sheep for twenty pence, a bushel of wheat for four or six pence. And that sithence this new religion (for which I now plead) came up there was never such plenty, neither was it ever so merry with us.

It seems that eggs were the key ingredient in the popular price index, and eggs had got much dearer—so the world was getting worse. Arthur Dent's Asunetus was a nostalgia-monger too, blaming expensive modern fashions for 'covetousness, oppression and deceit'. The old days of merriment and neighbourliness had gone, and the 'busy controllers' were getting their way.[5]

There was too much novelty, and not enough respect for old values and the way things used to be. In 1568 the churchwardens of Trowbridge, Wiltshire, admitted they that were not keeping a poor box as instructed, 'but the poor of the parish are better relieved with our devotion and better contented there withal than they should be if it were so kept'. Other parishes made the same point. At Wantage, Berkshire, in 1582 the wardens were saying it again: there was no poor rate, 'but we think the poor are better relieved at our houses than they should be by any such collection'. Traditional private charity was better than enforced rates and newfangled poor boxes. John Fry of Bedhampton, Hampshire, asked for help from the Virgin Mary in 1570. William Dowtie of Moreton, Essex, thought there was no harm in swearing 'by the Mass' in 1572—it was just a manner of speaking. Gifford's Atheos swore 'By my faith', and our old friend Asunetus swore 'by St Mary'. It was hard to make people change their ways—and especially to stop them praying for the dead. Thomas Allen told the preacher at Wing,

Northamptonshire in 1579, 'If we may not be prayed for when we are dead, then God help us.' In 1592 John Pulford of Horningsham in Wiltshire said that praying to the saints was a good remedy for sickness—but the churchwardens thought he might have been drunk. William Wolgar of Fareham, Hampshire, just couldn't get used the singing of metrical psalms, and protested in 1583 that they should not be allowed in the service.[6] When George Gifford wrote *The Country Divinity* in 1581, the vestiges of popery were all around—not just in some of the rituals of the new Church, but in the hearts of its people. So Atheos was constructed as a superstitious Catholic dressed up as a loyal Protestant: strip away the fancy loyalist dress, says Gifford, and you will find a papist underneath. The enemy is with us, and within us.

Twenty years later, things seemed different—when Arthur Dent wrote *The Plain Man's Pathway* in 1601. There, ignorant Asunetus and cavilling Antilegon were not crypto-papists, they were Protestants of a sort: they knew they would be saved through Christ's death and by faith in him. Papists were mentioned here and there in the book as holding different views from Protestants—but popery was not the problem. After all, most of those who remembered the old days with affection were now dead. Instead, godly Philagathus found worldliness and indifference rife among 'hollow-hearted hypocrites': 'Their heart is with atheism, their heart is with popery: they have a pope in their belly; they be church-papists'—they go to church, 'yet their heart goeth after covetousness'. This appropriation of the language of anti-popery is striking: the worldling's pope is not now in Rome, he is in the stomach; the worldly man goes to church not to hide his Catholicism but to hide his indifference to religion. By 1601, it seems, the preachers thought they had defeated the old enemy, popery, but they had not defeated materialism and profanity. Asunetus and Antilegon did not mouth watered-down Catholicism, as Atheos had done; instead, they mouthed watered-down Protestantism—it's all too difficult for us, do we really have to try so hard? 'As for sermons, they care not how few they hear. And for the Scriptures, they regard them not, they read them not, they esteem them not worth the while,' complained Master Theologus.[7]

Lack of religion and the depravity of mankind are common enough themes among Christian writers, but they were particularly prominent in the last years of Queen Elizabeth's reign. In 1595 the Reading preacher William Burton published seven sermons on 'the rousing of the sluggard'—the need to awaken the lazy Christian. 'What shall we find but in the most of them through the land a general numbness and apostasy, having put off the shoes of preparation for all kinds of vanity, preferring plays before preaching, tables and cards before the Old and New Testament.' Godliness was thought an oddity, he protested: 'What, are you so precise? Why, this is but a little oath, a little merriment, a little of the fashion,' was what people said. In 1596 Josias Nichols warned his readers that religion, morals, and good order were in decline: 'The great carelessness and coldness (that I say not contempt) of religion may hereby appear, that atheism, drunkenness and other very great sins are waxen bold and shameless'. 'For now the world abounds with atheists, epicures, libertines, worldlings, neuters that are of no religion, and sundry that have heretofore showed some forwardness begin to fall and stagger and look another way,' declared the favourite theologian of the godly, William Perkins. 'We in England have heard the calling of God more than forty years, and yet very few of us are moved to change and amend our lives. This shows our atheism and unbelief: here is almost nothing but heaving, shoving and lifting for the world.'[8]

Well, people are like that—and preachers are like that. People will do as they do, and preachers will preach as they preach, whatever. But irreligion seemed especially shocking in Elizabeth's last years, because God had spoken and the English had not listened. God had sent his warnings—threats of invasion from Spain, military failures in Ireland, crime and disorder at home, high unemployment, poor harvests, inflation, and disease—what more could he say? And still the worldly had not heard him. Edmund Topsell thought the country was going to the dogs in 1596: 'Such pollution of sabbaths as never was, yea even in this time of dearth and famine; drinking and drunkenness, dancing and riot, feasting and surfeiting, chambering and wantonness, swearing and forswearing, accounting gain for godliness and godliness to be the burden of the world, with a thousand greater and more grievous calamities.' By 1601, when Dent wrote *The Plain Man's Pathway*, things were not quite so bad. Harvests had improved, prices had dropped somewhat, and the Spanish had not come: Ireland was still a mess, though Ireland always was. But there was factionalism at the royal court, there were rumours of corruption among the politicians, the old queen seemed to be losing her grip, crime levels were thought still to be high—and people were slack in their religion. 'I think the Gospel was never so openly condemned in any age (of a people living under the profession of it and under a godly and Christian prince) as it is in this age,' wailed Theologus. So Dent wrote his book: 'This book meddleth not at all with any controversies in the Church, or anything in the state ecclesiastical, but only entereth into a controversy with Satan and sin.'[9] Or so he said. But his stress on the role of a dedicated ministry and powerful preaching in the scheme of salvation had political implications for a regime that demanded conformity from its clergy—and suspended the disobedient preachers.

We cannot tell if the ministers were right about the growing carelessness in religion, and for our purposes it does not much matter. For, as we have already seen, there was enough carelessness about to persuade them they were right. Henry Enewe walked out of a service at Coggeshall, Essex, in 1595, 'and being admonished to tarry service he answered he had business to do'. In 1608 Widow Wager, of Woodham Walter, 'being sundry times admonished to come to church, she made answer that she would come when she had leisure'. When Thomas Little of Great Burstead was reproved by the churchwardens in 1616 for driving his cattle in sermon time, he 'gave them very bad and unseeming

speeches, saying that he would come to church when he listed himself'. Robert
Smith of East Hornden would not come 'but when he list himself', and Hayward
of Harwich 'but when he listed', both in 1621. Robert Fryer of Ingrave was
caught fishing on Whit Sunday 1624 when he should have been at church,
and when reminded that he had not been to services for eight weeks 'answered
that he would be absent eighteen weeks, do he what he could'. Robert Grey of
Springfield was challenged over his absence from evening service on 1 August
1632, but 'he in a chafing manner answered that he was there in the forenoon
and it might hap he would be there the next Sunday'. Robert Hatch was late
for a service at Earl's Colne in 1633, and told the wardens that 'he would come
when he listed', and, when a warden went to Grisell Gardner's house in Elmsted
in 1634 to persuade her to go to church, she retorted 'that she was there a
fortnight ago and she would come when she list for all such a knave as he was'.
Master Theologus had wanted godly attentiveness to the demands of religion,
but what he often got was nonchalance: 'I marvel what good men get by gadding
to sermons and pouring so much in the Scriptures,' said Antilegon, 'or what, are
they better than others?'[10]

For George Gifford in 1581, the enemy of true religion was false religion:
popery. For Arthur Dent in 1601 the dangerous enemy was not false religion
but irreligion: worldliness. But by the late 1620s Robert Bolton thought the
main enemy was anti-religion: hostility to godliness. Bolton knew all about
anti-religion, for he had been there himself. As a student and a young lecturer
at Oxford, he had despised godliness and the godly: he 'could not abide their
company that were of a strict and holy conversation,' wrote his pupil, friend, and
biographer Edward Bagshawe. Bolton had 'loved stage-plays, cards and dice, he
was a horrible swearer and Sabbath-breaker and boon-companion'—an educated
Antilegon. In Bagshawe's biography, the young Bolton was an archetypal anti-
puritan, and Bagshawe may have exaggerated for literary effect the contrast
with Bolton's pious life and godly teaching after his conversion in about 1609.
Nevertheless, Bolton certainly knew the temptations of worldliness—and he
knew the danger of popery too, since he came from Catholic Lancashire and had
almost become a Catholic priest. But when he adopted the voice of common
Christians, when he quoted what the profane had to say for themselves, it was
their hostility to the godly that was most prominent. Such people were always
on the lookout to damn the godly. They accused any 'religious professor' of
'surliness and pride'—'You see now what these professors are … , they are even
all alike.' 'This it is now to be so bookish, to follow preachers so much, to be
more holy than their neighbours, never to have done with serving of God. Her so
much reading the Scriptures, and such pouring over precise books … hath made
her stark mad: "The puritan is beside herself." '[11]

It was this use of the word 'puritan' that now enraged Bolton—perhaps
because at Oxford he too had dismissed the godly as 'puritans'. He now saw it as
a trick that the profane used to discredit godliness as spiritual pride and so excuse

their own sinful lives: 'through the name of puritan, by a malicious equivocation, they strike at the very heart of grace and the power of godliness'. He had associated this usage with the alehouse counter-culture of 'good fellowship'—' "He was a good fellow", will they say, "but he is now quite gone; a proper man, and of good parts, but his puritanism hath marred all".' Poor chap, he has got religion and gone puritan. Such 'good fellows, as they call them' had their own value system: ' "We", say they, "are plain-dealing men, and appear as we are; we are flesh and blood and must have our pleasures, and therefore refresh ourselves at merry and jovial meetings. We swear sometimes, and drink and game, and, to tell you true, do a great deal worse, but without hypocrisy".' Plain, honest Christians, who knew themselves to be sinners, were 'good fellows': self-important hypocrites, the professors of the word, those who thought themselves better than the rest, were 'puritans'. But the use of the term 'puritan' was shifting: it was not only the ungodly Antilegons who were mouthing it.[12]

At the Northampton assizes in 1629 Bolton had preached fiercely on the duties of magistrates and patrons. He feared some in the congregation would say, 'I think he would have us all so righteous that we should turn puritans!'—but 'let me acquaint you with the truth about this unhappy imputation, ordinarily laid by Protestants at large upon the power of godliness'. He tried to deflate the term by arguing that almost everyone was some sort of puritan: 'the natural puritan', 'the moral puritan', 'the superstitious puritan', and so on—in short, all who 'think themselves to be the only men, and all others hypocrites' were puritans of a sort. His 'pharisaical puritan' is a particularly interesting category: 'who, being passingly proud of the godly flourish of outside Christianity, thinks himself to be in the only true spiritual temper, and whatever is short of him is profaneness and whatever is above him to be preciseness'—a dig at the conformists who criticized the godly. True puritans, 'I mean only such as Jesus Christ his own mouth styleth so', were those who had been purified by the Word of God—but now the description 'is put upon such as these in contempt and reproach'. In 1629, and in a sermon before the visiting judges and county notables, such a defence of 'puritanism', and an attack on those who used the term, was a highly political statement. For some senior churchmen were 'tampering with our articles of religion', and 'labouring to put false glosses upon them, and talking of some reconcilement of our church to the Romish synagogue'—and they were classing mainstream Calvinist Protestantism as 'puritanism'. Bolton's prime target was obvious—Richard Montagu, author of *A New Gag for an Old Goose*, who had argued in 1624 that predestination was a puritan aberration, not, as Calvinists supposed, a key doctrine of the Church of England. Charles I supported Montagu: by 1629 he was bishop of Chichester, and the preaching of predestination had been restricted. Bolton was suggesting in his Northampton sermon that the so-called Arminians who thought like Montagu were no better than the alehouse idlers who traduced the godly as puritans. They too were foes of true religion.[13]

These texts by Gifford, Dent, and Bolton encapsulate the experience of the godly ministers across the period we have considered: anxiety in 1581, frustration in 1601, and anxiety again by 1629. When George Gifford wrote *The Country Divinity* in 1581, he was afraid of popery: his bugbear was Atheos, who hated the Pope but in many respects still thought like a papist. When Arthur Dent published *The Plain Man's Pathway* in 1601, he was frustrated by worldliness: his bugbears were carping Antilegon and ignorant Asunetus—though at least Asunetus could be scared into reforming himself. And when Robert Bolton was writing in the 1620s he too was afraid of the enemies of godliness: his bugbears were 'good fellows' in the alehouse and the so-called Arminians close to the king. Between them our writers offer a short history of English religion between 1570 and 1640: first, a battle between new Protestantism and residual popery; next, a battle by the godly to make conforming Christians into zealous believers; and, third, a battle to defend godliness against the alehouse and the royal court. The godly won the first struggle, drew the second, and lost the third in the short term (but won in 1641). The key to their fortunes may have been the attitude of prominent royal councillors. In fighting popery, the godly had the support and protection of the most influential councillors. In fighting indifference, they could assume at least benevolent neutrality if they behaved themselves. However, after 1625 they faced growing hostility from councillors and a increasing number of bishops, who came to see the professors as disruptive radicals. The godly had thought they were the central trunk of English religion—but in the 1630s they found themselves out on a limb.

This isolation is quite surprising, for in the 1630s Charles I, Archbishop Laud, and the bishops were doing some pretty unpopular things—insisting that neglected rituals prescribed in the Prayer Book and the Canons of 1604 were followed punctiliously; demanding that communion tables be railed in at the east end of every church; requiring communicants to kneel at the rail to receive their bread and the wine; expecting parishes to spend and spend on church fabric repairs, plate, and decoration; and so on. These stipulations were enforced by a tighter disciplinary regime—with much more detailed instructions from bishops to parishes, careful inspections of churches, and interrogations of churchwardens; and separate reports from clergy as well as wardens. As we have seen in Chapter 5, such measures were hated as authoritarian popery by the godly, and resented as intrusive novelties by some of the less-godly. But these objectionable policies were accompanied by moves that were more attractive to the profane, though not to the professors: the prohibition of preaching on predestination, a more relaxed attitude towards Sunday recreations, and perhaps a more inclusive and less confrontational approach to pastoral care.[14] Nevertheless, the package of demands made by the king and his bishops was something close to a religious revolution, almost as momentous as the changes introduced in the reigns of Edward VI and Mary I, and again in the early years of Queen Elizabeth. But there was less resistance to orders from above in the 1630s than there had been under Edward or Elizabeth, and nearly as much success for the authorities as there had been under Mary. There was more nonconformity among the laity than had been usual, but not much more. Criticism of the clergy and the Church courts was hardly more frequent than before. The few godly resisters did not find themselves supported by the mass of their neighbours, and they were easily harried into obedience or emigration. The top-down Laudian revolution was a quiet one, with no need for terror and very few martyrs.

What is most striking about the Church court and visitation records of the 1630s is how little they differed from what had gone before. There were, it is true, local oddities and signs of disaffection. William Sharpe was paid 4*s.* by two neighbours to go to church at Burton Latimer, Northamptonshire, on a July Sunday in 1630 'with his shirt hanging out over his britches down to his knees before, and also hanging out behind, to the moving of laughter amongst the profane sort and grief amongst the devout'. This may have been a calculated protest against Dr Sibthorpe, the rector, and his insistence on dignified ritual, or it may have been an expensive private joke. There were more obvious protests, however. In 1634 Ralph Haines of Ditcheat in Somerset protested that 'my Lord Bishop Curle was blind and did not understand the Scripture, because he suffered maypoles to be set up in the town of Wells'. The curate of Lilbourne, Northamptonshire, told his people that 'the bishop of this diocese is a superstitious bishop, for that he bows to the altar and at the name of Jesus'. The rector of Thistleton, Rutland, thought there were only two or three worthy bishops in England, and the way services were done at Peterborough Cathedral was 'wonderful'—by which he meant shocking. The churchwardens of Great Baddow, Essex, had not moved their communion table to the east end of the church and railed it in by September 1636, and still had not obeyed a direct order by January 1637—more than a year after the first instruction. The wardens of All Saints, Northampton, were given detailed orders on the size, placing, and rails of their communion table, but in January 1637 they failed to certify their compliance and were excommunicated. At Barrington, Somerset, in 1637 the churchwardens had set tiny rails around the edges of their communion table, 'in a scoff and derision' of the bishop's order. During the night before a communion service at Terling, Essex, in 1638, the communion table was secretly moved outside the new rails and placed in the middle of the chancel. At half a dozen churches in the archdeaconry of Colchester in 1638, the minister stepped outside the communion rail to deliver the bread and wine to the people—though two of the clergy said they had now conformed.[15]

In 1638 the wardens of Winchelsea in Sussex confessed they had not moved their table or railed it in as instructed, because the pews of the mayor and jurats of the town stood at the east end where the table ought to be put—'not that any desire it should be so, but that the charge thereof, in removing the seats, placing the altar, severing the chancel from the church, and paving and beautifying the chancel will be so great, besides the annual charge, that the parish is neither able nor willing to undergo it'. This could be an excuse for non-compliance or a delaying tactic—but the wardens claimed that they were applying for a licence for a collection from other parishes towards the heavy costs involved. Perhaps the expense of major works was sometimes more of an issue than any religious objection to popish altars—and at Ditchling, Maresfield, Hailsham, and Etchingham there was resistance to paying the church rates that were then necessary. There were moans elsewhere too, and in 1637 Robert Godd complained that the churchwardens of St James's, Taunton, 'have laid out about £40 about toys in the church'. Nicholas Saunders of South Petherton, Somerset, objected to paying his church rate in 1637, wishing 'that my lord bishop were gone and another bishop come of a better mind than to put the parish to such unnecessary charges to buy cuckoo pipes, meaning the organs'. And we should keep the examples of opposition in proportion. In east Sussex in 1638, Winchelsea and four other parishes admitted they had not rearranged their churches as ordered, and seven more had not yet finished the work: of course, we cannot be certain that the other 132 churches listed had obeyed, but complete concealment of disobedience was not easy. There were a few parishes where there was substantial resistance to Laudian demands—the notorious refusal of Beckington, Somerset, to move its communion table, and a widespread opposition to communion at the rail in St Peter's, Colchester, in 1637, for example. But these cases were no more serious than what had gone before—the sixty people who would not kneel for communion in All Saints, Northampton, at Easter 1614, or the 100 who would not kneel at Ashby-de-la-Zouch in Leicestershire at Easter 1615.[16]

In the main, it was business as usual in the Church courts, and the 1630s do not look very different from the 1580s: sex offences, Sabbath-breaking, misbehaviour in church, and abuse of ministers and churchwardens. In 1634 Richard Buckeridge of Chithurst, Sussex, called a warden 'a knave and an old fool', and said 'that even a very shitbritch might have an office'. But that sort of insult was nothing new. There were, as ever, cases of people sleeping or chattering or vomiting in church, and of having a bit of fun at someone else's expense—William Harding of Whissendine, Rutland, chalked on Nicholas Bickerstaffe's back during a service in 1634, and at Pleshey in Essex in 1638 Judith Brett plucked flowers out of Elizabeth Soane's hat and threw them around. On Sundays people still played cards or sat drinking in the alehouse when they should have been at church, and the young still went dancing instead of turning up for catechism classes. John Kitchener missed both morning and evening services at Meeching in Sussex on 23 September 1638, and had people drinking in his house all day—which was cheeky, as he lived next door to the minister. There was working and trading on Sundays and holy days, as there had always been. Robert Soane of Hadstock told the Colchester court in 1633 that he worked on holy days out of principle—'he sayeth that he ought to work six days by the law of God'. But most working on forbidden days was for profit or pleasure: in 1636 Robert Nation of Wellington, Somerset, 'doth usually sell cabbage, carrots and turnips and suchlike fruits upon Sundays', and in the summer of 1637 Robert White of Huish Episcopi watered his garden on a Sunday. Religion was no more and no less important than it had ever been: the churchwardens of Lyme Regis, Dorset, reported in 1638 that they 'have used their diligence for removing of loiterers out of the churchyard during the time of divine service, but little reformation hath followed, for that many women with their children do sit about the church walls'.[17]

This appearance of normality may be misleading, of course. We know that Robert Woodford, steward of Northampton, confided his godly rage to his diary and perhaps to trusted friends, but his discretion kept him out of courts and their records. Some hypersensitive ecclesiastical officials and clergy saw occasional delays in obeying instructions as deliberate obstruction, and individual objections as evidence of widespread disaffection and puritanical conspiracy—and some historians have done the same. But parishes had rarely leapt to obey a bishop's commands, and there had always been reluctance to spend money on official whims. The bishops of the 1630s seem to have been at least as successful at getting parishes to pay for putting altars up as the early Elizabethan bishops had been in the cheaper task of getting altars taken down. But then, with the uprising in Scotland and the outbreak of war, things changed: it was one thing to set up an altar in one's own parish church, and quite another to fight a war to make the Scots have them. In June 1639 Robert Sibthorpe was protesting that what some in England called *bellum episcopale* (the Bishops' War) was in truth *rebellio puritanica*—the puritan rebellion. When Robert Goodwin of Wells objected to the invading Scots' religious programme in May 1640, Robert Bolsome, curate of Upton Noble, Somerset, responded that bishops were unnecessary and any minister could ordain other clergy. In August about thirty ministers from Northamptonshire and Leicestershire met at the Swan in Kettering to express their sympathy for the Scottish cause and their opposition to recent proceedings in Convocation. In October 1640 the incendiary William Erbury preached a six-hour marathon sermon at Chew Stoke in Somerset against having bishops in Christ's Church, and prayed that the Church of England might be reformed and ruled by the godly. This was a wholly new level of protest, and it was not confined to the clergy. At Netherbury, Dorset, in 1641, thirty-one parishioners refused to pay their church rate on demand, and after eleven of them had paid up late the minister asked the court not to summon them—'I know it will breed a great deal of clamour and murmuring and discontent among them if they should be further troubled.' At Calne in Wiltshire 121 parishioners refused their rate in that year, and only twenty-six paid it when threatened with prosecution.[18]

There are two ways of interpreting this evidence. One is that there was simmering and mounting anger throughout the 1630s, against the religious policies of the crown and the episcopate—anger from the godly at popish superstition, and from the less-godly at the cost of conformity. But this hostility was largely concealed, because of fear of the Church courts, especially the powerful High Commission in London, and the secular court of Star Chamber. In 1640, however, when the regime was weakened by the Scottish invasion, pent-up fury broke out into the physical destruction of the hated altar rails and physical attacks on the Laudian clergy who had enforced them. The violence of 1640 thus shows the suppressed fury of the 1630s.[19] The weakness of this argument is that only a few critics of the Church had been seriously harassed, and the notorious mutilation by Star Chamber of Bastwick, Burton, and Prynne in 1637 was highly unusual. Most of those who complained about altars or rails or organs were ticked off and told to apologize. There was no reign of terror to quell an angry nation into near-silence. An alternative interpretation is that there was some popular support for the bishops' campaign to silence the godly, and that the Laudian altar programme built on a fashion for church decoration and improvement that had been growing since the 1590s. There were certainly over-fussy bishops who got backs up—especially Wren at Norwich and Montagu at Chichester: nevertheless, despite the costs involved, bishops and parish clergy were generally able to pursue their goals with little serious resistance. But the Scottish invasion changed everything. The bishops were blamed for the war, and war taxation was hard to collect in difficult economic circumstances. Artisans and labourers pressed into the army against the Scots mutinied, notably against Catholic officers, and in many churches they tore down the rails that had now come to symbolize the policies that had led to war.[20] These two interpretations need to be assessed within the broader context of overall royal policies in the 1630s and responses to them—but the ecclesiastical court evidence suggests that the second one is more likely to be true.[21] The war turned opinion against policies and perpetrators that had hitherto been accepted, even if not welcomed.

So when conformists from more than thirty counties petitioned Parliament in 1641–2 to defend the Prayer Book and episcopacy, they distanced themselves from the now-discredited Laudian clergy and their doings. Petitions from Somerset and from Gloucestershire in December 1641 wished that 'the wittingly and maliciously guilty of what condition soever they be, whether bishops or other inferior clergy, may receive condign punishment' for their innovations in religion. But they insisted that the misdeeds of individuals must not lead to the destruction of the institution of episcopacy—'for the miscarriage of governors to destroy the government, we trust it shall never enter into the hearts of this wise and honourable assembly'. These and other petitions were usually explicit responses to the godly demands for a 'root and branch' reform of the Church of England. They had enough variation in language and content to suggest local initiatives, but their requests were consistent. The Oxfordshire petition put them succinctly: 'that the government of this Church may continue as is now by law established, and that the liturgy may be settled with such alterations (if there be cause) as your wisdoms shall approve'. It was tactfully accepted that Parliament might see a need for minor reforms of the Prayer Book liturgy, but there was a horror of nonconformity and the disruption of church services: 'for the depraving or despising of so wholesome an ordinance, we humbly tender it to your wise considerations whether fit to be suffered in a peaceable commonwealth', declared the Gloucestershire petitioners. They even wanted the godly to be stopped from gadding, and made to go to their own parish churches.[22] Archbishop Laud and his colleagues had made nuisances of themselves, but they had not driven the godly and the less-godly into alliance. 'Honest' Philagathus and carping Antilegon were still at loggerheads—and soon they would be at war.

Writing in the 1680s, Richard Baxter had represented the Civil War as a conflict between the godly and the profane. It was the godly who supported the Parliament and joined its army: 'the generality of the people through the land (I say not *all*, or *every one*) who were then called puritans, precisians, religious persons, that used to talk of God and heaven and Scripture and holiness … , both preachers and people, adhered to the parliament'. The king's support came from

the gentry that were not so precise and strict against an oath, or gaming, or plays, or drinking, nor troubled themselves so much about the matters of God and the world to come, and the ministers and people that were for the king's book, for dancing and recreations on the Lord's days, and those that made not so great a matter of every sin, but went to church and heard common prayer, and were glad to hear a sermon which lashed the puritans.

The moral temper of the two armies was therefore different: while the parliamentary troops went to sermons and sang psalms when on guard duty, the king's men drank and swore. Baxter claimed that at Kidderminster in Worcestershire all the drunkards joined the king's army, 'and were quickly killed, so that scarce a man of them came home again and survived the war'. Served them right, of course. The king's supporters called the parliamentary forces 'Roundheads' ('some say it was because the puritans then commonly wore short hair'), and the Parliament's men abused the Royalists as 'Damn-me's'—because of their swearing. In some places, said Baxter, anyone with short hair and modest dress was liable to be knocked down as a 'Roundhead', and in his native Shropshire those with a local reputation for prayer and sermon-going were later plundered by Royalist soldiers.[23]

All this looks like caricature, and so in part it was. Baxter was writing long after the event, and to justify his own stance: the parliamentarians were the good guys, so naturally he had been on their side. But there is something in what he tells us. It obviously suited Parliament's supporters to represent themselves as the men of God, and their cavalry rode into battle with godly slogans on their standards—'the word of God', 'holy scripture', 'Antichrist must down', and 'against the ungodly'. And it suited the Royalists to capitalize on anti-puritan sentiment and try to recruit the 'good fellows', so their standards mocked the sober-sided 'Roundheads'.[24] In a sense, the Civil War *was* fought between Philagathus and Antilegon—they were the competing stereotypes that identified friend and foe, and made men willing to kill. But slogans and stereotypes work only if they are plausible, if they bear some relationship to real experience—and the real experience of the godly was that they were traduced as 'the puritans', and the real experience of the less-godly was that they were traduced as 'the profane'. The professors and the profane didn't like each other, but in normal circumstances they didn't fight each other. We have seen that the godly and the 'good fellows' usually managed to get along together in their parish: it was only in very specific circumstances that orderly coexistence broke down and they dragged each other before the Church courts in any numbers—the godly for nonconformity, the profane for Sabbath-breaking, for example. An aggressive minister, a visiting preacher, a grumpy churchwarden, an unfortunate pairing of wardens, or a provocative diktat from the bishop or the king had sometimes made religious differences seem more important than communal cooperation—and so led to trouble. That is what happened in spades in 1638–42—and Philagathus and Antilegon were set against each other.

The godly had never liked the Laudian programme of the 1630s. Some of them had refused to take communion at the new rails—and probably more of them had done so only with the deepest misgivings. But their less-godly neighbours had expected them to conform, and they had been surprisingly compliant. The Bishops' War against the Scots had then generated more hostility to altars and rails and bowing, and to the particular bishops who had most enthusiastically enforced them—so there was often local sympathy for the soldiers and youths who now threw down the rails in 1640. There were, as we have seen, rumours of popish plots—and some thought the king himself was in league with the papists. There was a lot for a Philagathus to be cross about, and look to Parliament to reform. But undoing what Laud had done was one thing: threatening episcopacy and the Prayer Book was going far too far. The godly campaign of county petitions for 'root and branch' reform of the Church, and Parliament's own assertion of control over religion, prompted defensive petitioning by conformists. Now Antilegon had a lot to be cross about. The attacks on altars and rails of 1640 were followed in some places in 1641 by desecration of the Prayer Book, soiling of surplices, smashing of church windows, and disruption of services. Sectarian meetings were more common, nonconformity flourished, and the godly were getting their way—in the localities and at the centre. In September 1641 the House of Commons ordered 'That the Lord's day shall be duly observed and sanctified; all dancing or other sports, either before or after divine service, be forborne and restrained.' The king's declaration on sports was abrogated—one good reason to make Antilegon a Royalist.[25]

'The war was begun in our streets before the king or parliament had any armies,' wrote Richard Baxter in 1659. Perhaps he had two things in mind. First, the loyalties and the antagonisms that provided each side with its forces were already there—and a key antagonism was that between Philagathus and Antilegon. We saw it at Chilworth near Southampton in 1607—'some being forward in religion, and therefore termed by the other to be puritans, and they on the other side terming the other to be profane men'. There the profane had accused the puritans of nonconformity, and the puritans had accused the profane of Sabbath-breaking—'that Hamon hath played at bowls and skittles upon one Sunday within this year past, and that Whetall did hunt upon the Sabbath day'. The diocesan commissioners had advised them 'to agree amongst themselves concerning these brabbles between them, friendly if they can'—and probably they did, since the parish was quiet thereafter. But the 'brabbles' in England by 1642 could not be settled, because tempers were too high. And that was the second thing Baxter was thinking of—that recent events had so sharpened antagonisms that violence had started before the war. There was godly violence, against altars and rails, against papists and Laudian clergy, and against the Book of Common Prayer. And there was profane violence too. Baxter tells that after the Commons order for the removal of religious pictures, images, and statues from churches had reached Kidderminster in the autumn of 1641, those he called 'the rabble' searched for him and the churchwarden to prevent any such destruction. Baxter's supporters, 'sober, pious men', were beaten up, 'merely because they were accounted puritans', and Baxter fled for his life. 'The hatred of the puritans and the parliament's reformation inflamed the ignorant, drunken and godly rout, so that I was forced to be gone even before the wars.'[26]

Scuffles on the streets of Kidderminster did not cause the Civil War—but it was the bitterness that such scuffles reflect that helped make war happen. When Parliament and the king could not settle their political differences in 1642 and instead sought to raise armies, the recruits were there ready. The godly were drawn to Parliament, to build a Protestant commonwealth, and do down popery and sin. The less-godly were drawn to the king, to defend the Church of England and do down hypocrites and 'busy controllers'. The godly revolted against the profane and the less-godly revolted against the puritans: they all knew who they were against, even if they were less clear on what they were for. This is not to suggest that civil war was in any sense inevitable, that Philagathus and Antilegon were bound to slug it out eventually. They had settled their little local differences countless times before. But by 1642 their differences were neither little nor local, and with Parliament and the king at each other's throats they were not going to be settled. Political failures in London had made a war likely: religious antagonisms in the counties made a war possible.

Conclusion: Pathways to Heaven

Despite the last few paragraphs of Chapters 9 and 10, this is determinedly not a book about the origins of the English Civil War. Instead, it is a book about how Theologus, Asunetus, Philagathus, Antilegon, and the Papist saw their own and each other's religion, and how they got along together, in the seventy years or so before the war came. Usually they managed to rub along together, and sometimes they rowed together—and the rows between the professors and the profane could be just as disruptive as the rows between the Protestants and the papists. But normally life went on, and religious differences were facts of daily life. Theologus and Philagathus wanted to make Asunetus less ignorant and Antilegon less awkward: it looks as if, in reality as well as in Dent's book, they had some success with Asunetus but none with Antilegon. Asunetus and Antilegon wanted to make Theologus and Philagathus less demanding, a bit more realistic about the requirements of religion—but they failed. And all four wanted to make the Papist into some sort of Protestant, a reliable fellow citizen who went to church and obeyed the law: they didn't have much impact either. Protestant failed to persuade Papist in George Gifford's book, and in England the papist population stabilized after 1606. All in all, it seems, not much changed in religious relationships between 1570 and 1640 (or 1638, at least).

Theologus, the divine, changed his coat. He was a black-coat by the 1630s, wearing a uniform that distinguished him from the laity and gave him a professional and social status. What that status should be was, however, contested. As more and more university graduates became parish incumbents, as more of them married the daughters of gentlemen and of other clerics, as rising tithe values made them more prosperous, ministers demanded deference. Perhaps that caused more friction with the laity and more hostility towards priests. When Dr Thomas Temple, rector of Bourton-on-the-Water, Gloucestershire, set up a prestigious new pew for his family in the parish church, he precipitated a running status-conflict with a local gentleman that lasted from 1631 to 1637 and ground through the wearying processes of the Gloucester consistory court, the Court of Chivalry, and Star Chamber. But it is quite likely that clerical touchiness about status had created an illusion of heightened opposition. The Newcastle preacher Robert Jenison wanted to be sure his doctorate was recognized by the laity in 1630, and Thomas Temple was on the lookout for any social slight from Bray Ayleworth.[1] The issue of clerical status may have influenced the rhetoric of lay–clerical relations, but it would be hard to prove that it significantly worsened them. Some of the vocabulary of anticlerical abuse had been inherited from before the Reformation, and much the same insults were employed across the whole of our period. Theologus did not have a harder time of it in the 1630s than he had done in the 1570s—nor, it seems, did he have an easier one.

There was, of course, more than one kind of clergyman. William Seredge, rector of East Hanningfield, Essex, was a hard-line Calvinist disciplinarian in the 1580s, the kind of cleric who gave godliness a bad name. He was a liturgical nonconformist, and would not baptize with the sign of the cross when parents asked for it. He examined his congregation strictly before communion, set high standards, and rejected many from the sacrament. He had private meetings in his house for the godly only, with prayers and psalm-singing, welcoming zealots from other parishes but excluding his own people. He was denounced as a 'false prophet', and his followers were mocked as 'saints and scripture-men'. Seredge alienated many of his parishioners, and they eagerly shopped him for nonconformity year after year.² Dr Robert Sibthorpe was a different kind of clergyman, but he also had confrontational relationships with his people. He was a hard-line conformist disciplinarian, and by the 1630s was the kind of cleric who gave Laudianism a bad name—partly because of his sermons on obedience to kings. At Northampton in the 1610s, he had struggled to enforce reverence on an unruly congregation and to make the godly kneel for the communion—using his position as a judge in the consistory court to make men kneel precisely as he wished. All this provoked opposition: Richard Holman was determined in 1616 that Sibthorpe would not 'rule them as a gentleman amongst them', and William Prim declared in 1620 that 'he cared not a fart for him'. After his move to Brackley in 1622, leaving behind the godly of Northampton, Sibthorpe had fewer problems. He still took parish discipline seriously, but when he stamped on a possibly adulterous relationship in 1623 he did so in concert with the mayor. At Burton Latimer in the 1630s, said a churchwarden, Sibthorpe's people were divided between 'the profane sort' and 'the devout'—though doubtless that was true of all parishes. In 1630 one parishioner deliberately mocked his insistence on dignified worship, and in 1636 Susan James derided him for having her husband carted off to gaol.³ Seredge and Sibthorpe were almost stereotypical cases, the godly preacher and the Laudian ceremonialist: they were both divisive, and they both had trouble—one early in our period, the other towards the end.

There were quieter men, too, at the beginning and at the end of our period. George Gifford's Atheos praised his peacemaking curate 'Sir R'—who seems to have been based on Christopher Ampleforth, vicar of Great Baddow, Essex, in the 1570s. Parish clergy were sometimes given testimonials by the people, and commended for their qualities. In 1586 the church of Bisham in Berkshire had no vicar and was served by George Ashborne as curate, 'which the parish doth like very well, and he is a very honest man and would gladly come if your lordship would appoint him'. In about 1591 the wardens of Sherborne

in Dorset complained about Francis Scarlett's nonconformity, especially that
he would not baptize with a cross—but perhaps he mended his ways, and
a decade latter they said, 'our vicar is of honest reputation, good life and
doctrine, and doth carefully observe the thirteenth article'. In 1620 the people
of South Petherton, Somerset, submitted a lengthy defence of Robert Marks,
their vicar, against the allegations of his enemies among the local gentry: he
was conscientious in his preaching and other duties, and went to the alehouse
only when he had to meet someone on business. Bridget Hamer of Yeovil
declared in 1628 that she hoped their vicar would break his neck 'before divers
of the parish, which much grieved them to hear her abuse such a worthy man
in his place and calling'.[4] When Thomas Pestell was hounded before High
Commission by a few enemies in 1633, he was supported by local gentlemen and
more than thirty tradesmen and husbandmen from his Leicestershire parishes of
Coleorton and Packington. William Sherman, gentleman, described him as 'a
man of religious life and conversation and a man well accepted and esteemed
amongst the gentry and other of good quality, and that he hath been and is
accounted a grave, painful preacher of God's holy word'. John Husband, collier,
testified that Pestell was charitable and hospitable to his neighbours, and Richard
Bailey, another collier, said he was 'a grave, painful, religious, peaceable and
conformable minister'. 'Peaceable' may have been stretching the truth, but Pestell
was an effective pastor and the investigation proved his popularity. He was a
model new black-coat, a conformist, a graduate, a poet, and a preacher, a friend
of Laudian bishops and deans and, for a time, of the earl of Huntington. But his
people stood up for him when he got into trouble.[5] So there were troublesome
clergy and popular clergy: William Seredge and George Ashborne in the 1580s,
Robert Sibthorpe and Thomas Pestell in the 1630s. *Plus ça change, plus c'est la
même chose.*

Just like Theologus, Asunetus himself changed, but his relations with others
did not. As the Church's catechizing regime intensified, so Asunetus the ignorant
became less ignorant. In the 1570s, failure to catechize children and servants was
one of the most frequently reported offences of the clergy: by the end of the
century, such laxity was rare. In the 1570s and 1580s, parents were often cited
for not sending their children to be catechized, and in these decades it was quite
common for adults to be refused communion because they could not recite the
official catechism. But by 1600 cases of exclusion for ignorance were much less
frequent, and after 1610 they were quite rare. Indeed, by the 1620s and 1630s
cases of profound ignorance were being reported by clergy and churchwardens
in shocked terms. So Asunetus finally learned his catechism. This was no mean
achievement for the clergy, given the levels of resistance they encountered and
the indiscipline of the youth assembled in church on Sunday afternoons. But
Theologus and godly Philagathus were not impressed: Asunetus could recite the
Prayer Book catechism by rote, but that did not mean he understood it—still
less that he had any real grasp of what Protestant Christianity was all about. For

them, Asunetus remained ignorant—ignorant of the things he needed to know if his soul were to be saved.[6]

But, as we have seen, Asunetus thought himself to be a religious man. For people like him, the services, sacraments, and rites of passage mattered, and they had to be done properly. That meant that ministers had to perform the prescribed rituals, and that the laity had to be in the right frame of mind. Lay attitudes towards communion are particularly striking—a determination to receive it if possible, and a reluctance to receive when troubled in conscience or out of charity with neighbours. We have seen lots of evidence of conventional religiosity and habitual practice, and enough evidence that parishioners expected their neighbours to do their duty to God and to their fellows. But there is nothing in the court books to suggest that levels of commitment and religious practice increased over time: in that sense, Theologus was right, and learning the catechism did not make much difference to how life was lived and God was served. This is not something that could be proved statistically, even if this were a statistical kind of book, but it is a strong impression. Throughout our period there was plenty of religion, but for most people it was kept in its place—and its place was on Sundays in service time, if that was convenient. Though almost everyone knew they should go to church and, indeed, wanted to go to church, other things might crop up—an invitation not to be missed, a piece of work not completed on Saturday, a round of drinks not finished, or a spontaneous game of bowls that got exciting. God expected his servants to meet him in church, but he was a realistic God who knew that other things mattered too. And his expectations were limited. His people ought to go to church on Sundays, and they ought to do only really essential work—but the rest of the day was their own. Strict sabbatarianism never really caught on in England, for all the efforts of the godly. Every Sunday there was dancing and drinking, selling and shopping, fishing and football—the game between Warmington and Clapton in 1603, or between Slindon and Madehurst in 1614; the match at Great Bedwyn in 1619 that ended in a brawl; and the regular games after evening prayer at Burnham in 1638. Robert Bath of Stone Easton thought his holy dog took Sunday more seriously than some humans—'I think he breaketh the Sabbath day less than some people do.'[7] Such was the English Sunday, from 1570 through to 1640. And it is not obvious that the Book of Sports changed habits: like God, the king had simply recognized realities.

Philagathus did not change very much, though the world about him did, and that made him a little angrier and rather more evident. There was much gadding to preachers in the 1570s and 1580s, because most parishes did not have regular sermons and the godly had to find them when and where they could. Some would not go to church unless there were a sermon, but as the number of preachers rapidly increased the godly became more choosy: John Pickman avoided services in 1589 because 'the word of God is not truly preached in Hornchurch by Mr Lambert the minister there', and Leonard Major of Northampton complained in

1615 that 'the preachers of this town do not preach powerfully'. No doubt later Laudian sermons on the beauty of holiness and the sanctity of the Virgin were even more objectionable. The court books seem to record about the same volume of gadding, but that may be an illusion. Whereas some Elizabethan officials had been willing to tolerate controlled gadding when there were no sermons in home parishes, Caroline bishops were determined that parishioners should hear their own preaching minister—so it is likely that the level of gadding declined, but a higher proportion of it was prosecuted. It was slightly different with lay nonconformity, which appears to have declined in the 1610s and then to have increased in the 1630s. This may conceal a fairly stable level of godliness: refusal to kneel for communion was less likely to be reported under Archbishop Abbott than it had been under Whitgift, but more likely under Laud. Further, other forms of nonconformity were much more frequently recorded in the 1630s. It is much more probable that standing and bowing in the service were neither observed nor much expected before the 1620s, than that there was a new outburst of disobedience—but neglecting these gestures was reported in the 1620s and enforced with some rigour in the 1630s. Going up to receive communion at a rail was a new requirement from 1634, and the godly who had conformed in other ways found this an intolerable piece of popery. The rail forced the conforming godly (usually concealed from us) into the open, and George Wright and his wife of Great Chishall, Essex, asked in 1638 'that they may have liberty to resolve their consciences about the lawfulness of their coming up to the rail to receive the communion'.[8] But not all those who rejected the rail were godly, and some objected that it was just an expensive novelty.

Arthur Dent's Philagathus got on well with Theologus: he admired the preacher, and enjoyed his confidence. But with other clergy it could be different. The godly abhorred the negligent Martin Clipsam of Stanford-le-Hope, Essex, and the strict conformist David Owen at Northampton. At All Saints, Northampton, at Easter 1614, some parishioners refused to take communion from Owen, but said they would receive from the deprived nonconformist Robert Catlin. At Colchester in the late 1630s, Richard Aske and Samuel Burrows campaigned to discredit the Laudian Thomas Newcomen, and Burrows deliberately disturbed church services. The relationship between Philagathus and the ungodly was always tense and sometimes publicly hostile. At Moreton Valence in Gloucestershire in 1569, Thomas Bradford and other zealots would not socialize or take communion with ordinary churchgoers, though they were a particularly uncompromising lot. The godly of Ringwood in Hampshire met together in 1607 to sing psalms and read from the Bible, and protested loudly against drunkards and other offenders in the parish.[9] We have seen that the godly could be a disruptive force in parish life—trying to stop the minister wearing a surplice at Badby in 1600, trying to prevent the Whitsun feasting at Lyme Regis in 1609 and the May festivities at St Peter-le-Bailey in Oxford in 1634. And when that happened a parish could be polarized, with allegations and recriminations all round, and sometimes violence—then the godly were damned as factious puritans and, in return, the conformists were slighted as vicious and profane. But it didn't last. The ordinary routines of communal living worked against segregation and open discord, and things got back to normal: the alternative was too disruptive and expensive. The nonconformists of Yapton in Sussex were hauled off to court in 1622, the dancers in 1623, and that was that. Yapton, for all we can tell, went back to peaceful, if not amicable, coexistence.

Of Dent's four characters, Antilegon looks like the most obvious literary fiction, deliberately invented for his role in the dialogue as an un-ideal type—the worldly, irreligious sinner who thinks he is a Christian but refuses to be a better one. However, the characteristics of the fictional Antilegon were all too obvious out there in the real world. There were men and women with an offhand attitude towards drunkenness, thinking that an occasional lapse was normal and neighbours should meet in the alehouse for good-fellowship—so the drinkers of Corringham celebrated their ale-flushed camaraderie in 1599. There were people who did not think that sex should be confined to the marital bedroom, but who joked and groped and paid Thomasine Simms 5s. for a show in 1617. There were young people who cross-dressed and flaunted sexiness, strutting their borrowed stuff in the street and in church. There were, in short, many who would willingly break the dominant moral code for a bit of subversive fun—especially at midsummer and Christmas. It was impossible to control them all. They laughed or raged at ministers and churchwardens who tried to keep them in order, and they derided the Church courts and their officers. They held mock courts that turned the law upside down, enquiring for cuckolds and punishing those who did not drink enough. They slighted the penalty of penance—'What did he care to do his penance before a company of coxcombs, he did not care if he did do it every day,' Richard Cooper had declared in 1618. The Church's rules, the moral conventions of godly society, were there to be broken, and if they were broken it did not matter very much—'If the worst came to the worst it was but a ten groats matter and there's an end,' said John Grey of Manuden in Essex in 1622.[10]

The Antilegons of the world might treat religion with equal disdain. They mocked the ministers and their teaching, with imitations of a preacher's style and spoof sermons on the necessity of sinning. They saw the funny side of a sermon, and John Sutton knew there was no sewing thread in Eden. They spoke disparagingly of Christ and the Virgin Mary: she was no virgin at all, and Christ had died for Giles Cosbie's dog. A few thought there was no God nor heaven nor hell—'all things did come by nature or chance', according to Thomas Tuck. Organized religion could be a real nuisance, all that going to church in the rain and only to hear the parson prate, so why not have a bit of fun to liven things up—with a dog tied to a bell-rope, or by singing the wrong tune to a psalm. The church and churchyard were not special, not holy places—so smear excrement on the churchyard style, and dry the washing in the church. Why not? What mattered at communion was how much wine you got, and how much bread there was to eat. Religion was not to be taken too seriously, but it certainly could be useful—with fancy rituals that could be borrowed for any purpose. There were mock baptisms—to insult John A-Gaskins, and to admit a William to drink with the Chipping Norton Johns. There were mock marriages, sometimes as a ritual prelude to fornication, sometimes to make a joke about disparities. There were mock funerals, and bells were tolled because a wife was 'speechless'. Religion could be a laughing matter. All this should put early modern religiosity in a realistic context: there were those who took it seriously, and we have always known a lot about them—but there were those who went along with it for a giggle or with a groan, and we need to recognize that they were there too. There were Antilegons all around and always. In 1587 John Somerset had pronounced 'that christendom is nothing worth'. 'Shit on the church, what care I for the church?' said Nicholas Crisp in 1633.[11]

Like the poor, the profane and the papists are always with us, and somehow they have to be endured. The papists were a problem for everyone, and even Asunetus and Antilegon knew they were supposed to hate them. But were they so hateful, and what about the good papists?—if there were good papists. On the face of it, they seemed harmless enough. They said they kept to the faith of their forefathers, and pleaded conscience in their own defence—but they were loyal to the Pope, and perhaps they were loyal to the king of Spain too. Usually they kept quiet, but some revealed their evil minds. What was a Protestant to do? William Redman had spoken up in defence of the recusant Henry Foxwell in 1605—'I think in my conscience he liveth a better life than we do.' But Mary Lyne wanted Foxwell punished: 'he will be seen unto well enough I warrant you'. The minister buried the Catholic Anne Freele at Rye in 1641 as 'our dear sister', but Samuel Jeake objected, 'Nay, she was an infidel for being a papist.' In normal times Mary Lyne and Samuel Jeake were in the minority, and in 1619 twenty-six people from Wellingborough and villages around were present at a wedding dinner with a couple of excommunicated papists. But there were anti-Catholic scares whenever there was a political crisis or some reason for worry, as in 1625, 1633, and 1639–40. And even in 1640 the mayor and jurats of Rye would issue a certificate of loyalty for Thomas Threele, saying he was a good papist 'so far as we know'.[12]

Religion was divisive. It made Theologus and Philagathus despise Asunetus and abhor Antilegon, and it made all four of them suspicious of papists—at best. It might bring the professors and the profane to blows, and make the Protestants of Colchester believe the papists were going to blow them up. In the highly unusual circumstances of 1642, religious division was to bring civil war: Philagathus *versus* Antilegon. But religion could also bring people together. For most of them it was a shared experience, and for all of them a shared interest—even for those who laughed at it or used it to laugh. We see this shared interest in the many intense discussions of religious issues that took place in alehouses and shops, as well as in church and churchyard. In 1566 there was a conversation about communion between at least four people at the house of John and Elizabeth Smith in Headbourne Worthy, Hampshire. Elizabeth was ill, and wanted to take the Easter communion: 'I feel myself ill, therefore I would to God I might receive.' But Richard Smith warned her, 'Oh, cousin, what will you receive?' Elizabeth said she would receive 'as other Christian folks do'—but Richard again warned, 'Take heed what you receive, for there is no virtue therein and it is contrary to God's word as it is now set forth.' Richard Smith and John Jarvis argued the issue, until Elizabeth ' being disquieted bade them get them out of doors and hold their peace'. It looks as if Richard was a Catholic, trying to dissuade Elizabeth from the Protestant communion. This was no inconsequential chat: religion was a matter of life and death, of salvation or damnation. In 1568 one of the parishioners of Lullington in Somerset discussed with the curate whether children would be saved if they died unbaptized, and thought that they would because their parents were Christians.[13]

People talked about religion because it was important to them. After a morning sermon at Bocking in Essex in 1577, Master Wentworth's servants sat at dinner discussing what the preacher had said. John Howard, a visitor, regretted that the Scriptures were preached about, and then discussed 'among such persons as they were'—but William King declared that he hoped the gospel would always be preached in England. The occasion of Ralph Byckenell's assertion that there was no God was a conversation between neighbours at Over Compton, Dorset, in 1601, 'reasoning and talking of the Scriptures'. The vicar and churchwardens of Roxton, Bedfordshire, made a collection for Geneva before morning service on 11 December 1603, but Thomas Lake said they should not contribute because 'it was unknown to him whether the citizens of Geneva were the king's friends'. The vicar pointed out that English exiles had fled there from persecution under Mary and the Bible had been translated at Geneva, but Lake quibbled 'that the English Bibles did not agree but were contrary one to another'—and when the vicar asked him whether he would contribute to the collection he declared, 'Let other men do as they will, he purposed to give nothing'. There was a true Antilegon—'a caviller'.[14]

In 1618 there was a heated argument at the bishop's office in Wells over whether a man could live in the faith of Christ if he was excommunicated. Richard Bellamy said he would not return for an absolution as he could be a Christian without it, and Ralph Trevillian said a Christian must obey the law—'This law (meaning the ecclesiastical law) is not God's law but the devil's law,' responded Bellamy. At the town hall of Axbridge, Somerset, after supper at the Angel inn, in a churchwarden's house, and on the highway, there were debates over several religious issues in 1619–20, such as why a man should go to church and what happened to the soul after death. Thomas Morton thought that people should go to pray rather than to hear sermons, and cited the Book of Common Prayer in support. They did not need sermons, because they could learn what they needed by reading books at home. It was thought that the ghost of William Locke was walking in the town, and Morton explained where he thought the souls of Locke and others would be: not yet in heaven or hell, but 'there is a *tercius locus* [third place] where their souls shall rest until the day of judgement'—which looks like Luther's doctrine of psychopannychia, or soul-sleeping. Those who heard Morton thought he was talking of purgatory, but he answered, 'I do not speak of purgatory, but there is a *tercius locus* wherein the souls of all that do depart out of this life do rest, until the day of judgement.' Morton was a quirky character, with an odd set of views and a good knowledge of the Bible—and others wanted to know what he thought and asked him to explain his beliefs. His opinions were suspect, however, and he was cited to court. In the churchyard of Pawlett in 1620, Atherwyn Parsons and George Yowe discussed Christ's family descent. Yowe suggested 'that Christ was descended from Phares according to the flesh', and that Phares was a bastard, as he had learned from the Old Testament. There was much talk and anxiety among the men and women of Middlezoy in 1622, after Christian Godfrey's ghost appeared to Joan Wyn and said that she was in hell for stealing beans and that others from the village would be joining her soon. Early in June 1624, Richard Wayte and three other men from Wells were sitting in Mendip forest eating their picnic dinner when they heard thunder. They talked about what thunder was. William Denby thought it was air crashing together, but Humphrey Spigot said it was a spirit making the noise. ' "No", quod the said Wayte, "it is no spirit, it is the devil, and no man knows it better than I." ' He explained that Lucifer had been an angel who had presumed to sit on God's throne, so God cast him down into hell, but then he became a Christian and was christened Barabbas, as Wayte claimed he had read in the Bible.[15]

Such religious conversations as are recorded from the reign of Charles I usually focused on ecclesiastical novelties and policy. They were often initiated by critics, perhaps the godly, but others took part and sometimes defended authority. There was much discussion in the churchyard at Bedminster near Bristol on 28 December 1628, after the curate of Chew Magna preached a sermon on the Virgin Mary and the birth of Christ—and a sermon by the vicar of Bedminster against gadding away to other preachers was discussed at the George inn at the end of November 1629. There was talk about nonconformity and the Prayer Book at Elizabeth Combe's shop in Yeovil in 1629, when Susan Dennis tried to defend a nonconforming minister and justify her own doubts about the Church's liturgy—but Thomas Rock and others thought the state's policy and the judgements of 'the learned men of the kingdom' should be followed. About 1632 a group of Taunton tailors at work discussed the installation of an organ in St Mary Magdalene church, which Thomas Davis had favoured and Hugh Willis did not. Some of the parishioners of Ditcheat talked in the churchyard about maypoles in 1632, after the vicar had defended them in a sermon, and Arthur Dorvall insisted 'that the maypole is an idol, and setting him up is idolatry'. Ralph Haynes argued that their bishop did not understand the Bible, 'in respect he suffered maypoles to be set up in the town of Wells'. And at Thomas Grigson's house at Ditcheat, neighbours 'fell into discourse of the Scriptures'. The conversation must have turned to the Commandments, since there was debate over whether they could play bowls on the Sabbath—Dorvall argued that Sabbath-breaking was as bad as adultery, but William Ewes thought bowling should be allowed. And there were arguments for and against May games and church ales in Oxford in the run-up to Whitsun 1634, and eventually a fight over them.[16] We sometimes find ignorance and misunderstanding in these conversations, and probably the men talked about football and sex more often. But talking about religion was obviously a day-to-day activity: it did not only happen on Sundays when a minister had said something controversial, it also happened at home, at work, in the street, and at the alehouse. Religious issues were inescapable and they preyed on people's minds: would taking communion help a sick woman, could an unbaptized baby be saved, does it matter if we don't attend church regularly, who will be going to hell from Middlezoy, and is it safe to set up a maypole or to play bowls on Sundays?

Everyone—well, almost everyone—talked and thought and cared about religion. But they did so with different levels of concentration and enthusiasm. Serving God was rather like saving the planet. A few determined zealots see it as the crucial task for humanity, do all they can to achieve it, and insist everyone else must be like them. A larger number know it matters and do their best when they remember, but get on with living without worrying too much. Others just can't really be bothered, and don't see what difference their actions would make anyway. And a few just don't believe there's a problem and nature will take its course—'all things did come by nature or chance'. The zealots despise the lazy and hate the indifferent and the sceptics. The lazy are tired of being hectored by the zealots, and the indifferent wish the others would just leave them alone to enjoy their sinning. The sceptics can be zealots too, but they know the weight of opinion is against them. Everybody but the absolute sceptics know that they are all part of the problem, even if they don't agree that they are part of the solution. For some in our period, God was immediate and his demands urgent, life was a constant struggle to do his will, and salvation was only for his chosen few. For others God was a benign but distant presence, he had a tolerant understanding of human frailty, and he would save the souls of those who had made some effort to be good. And the rest wished everyone would stop making so much fuss about God, and get a life. Our Theologus, Philagathus, Asunetus, and Antilegon, and the Papist too, agreed there was an issue about how to serve God: they did not agree about how to do it, nor how much effort was required. But they knew there was a heaven, and they all wanted to get to it. They took their different pathways.

Notes

INTRODUCTION

1. E. Culverwell, 'The Epistle Dedicatory', in A. Dent, *The Ruine of Rome* (1607), sig. A$_2$; I. Green, *Print and Protestantism in Early Modern England* (2001), Appendix 1, *sub* Dent; A. Dent, *A Sermon on Repentance* (1637 edn.), 26; *PMP*, Epistle to the Reader.

2. J. Bate, *The Portraiture of Hypocrisy, lively and pithilie pictured in her colours* (1589), 35–6. 'Philoxenus' probably refers to a Macedonian Greek who sought the truth in a dispute, and 'Autophilus' is 'self-loving'.

3. *PMP*, 21, 295, 302, 356, 409, 429.

4. S. Hieron, *The Preacher's Plea, or a Treatise in the Form of a Plain Dialogue* (1604), sig. A$_3$; T. Turvill, *The Poore Man's Path-way to Heaven* (1616), 267; T. Granger, *Paul's Crowne of Rejoycing, or The Manner how to heare the Word with profit* (1616), 24; R. Bolton, *Some Generall Directions for a Comfortable Walking with God, delivered in the lecture at Kettering in Northamptonshire* (1625); R. Bolton, *Instructions for a Right Comforting Afflicted Consciences* (1631); R. Bolton, 'The Saints' Self-Enriching Examination', in *A Three-Fold Treatise* (1634). Epaphras and Timothy were Christian companions of St Paul, and Ananias the high priest who prosecuted Paul. (Ananias was also a character in Ben Jonson's *The Alchemist*, but there he is a puritan.) Aquila was an early Christian at Corinth; Nymphas was a Greek place name, so perhaps the character was to be thought of as a countryman.

5. G. Gifford, *A Briefe discourse of certaine points of the religion which is among the common sort of Christians, which may be termed the countrie divinitie* (1582 edn.), Epistle Dedicatory; *PMP*, Epistle Dedicatorie; Hieron, *The Preacher's Plea*, sig. A$_2$.

6. *PMP*, Epistle Dedicatorie; *PMP*, Epistle to the Reader; R. Bolton, *Two Sermons Preached at Northampton at Two Severall Assizes There* (1635), 85.

7. *PMP*, 2, 4. The classic study of the omnipresence of religion is L. Febvre, *The Problem of Unbelief in the Sixteenth Century: The Religion of Rabelais*, trans. B. Gottlieb (1982), esp. chapter 9. For religious explanations of events, see esp. K. Thomas, *Religion and the Decline of Magic* (1973) and A. Walsham, *Providence in Early Modern England* (1999). For the Church courts, see esp. M. Ingram, *Church Courts, Sex and Marriage in England, 1570–1640* (1987).

8. GRO, GDR 31, p. 164; SRO, D/D/Ca.160, deanery of Dunster, 19 Oct. 1609; ERO, D/AE/A25, fo. 313; D/AB/A2, fos. 33v, 40v; D/AC/A52, fo. 28; NRO, X614/41, p. 376; WRO, D5/28/20/70.

9. NRO, X612/32, fo. 177; X614/40, fo. 13; X617/48, p. 66; X618/55, fo. 32; SRO, D/D/Ca.162, deanery of Wells, 15 Sept. 1609; D/D/Ca.171, p. 368; HRO, 21M65/C3/13, pp. 1–2, 7–8, 85.

10. ERO, D/AC/A22, fo. 73v; D/AE/A27, fo. 83; D/AC/A42, fo. 104; D/AE/A36, fo. 26v; D/AC/A50, fo. 158; ORO, Oxford archdeaconry papers, c.12, fo. 237. Attempts to establish guilt and punish offenders at parish level are considered in C. Haigh, 'Clergy and Parish Discipline in England, 1570–1640', in B. Heal (ed.), *The Impact of the European Reformation* (forthcoming).

11. ERO, D/AC/A33, fo. 33; D/AE/A27, fos. 38v, 73v; D/AC/A47, fos. 210, 214; NRO, X615/44, [p. 644]; X621/67, 15 Aug. 1637; SRO, D/D/Ca.282, fos. 15v, 91v.
12. LA, Vj 16, fo. 82; ERO, D/AC/A15, fo. 3v; WRO, D5/28/22/35, D/5/28/38/56, D5/28/34/41, D5/28/34/2, D5/ 28/35/73.
13. GRO, GDR 66, fo. 24v.
14. SRO, D/D/Ca.282, fo. 178; WSRO, Ep.I/17/15, 10 July 1613; NRO, X618/52, fos. 73v, 77, 85v.
15. G. Gifford, *A Dialogue betweene a Papist and a Protestant, applied to the capacitie of the unlearned* (1582); E. Bagshawe, 'The Life and Death of Mr Bolton', in *Mr Bolton's Last and Learned Worke of the Four Last Things* (1632), sigs. b$_{3v-b4}$.

CHAPTER 1

1. *PMP*, 363–4, 368; BLO, MS Rawlinson C.764, fo. 63. For the self-image of the godly minister, see T. Webster, *Godly Clergy in Early Stuart England: The Caroline Puritan Movement, c.1620–1643* (1997), 95–121.
2. *PMP*, 372; WSRO, Ep.I/23/7, fo. 27; Ep.I/17/9, 28 Mar. 1598; WRO, D1/39/2/5, fo. 20v; ERO, D/AC/A35, fo. 59v; NRO, X617/48, p. 549; X619/58, 14 July 1626; H. Johnstone (ed.), *Churchwardens' Presentments (17th Century): Part 1. Archdeaconry of Chichester*, Sussex Record Society, 49 (1948), 116.
3. NRO, X615/44, p. 401; SRO, D/D/Ca.200, 16 Nov. 1618; ERO, D/AC/A44, fo. 119v; D/AC/A47, fos. 45v, 153; D/AC/A52, fo. 256v.
4. R. Bernard, *The Faithfull Shepheard amended and enlarged* (1609 edn.), 72; *PMP*, 346–52, 407–8, 410–11 (the statement on p. 411 is ascribed there to Philagathus, but this is obviously an error for Asunetus); Bolton, *Instructions for a Right Comforting Afflicted Consciences*, 354–5.
5. Granger, *Paul's Crowne of Rejoycing*, 29; HRO, 21M65/C3/4, p. 76; NRO, X609/21, fo. 208v; X614/40, fos. 114v, 133, 140v; ERO, D/AE/A16, fo. 125.
6. ERO, D/AE/A26, fo. 159v; D/AE/A35, fo. 68v; D/AB/A6, fos. 54v, 63v; SRO, D/D/Ca.200, 29 Sept. 1621; NRO, X649/1, p. 476; X614/40A, fo. 47.
7. NRO, X608/15, fo. 98v; X609/21, fo. 116; X610/25, fo. 9; SRO, D/D/Ca.81, 18 Jan. 1588.
8. LA, Court Papers, 58/1/5; NRO, X612/32, fos. 131v, 145; HRO, 21M65/C1/28, fos. 14, 21.
9. NRO, X612/33, fos. 177, 184v–185v, 186v, 190v, 208, 232v, 234–v.
10. WSRO, Ep.I/17/14, 13 Mar. 1613; SRO, D/D/Ca.189, fos. 357v–358, 360; D/D/Cd.72, Saunders v. Gapper; ERO, D/AB/A2, fo. 92; D/AB/A4, fos. 43, 48v, 105.
11. BLO, Rawlinson Letters 89, fo. 28; SRO, D/D/Ca.189, fos. 184–v, 276v; D/D/Ca. 299, fos. 56v–58, 61–v.
12. *PMP*, 307, 309, 310, 313, 314, 320, 323; BRO, D/A/V/1, fo. 51; WRO, D5/28/7/29; LA, Ch.P/9/7–8; SRO, D/D/Ca.189, fo. 175; D/D/Ca. 220, 8 Sept. 1620; D/D/Ca. 299, fo. 10v.
13. Gifford, *A Briefe discourse*, fos. 24v, 59, 75; Bolton, *A Three-Fold Treatise*, 88; A. Dent, *The Opening of Heaven Gates* (1624 edn.), 83, 90.
14. *PMP*, 367; R. Bernard, *Two Twinnes: or Two parts of one portion of Scripture* (1613), 8, 17–18; SRO, D/D/Ca.299, fo. 61v; R. Cawdrey, *A Short and Fruitfull Treatise*

of the profit and necessitie of catechising (1604 edn.), 10; LA, Court Papers 69/2/15; NRO, X614/41, p. 341; X617/48, 10 Feb. 1618. For the theory and practice of catechizing, see I. Green, *The Christian's ABC: Catechisms and Catechising in England, c.1530–1740* (1996).

15. C. Haigh, 'Success and Failure in the English Reformation', *Past & Present*, 173 (2001), 28–49; ERO, D/AE/A14, fo. 175; D/AE/A25, fo. 11v; D/AC/A20, fo. 112v; NRO, X610/24, fos. 124v–125; X615/43, fo. 1v.

16. SRO, D/D/Ca.196, fo. 36v; D/D/Ca.226, fo. 137; ERO, D/AE/A30, fo. 38v; D/AB/A1, fo. 194; NRO, X617/52, fo. 5; WRO, D5/28/21/12.

17. NRO, X648/2, pp. 238, 247; Leics. RO, 1D41/13/59, fo. 309v; 1D41/13/60, fo. 36; ERO, D/AC/A52, fo. 15v.

18. WSRO, Ep.I/17/14, 13 Feb. 1613; NRO, X615/44, p. 270; ERO, D/AE/A31, fos. 265v–266v; D/AC/A42, fo. 175v; SRO, D/D/Ca.261, fo. 181; D/D/Ca. 267, Ilchester deanery, 11 Sept. 1629.

19. Granger, *Paul's Crowne of Rejoycing*, 28–9; SRO, D/D/Ca.160, Crewkerne deanery, 20 Oct. 1609; *PMP*, 365.

20. ERO, D/AE/A10, fos. 115v, 120; D/AE/A12, fo. 129v; A. Peel (ed.), *The Seconde Parte of a Register* (1915), ii, 164; ORO, Oxford diocesan papers, d.4, fo. 54; WSRO, Ep.I/17/11, fo. 113v; NRO, X614/40, fos. 82, 106, 147v, 230v.

21. Lichfield RO, B/V/1/13, p. 143; LA, Vj 16, fo. 51; NRO, X610/24, fo. 75v; GRO, GDR 66, fos. 73, 81v, 87v; WRO, D/5/28/2, 28; NRO, X618/52, fos. 57v–58; X619/58, 31 Mar., [?] May, 27 May 1626 (some bishops were willing to tolerate clergy who wore a surplice 'usually', but others demanded 'always'); ERO, D/AB/A5, fo. 71v.

22. GRO, GDR 40, fo. 83v; ERO, D/AE/A12, fo. 55v; D/AE/A16, fo. 64; D/AE/A30, fo. 22; D/AE/A31, fo. 12; D/AE/A32, fo. 247; SRO, D/D/Ca.134, Winford, Wrington; S. Crooke, 'The Ministeriall Husbandry and Building', title page, in *Three Sermons* (1615).

23. GRO, GDR 24, p. 709; NRO, X607/8, fo. 2; X613/34, fos. 20v, 59, 114; ERO, D/AE/A8, fo. 87; D/AC/A13, fo. 164v; SRO, D/D/Ca.102, fos. 3v–4, 23.

24. GRO, GDR 40, fo. 37v; ERO, D/AE/A12, fo. 16v; D/AC/A47, fo. 140v; WRO, D1/43/6, fo. 15a; D5/28/10/30, 62; NRO, X609/21, fo. 215v; X610/24, fo. 75; X610/25, fo. 18v; SRO, D/D/Ca.172, 3 Nov. 1612.

25. SRO, D/D/Ca.267, Merstone deanery, 11 Sept. 1629; D/D/Cd.66, pp. 107–10.

26. *PMP* (1631 edn.), 19.

CHAPTER 2

1. *PMP*, 364; P. Collinson, 'Shepherds, Sheepdogs and Hirelings: The Pastoral Ministry in Post-Reformation England', *Studies in Church History*, 26 (1989), 194–8; GRO, GDR 20, pp. 13, 63–4.

2. HRO, 21M65/C3/3, p. 275; 44M69/F2/11/56; LA, Court Papers, 69/1/3/2,3; 69/1/4; Vj 16, fo. 74; Ch.P/9/2; ERO, D/AE/A41, fo. 155.

3. ERO, D/AC/A11, fo. 72; D/AE/A24, fos. 96v–97; D/AC/A35, fo. 254; ORO, Oxford diocesan papers, d.6, fo. 13v; WSRO, Ep.I/17/14, 20 Mar. 1613; NRO, X618/56a, pp. 447–8; GRO, GDR 20, p. 13.

4. GRO, GDR 40, fos. 128v, 146–v; GDR 46, p. 23; HRO, 21M65/C3/8, p. 186; ORO, Oxford diocesan papers, d.16, fos. 199v–200, 201v; ERO, D/AE/A17, fo. 244; D/AE/A19, fo. 39; D/AE/A25, fo. 359; SRO, D/D/Cd.49, Office v. Browse.

5. WRO, D1/43/5, fo. 34; SRO, D/D/Ca.140, p. 308; D/D/Cd.60, Office v. Hix; ORO, Oxford archdeaconry papers, c.118, fos. 109v–111, 120v; WRO, D5/21/3/9/1, 25; D5/28/30/44.

6. GRO, GDR 40, fos. 9, 36v, 40v, 62, 87, 104v, 105v; HRO, 21M65/C1/22, fo. 28v; LA, Vj 16, fo. 93v; WRO, D1/43/6, fo. 4v (the name of the parish is missing); WSRO, Ep.I/17/9, 1 Oct. 1597; ERO, D/AE/A19, fos.198v–199; D/AE/A28, fo. 32; NRO, X612/32, fo. 132; X613/34, fo. 139.

7. WRO, D5/28/7/2; SRO, D/D/Cd.34, Office v. Calvert.

8. Gifford, *A Dialogue betweene a Papist and a Protestant*, fo. 51; Gifford, *A Briefe discourse*, fo. 47v; *PMP*, 17–21; LA, Court Papers, 58/1/5; WRO, D3/4/1, fo. 259; D1/39/2/6, fo. 25v; D5/21/3/9/29.

9. SRO, D/D/Cd.66, fo. 173; D/D/Ca.313, fo. 96v; NRO, X620/63, p. 197; ERO, D/AB/A8, fo. 47v; Granger, *Paul's Crowne of Rejoycing*, 28; BLO, Rawlinson Letters 89, fo. 27v.

10. C. Haigh, 'Communion and Community: Exclusion from Communion in Post-Reformation England', *Journal of Ecclesiastical History*, 51 (2000), 722–9; LA, Vj 16, fo. 134; G. Gifford, *A Short Treatise against the Donatists of England, whome we call Brownists* (1590), 57; NRO, X608/14, fo. 31.

11. WRO, D5/28/5/95; ERO, D/AC/A22, fo. 195; NRO, X614/40, fo. 216v; Leics. RO, 1D41/4/Box VII/149.

12. ERO, D/AE/A16, fos. 43v, 52v, 94; D/AE/A27, fo. 73; D/AE/A28, fo. 192v; D/AE/A38, fo. 69; SRO, D/D/Ca.98, p. 33; WRO, D5/28/8/80; Johnstone (ed.), *Churchwardens' Presentments (17th Century): Part 1*, 93.

13. ERO, D/AC/A20, fos. 101v–103v, 112v; D/AE/A12, fos. 10, 49v, 98; D/AE/A13, fo. 168v; D/AE/A14, fos. 288, 304v; D/AE/A17, fos. 110–111v; D/AC/A22, fos. 110v–111, 224; SRO, D/D/Ca.98, p. 89; D/D/Ca.134, Widford; D/D/Ca.142, p. 30.

14. ORO, Oxford diocesan papers, c.21, fos. 75–76v; HRO, 21M65/C1/29, fo. 36; WRO, D5/28/18/8; SRO, D/D/Ca.214, fo. 12v; D/D/Ca.215, fo. 183; NRO, X617/54, 20 Feb., 6 Mar. 1621, [?] June, 3 Aug. 1622.

15. NRO, X607/12, fo. 15v; X609/20, fo. 62v; X609/21, fos. 11v, 71–v, 151v; X610/23A, fo. 151v; ERO, D/AE/A14, fo. 288; D/AE/A23, fo. 166v; D/AE/A24, fo. 36; D/AC/A35, fos. 87, 96v–97; D/AE/A31, fo. 69v; GRO, GDR 66, fo. 93.

16. SRO, D/D/Ca.224, fo. 323; ERO, D/AE/A39, fos. 92–v, 113; WSRO, Ep.II/15/1, p. 5.

17. LA, Ch.P/9/11; Turvill, *The Poore Man's Path-way to Heaven*, 160; WRO, D1/39/2/11, fo. 42 ('the king doth allow of it' is a reference to the 1618 declaration on Sunday recreations).

18. Gifford, *A Briefe discourse*, fo. 2; BLO, MS Rawlinson D.1346; LA, Ch.P/5/22; HRO, 21M65/C1/29, fo. 30v; Leics. RO, 1D/41/13/51, fos. 3v, 4a; ERO, D/AE/A42, fo. 168v. There was a legal process for absolving excommunicates *in forma pauperis*, but ministers had chosen to help parishioners with it.

19. HRO, 21M65/B1/9, fos. 116v–117; ORO, Oxford diocesan papers, d.9, fo. 103; Leics. RO, 1D/41/13/50, fo. 149v; NRO, X618/56A, pp. 268, 311, 317, 322.

20. GRO, GDR 31, pp. 374, 390; NRO, X609/21, fo. 206; X614/40, fo. 233v; X618/56A, p. 181; X621/69, fo. 41v; SRO, D/D/Ca.134, Cutcombe; D/D/Ca.189, fo. 241; ERO, D/AE/A22, fo. 164; D/AE/A25, fo. 85.

21. GRO, GDR 46, p. 7; SRO, D/D/Cd.34, King v. Walmesley; D/D/Ca.283, fo. 199v; D/D/Ca.313, fo. 179; D/D/Ca. 226, 3 Dec. 1622; NRO, X614/41, p. 480; X621/68, fo. 23v; ORO, Oxford diocesan papers, c.2, fos. 20v–21, 56–v; WRO, D5/28/30/12.

22. *PMP*, 1, 205, 291; *PMP* (1631 edn.), 127; NRO, X617/54, 20 Mar. 1621; ERO, D/AB/A3, fo. 87v.

23. HRO, 21M65/C1/13/1, fo. 25; 21M65/C1/21, fo. 146; 21M65/C1/29, fos. 46, 51v; NRO, X607/11, fos. 27v, 87; X607/12, fo. 18v; X610/25, fo. 18v; X612/32, fo. 61v; X613/36, fo. 265; X614/40, fos. 102, 273v; X615/42, p. 59; X614/41, p. 264; X617/54, 20 Mar. 1621; GRO, GDR 46, pp. 2–3; GDR 45, fo. 167v; E. R. Brinkworth (ed.), *The Archdeacon's Court: Liber Actorum, 1584*, Oxfordshire Record Society (1942), 9; LA, Vj 16, fo. 74; LQS, A/1/2/153; WRO, D1/43/6, fo. 7v; D5/28/26/38; SRO, D/D/Ca.134, Luxborough; D/D/Ca.160, Taunton deanery, Pitminster; D/D/Cd.44, Office v. Webber; D/D/Ca.282, fo. 26; ERO, D/AC/A31, fo. 17; D/AE/A26, fo. 29; S. A. Peyton (ed.), *Churchwardens' Presentments in the Oxfordshire Peculiars of Dorchester, Thame and Banbury*, Oxfordshire Record Society (1928), 194; WSRO, Ep.I/17/14, 13 Mar. 1613; Ep.I/17/17, 22 Feb. 1617; Johnstone (ed.), *Churchwardens' Presentments (17th Century): Part 1*, 53; PRO, SP 16/388, fo. 166v.

24. ERO, D/AE/A25, fo. 90; D/AB/A6, fo. 57v; D/AC/A10, fo. 22v; WSRO, Ep.I/17/15, 26 Mar. 1614; NRO, X616/46, fo. 47; X615/44, p. 624; WRO, D5/21/3/9/29; HRO, 21M65/C3/8, pp. 294–5 ('thou' was a familiar term, to be used only to equals or inferiors); SRO, D/D/Ca.224, fo. 65 ('sirrah' might be used to address a youth or a servant); Leics. RO, 1D41/4/Box VII/150; 1D41/13/64, fo. 126v. On clerical assertiveness, see C. Haigh, 'Anticlericalism and Clericalism, 1580–1640', in N. Aston and M. Cragoe (eds.), *Anticlericalism in Britain, 1500–1914* (2000); A. Foster, 'The Clerical Estate Revitalised', in K. Fincham (ed.), *The Early Stuart Church, 1603–1642* (1993).

25. ERO, D/AE/A13, fo. 111; D/AE/A26, f. 29; D/AE/A27, fo. 195v; SRO, D/D/Ca.134, Skilgate; D/D/Ca.260, fo. 238; NRO, X614/40, fo. 81v; WSRO, Ep.I/17/13, 15 Dec. 1610; Ep.I/17/15, 26 Mar. 1614; Leics. RO, 1D41/4/Box XIII/93; BLO, MS Tanner 71, fo. 30v.

26. GRO, GDR 46, p. 6; GDR 76, fo. 291; NRO, X608/14, fos. 30, 131; X613/36, fo. 271v; X617/54, 20 Mar. 1621; X618/56A, p. 115; X621/66, fo. 59v; X621/68, fo. 26; Lichfield RO, B/V/1/17, fo. 230; HRO, 21M65/C3/10, pp. 430–1; ERO, D/AC/A22, fo. 258v; D/AE/A25, fo. 313; D/AC/A42, fo. 13; Peyton (ed.), *Churchwardens' Presentments in the Oxfordshire Peculiars*, 286; SRO, D/D/Cd.44, King v. Walmesley; D/D/Ca.189, fo. 20; D/D/Cd.56, Office v. Robins; D/D/Ca.247, fo. 168; D/D/Ca.261, fo. 112v; D/D/Ca.313, fo. 151v; WRO, D5/28/16/28; BRO, D/A/V/2, fo. 104; LA, Vj 30, fo. 103.

27. Culverwell, 'Epistle Dedicatory', in Dent, *The Ruine of Rome*, sig. A₂; W. Garrett, *Anthologia: the life and death of Mr Samuel Crook, late pastor of Wrington* (1651), 21, 29–30, 40, 42; Bagshawe, 'The Life and Death of Mr Bolton', in *Mr Bolton's Last and Learned Work*, sigs. b₄–c₄; S. Clarke, *A Collection of the Lives of Ten Eminent Divines* (1662); S. Clarke, *The Lives of Thirty-Two English Divines* (1677).

On Clarke's various 'lives', see P. Collinson, 'A Magazine of Religious Patterns', in his *Godly People* (1981). I am grateful to Alexandra Walsham for suggesting that a contrast with the godly lives would be useful.

28. HRO, 21M65/C1/14/1, fos. 90v–92, 166, 189v; NRO, X607/11, fo. 87; X607/12, fo. 17v; ERO, D/AC/A8, fos. 215, 234; D/AE/A11, fo. 20v; D/AE/A25, fo. 319v; Anon., *The Manner of the Cruell Outrageous Murther of William Storre, Mast. Of Art* (1603), sig. A₃; NRO, X615/43, fo. 77; SRO, D/D/Ca.207, fos. 244v–245; PRO, SP 16/388, fo. 167.

29. Granger, *Paul's Crowne of Rejoycing*, 6–7; SRO, D/D/Cd.49, Office v. Rowswell; WRO, D5/28/22/52; WSRO, Ep.I/17/23, fo. 157; NRO, X620/63, p. 137; X621/66, fo. 13v; LA, Vj 30, fo. 24.

30. PRO, SP 16/261, fo. 95; *PMP*, 366.

CHAPTER 3

1. *PMP*, 2, 19–20, 29–30, 31–2, 287, 377; *PMP* (1635 edn.), 125; Gifford, *A Briefe discourse*, Epistle Dedicatory, fos. 3, 15; Turvill, *The Poore Man's Path-way to Heaven*, 82; Bolton, *A Three-Fold Treatise*, 212; Bolton, *Two Sermons Preached at Northampton*, 85.

2. *PMP*, 28, 354–5; G. Gifford, *Foure Sermons upon the seven chiefe virtues or principall effectes of faith, and the doctrine of election* (1582), sig. C₃; Bolton, *Some Generall Directions*, 300–1; BLO, MS Rawlinson C.764, fo. 127v.

3. ERO, D/AC/A3, fos. 45v–46; WSRO, Ep.I/23/1, fos. 13, 28, 29, 46, 73; HRO, 21M65/C1/14/1, fo. 23; 21M65/C1/15, fos. 88, 101, 119; 21M65/C1/17, fos. 23–27v; GRO, GDR 40, fos. 3v, 6v, 14v, 19, 261v; Haigh, 'Success and Failure', 36, 44–5.

4. SRO, D/D/Cd.15, fo. 72; D/D/Ca.73, 8 July 1585; HRO, 21M65/C1/19, fos. 8v–9v, 125–v; ERO, D/AE/A10, fo. 137; D/AE/A12, fo. 137; D/AC/A15, fo. 15; GRO, GDR 50, Gloucester deanery, Frethern.

5. NRO, X613/34, fo. 30v; X613/36, fo. 256; ERO, D/AE/A25, fos. 47, 155v; D/AE/A29, fo. 149v; D/AE/A30, fo. 38v; D/AE/A40, fo. 110v; SRO, D/D/Ca.162, Bedminster deanery, 16 Oct. 1609; D/D/Ca.220, 15 Sept. 1620; WSRO, Ep.I/17/13, 16 June 1610; Ep.I/17/25, fo. 12; WRO, D5/28/20/28.

6. GRO, GDR 40, *passim*; NRO, X608/14, fo. 29; X619/58, [?] Mar. 1627; WSRO, Ep.I/23/7, fo. 13v; SRO, D/D/Ca.98, p. 65; D/D/Ca.120, Hutton; D/D/Ca.140, pp. 220–3; D/D/Ca.191, Winscombe; WRO, D5/28/10/78; Peyton (ed.), *Church-wardens' Presentments in the Oxfordshire Peculiars*, 292–3; ERO, D/AC/A48, fo. 154.

7. *PMP*, 342–56; ERO, D/AC/A20, fo. 112v; D/AE/A13, fo. 128; R. Gawton, *A Short Instruction for All Such as Are to be Admitted to the Lord's Supper* (1612), sig. A₂; NRO, X616/45, [?] Jan. 1618; X617/48, 31 Jan. 1618; Huntington Library, San Marino, CA, STT Correspondence, 1880.

8. *PMP*, 2; R. Bernard, *A Guide to Grand-Jury Men* (1627), 77–8; G. Gifford, *A Dialogue concerning Witches and Witchcraftes* (1593), sigs. B₂, B₄, D₄, E₃, T₄; ERO, D/AE/A9, fo. 72v; D/AC/A10, fo. 47; D/AE/A19, fo. 198; D/AE/A18, fo. 151; D/AE/A22, fo. 3v; NRO, X615/43, fos. 110, 216v; X611/26, fos. 81, 107v, 135; X617/48, p. 289; X617/47, fos. 122v, 63, 67v; X620/62, fo. 35; HRO,

21M65/C1/18, fos. 14v–15; WSRO, Ep.I/17/15, 26 Feb. 1614; Ep.I/17/17, 8 Feb. 1617; Peyton (ed.), *Churchwardens' Presentments in the Oxfordshire Peculiars*, 294.

9. NRO, X610/23A, fo. 72; X611/26, fo. 172v; X616/46, fo. 86–v; X618/56A, p. 246; X619/61, 8 July 1629; WRO, D3/7/1, fo. 92; D5/28/17/37; ERO, D/AE/A20, fo. 237; D/AE/A22, fo. 69; D/AE/A31, fo. 69; ORO, Oxford archdeaconry papers, c.118, fos. 223–224v, 231–v.

10. Turvill, *The Poore Man's Path-way to Heaven*, 4–6; WRO, D5/28/4/9; D1/39/2/1, fo. 7v; D5/28/11/24; HRO, 21M65/C1/22, fo. 146; SRO, D/D/Ca.73, 16 July 1585; D/D/Ca.134, deanery of Crewkerne, loose sheet; D/D/Ca.189, fo. 378; D/D/Ca.215, fo. 116–v; NRO, X609/21, fo. 220a; X612/33, fo. 16v.

11. WRO, D3/4/7, fo. 19v; D5/28/35/73; SRO, D/D/Ca.299, fo. 1v; D/D/Cd.78, Office v. Dorvall; ORO, Oxford archdeaconry papers, c.12, fos. 278v–279; Oxford diocesan papers, c.27, fos. 43v–48.

12. HRO, 21M65/C1/12, *passim*; 21M65/C3/5, p. 289; GRO, GDR 40, *passim*; SRO, D/D/Ca.40, deanery of Frome; NRO, X607/10, fo. 64; X611/28, fo. 33v; X613/34, fos. 27v, 205; X613/36, fos. 13v, 107; LA, Court papers, 69/1/17; Lichfield RO, B/V/1/17, fo. 207; ERO, D/AE/A14, fos. 165v–166.

13. WSRO, Ep.I/17/13, 20 July 1611; NRO, X617/47, fos. 132v–134; X619/58, 19 Sept. 1626; X621/65, fo. 101v; Johnstone (ed.), *Churchwardens' Presentments (17th Century): Part 1,* 126; SRO, D/D/Ca.267, deanery of Frome; ORO, Oxford diocesan papers, c.2, fo. 309v; ERO, D/AC/A53, fo. 77.

14. *PMP*, 344; NRO, X608/13, fo. 67; X613/34, fos. 13v, 168v; X617/54, 3 July 1623; X619/58, 9 Feb. 1626; X620/64, p. 47; ERO, D/AE/A22, fo. 211; SRO, D/D/Cd.51, Office v. Hix; ORO, Oxford diocesan papers, c.26, fo. 30; BRO, D/A/V/2, fo. 18. For involvement in parish religion, see C. Marsh, *Popular Religion in Sixteenth-Century England* (1998), 27–95, 195–219.

15. WRO, D1/43/5, fo. 23v; ORO, Oxford diocesan papers, d.5, fo. 107v; Oxford archdeaconry papers, c.118, fo. 110; ERO, D/AE/A20, fo. 32v; D/AC/A46, fos. 39v, 44. For churching, see D. Cressy, *Birth, Marriage and Death: Ritual, Religion, and the Life-Cycle in Tudor and Stuart England* (1997), 197–229.

16. LA, Court Papers, 69/2/9; 69/1/23; ORO, Oxford diocesan papers, c.2, fo. 217; WRO, D3/4/7, fo. 4v; ERO, D/AC/A52, fo. 17. On the importance of baptism, see Cressy, *Birth, Marriage and Death*, 97–123.

17. SRO, D/D/Ca.220, 11 Sept. 1620; D/D/Ca.299, fo. 84; D/D/Ca.260, fo. 98v; D/D/Ca.316, fos. 129v, 156v; D/D/Ca.330, fo. 15; NRO, X648/2, p. 266; X619/61, fos. 6v–7.

18. NRO, X611/28, fos. 72v, 74v, 77v–78, 85v; ERO, D/AC/A33, early 1610; WRO, D5/28/13/24; SRO, D/D/Ca.267, Wells, 7 Sept. 1629; ORO, Oxford diocesan papers, c.2, fos. 194v, 197.

19. SRO, D/D/Ca.57, deanery of Crewkerne, 30 Jan. 1577; D/D/Cd.15, fos. 144–5; D/D/Ca.85, 18 Sept. 1588; NRO, X614/40, f. 62; Johnstone (ed.), *Churchwardens' Presentments (17th Century): Part 1,* 37; ERO, D/AC/A9, fo. 123; BRO, D/A/V/2, fo. 123v. On the significance of communion, see A. Hunt, 'The Lord's Supper in Early Modern England', *Past & Present*, 161 (1998), 41–6.

20. ERO, D/AC/A10, fo. 52; D/AC/A33, fo. 177; Brinkworth (ed.), *The Archdeacon's Court*, 159; ORO, Oxford diocesan papers, d.13, fos. 49, 89; WRO, D5/28/27/26; LA, Vj 30, fo. 64; GRO, GDR 31, p. 359.

21. GRO, GDR 26, p. 61; GDR 37, fos. 16v–17v; NRO, X608/13, fo. 118; X613/34, fo. 157; X615/44, p. 42; ORO, Oxford diocesan papers, d.9, fos. 27, 74v; Oxford archdeaconry papers, c.13, fo. 179v. Cf. D. W. Sabean, *Power in the Blood: Popular Culture and Village Discourse in Early Modern Germany* (1984), 38–41, 45–54.
22. HRO, 21M65/C1/21, fo. 132v; ERO, D/AE/A15, fo. 119v; D/AE/A16, fo. 71; D/AC/A52, fo. 234; D/AC/A53, fo. 13v.
23. ERO, D/AE/A16, fos. 14v, 45; D/AE/A32, fo. 124; HRO, 21M65/C1/25, fo. 34; 21M65/C29, fo. 62; WRO, D5/28/17/87.
24. ORO, Oxford diocesan papers, d.16, fos. 199v, 201v, 206; ERO, D/AE/A20, fos. 64, 81v; D/AB/A5, fo. 156; WRO, D1/39/2/5, fo. 34; NRO, X615/44, p. 26.
25. NRO, X618/52, fo. 155; Peyton (ed.), *Churchwardens' Presentments in the Oxfordshire Peculiars*, 68; H. Smith, *The Sermons of Master Henrie Smith* (1592 edn.), 155; ERO, D/AC/A51, fo. 103.
26. SRO, D/D/Ca.102, fo. 31v; D/D/Cd.56, Office v. Chicke; D/D/Ca.172, 24 Nov. 1612; ERO, D/AE/A28, fo. 92; D/AC/A8, fo. 257; D/AC/A51, fo. 253v; D/AC/A52, fo. 13; ORO, Oxford diocesan papers, c.25, fo. 83; NRO, X618/56A, p. 521; X617/54, 12 July 1621.
27. ORO, Oxford diocesan papers, d.9, fo. 104; c.2, fo. 138v; SRO, D/D/Ca.189, fo. 213; D/D/Cd.56, Office v. Wyn; ERO, D/AE/A42, fo. 14.
28. NRO, X614/40, fo. 186v; X616/45, p. 676; ERO, D/AC/A42, loose letter, Griffin to Aylett; D/AC/A54, loose letter, Harrell to Tillingham.
29. *PMP*, 342, 355–6.

CHAPTER 4

1. *PMP*, 27; Bate, *The Portraiture of Hypocrisy*, 96; Bolton, *Some Generall Directions*, 303; SRO, D/D/Ca.215, fo. 28v; ERO, D/AE/A8, fo. 282.
2. ERO, D/AE/A18, fo. 2; D/AE/A24, fo. 42; D/AC/A42, fo. 1; D/AC/A47, fo. 140; D/AE/A15, fo. 69v; D/AE/A26, fo. 107v; D/AC/A35, 8 Dec. 1613; D/AE/A36, fo. 238v; D/AC/A48, fo. 185v; D/AC/A51, fo. 130v; NRO, X614/40, fo. 41v; SRO, D/D/Ca.142, p. 126; D/D/Cd.54, Office v. Morton; WSRO, Ep.I/17/23, fo. 172; WRO, D5/28/38/27.
3. NRO, X616/45, p. 18; SRO, D/D/Ca.215, fo. 242v; ERO, D/AE/A36, fo. 103; D/AE/A39, fo. 34v; D/AE/A42, fo. 22.
4. GRO, GDR 40, fos. 105, 116v, 256v, 257v; WRO, D5/28/11/24; D5/28/20/36, membranes 3–4; SRO, D/D/Ca.191, Wells, 28 Sept. 1615; D/D/Ca.214, fo. 36v; D/D/Ca.267, deanery of Wells, 7 Sept. 1629; NRO, X617/47, fo. 133v.
5. SRO, D/D/Ca.85, fo. 42v; D/D/Ca.142, p. 116; D/D/Ca.200, 30 Sept. 1619; D/D/Ca.224, fo. 233v; WSRO, Ep.I/17/13, 7 Oct. 1609; NRO, X614/41, p. 263; ERO, D/AE/A27, fo. 326; D/AC/A45, fo. 96v.
6. WSRO, Ep.I/23/5, fo. 37v; ERO, D/AE/A15, fo. 9; D/AE/A22, fo. 6; D/AE/A32, fo. 153; D/AC/A44, fo. 18v; D/AC/A45, fo. 241v; D/AE/A38, fo. 4; D/AC/A50, fo. 9; D/AC/A51, fo. 46; D/AC/A54, fos. 95,112v; SRO, D/D/Ca.283, fo. 116v.
7. ERO, D/AC/A35, fos. 68, 76v; D/AB/A1, fo. 208v; D/AE/A34, fo. 291v; D/AE/A41, fo. 159v; WRO, D1/39/2/1, fos. 38–9; D3/7/1, fo. 170v; SRO, D/D/Ca.267,

deanery of Axbridge, 10 Sept. 1629; D/D/Ca.226, fo. 108v; D/D/Ca.308, fo. 83v; HRO, 21M65/C1/21, fo. 127v; NRO, X619/58, 4 Apr. 1627.

8. ERO, D/AE/A23, fo. 4v; D/AE/A7, fo. 46; D/AE/A12, fo. 147; D/AE/A22, fo. 238; D/AE/A33, fo. 328; D/AE/A34, fo. 42; GRO, GDR 66, fos. 92, 93; WSRO, Ep.I/17/13, 6 July 1612; WRO, D3/4/7, fo. 51.

9. GRO, GDR 50, deanery of Gloucester, deanery of Stow; ERO, D/AE/A16, fo. 64v; D/AE/A22, fo. 253v; D/AB/A6, fo. 117; D/AB/A7, fo. 108v; SRO, D/D/Ca.113, fo. 151–v; NRO, X615/44, pp. 125, 244; X617/47, fo. 133v; WRO, D5/28/16/51; D5/28/28/24.

10. ERO, D/AC/A6, fo. 274; D/AC/A45, fo. 30; D/AE/A42, fo. 15–v; NRO, X609/19, fo. 39; X615/42, [p. 632]; SRO, D/D/Cd.34, Office v. Stibbs; WSRO, Ep.I/17/23, fo. 30; ORO, Oxford diocesan papers, c.2, fo. 35.

11. ERO, D/AC/A13, fo. 117v; D/AE/A17, fo. 1v; D/AE/A41, fo. 99v; NRO, X615/42, p. 566; X614/41, pp. 201, 230; SRO, D/D/Ca.222, fo. 118v; WSRO, Ep.I/17/15, 2 Apr. 1614.

12. ERO, D/AE/A13, fo. 54; D/AC/A47, fo. 46v; D/AE/A30, fos. 62v, 88; D/AE/A39, fos. 88v, 114; D/AC/A33, fo. 99; SRO, D/D/Ca.134, Bridgwater; D/D/Ca.214, fo. 45; D/D/Ca.215, fo. 242; D/D/Ca.226, fo. 178; WSRO, Ep.I/17/13, 10 Feb. 1610; HRO, 21M65/C1/27, fo. 30v; NRO, X614/41, p. 466; X612/68, fo. 26.

13. ERO, D/AC/A5, fo. 115; D/AC/A7, fo. 43v; D/AC/A8, fo. 233v; D/AC/A22, fo. 161v; D/AC/A51, fos. 182v, 262; NRO, X610/24, fo. 107; X617/48, p. 286; SRO, D/D/Cd.49, Office v. Bodye.

14. NRO, X610/24, fo. 21; X613/34, fo. 91; X617/48, pp. 183, 187; X620/62, fos. 86, 141; SRO, D/D/Ca.200, 16 Nov. 1618; WRO, D3/4/7, fo. 20v; D5/28/38/7.

15. NRO, X613/36, fo. 118v; X617/48, p. 205; X618/56A, p. 399; X621/68, fo. 81v; ORO, Oxford archdeaconry papers, c.12, fo. 166; ERO, D/AE/A27, fo. 209; D/AE/A41, fo. 121v; D/AC/A52, fo. 114; D/AC/A53, fos. 167–v, 172v; SRO, D/D/Ca.317, fo. 110.

16. NRO, X612/32, fos. 69, 71; X615/44, p. 510; X616/45, pp. 17–18; WRO, D5/28/10/68.

17. NRO, X609/20, fo. 183v; X610/24, fo. 169; X614/40, fo. 307; X614/41, pp. 154–5; SRO, D/D/Ca.120, Croscombe; D/D/Ca.140, p. 34; WSRO, Ep.I/17/15, 10 July 1613; ERO, D/AB/A1, fo. 97; D/AC/A51, fo. 182v; D/AE/A41, fo. 145; D/AC/A53, fo. 59v.

18. ERO, D/AB/A4, fo. 4; GRO, GDR 20, p. 32; GDR 40, fo. 162v; HRO, 21M65/C1/20, fo. 34v; SRO, D/D/Cd.34, Office v. Calvert; NRO, X613/36, fo. 117v; X621/66, fo. 149v; WRO, D1/39/2/11, fo. 37; D10/4/1, 12 Apr. 1627; D5/28/34/34, fo. 1.

19. NRO, X610/23, fo. 60; X610/23A, fos. 81, 123; X615/43, fo. 45; ERO, D/AE/A15, fo. 163v; D/AE/A38, fo. 122v; SRO, D/D/Ca.142, p. 130; WRO, D5/28/20/7, 25.

20. *PMP* (1631 edn.), 123; ORO, Oxford diocesan papers, d.9, fo. 90; SRO, D/D/Ca.162, deanery of Bedminster, 16 Oct. 1609; D/D/Cd.56, Office v. Bath; Peyton (ed.), *Churchwardens' Presentments in the Oxfordshire Peculiars*, 283.

21. WRO, D5/28/10/89; ERO, D/AE/A29, fo. 46; BLO, MS Rawlinson C.766, fos. 154v–157; NRO, X620/63, p. 197; PRO, SP 16/261, fo. 207; SRO, D/D/Ca.222, fos. 9, 10, 16; Johnstone (ed.), *Churchwardens' Presentments (17th Century): Part 1*, 66, 75; ORO, Oxford archdeaconry papers, c.12, fos. 291, 313.

22. ERO, D/AC/A15, fo. 63v; D/AE/A42, fo. 17; NRO, X613/36, fos. 39–40, 99–v; WRO, D5/28/9/27; D5/28/20/17, 21, 22; WSRO, Ep.I/17/15, 1 Oct. 1614; Ep.I/17/23, fo. 172.
23. SRO, D/D/Ca.73, 10 July 1585; D/D/Ca. 220, Middlezoy; D/D/Ca.260, fo. 151–v; D/D/Cd.78, Office v. Dorvall; D/D/Ca.282, fo. 141; D/D/Ca.215, fo. 217; ERO, D/AC/A9, fo. 226v; D/AC/A42, fo. 92; NRO, X615/43, fo. 211; X613/36, fos. 50v–51, 60.
24. WSRO, Ep.I/17/13, 21 Oct. 1609; WRO, D5/28/17/16; D5/28/22/21; ERO, D/AC/A45, fo. 141v; D/AE/A36, fo. 89; D/AE/A39, fo. 134v; ORO, Oxford diocesan papers, c.2, fos. 226v, 234–v.
25. GRO, GDR 66, fo. 83v; NRO, X610/24, fo. 176; X613/36, fo. 170; WSRO, Ep.I/17/15, 21 Jan. 1614; SRO, D/D/Ca.207, fos. 229v–230; ERO, D/AE/A34, fo. 247v; D/AC/A49, fo. 136v; D/AC/A51, fo. 4v; D/AE/A42, fo. 140.
26. GRO, GDR 76, fo. 51; SRO, D/D/Ca.196, fo. 360v; D/D/Ca.85, 25 Sept. 1588; D/D/Ca.113, fo. 74; ERO, D/AC/A52, fo. 263; D/AC/A47, fo. 41v; D/AC/A51, f. 114; D/AE/A15, fo. 207v; D/AE/A36, fos. 41v, 77v; NRO, X617/51, pp. 424, 431; HRO, 21M65/C1/30, fo. 34; ORO, Oxford archdeaconry papers, c.12, fo. 273b.
27. SRO, D/D/Ca.189, fo. 248v; D/D/Ca.214, fo. 267v; D/D/Ca.224, fo. 329; D/D/Ca.282, fos. 11v, 91v; WRO, D5/28/17/57, fo. 1v; NRO, X618/56A, p. 346.
28. *PMP*, 19–20, 292, 346; H. Scudder, *The Christian's Daily Walke in Holy Securitie and Peace* (1631 ed.), 456–57; SRO, D/D/Ca.207, fos. 39v, 119–v; ERO, D/AE/A40, fo. 225v; Bate, *The Portraiture of Hypocrisy*, 34; Turvill, *The Poore Man's Path-way to Heaven*, 31, 58, 61.

CHAPTER 5

1. *PMP*, 1–3, 13–16, 82–3, 108, 302, 323, 356. Many of the themes of this chapter were set out by Patrick Collinson in his *Godly People: Essays on English Protestantism and Puritanism* (1983), 1–17, 399–428, 527–50.
2. *PMP*, 7; Turvill, *The Poore Man's Path-way to Heaven*, 53; Bolton, *Some Generall Directions*, 79; ERO, D/AC/A13, fo. 28; D/AE/A13, fo. 65v; D/AE/A26, fo. 43v; NRO, X610/23A, fo. 157; SRO, D/D/Ca.266, deanery of Dunster, 17 Sept. 1629.
3. Turvill, *The Poore Man's Path-way to Heaven*, 238; HRO, 21M65/C1/14/2; WSRO, Ep.I/23/7, fo. 21; ERO, D/AE/A13 fo. 65; D/AE/A20, fo. 213v; D/AC/A15, fo. 92v; SRO, D/D/Ca.102, fo. 18; D/D/Ca.189, fo. 175; D/D/Ca.299, fo. 61v; D/D/Ca.313, fo. 86v; NRO, X612/32, fo. 214.
4. Matthew 5:11; GRO, GDR 21, p. 304; NRO, X607/9, fo. 14; LA, Ch.P/12/3, fo. 3; ERO, D/AE/A34, fo. 66v; Bolton, *Some Generall Directions*, 5–6.
5. GRO, GDR 26, pp. 31, 44; GDR 29, p. 88; ERO, D/AC/A10, fos. 66v–67, 75; D/AC/A35, fo. 232; R. Baxter, *The Autobiography*, ed. N. H. Keeble (1974), 4, 6; ORO, Oxford diocesan papers, c.27, fos. 53v, 54v, 58v, 62.
6. ERO, D/AC/A35, fo. 131v; D/AB/A7, fo. 36; SRO, D/D/Ca.261, fo. 250v; D/D/Cd.66, pp. 107–10; D/D/Ca.299, fo. 10v.
7. ERO, D/AE/A23, fo. 7; D/AB/A1, fo. 135; D/AB/A6, fos. 139, 170v; D/AB/A7, fo. 11; D/AB/A8, fo. 113; NRO, X619/60, fo. 114; SRO, D/D/Ca.171, fo. 408.
8. ERO, D/AC/A12, fo. 67; D/AE/A32, fo. 124v; NRO, X615/42, p. 177; Johnstone (ed.), *Churchwardens' Presentments (17th Century): Part 1*, 2.

9. ERO, D/AE/A13, fo. 104v; D/AB/A1, fo. 185; WSRO, Ep.I/17/9, 25 May 1598; NRO, X615/44, p. 584; X609/21, fos. 185, 196v; X614/40, fo. 18v.

10. ERO, D/AC/A13, fos. 87, 93v; D/AE/A14, fo. 274; D/AE/A16, fo. 55v; D/AE/A27, fo. 288; NRO, X611/28, fo. 29v; X648/2, p. 163; HRO, 21M65/C1/29, fos. 22v, 27v.

11. WSRO, Ep.I/17/9, 23 July 1597; Ep.II/15/1, p. 58; ERO, D/AC/A35, 24 Oct. 1611; D/AE/A22, fo. 30; D/AE/A24, fos. 184, 216; D/AE/A27, fo. 38; D/AE/A32, fos. 125, 164–v; NRO, X611/28, fo. 42; HRO, 21M65/C1/34, fo. 9; WRO, D1/39/2/11, fo. 116.

12. GRO, GDR 76, fo. 266v; NRO, X611/27, fo. 41; X616/45, [p. 606]; Peyton (ed.), *Churchwardens' Presentments in the Oxfordshire Peculiars*, 201–2, 209; Clarke, *The Lives of Thirty-Two English Divines*, 118–19; Leics. RO, 1D41/13/39, fos. 99–102; WRO, D1/39/2/11, fo. 3v; ERO, D/AE/A36, fos. 103, 173.

13. ERO, D/AE/A37, fos. 201v–202; D/AE/A38, fo. 70; D/AB/A5, fo. 165; D/AC/A52, fo. 171v; D/AC/A47, fo. 210; NRO, X621/67, 15 Aug. 1637; X649/1, pp. 475–6, 497, 519–22.

14. BRO, D/A/V/1, fo. 29v; NRO, X610/23, fo. 75v; X608/13, fo. 77v; X609/20, fo. 20; X615/44, pp. 42, 44, 257; X614/41, pp. 132, 152; SRO, D/D/Ca.102, fo. 54; D/D/Ca.162, deanery of Bedminster, 16 Oct. 1609; ORO, Oxford diocesan papers, d.5, fos. 47, 67.

15. ERO, D/AE/A13, fo. 131; D/AE/A21, fo. 222; D/AC/A54, fo. 96; ORO, Oxford archdeaconry papers, c.13, fo. 159v.

16. NRO, X609/20, fo. 33v; ERO, D/AC/A35, fos. 5, 24v; D/AC/A46, fos. 122v, 130v; D/AC/A49, fo. 57v; D/AE/A42, fo. 35; BRO, D/A/V/2, fo. 213.

17. *PMP*, 369; WSRO, Ep.I/23/7, fo. 27; Ep.I/17/15, 17 June 1615; GRO, GDR 76, fo. 288; SRO, D/D/Ca.172, 11 Jan. 1613; NRO, X617/48, p. 549; ERO, D/AB/A5, fo. 25v.

18. ERO, D/AE/A14, fo. 127v; D/AE/A15, fo. 129v; D/AC/A43, fo. 137v; WRO, D1/39/2/11, fo. 119; NRO, X621/65, fo. 31v.

19. ERO, D/AE/A13, fo. 41; AC/A42, fos. 162, 171, loose letter, Parker to Tillingham; NRO, X610/24, fo. 76; SRO, D/D/Ca.282, fo. 177v; ORO, Oxford archdeaconry papers, c.12, fo. 81v.

20. ERO, D/AE/A14, fos. 273v–274v; D/AE/A15, fo. 129–v; D/AE/A17, fo. 111v; D/AE/A19, fo. 119; D/AC/A45, fo. 180–v; D/AC/A48, fo. 52; D/AC/A47, fo. 167v; NRO, X614/40, fos. 62v, 82; X615/43, fo. 16; X620/62, fo. 153v; X621/66, fos. 55, 66v; X620/63, fos. 408v, 417v; SRO, D/D/Ca.189, fos. 183v–184, 276v; D/D/Ca.191, Stoke Lane, 6 Oct. 1615, Farringdon, 13 Oct. 1615; D/D/Ca.222, fo. 13; ORO, Oxford diocesan papers, c.2, fo. 272v.

21. ERO, D/AE/A12, fos. 103–4, 115v–116, 267–v; D/AC/A48, fos. 195, 196v, 206–v; BL, Additional MS 48064, fo. 85v; NRO, X616/45, Jan. 1618; X617/48, 31 Jan. 1618; SRO, D/D/Ca.299, fo. 57; D/D/Ca.313, fos. 28, 35v–36; BLO, Rawlinson Letters 89. On conventicles, see P. Collinson, 'The English Conventicle', in his *From Cranmer to Sancroft* (2006); P. Collinson, *The Elizabethan Puritan Movement* (1967), 374–80.

22. GRO, GDR 40, fo. 164–v; SRO, D/D/Cd.20, fo. 82; D/D/Ca.81, Stoke Difford; WSRO, Ep.I/23/7, fo. 27; ERO, D/AE/A13, fos. 20v, 92v, 125v–126, 128; WRO, D5/28/8/151; D1/39/2/5, fos. 65–6.

23. ERO, D/AE/A29, fo. 149–v; WRO, D5/28/17/46; SRO, D/D/Ca.200, 30 Sept. 1619; D/D/Cd.66, pp. 113, 115; NRO, X619/61, 1 Dec. 1630, 20 Jan. 1631; ORO, Oxford archdeaconry papers, c.12, fo. 344–v.

24. SRO, D/D/Cd.66, pp. 111–15; D/D/Cd.72, Office v. Willis; D/D/Ca.283, fo. 26; D/D/Ca.315, fo. 104; D/D/Ca.316, fos. 83v, 99v. In 1637 thirteen parishioners of St Mary Magdalene, Taunton, were cited for refusing to contribute towards the cost of the organs, but Willis was not among them, see SRO, D/D/Ca.313, fos. 101, 106v–107.

25. ORO, Oxford diocesan papers, c.27, fo. 44v; Oxford archdeaconry papers, c.12, fos. 79v–80; NRO, X621/65, fos. 61–v, 82; ERO, D/AB/A8, fo. 3; D/AE/A42, fo. 34v; WSRO, Ep.II/15/1, p. 33.

26. ERO, D/AE/A13, fo. 97v; WRO, D5/28/22/88; NRO, X615/42, pp. 31, 108, 154; Johnstone (ed.), *Churchwardens' Presentments (17th Century): Part 1*, p. 37.

27. WSRO, Ep.I/17/23, fo. 8; SRO, D/D/Ca.282, fo. 178; NRO, X621/65, fos. 50v, 147, 161; WRO, D5/28/34/34–7.

28. ERO, D/AC/A47, fo. 100v; D/AE/A38, fo. 294v; D/AB/A7, fo. 165; D/AE/A41, fo. 102v; ORO, Oxford diocesan papers, c.27, fos. 43v–48v, 53v–58v; SRO, D/D/Ca.308, fos. 45–6, 74v; NRO, X621/68, fo. 38.

29. ERO, D/AE/A41, fos. 182v–183; D/AC/A52, fos. 186v, 193, 196, 227, 228v, 232–v; D/AE/A42, fo. 5; D/AC/A53, fos. 95, 208v.

30. ERO, D/AC/A51, fos. 184, 196, 206v, 207v, 237v; D/AC/A52, fo. 22v; D/AB/A9, fo. 92v; SRO, D/D/Ca.313, fo. 27v.

31. SRO, D/D/Ca.224, fo. 330; D/D/Ca.313, fo. 86v; D/D/Ca.315, fo. 112; Johnstone (ed.), *Churchwardens' Presentments (17th Century): Part 1*, 83; ERO, D/AC/A47, fo. 99v; D/AB/A8, fo. 171v.

32. NRO, X620/63, fo. 333; ERO, D/AE/A41, fos. 241v, 243v; D/AE/A42, fos. 52v, 54; D/AC/A50, fo. 179v.

33. ERO, D/AC/A53, fos. 112, 164; SRO, D/D/Ca.313, fo. 28; NRO, X621/65, fo. 38; X621/68, fo. 29v; *PMP*, 70.

CHAPTER 6

1. *PMP*, 20, 245–6, 296; Bolton, *Some Generall Directions*, 288; Bolton, *Instructions for a Right Comforting*, 341; ERO, D/AE/A10, fo. 64v.

2. Bolton, *Two Sermons Preached at Northampton*, 84; NRO, X607/9, fo. 12v; WRO, D5/28/7/2, 26, 28, 29, 100; ORO, Oxford diocesan papers, c.24, fo. 106v.

3. HRO, 21M65/C1/28, fos. 21v–22, 31v–32; W. Perkins, *The Workes* (1608–12), i, 311.

4. Bolton, *Instructions for a Right Comforting*, 61; SRO, D/D/Ca.191, Wincanton, 6 Oct. 1615; D/D/Ca.260, fos. 75v, 79v; WRO, D5/28/18/26; D1/39/2/11, fo. 42–v.

5. Bolton, *Some Generall Directions*, 24; Lichfield RO, B/C/5/1629, Handsworth, fos. 1v, 4, 7v–8; SRO, D/D/Cd.72, Office v. Willis, loose letter, mayor to bishop.

6. NRO, X610/25, fo. 19; W. J. Sheils, *The Puritans in the Diocese of Peterborough, 1558–1610*, Northamptonshire Record Society (1979), 128 ('Brownists' were those thought to be followers of the separatist Robert Browne; 'Martinists' were those thought to be sympathetic to the anti-episcopalian tracts of Martin Marprelate); SRO, D/D/Ca.101, 19 and 30 July 1594; D/D/Ca.102, fo. 12; D/D/Ca. 215, fos.

133v–134 (John Traske had been preaching in Somerset in 1614. For his teachings, see D. Como, 'The Kingdom of Christ, the Kingdom of England and the Kingdom of Traske', in M. C. McClendon, J. P. Ward and M. MacDonald (eds.), *Protestant Identities: Religion, Society and Self-Fashioning in Post-Reformation England* (1999), 62–82); D/D/Ca.220, 8 Sept. 1620; ERO, D/AE/A22, fo. 2; D/AE/A23, fo. 6; D/AE/A27, fo. 295; D/AC/A46, fo. 111; D/AC/A47, fo. 98; D/AC/A51, fo. 253v; D/AC/A53, fo. 201v; HRO, 21M65/C1/28, fo. 21v.

7. NRO, X610/24, fo. 93; X613/36, fos. 114–v, 116; SRO, D/D/Ca.121, Stoke; D/D/Ca.134, Stogursey.

8. PRO, STAC 8/94/17, nos. 2, 12, 14; WRO, D5/28/9/59. For the background to the Dorchester libels, see D. Underdown, *Fire from Heaven: Life in an English Town in the Seventeenth Century* (1993 edn.), 27–37.

9. SRO, D/D/Ca.248, fo. 116; D/D/Ca.282, fo. 218v; ERO, D/AC/A48, fos. 154v, 186v, 199v; D/AC/A51, fos. 14v, 26v.

10. ORO, Oxford diocesan papers, c.27, fos. 43v–48v, 53v–58, 64v; PAR214/4/F1/78.

11. *PMP*, 26, 302, 368–9; ERO, D/AE/A19, fo. 315; D/AC/A49, fo. 18v; D/AE/A31, fo. 117v; *Historical Manuscripts Commission 13th Report: Rye* (1892), 99; R. P. Sorlien (ed.), *The Diary of John Manningham* (1976), 29, 77, 163, 218; LA, Vj 16, fo. 94v; SRO, D/D/Ca.215, fo. 150; PRO, STAC 8/94/17, no. 2; Johnstone (ed.), *Churchwardens' Presentments (17th Century): Part 1*, 66; Lichfield RO, B/C/5/1629, Handsworth, fo. 4; Granger, *Paul's Crowne of Rejoycing*, 31.

12. ERO, D/AE/A26, fo. 139; D/AE/A31, fo. 68–v; D/AE/A36, fo. 263; D/AC/A46, fo. 162; N. Tyacke, 'Popular Puritan Mentality in Late Elizabethan England', in P. Clark, A. G. R. Smith, and N. Tyacke (eds.), *The English Commonwealth, 1547–1640* (1979), 77–92 (the illegitimate child of Anne Stephens of Marks Tey was named Repentance in 1632: see ERO, Q/SR 278/19); ERO, D/AE/A41, fo. 102v; NRO, X615/44, p. 104; X619/61, 30 Sept. 1629.

13. Bolton, *A Three-Fold Treatise*, 256; Perkins, *The Workes*, i, sig. A₂, 311, 361; ii, 87, 332; iii, 447; Bate, *The Portraiture of Hypocrisy*, 89; Turvill, *The Poore Man's Path-way to Heaven*, 11–12, 53; Granger, *Paul's Crowne of Rejoycing*, 6, 9, 54; *PMP*, 287; WRO, D5/28/29/39.

14. ERO, D/AE/A14, fos. 95v, 253–v; D/AE/A15, fos. 154v, 155v. Blaby apparently held a rectory in Worcestershire.

15. ERO, Q/SR 118/32–3, 39, 40, 40a; J. S. Cockburn (ed.), *Calendar of Assize Records: Essex Indictments, Elizabeth I* (1979), 383.

16. ERO, Q/SR 118/40a, 55–9; D/AE/A15, fos. 166, 183v, 190v, 194; Cockburn (ed.), *Calendar of Assize Records: Essex Indictments, Elizabeth I*, 382–3, 385.

17. ERO, D/AE/A14, fo. 95v; Q/SR 104/39, 118/39; Cockburn (ed.), *Calendar of Assize Records: Essex Indictments, Elizabeth I*, 382.

18. NRO, X613/34, fos. 20v, 59, 114v–115, 125v.

19. NRO, X608/13, fos. 1v, 148; Sheils, *The Puritans in the Diocese of Peterborough*, 135–6.

20. NRO, X615/42, pp. 554–5; X615/44, pp. 26–44, 257, 362, 565, 27 May 1616, 638, 670, 692, 693; X616/45, 29 Oct. 1617.

21. NRO, X615/44, p. 401; X616/45, 14 July 1617, 27 Sept. 1617; X614/41, pp. 403–4, 412.

22. NRO, X615/44, pp. 510, 584; X616/45, p. 198, 12 Nov. 1617, Jan. 1618; X614/41, pp. 316, 394, 409, 424; X617/48, 31 Jan. 1618, p. 437; X618/56A, pp. 447–8; X648/2, pp. 190, 397, 411; J. Fielding, 'Opposition to the Personal Rule of Charles I: The Diary of Robert Woodford, 1637–1641', *Historical Journal*, 31 (1988), 779–85.

23. PRO, SP 14/122, fo. 285v; NRO, X614/41, pp. 25, 99; X615/44, p. 561; X616/45, p. 18, 29 Oct. 1617, 14 Nov. 1617.

24. WSRO, Ep.I/17/11, fos. 95, 113v, 166; Ep.I/17/15, 9 July 1614; Ep.I/17/17, 8 Mar. 1617; Ep.I/26/2, fo. 26; Johnstone (ed.), *Churchwardens' Presentments (17th Century): Part 1*, 48–9, 57, 66, 75.

25. ERO, D/AC/A47, fo. 99v; D/AB/A5, fo. 25v, D/AC/A50, fos. 9, 103, 115, 127, 201v; D/AC/A48, fo. 154; D/AC/A49, fo. 136v.

26. ERO, D/AC/A51, fos. 15v, 27v–28, 51, 61, 78v, 81, 87–v, 119v, 120, 125, 161, 252v; D/AC/A52, fo. 17; D/AC/A54, fo. 96; J. Walter, 'Popular Iconoclasm and the Politics of the Parish in Eastern England, 1640–1642', *Historical Journal*, 47 (2004), 285.

27. PRO, SP 16/261, fos. 179–180v; SP 16/339, fo. 82; BLO, MS Tanner 70, fos. 107–11; J. Walter, *Understanding Popular Violence in the English Revolution: The Colchester Plunderers* (1999), 171–3; ERO, D/AC/A52, fos. 17, 19, 94; D/AC/A54, fo. 10v; D/AC/A51, fo. 253v; D/AC/A53, fos. 164, 201v.

28. Walter, *Understanding Popular Violence*, 172; ERO, D/AC/A51, fo. 125; D/AC/A52, fos. 66, 92, 249; D/AC/A54, fo. 49v. There was much more trouble in Colchester in 1640, in the new situation brought about by the Bishops' War. My interpretation of the earlier evidence differs somewhat from that of Walter, *Understanding Popular Violence*, 161–200, primarily because the recorded nonconformity and protest in the town in the 1630s does not seem to me to amount to very much. See below, pp. 210–14.

29. ERO, D/AE/A12, fos. 10, 49v, 98, 103–4, 115v–116, 150v, 266–8, 287, 311v; D/AE/A13, fos. 71v, 137v; BL, Additional MS 48064, fos. 85v–86v; NRO, X610/23, fos. 60, 143v, 144v–146, 220v; X609/21, fo. 116–v; X610/23A, fos. 13, 14, 16, 24; Peyton (ed.), *Churchwardens' Presentments in the Oxfordshire Peculiars*, 201–2; Clarke, *The Lives of Thirty-Two English Divines*, 118–19; Leics. RO, 1D41/13/39, fos. 99–102; WRO, D1/39/2/11, fos. 35v–43; D5/28/11/24; D5/28/35/73; SRO, D/D/Ca.299, fos. 1v, 11, 56v–58, 61–v; D/D/Ca.78, Office v. Dorvall, Office v. Haines.

30. ORO, Oxford diocesan papers, c.27, fos. 43v–48v, 53v–64v; PAR214/4/F1/78; *PMP*, 301–5. These issues of religious conflict and coexistence are discussed in A. Walsham, *Charitable Hatred: Tolerance and Intolerance in England, 1500–1700* (2006), 106–59, 207–14, 269–80. See also P. Collinson, 'The Cohabitation of the Faithful with the Unfaithful', in O. P. Grell, J. I. Israel, and N. Tyacke (eds.), *From Persecution to Toleration: The Glorious Revolution and Religion in England* (1991).

CHAPTER 7

1. *PMP*, 35, 275, 279, 295, 300, 304, 307, 309, 310, 314, 320.

2. *PMP*, 186; ERO, D/AE/A19, fo. 212; D/AE/A12, fo. 145v; D/AE/A16, fos. 72, 74; S. Ward, *Woe to Drunkards* (1622), 27–8; GRO, GDR 28, p. 89; NRO, X609/19, fo. 39.

3. ORO, Oxford diocesan papers, d.13, fo. 50v; WRO, D5/28/13/98; WSRO, Ep.I/17/13, 18 Jan. 1612; ERO, D/AE/A27, fo. 215; D/AE/A33, fos. 142v, 164v, 265; D/AE/A38, fos. 172v–173, 269v; D/AE/A42, fo. 149v; NRO, X617/54, 24 Jan., 20 Mar., 13 Apr. 1621; Leics. RO, 1D41/13/59, fo. 349. The classic study of the values of alehouse and church is K. Wrightson, 'Two Concepts of Order: Justices, Constables and Jurymen in Seventeenth-Century England', in J. Brewer and J. Styles (eds.), *An Ungovernable People: The English and their Law in the Seventeenth and Eighteenth Centuries* (1980).

4. *PMP*, 63; SRO, D/D/Ca.86, Hill Farrance; D/D/Ca.189, fos. 304–v, 327–8, 337v–338; D/D/Ca.267, deanery of Carey, 9 Sept. 1629; WRO, D5/28/8/48; NRO, X648/2, pp. 130, 138, 149; ERO, D/AE/A38, fo. 89v; D/AC/A49, fo. 92. For the mistreatment of pregnant women, see esp. M. Ingram, *Church Courts, Sex and Marriage in England, 1570–1640* (1987), 230–6, 261; for sympathy towards them, see ibid. 285–91, though Dr Ingram suggests that it was unusual.

5. GRO, GDR 46, p. 76; ERO, D/AE/A17, fo. 70v; D/AE/A25, fo. 290; WRO, D5/28/11/14; NRO, X615/43, fo. 216v; SRO, D/D/Ca.196, 4 July 1615; D/D/Ca.200, 16 Nov. 1618; D/D/Ca.320, fo. 74; D/D/Ca.330, fo. 17.

6. NRO, X612/33, fo. 173v; WRO, D1/39/2/6, fo. 128; SRO, D/D/Ca.172, 17 Nov. 1612; D/D/Ca.207, fos. 39–v, 40v–41; Leics. RO, 1D41/13/59, fos. 350v–351.

7. WSRO, Ep.I/17/13, 13 July 1611; NRO, X615/42, pp. 376, 444; X620/64, fo. 21; WRO, D5/28/28/27; ORO, Oxford archdeaconry papers, c.12, fo. 75–v; ERO, D/AE/A17, fo. 149v; D/AE/A24, fo. 182v; *PMP*, 64. Cf. D. Cressy, 'Cross-Dressing in the Birth Room: Gender Trouble and Cultural Boundaries', in his *Travesties and Transgressions in Tudor and Stuart England* (2000), 92–115.

8. *PMP*, 103, 107; WRO, D5/28/8/30; D5/28/17/35; D5/28/22/84; ORO, Oxford diocesan papers, c.2, fos. 226v, 234–v; SRO, D/D/Ca.308, fos. 176v–177v; D/D/Ca. 196, fo. 218v; D/D/Ca.215, fo. 28v; NRO, X621/68, fo. 50; X610/23A, fo. 95; X617/54, 26 Jan. 1624; GRO, GDR 76, fo. 221; ERO, D/AE/A32, fo. 156v; D/AE/A34, fo. 140v; D/AE/A19, fo. 352v; D/AE/A39, fo. 135–v; D/AB/A4, fo. 54.

9. *PMP*, 303; SRO, D/D/Ca.65, 16 Oct., 31 Oct. 1581; D/D/Ca.172, 24 Nov. 1612; ERO, D/AE/A14, fo. 102; NRO, X617/48, p. 415; HRO, 21M65/C1/34, fo. 43.

10. SRO, D/D/Ca.140, p. 397; D/D/Ca.172, 24 Nov. 1612; D/D/Cd.66, pp. 196–8; ERO, D/AC/A33, fo. 31v; D/AE/A17, fo. 164; D/AE/A25, fos. 3, 75v; D/AE/A27, fo. 326; D/AE/A31, fos. 247v–248; D/AC/A42, fo. 175v; D/AC/A45, fo. 96v; WSRO, Ep.I/17/17, 7 Dec. 1616 (he meant that he was now within the jurisdiction of the dean of Chichester, not the diocesan court); Ep.I/17/24, 22 June 1632; NRO, X616/45, p. 127; X619/61, 16 June 1629; X614/41, p. 23; X621/66, fo. 24v; Johnstone (ed.), *Churchwardens' Presentments (17th Century): Part 1*, 53.

11. Ingram, *Church Courts, Sex and Marriage in England*, 323–63; GRO, GDR 43, fo. 55v; ERO, D/AE/A17, fo. 136; D/AC/A34, fo. 182; D/AB/A1, fos. 20, 81v; NRO, X614/40, fo. 308v; ORO, Oxford diocesan papers, c.2, fo. 324; BRO, D/A/V/2, fo. 143v; SRO, D/D/Cd.56, Office v. Light; D/D/Ca.226, fo. 222v; D/D/Ca.261, fo. 134; D/D/Ca.171, fo. 277–v; WRO, D5/28/22/21, 26, 34.

12. SRO, D/D/Ca.65, 19 Jan., 26 Jan. 1582; D/D/Ca.134, Office v. Masters; D/D/Cd.54, Office v. Dolling; ERO, D/AE/A24, fos. 4, 33; NRO, X614/41, pp. 132, 152; X648/2, p. 114 (Edward meant that he would employ Richard even if he

was not absolved from excommunication); Leics. RO, 1D41/13/60, fo. 224; ORO, Oxford archdeaconry papers, c.12, fo. 54.

13. GRO, GDR 43, fos. 49v, 50v; F. D. Price, 'An Elizabethan Church Official: Thomas Powell, Chancellor of Gloucester Diocese', *Church Quarterly Review*, 128 (1939), 94–112; SRO, D/D/Ca.65, 16 Oct. 1581; D/D/Ca.85, 4 Nov. 1588; D/D/Ca.113, fo. 101; D/D/Ca.189, fo. 18v; D/D/Ca.283, fo. 92; ERO, D/AE/A14, fo. 32v; D/AC/A50, fos. 115, 127, 168v; D/AB/A8, fo. 6v.

14. HRO, 21M65/C1/11, fo. 32; ERO, D/AC/A15, fo. 8v; D/AE/A33, fos. 283v–284; SRO, D/D/Ca.207, fo. 271v; D/D/Ca.226, fo. 100; D/D/Ca.248, fos. 122 ('polling' literally means taxing), 126v; D/D/Ca.260, fo. 243v; D/D/Ca.283, fo. 92; NRO, X621/65, fo. 15v.

15. LA, Vj 16, fo. 99v; SRO, D/D/Ca.85, 2 Oct., 4 Nov. 1588; D/D/Ca.260, fo. 191; ERO, D/AC/A21, fos. 19v–20; D/AC/A22, fo. 258; D/AC/A31, fo. 17; D/AE/A26, fo. 87; D/AE/A27, fo. 281v; D/AE/A29, fo. 76v; D/AC/A54, fo. 23; WSRO, Ep.I/17/13, 3 Feb. 1610; NRO, X621/66, fo. 12v.

16. GRO, GDR 40, fo. 63v; WRO, D1/43/5, fo. 9; D3/7/1, fo. 169; D1/39/2/6, fo. 82v; NRO, X612/29, fo. 8v; SRO, D/D/Ca.142, pp. 113–14; WSRO, Ep.I/17/15, 30 July 1614; ERO, D/AE/A32, fo. 124v.

17. NRO, X617/51, p. 500; X619/60, fo. 6v; X649/1, p. 40; X621/68, fo. 102v; WSRO, Ep.I/17/25, fo. 21v; Ep.II/15/1, p. 17; SRO, D/D/Ca.300, fo. 135; ERO, D/AC/A54, fo. 56.

18. ORO, Oxford diocesan papers, d.11, fos. 241v, 281, 337; Oxford archdeaconry papers, c.13, f. 126; ERO, D/AC/A51, fo. 45v. On churchwardens and their work, see E. Carlson, 'The Origins, Function and Status of the Office of Churchwarden, with Particular Reference to the Diocese of Ely', in M. Spufford (ed.), *The World of Rural Dissenters, 1520–1725* (1995), 164–207; J. Craig, *Reformation, Politics and Polemics: The Growth of Protestantism in East Anglian Market Towns, 1500–1610* (2001), 34–63.

19. ERO, D/AB/A4, fos. 112v, 115; D/AC/49, fo. 83; D/AB/A8, fo. 179; ORO, Oxford diocesan papers, c.2, fos. 18v, 36v, 241.

20. LA, Vj 16, fo. 97v; ERO, D/AC/A22, fos. 161v, 181; SRO, D/D/Ca.142, fo. 96; D/D/Ca.200, 27 Sept. 1621; NRO, X614/41, p. 475. Purgation was the production of character-witnesses who would swear that the accused's denial could be believed.

21. ERO, D/AE/A9, fo. 32v; NRO, X612/33, fo. 184v; X615/42, 8 Feb. 1614; X615/43, fo. 293v; X617/47, fo. 113–v; X621/68, fos. 102v, 113v; X621/69, fo. 4v; WSRO, Ep.I/17/15, 23 July 1614; Ep.II/15/1, p. 20.

22. ERO, D/AC/A9, fo. 218; D/AC/A51, fos. 207v, 229; NRO, X617/50, pp. 297, 331; WRO, D5/28/22/16; SRO, D/D/Ca.267, deanery of Frome, 8 Sept. 1629; D/D/Ca.282, fos. 224v–225; BRO, D/A/V/2, fo. 101.

23. GRO, GDR 9, p. 106; ERO, D/AE/A14, fo. 273v; D/AE/A17, fo. 58; D/AC/A35, fo. 87; NRO, X613/36, fos. 116v, 122, 130; SRO, D/D/Ca.207, fo. 119v.

24. NRO, X614/40, fo. 87v; X617/48, pp. 132, 158; X619/58, 9 Feb., 31 Mar. 1626; SRO, D/D/Ca.220; D/D/Ca.267, deanery of Frome, 8 Sept. 1629; ERO, D/AC/A47, fos. 42v, 152v; D/AC/A50, fo. 131v; D/AC/A51, fo. 229v; ORO, Oxford archdeaconry papers, c.12, fo. 28.

25. *PMP*, 2.

26. Gifford, *A Briefe discourse*, fo. 2–v; *PMP*, 303.

CHAPTER 8

1. *PMP*, 129, 353–4.
2. ERO, D/AC/A13, fo. 160; SRO, D/D/Ca.141, [5] Mar. 1605; D/D/Ca.171, fo. 269v; D/D/Ca.207, fo. 3; D/D/Ca.215, fo. 150; D/D/Ca.220, 15 Sept. 1620; D/D/Ca.247, fo. 2v; D/D/Ca.266, deanery of Crewkerne, 18 Sept. 1629.
3. ORO, Oxford diocesan papers, c.26, fos. 341–v, 347–v; SRO, D/D/Ca.313, fos. 71v–72; D/D/Ca.330, fo. 54v.
4. NRO, X607/9, fo. 7v; X609/21, fo. 206; X619/58, 28 July 1626; X620/63, fo. 400; ERO, D/AC/A6, fo. 304; D/AE/A14, fos. 165v–166; D/AE/A32, fo. 64v; SRO, D/D/Ca.57, deaneries of Taunton and Dunster; D/D/Ca.120, East Pennard; WRO, D5/28/10/30, 62; WSRO, Ep.I/17/14, 20 Mar. 1613; Ep.I/17/17, 28 June 1617.
5. ERO, D/AE/A11, fo. 127v; D/AE/A12, fo. 14; BRO, D/A/V/1, fo. 30v; SRO, D/D/Cd.34, Office v. Hillard; D/D/Ca.172, 19 Jan. 1613; D/D/Ca.189, fos. 102, 104v–105v; D/D/Ca.207, fos. 166v–167, 179v, 195v, 226v.
6. SRO, D/D/Ca.196, fo. 321; D/D/Ca.260, fo. 166v; D/D/Ca.282, fo. 120v; D/D/Ca. 283, fo. 29; D/D/Ca.317, 24 July 1638; WRO, D5/28/22/52; ERO, D/AE/A37, fos. 4v, 75v; D/AC/A47, fo. 142; D/AC/A53, fo. 167; NRO, X619/61, 17 Sept. 1631; Leics. RO, 1D41/13/57, fo. 162v.
7. G. E. Aylmer, 'Unbelief in Seventeenth-Century England', in D. Pennington and K. Thomas (eds.), *Puritans and Revolutionaries* (1978), 22–32; WRO, D5/28/8/68; D5/28/10/66; SRO, Q/SR 57/1, fos. 31, 63; NRO, X621/65, fo. 75v. See M. Hunter, 'The Problem of Atheism in Early Modern England', *Transactions of the Royal Historical Society*, 5th ser., 35 (1985) 135–57.
8. GRO, GDR 31, p. 359; SRO, D/D/Ca.66, Edington; D/D/Cd.54, Office v. Smith; D/D/Ca.215, fo. 80v; ERO, D/AC/A20, fo. 65–v; D/AC/A33, fo. 6; D/AE/A25, fo. 319v; D/AE/A26, fo. 171v; D/AB/A6, fo. 117; D/AC/A49, fo. 224; WRO, D5/28/3/42; NRO, X617/51, p. 424.
9. NRO, X621/68, fo. 45; X609/21, fos. 151, 175; X617/47, fo. 59; X617/48, pp. 191, 230; X620/62, fo. 2; ERO, D/AC/A35, fo. 130v; D/AE/A36, fo. 208v; D/AE/A41, fos. 43v, 241; SRO, D/D/Ca.247, fo. 233.
10. ERO, D/AE/A17, fos. 123, 132v; SRO, D/D/Ca.189, fos. 268v–269; D/D/Ca.200, 15 Nov. 1616; NRO, X617/47, fo. 85v; X619/61, 8 Feb. 1631.
11. ERO, D/AC/A21, fo. 20; D/AE/A25, fo. 39v; D/AC/A44, fo. 49; GRO, GDR 76, fo. 276v; WRO, D5/28/6/174; SRO, D/D/Ca.196, fo. 351v; D/D/Ca.214, fo. 180; D/D/Ca.300, fos. 25v–26; ORO, Oxford diocesan papers, c.2, fos. 187v–189v, 192v. For some other mock ceremonies, see D. Cressy, 'Baptized Beasts and Other Travesties: Affronts to Rites of Passage', in his *Travesties and Transgressions*, pp. 171–85.
12. SRO, D/D/Ca.214, fo. 6v; NRO, X617/47, fos. 200, 221v; ERO, D/AB/A4, fo. 93v; ORO, Oxford archdeaconry papers, c.13, fo. 34.
13. PRO, SP 16/375, fos. 145–7; ERO, D/AE/A42, fo. 191; D/AC/A54, fo. 67.
14. ORO, Oxford diocesan papers, c.2, fo. 188v.
15. ERO, D/AC/A21, fos. 368v, 391; NRO, X613/36, fo. 13; X617/48, p. 555; X620/62, fo. 96v; X621/66, fo. 108; SRO, D/D/Ca.224, fo. 34.
16. ERO, D/AC/A13, fo. 111v; D/AE/A27, fo. 294v; D/AE/A37, fos. 131v, 138v; NRO, X610/23A, fo. 123; ORO, Oxford diocesan papers, c.24, fos. 169–170v;

WSRO, Ep.I/17/15, 26 Mar. 1614; Ep.II/15/1, p. 33; SRO, D/D/Ca.200, 15 Nov. 1616; D/D/Ca.224, fo. 17; D/D/Ca.320, fo. 55.

17. SRO, D/D/Ca.299, fos. 22v, 39v; D/D/Ca.171, fo. 135; D/D/Ca.315, fos. 67, 76v; D/D/Ca.330, fo. 33v; WSRO, Ep.II/15/1, p. 4; NRO, X617/53, fo. 243v; X613/36, fo. 202; WRO, D1/39/2/11, fo. 37v; D5/28/8/101; HRO, 21M65/C1/27, fo. 51v; ERO, D/AC/A44, fo. 33v; D/AC/A43, fo. 108.

18. HRO, 21M65/C1/29, fo. 3; NRO, X615/44, p. 466; X617/54, 24 Jan. 1622; X619/58, 19 Sept, 4 Oct. 1626; Peyton (ed.), *Churchwardens' Presentments in the Oxfordshire Peculiars*, 194; SRO, D/D/Ca.171, fos. 113, 116, 143, 148v; WSRO, Ep. I/17/23, fo. 128v.

19. ERO, D/AE/A20, fo. 194; D/AC/A13, fo. 164; D/AE/A34, fo. 192; D/AE/A36, fo. 311; D/AE/A37, fo. 17; D/AC/A46, fo. 174; D/AC/A49, fo. 28v; GRO, GDR 67, fo. 80v; NRO, X617/51, p. 517; SRO, D/D/Ca.260, fos. 108v, 225v; D/D/Ca.261, fo. 258.

20. *PMP*, 274–6.

21. Ibid. 274.

22. SRO, D/D/Ca.215, fo. 28v; Q/SR 57/1.

23. *PMP*, 407.

CHAPTER 9

1. Gifford, *A Dialogue betweene a Papist and a Protestant,* 3; Gifford, *A Dialogue concerning Witches and Witchcraftes* , sigs. M$_{2-4}$.

2. BL, Lansdowne MS 68, fo. 110.

3. Gifford, *A Dialogue between a Papist and a Protestant*, Epistle, fos. 1–2v.

4. Ibid., fos. 3, 9v, 19v–18 [*sic*], 26, 30, 68, 85v. For Catholic identity and self-image, see L. McClain, *Lest we be Damned: Practical Innovation and Lived Experience among Catholics in Protestant England, 1559–1642* (2004), esp. 233–71.

5. The examinations are printed in A. Raine (ed.), *York Civic Records*, vii, Yorkshire Archaeological Society, Record Series (1949), 130–7. The replies may have been somewhat standardized by the York scribe, but there is enough variation to suggest the flavour of individual responses.

6. PRO, SP 12/136, fos. 44v–45.

7. ERO, D/AE/A9, fo. 74; HRO, 21M65/C1/22, fos. 136v–138v.

8. SRO, D/D/Ca.101, 19 July 1594; HRO, 21M65/C1/26, pp. 4, 12, 33.

9. HRO, 21M65/C1/26, pp. 15, 64; 21M65/C1/28, fos. 37v–38; ERO, D/AE/A31, fo. 304v; D/AE/A34, fo. 149; D/AE/A35, fo. 11.

10. Cockburn (ed.), *Calendar of Assize Records: Sussex Indictments, Elizabeth I*, 105; ERO, Q/SR 64/44–5; Cockburn (ed.), *Calendar of Assize Records: Essex Indictments, Elizabeth I*, 331–2, 390, 391; SRO, D/D/Ca.142, p. 68.

11. NRO, X608/13, fo. 118–v; X612/32, fos. 8v, 14; X612/33, fo. 3v; ERO, D/AE/A12, fo. 135; D/AE/A23, fo. 132.

12. LA, Ch.P/9/7–8, 32; Vj 22, fo. 38v; J. S. Cockburn (ed.), *Calendar of Assize Records: Essex Indictments, James I* (1982), 70; SRO, D/D/Ca.162, Glastonbury jurisdiction; D/D/Ca.200, 15 Nov. 1616; ERO, D/AE/A27, fo. 111v; NRO, X618/55, fo. 14.

13. HRO, 21M65/C1/28, fo. 2; ERO, D/AC/A44, fo. 65v; WSRO, Ep.II/15/1, p. 77.

14. Raine (ed.), *York Civic Records*, vii, 133; WRO, D1/39/2/2, fo. 11; ORO, Oxford diocesan papers, d.13, fo. 50; d.9, fos. 14, 97v; SRO, D/D/Ca.142, p. 20, 17 Oct. 1620.

15. HRO, 21M65/C1/27, fo. 48v; ERO, D/AE/A29, fo. 40v; D/AC/A51, fos. 66v, 74; D/AC/A52, fos. 55v, 102v; WSRO, Ep.II/15/1, p. 60.

16. M. C. Questier, *Conversion: Politics and Religion in England, 1580–1625* (1996), 135–7; D. M. Clarke, 'Conformity Certificates among the King's Bench Records: A Calendar', *Recusant History*, 14 (1977–8), 57–63; LA, Ch.P/12/16.

17. HRO, 21M61/C1/22, fo. 137; 21M61/C1/23/1, fo. 7; 21M61/C1/26, p. 59; ORO, Oxford diocesan papers, d.4, fo. 17; PRO, SP 12/279, fos. 168v–169; NRO, X614/40, fo. 101v; ERO, D/AE/A27, fo. 301–v; SRO, D/D/Ca.244, pp. 94–5, 108, 110.

18. SRO, D/D/Ca.244, pp. 5, 127, 140; NRO, X619/58, 17 Apr. 1626, and mutilated note attached; ERO, D/AC/A50, fo. 125v; D/AE/A42, fo. 195; ORO, Oxford archdeaconry papers, c.13, fo. 310.

19. Cockburn (ed.), *Calendar of Assize Records: Essex Indictments, Elizabeth I*, 425–6; Cockburn (ed.) *Calendar of Assize Records: Essex Indictments, James I*, 9.

20. ORO, Oxford diocesan papers, c.2, fo. 31; NRO, X614/40, fo. 48; X619/58, 3 Apr. 1628; WRO, D1/39/2/6, fos. 102, 109v–110v; ERO, D/AC/A42, fos. 12v, 18–v; SRO, D/D/Ca.299, fos. 13v, 15v–16, 17v.

21. NRO, X613/34, fo. 36; X614/40, fo. 20v; WRO, D5/28/21/17; ERO, D/AC/A45, fo. 107v.

22. ORO, Oxford diocesan papers, c.2, fos. 145v–197, *passim*. This case is discussed by D. Cressy, 'Who Buried Mrs Horseman? Excommunication, Accommodation and Silence', in his *Travesties and Transgressions*, 116, 120–6.

23. Gifford, *A Dialogue betweene a Papist and a Protestant*, fos. 101v–102; SRO, D/D/Cd.34, Office v. Redman.

24. P. Lake, 'Anti-Popery: The Structure of a Prejudice', in R. Cust and A. Hughes (eds.), *Conflict in Early Stuart England* (1989); HRO, 21M65/C3/5, pp. 22, 24; SRO, D/D/Ca.57, Ash Priors; D/D/Cd.54, Office v. Morton; D/D/Ca.172, 9 June 1612; ERO, D/AC/A13, fo. 57v; LA, Vj 22, fo. 16; WRO, D5/28/22/52; PRO, SP 14/260, fo. 97; WSRO, Ep.II/15/1, p. 76; A. Fletcher, *A County Community in Peace and War: Sussex, 1600–1660* (1975), 103.

25. C. W. Foster (ed.), *The State of the Church*, Lincoln Record Society (1926), p. lxxxix; WSRO, Ep.I/17/14, 20 Mar. 1614 (Midhurst had probably the highest concentrations of Catholics in Sussex); ERO, D/AE/A40, fo. 110v.

26. Gifford, *A Dialogue betweene a Papist and a Protestant*, fo. 101v; NRO, X612/33, fos. 164v–165; X613/36, fo. 11v; X615/43, fo. 44v; X617/50, pp. 158–9, 208; X617/54, Feb. 1623; ORO, Oxford diocesan papers, c.2, fos. 298v, 358; PRO, SP 16/239, fo. 80; Fielding, 'Opposition to the Personal Rule of Charles I', 773–4.

27. R. Clifton, 'Fear of Popery', in C. Russell (ed.), *The Origins of the English Civil War* (1973), 163–5.

28. PRO, SP 16/7, fo. 47; SP 16/237, fos. 39–v, 42–v, 44, 54, 60, 87–v; SP 16/238, fos. 51–2; SP 16/239, fos. 77–80, 111.

29. *Historical Manuscripts Commission Ninth Report*, 3 vols. (1883–4), iii, 498; Huntington Library, San Marino, CA, STT Correspondence, 1876, 1877, 1880. For the local troubles over recruitment, see V. L. Stater, 'The Lord Lieutenancy on the Eve

of the Civil Wars: The Impressment of George Plowright', *Historical Journal*, 29 (1986), 279–96.

30. PRO, SP 16/458, fos. 24–v, 26–v; SP 16/457, fo. 59–v; Walter, *Understanding Popular Violence*, 201–4; PRO, Privy Council Registers, Charles I (facsimile ed.), x, fo. 263.

31. PRO, SP 16/467, fos. 209, 211, 213. My attention was drawn to some of the above cases by R. Clifton, 'Fear of Catholics in England, 1637–1645' D.Phil. thesis, University of Oxford, 1967.

32. Gifford, *A Dialogue betweene a Papist and a Protestant*, fos. 101–102v, 105, 114 (wrongly numbered as 94). Gifford is deliberately presenting Catholics as a political threat, hence the Papist's endorsement of regicide.

CHAPTER 10

1. ERO, D/AE/A9, fos. 9, 13v–14; Gifford, *A Briefe discourse*, Epistle Dedicatory.

2. Gifford, *A Briefe discourse*, fos. 1–2, 22, 31–v, 38v, 72; Gifford, *A Dialogue betweene a Papist and a Protestant*, Epistle Dedicatorie, fo. 1–v.

3. Gifford, *A Briefe discourse*, fos. 4v–5, 17v; BLO, MS Tanner 50, fo. 25v; R. Greenham, *The Workes* (1601 edn.), 425–6; SRO, D/D/Cd.15, fos. 134, 137, 165–v; D/D/Cd.78, Office v. Day; ERO, Q/SR 65/61; F. Emmison, *Elizabethan Life: Disorder* (1970), 48; J. Fielde, *A Caveat for Parsons Howlet* (1581), sigs. D₈–E₁; F. Trigge, *An Apologie or Defence of Our Dayes* (1589), 24, 32, 35; Peyton (ed.), *Churchwardens' Presentments in the Oxfordshire Peculiars*, 286.

4. HRO, 21M65/C1/10, fo. 59v; SRO, D/D/Cd.15, fo. 133v; D/D/Cd.49, Office v. Sholeford; ERO, D/AC/A4, fo. 146; GRO, GDR 43, fos. 56, 108, 112v; GDR 57, pp. 206–7; GDR 45, fo. 92; NRO, X613/34, fo. 84v; X615/42, p. 367; X617/50, p. 273; X614/40, fo. 84v; ORO, Oxford archdeaconry papers, c.12, fo. 166v.

5. NRO, Archdeacon's Visitation Book 7, sheet at fo. 20; [M. Marprelate], *A dialogue, Wherein is plainly laide open the tyrannical dealings of l[ord] bishopps against God's children* (1589), sig. D; Turvill, *The Poore Man's Path-way to Heaven*, 2, 10; Gifford, *A Dialogue betweene a Papist and a Protestant*, fo. 2; Bate, *The Portraiture of Hypocrisy*, 17–18; T. Stoughton, *A Generall Treatise against Poperie* (1598), 138; *PMP*, 48.

6. WRO, D5/28/1/122; D5/28/5/28; D5/28/6/20; HRO, 21M65/C1/14/1, fo. 106; 21M65/C1/22, fo. 89v; ERO, D/AE/A7, fo. 34v; Gifford, *A Briefe discourse*, fo. 63v; *PMP*, 348; NRO, X608/15, fo. 44v.

7. *PMP*, 21; *PMP* (1631 edn.), 125.

8. W[illiam] B[urton], *The Rowsing of the Sluggard* (1595), 58, 74–5, 77–9, 114; J. Nichols, *An Order of Household Instruction* (1596), sig. B₂; Perkins, *The Workes*, ii, 260, 372.

9. E. Topsell, *The Reward of Religion* (1613 edn.), 7; *PMP*, Epistle to the Reader, 124.

10. ERO, D/AC/A22, fo. 161v; D/AE/A25, fo. 52v; D/AE/A29, fo. 138v; D/AE/A32, fo. 206v; D/AB/A1, 10 Jan. 1621; D/AE/A34, fo. 66v; D/AE/A39, fo. 53; D/AC/A49, fo. 131v; D/AC/A50, fo. 10v; *PMP*, 26.

11. Bagshawe, 'The Life and Death of Mr Bolton, sigs. b₃ᵥ–b₄; Bolton, *Some Generall Directions*, 349–50; Bolton, *Instructions for a Right Comforting*, 200.

12. Bolton, *Two Sermons Preached at Northampton*, 88; Bolton, *Instructions for a Right Comforting*, 96, 98; Bolton, *Some Generall Directions*, 352. For the changing usage

of 'puritan', see N. Tyacke, 'Puritanism, Arminianism and Counter-Revolution', in Russell (ed.), *The Origins of the English Civil War*, 133–4, 139.

13. Bolton, *Two Sermons Preached at Northampton*, 76, 83–88; N. Tyacke, *Anti-Calvinists: The Rise of English Arminianism, c. 1590–1640* (1987), 125–80.

14. K. Fincham and P. Lake, 'The Ecclesiastical Policies of James I and Charles I', in K. Fincham (ed.), *The Early Stuart Church* (1993), 36–49; K. Fincham, 'The Restoration of Altars in the 1630s', *Historical Journal*, 44 (2001), 919–40; C. Haigh, 'The Taming of the Reformation: Preachers, Pastors and Parishioners in Elizabethan and Early Stuart England', *History*, 85 (2000), 573–88.

15. NRO, X619/61, 3 Aug., 20 Oct. 1630; X620/64, p. 72; X621/65, fo. 79; X620/63, p. 431; SRO, D/D/Ca.299, fo. 1v; D/D/Ca.313, fo. 138v; ERO, D/AE/A41, fos. 75, 111; D/AC/A52, fos. 56, 186v, 193, 196, 226v–227, 228v, 232–v, 250.

16. WSRO, Ep.II/15/1, pp. 2, 8, 12, 43, 46–60; SRO, D/D/Ca.316, fo. 25; D/D/Ca.313, fo. 178v; Walter, 'Popular Iconoclasm and the Politics of the Parish', 285; M. Steig, *Laud's Laboratory: The Diocese of Bath and Wells in the Early Seventeenth Century* (1982), 297–300; NRO, X615/44, pp. 42–4; Leics. RO, 1D41/13/39, fos. 99–102.

17. WSRO, Ep.I/17/25, fo. 57v; Ep.II/15/1, p. 48; NRO, X620/64, p. 84; ERO, D/AB/A8, fo. 198; D/AE/A49, fo. 57v; SRO, D/D/Ca. 313, fo. 219; D/D/Ca.316, fo. 24; WRO, D5/28/38/43.

18. Fielding, 'Opposition to the Personal Rule of Charles I', 777–87; Huntington Library, San Marino, CA, STT Correspondence, 1390; SRO, D/D/Cd.90, Office v. Bolsome; D/D/Ca.334, fos. 94–5, 103v–105v; T. Webster, *Godly Clergy in Early Stuart England: The Caroline Puritan Movement, c. 1630–1643* (1997), 231–2; WRO, D5/28/39/2, 6, 26, 62.

19. See, for example, Walter, 'Popular Iconoclasm and the Politics of the Parish', 280–90; Walter, *Understanding Popular Violence*, 161–200.

20. W. G. Bittle and R. T. Lane, 'Inflation and Philanthropy in England: A Re-Assessment of W. K. Jordan's Data', *Economic History Review*, 2nd ser., 29 (1976), 209; Clifton, 'Fear of Catholics in England'; Walter, 'Popular Iconoclasm and the Politics of the Parish', 261–77; D. Cressy, 'The Battle of the Altars: Turning the Tables and Breaking the Rails', in his *Travesties and Transgressions*, 203–7. For the breakdown of order from 1640 and the dramatic new levels of criticism of religious policy, see D. Cressy, *England on Edge: Crisis and Revolution, 1640–1642* (2006), 110–210.

21. However, for warnings against reliance on official records in assessing levels of opposition, see Fielding, 'Opposition to the Personal Rule of Charles I', 777, 783; P. Lake, 'The Collection of Ship Money in Cheshire during the 1630s', *Northern History*, 17 (1981), 71.

22. J. Maltby (ed.), 'Petitions for Episcopacy and the Book of Common Prayer on the Eve of the Civil War, 1641–1642', in S. Taylor (ed.), *From Cranmer to Davidson: A Church of England Miscellany*, Church of England Record Society (1999), 126, 146, 162.

23. Baxter, *Autobiography*, 34–5, 36, 39, 40, 43.

24. Tyacke, 'Puritanism, Arminianism and Counter-Revolution', 143.

25. A. Fletcher, *The Outbreak of the English Civil War* (1981), 91–124, 191–227; J. Morrill, 'The Attack on the Church of England in the Long Parliament', in his *The Nature of the English Revolution* (1993), 69–90; Walter, 'Popular Iconoclasm

and the Politics of the Parish', 274–77; D. Cressy, 'Revolutionary England, 1640–1642', *Past & Present*, 181 (2003), 48–64; S. R. Gardiner, *Constitutional Documents of the Puritan Revolution, 1625–1660* (1906 ed.), 198.
26. R. Baxter, *A Holy Commonwealth, or Political Aphorisms* (1659), 456–7; Baxter, *Autobiography*, 38–9; HRO, 21M65/C1/28, fos. 31v–32; Gardiner, *Constitutional Documents*, 198.

CONCLUSION

1. C. Haigh, 'Anticlericalism and Clericalism, 1580–1640', in N. Aston and M. Cragoe (eds.), *Anticlericalism in Britain, 1500–1914* (2000); C. Haigh, 'Dr Temple's Pew: Sex and Clerical Status in the 1630s', *Huntington Library Quarterly*, 68 (2005). For Jenison, see above, p. 52.
2. See above, pp. 44, 140; ERO, D/AE/A14, fo. 288; BL, Additional MS 48064, fos. 85v–86v.
3. See above, pp. 135–6, 167; NRO, X616/45, pp. 17–18; X617/48, p. 437; X618/56A, p. 227; X619/61, 3 Aug. 1630; X620/63, fo. 400.
4. C. Haigh, 'The Character of an Antipuritan', *Sixteenth Century Journal*, 35 (2004), 678; J. Maltby, *Prayer Book and People in Elizabethan and Early Stuart England* (1998), 76–80; WRO, D1/43/6, fo. 55v; D5/28/6/5; D5/28/8/124; SRO, D/D/Ca.220, 15 Sept. 1620; D/D/Ca.261, fo. 114v.
5. C. Haigh, 'The Troubles of Thomas Pestell: Parish Squabbles and Ecclesiastical Politics in the 1630s', *Journal of British Studies*, 41 (2003); Huntington Library, San Marino, CA, HA Legal, Box 5 (9).
6. See above, pp. 60–3; Haigh, 'Success and Failure', 28–49.
7. NRO, X613/36, fo. 99–v; WRO, D5/28/20/17, 21, 22; WSRO, Ep.I/17/15, 1 Oct. 1614; ERO, D/AE/A42, fo. 17; SRO, D/D/Cd.56, Office v. Bath. For Sabbatarian teaching, see K. Parker, *The English Sabbath: A Study of Doctrine and Discipline from the Reformation to the Civil War* (1988).
8. ERO, D/AE/A14, fo. 127v; D/AC/A53, fo. 95; NRO, X615/44, p. 401.
9. NRO, X615/44, pp. 42, 44; BLO, MS Tanner 70, fos. 107–11; GRO, GDR 26, p. 31; HRO, 21M65/C1/28, fos. 21v–22.
10. NRO, X617/47, fo. 113v; ERO, D/AC/A42, fo. 175v.
11. SRO, Q/SR 57/1, fos. 31, 63; D/D/Ca.66, Edington; ERO, D/AB/A6, fo. 117.
12. SRO, D/D/Cd.34, Office v. Redman; A. Fletcher, *A County Community in Peace and War: Sussex, 1600–1660* (1975), 103; PRO, SP 16/467, fo. 211.
13. HRO, 21M65/C3/4, pp. 41–2; SRO, D/D/Ca.40, Lullington.
14. ERO, Q/SR 65/61; WRO, D5/28/8/68; LA, Court Papers, 69/1/47.
15. SRO, D/D/Ca.207, fo. 119v; D/D/Cd.54, Office v. Morton; D/D/Cd.56, Office v. Yowe (Yowe knew his Bible: in the Old Testament, Phares was the illegitimate son of Judah and Tamar; in the New Testament, Phares is named in the lineages of Christ. This looks like a subtle variant on the 'carpenter's bastard' theme); D/D/Cd.56, Office v. Wyn; D/D/Cd.58, Office v. Wayte.
16. SRO, D/D/Cd.66, pp. 107–10, 111, 114, 115, 130, 132–3; D/D/Cd.72, Office v. Willis; D/D/Cd.78, Office v. Dorvall; Office v. Haynes; D/D/Ca.299, fo. 1v; ORO, Oxford diocesan papers, c.27, fos. 43v–48v, 53v–59, 62–64v.

List of Manuscript Sources

Bodleian Library, Oxford

Rawlinson Letters 89
MS Rawlinson C.764
MS Rawlinson C.766
MS Rawlinson D.1346
MSS Tanner 50, 70–1

British Library, London

Additional MS 48064
Lansdowne MS 68

Buckinghamshire Record Office, Aylesbury

D/A/V/1–3   Archdeaconry of Buckingham, Visitations, 1584–1635

Essex Record Office, Chelmsford

D/AB/A1–9	Bishop's Commisssary for Essex, Act Book, 1616–1641
D/AC/A3–54	Archdeaconry of Colchester, Act Books, 1569–1641
D/AE/A1a–42	Archdeaconry of Essex, Act Books, 1561–1640
Q/SR 32–311	Quarter Sessions Rolls, 1570–1640

Gloucestershire Record Office, Gloucester

GDR 9–204	Consistory Act Books, Depositions Books, and Visitation Books, 1554–1640 (selected volumes)

Hampshire Record Office, Winchester

21M65/B1/9–12	Winchester Diocese, Visitation Books, 1567–73
21M65/C1/7–35	Winchester Consistory, Office Act Books, 1558–1624
21M65/C1/26	*Processus contra recusantes*, 1598–1603
21M65/C1/28	Act Book of Ecclesiastical Commissioners, 1606–8
21M65/C3/3–13	Depositions Books, 1564–1633
44M69/F2/11	Jervoise of Herriard Papers, 1592–1600

Huntington Library, San Marino, California

HA Legal, Box 5(9)	High Commission depositions on Thomas Pestell
STT Correspondence	Temple family correspondence

Leicestershire Record Office, Wigston Magna

1D41/4/Boxes VI–XV	Archdeaconry of Leicester, Cause Papers, 1629–35
1D41/13/35–65	Archdeaconry Correction Act Books, 1611–42

Lichfield Joint Record Office, Lichfield

B/C/2/20	Lichfield Consistory, Office Act Book, 1582–4
B/C/3/10	Consistory Office Act Book, 1583–94
B/C/5	Consistory Cause Papers
B/V/1/7–17	Visitation Books, 1570–84
B/V/2/1	Excommunication Book, 1581–5

Lincolnshire Archives, Lincoln

Ch.P/5–12	Churchwardens' Presentments, 1598–1633
Cj 3	Episcopal Court Book, 1525–62
Cj 12	Episcopal Court Book, 1598–1600
Court Papers, Boxes 56–80	Consistory Court, Cause Papers
LQS, A/1/2	Quarter Sessions Roll, 1629
Vj 13–16	Visitation Books, 1566–85
Vj 22	Visitation Book, 1607
Vj 30	Visitation Book, 1638

Northamptonshire Record Office, Northampton

Archdeacon's	Visitation Books 4–9, 1576–90
X607/6–X621/70	Peterborough Consistory, Correction Books, 1572–1641
X648/2	Peterborough Consistory, Correction Book, 1627–30
X649/1	Peterborough Consistory, Correction Book, 1629–31

Oxfordshire Record Office, Oxford

Oxford archdeaconry papers, c.2–13	Act Books, 1566–1638
Oxford archdeaconry papers, c.118	Depositions Book, 1616–20
Oxford archdeaconry papers, c.158	Peculiar of Dorchester, Act Book, 1625–1722
Oxford archdeaconry papers, d.13–14	Peculiar of Dorchester, Act Books, 1581–94
Oxford diocesan papers, c.2	Consistory Court Book, 1630–1

Oxford diocesan papers, c.18	Peculiar of Thame, Act Book, 1584–1640
Oxford diocesan papers, c.21–7	Depositions Books, 1570–1639
Oxford diocesan papers, d.4–11	Office Act Books, 1593–1623
Oxford diocesan papers, d.13	Peculiar of Dorchester, Act Book, 1591–4
Oxford diocesan papers, d.15–16	Depositions Books, 1581–93
PAR214/4/F1/76–8	Churchwarders' Accounts, St Peter-le-Bailey, Oxford, 1633–5

Public Record Office (National Archives), Kew

SP 12	State Papers, Domestic, Elizabeth I
SP 14	State Papers, Domestic, James I
SP 16	State Papers, Domestic, Charles I
STAC 8	Star Chamber Cases

Somerset Record Office, Taunton

D/D/Ca.40–330	Bath and Wells Diocese, Visitation *Comperta* and Office Act Books, 1568–1640 (all volumes fit for production)
D/D/Cd.15–90	Depositions Books, 1573–1640 (selected volumes)
Q/SR 57/1	Quarter Sessions Roll, 1626

West Sussex Record Office, Chichester

Ep.I/17/9–25	Archdeaconry of Chichester, Detection Books, 1596–1634
Ep.I/23/1–7	Archdeaconry of Chichester, Registers of Presentments, 1571–86
Ep.I/26/2	Archdeaconry of Chichester, Church Inspection Book, 1636
Ep.II/15/1	Archdeaconry of Lewes, Register of Presentments, 1637–8

Wiltshire and Swindon Record Office, Trowbridge

D1/39/2/1–12	Salisbury Diocese, Office Act Books, 1584–1635
D1/43/4–6	Salisbury Diocese, *Detecta* Books, 1565–86
D3/4/1–7	Archdeaconry of Wiltshire, Office Act Books, 1601–42
D3/7/1	Archdeaconry of Wiltshire, *Detecta* Book, 1586–99
D5/21/1	Dean of Salisbury's Peculiar, Citations
D5/21/3	Dean's Peculiar, Libels
D5/28/1–39	Dean's Peculiar, Presentments, 1558–1641
D10/4/1	Peculiar of Highworth, Presentments, 1624–9

Index

Abbess Roding, Essex 27
Abbey, Richard 64
Abbott, George, archbishop of Canterbury 222
Abel, William 82
Abingdon, Berkshire 111
Abington family 196–7
Abington, Northamptonshire 20, 48, 76, 77, 130, 167
absenteeism 8, 9, 10, 79–87, 156, 170, 212; alternative pursuits 84–7; due to poor sermons 17–18; excuses 82–3; fear of arrest 83–4; fines for 82, 84–5; regular offenders 82; *see also* attendance, church; Sabbath
absolution 47, 68–9, 77, 97, 108, 119, 131–2, 153, 155, 162, 163, 190, 193, 196, 225
Adam and Eve 168–9
Adams, Alice 28
Adams, Elizabeth 55
Adams, William 173
Adderbury, Oxfordshire 66
adultery 21, 48, 54, 71, 73, 86, 114–15, 130, 148, 153, 154, 159, 160; by clergy 53, 54
Agar, Joan 165
Agasseman, Mr (minister) 22–3
Ager, Margaret 72
Agwilliam, William 10
Aishe, James 23
Aisholt, Somerset 189
Akers, John 106
Alcock, Richard 82
Alcock, Robert 54
Aldcorne, Elizabeth 185–6
Alderton, Wiltshire 17
Aldwinkle, Northamptonshire 8
alehouses 85–6, 90, 91–2, 124, 140, 146–7, 152, 154, 162, 163, 166, 167, 169, 172–3, 212, 223, 224
ales, church 65–6, 141, 227
Alfield, Edward 90
All Cannings, Wiltshire 99
All Hallows 67
All Saints' Day 67
Alland, Thomas 146
Allen, Lucy 88
Allen, Thomas (of Oxford) 128
Allen, Thomas (of Wing) 205–6
Allen, William 173
Aller, Somerset 54
Allexton, Leicestershire 37

Allgood, John 68
Allum, Anne 194
Alresford, Essex 29, 37
Alresford, Hampshire 60
altars 118, 119, 213, 214, 216, 217
Alton, Wiltshire 93
Alton Pancras, Dorset 148
Amberley, Sussex 60
Ampleforth, Christopher 219
Amye, Andrew 104
Andover, Hampshire 187
Andrew, Dr 69
Andrewes, William 165
Andrews, William 102
Angel, Thomas 111
Anger, Bridget 74
Angmering, Sussex 67–8
animals: believed bewitched 64; in church 88, 90, 92, 176, 197; jokes about 29, 37, 175, 176, 178, 223; lost and stolen 64; as reason for Sabbath-breaking 83, 85, 91, 95, 96, 207–8
Ansell, William 37
Ansley, John, and wife 88
Antilegon (Arthur Dent's 'caviller') 3, 5, 12, 25, 26, 41, 54, 141, 206, 224; attitude to sinfulness 145–6, 147, 151, 163–4, 179, 180, 223; contempt for authority 152, 165; on the godly 128, 129, 208
apostasy, sermon on 24
apparitors 155–6
Appellation Day 67, 140
Archer, Richard, wife of 69
Ardleigh, Essex 88, 170
Arlington, Sussex 158
Arminians 209, 210
Armitage, Anthony 70
Arnold, Agnes 43
arrest warrants: served at church 83–4
Arthingworth, Northamptonshire 18, 69, 111, 195
Arundel, Sussex 117
Asfordby, Leicestershire 43
Ash Priors, Somerset 196
Ashborne, George 219, 220
Ashbrooke, Timothy 135
Ashby, Robert 168
Ashby-de-la-Zouche, Leicestershire 48, 52, 107, 140, 147, 150, 169, 212
Ashby St Ledgers, Northamptonshire 20–1

Ashcott, Somerset 88
Ashdon, Essex 82–3, 159–60
Asheldham, Essex 84, 176
Ashendon, Buckinghamshire 39, 129
Ashingden, Essex 84
Ashington, Sussex 82
Ashton, Northamptonshire 85, 146
Ashton Somerville, Gloucestershire 39
Ashurst, Sussex 72, 80, 93
Aske, Richard 139, 222
Aston, Robert 166
Aston Clinton, Buckinghamshire 25
Aston Rowant, Oxfordshire 65
Astwell, Northamptonshire 64
Asunetus (Arthur Dent's 'ignorant man') 3, 5,
    12; attitude to preachers 41, 50; attitude
    to religion 79, 97, 206; fear of damnation
    180, 210; ignorance 59–60, 63–4, 68,
    78, 220–1; nostalgia 205
atheists: those denying God's existence 11,
    169, 223, 225; used as term for the
    ungodly 68, 169, 170
Athy, John 45
attendance, church: by
    excommunicated 68–9; perceptions of
    requirements 80; *see also* absenteeism
Auden, William 48
Audley, Lady 200
Austin, Anne 197
Austin, Master (minister at Little Oakley) 197
Austin, Mr (rector at Aveley) 49
Austin, Robert 123
Aveley, Essex 27, 45, 49, 51, 74, 86, 147,
    153
Axbridge, Somerset 76, 80, 83, 96, 151, 156,
    225
Axminster, Somerset 196
Aylett, Mr (minister) 44
Aylett, Richard 86
Aylett, Robert, wife of 106
Ayleward, Nicholas 172
Ayleworth, Bray 218
Ayres, John, and family 89
Ayston, Rutland 21

Bachelor, Thomas 157
Backwell, Somerset 88, 92, 170
Bacon, Margaret 86
Badby, Northamptonshire 33, 133–5, 137,
    222
Badcock, John 152
Bagshawe, Edward 53, 54, 208
Bailey, Edith 77
Bailey, John 155
Bailey, Richard 220
Bailey, Robert 131, 132, 133

Bakehouse, Susan 158
Baker, John 166
Baker, Mr (minister) 49
Baker, Richard 171
Baker, Thomas 111
bakers 95, 151, 196
Balcombe, Sussex 176
Baldwin, Alice 71
Ball, Jacob 40
Bamford, Agnes 65
Bampton, Oxfordshire 159
Banbury, Oxfordshire 107, 113, 140
Band, John 66
Banks, Catherine 150–1
Banwell, Somerset 62–3
baptism 29, 39, 69–70, 79, 105–6, 126, 134,
    139; bad behaviour at 172; Catholics and
    185; crossing 30–1, 32, 33, 34, 105, 137,
    219, 220; mock 172–3, 174, 224
barbers 86, 151
Barford, Oxfordshire 76
Barford St Martin, Wiltshire 41
Barker, Master 200
Barker, Richard 168
Barking, Essex 61, 65, 69, 79, 153, 160
Barlow, Thomas 77
Barnard, Joan 49
Barnard, John 114
Barnes, Edward, and wife 139
Barnes, Thomas 73–4
Barnwell, Margaret, John and
    Lawrence 171–2
Barrett, William 85
Barrington, Somerset 166, 211
Barrowden, Rutland 170
Barston, Anne 65
Basingstoke, Hampshire 21–2, 44, 152
Bassett, Bridy 95
Bassett, William 192
Bastwick, John 139
Batcombe, Somerset 23, 24, 26, 103, 112,
    113, 140
Bate, John: *The Portraiture of Hypocrisy* 2, 4,
    79, 97, 130, 205
Bate, Sarah 163
Bath, Robert 92, 221
Bath, Somerset 32; St James's 70
Bath and Wells, diocese of 23–4, 34, 82,
    115–16, 211
Bathford, Somerset 125, 177
Bathwick, Somerset 80
Batsie, Thomas 138
Battersea, Surrey 60
Battison, Anne 48
Bawdrip, Somerset 66, 86
Bawles, Charles 189
Baxter, Richard 104, 215, 216, 217

Baxter, Robert 22
Baybrooke, Northamptonshire 177
Bayley, John 190
Bayley, Lewis: *The Practice of Piety* 2–3
Beacon, Nicholas 139
Beaconsfield, Buckinghamshire 69
Beale, Anne 83
Beaminster, Dorset 49–50, 91, 117
Beard, John 171
Beauchamp Roding, Essex 62, 64, 197
Beaulieu, Hampshire 177
Becke, John 86
Beckington, Somerset 33, 212
Beckley, William 190
Beckwith, Margery 27
Bedford 67
Bedhampton, Hampshire 205
Bedminster, Somerset 86, 115, 125, 226
Behoe, Henry 161
Behowe, Boniface 61
Belcher, Anne 151
bell-ringing 51, 67–8, 86, 166, 178–9, 195, 197, 224
Bellamy, Richard 97, 163, 225
Bellers, James 68
Belly, Stephen 152
Benbow, Nathaniel 119–20
Benefield, Northamptonshire 109
Bennett, Anthony 175
Bennett, John 148
Bennington, Isaac 36–7
Benson, Margery 75
Benson, Richard 139
Bent, John 189
Benton, Northamptonshire 87
Bere Regis, Dorset 96, 115
Bergholt, Essex 51
Bernard, Richard: catechizing 26, 140; conventicles 113; court cases 23–4; on ignorance 64; life 23; sermons 23–4, 112, 140; *The Faithful Shepherd* 18, 20, 23, 26; *Two Twinnes* 26
Berry, John (of Denton) 154
Berry, John (of White Staunton) 166
Berwick Bassett, Wiltshire 150
Berwick St John, Wiltshire 75
Bezant, William, wife of 196
Bible: associated with the godly 129; oaths on 76; reading 59, 104, 145, 168, 204; translations 103, 225
Bicester, Oxfordshire 112
Bickerstaffe, Master 113
Bickerstaffe, Nicholas 212
Bicknell, Somerset 30
Bicknoller, Somerset 7
Billericay, Essex 205
Billing, John 49

Billingshurst, Sussex 29, 86
Bindon, Henry 127–8
Binkes, William and George 188, 194
Binstead, Sussex 178
biographies: of clergy 53–4
Birch, Essex 83
Bird, Henry 189
Bird, William 113, 135, 136, 137
Birdham, Sussex 95
Birmingham 54
Bisham, Berkshire 219
Bishop, Thomas 141
bishops 210, 211, 213, 214, 216, 220
Bishop's Waltham, Hampshire 61
Bishops' War 213, 216
Bishopstone, Wiltshire 85, 92
Bisse, John 116
Blaby, Tristram 131–3
Black, John 49
'black-coats': as insult 54–5
Blackaby, Richard 106
Blackmore, Essex 149, 170, 189
Blacksmith, Miles 55
Blagdon, Somerset 105, 177
Blake, Averius 80
Blakesley, Northamptonshire 160
Bland, Mr (minister) 175
Bland, Nicholas 80
Blandford, Dorset 60
blasphemy 45, 46, 167–9
Blatherwyke, Northamptonshire 64
Bleason, Somerset 49
Blewbury, Berkshire 177
Blissett, Richard 157
Blisworth, Northamptonshire 97
Bloxham, Oxfordshire 72, 159
Boad, John 44
Board, Richard 112
Bobbingworth, Essex 102
Bocking, Essex 204, 225
Boddington, William 37, 136
Bodell, Richard, and wife 47
Bodye, John 87
Bolsome, Robert 213
Bolt, John 66, 104, 128, 141
Bolton, Robert: on Arthur Dent 5; Bagshawe's biography of 53, 54, 208; 'conventional Christian' character 79; dislike of 'puritan' label 208–10; on the godly 102, 103, 122, 124, 125, 130; guides by 4, 12; on ignorance 60; Kettering lecture 122; life 13, 208; Northampton assizes sermon (1629) 122, 209; on predestination 26; on Protestants 59; on sermons 19
Bolton, Thomas 76
Bond, Richard 150
Bonney, John 197

Book of Common Prayer: on baptism 69–70; on bowing and kneeling 116; and burial 197; catechism 26, 28, 60, 136; on communion wine 177–8; desecration of 216, 217; failure to observe 33–5, 202; Laud and 210; objections to 30, 104, 119, 139; petitions to defend (1641–2) 214–15, 216; on prayer and sermons 225; on quarrels as reaon for refusing communion 73, 74; on repentance 25
Book of Sports (1633) 66, 116, 221; *see also* Declaration of Sports
Booth, Helen 186
Booth, William 54
Boreham, William 179
Bosham, Sussex 17
Bottomley, William 154
Boughtill, Richard 147
Boughton, Northamptonshire 4, 53
Boulton, Marmaduke 20, 160
Bourne, Richard 71
Bourton-on-the-Water, Gloucestershire 218
Bover, John 174
Bowden, Francis 54
Bowden, George 25, 31, 123
Bowen, Robert 66
Bower, Luke 114
Bowers, Essex 190
bowing (in church) 116, 117, 118, 120, 128, 216, 222
Bowker, John 82
bowls 84, 85, 93–4, 146, 152–3, 227
Bowman, William and Katherine 185
Bowrer, Rowland 51
Boxgrove, Sussex 93
Boxted, Essex 87, 108
Boyce, John (of Ashby St Ledgers) 20–1
Boyce, John (of Stock) 167–8
Bozeat, Northamptonshire 43, 73, 153
Bracebridge, Lincolnshire 55
Brackley, Northamptonshire 65, 136, 219
Bradfield, Thomas 114
Bradfield, Essex 167
Bradford, John 103
Bradford, Thomas (of Moreton Valence) 222
Bradford, Thomas (at Northampton christening) 105
Bradford, Thomas (of Thurlaston) 103
Bradford, William 102
Bradley, Mary 39–40
Bradshaw, Frances 204
Bradshaw, Thomas 139
Bradwell, Essex 18, 34
Bradwell-on-Sea, Essex 188
Braintree, Essex 83
Bramber, Sussex 157
Bramdean, Hampshire 54

Branch, William, wife of 138
Brand, Robert 148
Brandon, Henry 60
Branwood, Thomas 172
Braunston, Northamptonshire 126, 148, 158
Bray, John 76
Braybrooke, Northamptonshire 68
Breckland, John 159
Bremhill, Wiltshire 41
Bremmett, Hampshire 66
Brentwood, Essex 183
Brett, Judith 212
Brett, William 85
Brewer, Hilda 96
Brewham, Somerset 155, 156
Brickworth, Robert 146
Bridge, Joseph 91–2
Bridgwater, Somerset 86, 114, 120, 154
'Brief advertisement how to answer unto the statute for not coming to church' 186
Brighstone, Isle of Wight 8–9
Brightlingsea, Essex 152, 154
Brigstock, Northamptonshire 151, 189
Brimley, Anne 186
Brinkelow, Robert 111
Brinkley, William 55
Britten, Richard 24, 103
Brixton, Surrey 54
Brixworth, Northamptonshire 69, 83, 163
Broadwater, Sussex 62
Brodripp, Augustine 115
Brompton Ralph, Somerset 103, 119
Brond, John 83
Brooke, Thomas 92
Broome, Thomas 139
Broomfield, Essex 32
Broughton, Northamptonshire 106, 113
Broughton Gifford, Wiltshire 114
Brown, David 204
Brown, Gilbert 157
Brown, John 90
Brown Candover, Hampshire 74
Browne, David 188
Browne, Francis 21
Browne, Henry 102
Browne, John 172, 174
Browne, William 51
Brownes, Robert 84
Brownists 125–6, 139
Brownley, John 80
Browse, Zachary 178
Broxted, Essex 9–10
Bruning, Ursula 106
Bruton, Somerset 87
Bryan, Elizabeth 193
Buck, Francis 44
Buck, John 112

Buckeridge, Richard 212
Buckingham, archdeaconry of 153
Buckinghamshire: rumours of Catholic
  plots 198–9, 200
Buckland, Robert 95
Buckland St Mary, Somerset 82, 176
Bufford, John 186
Bugbrooke, Northamptonshire 90
Bulgin, Thomas 156
Bull, Elizabeth 197
Bull, Henry 189
Bull, John 65
Bull, Thomas 70
Bullock, Elizabeth 173
Bullock, Lawrence 17
Buncombe, Agnes 10, 97
Burden, Elizabeth 91
Burden, John 91
Burdge, John 115
Burford, Oxfordshire 166
Burge, Thomas 158
Burgess, Anne 159
Burgess, Goodwife 163
Burghill, John 82, 153
Burham, Essex 106
burials 6, 39, 41, 70, 71; of Catholics 71,
  194–6, 197, 198; of excommunicates 71,
  77, 195; mock funerals 178, 224; of
  suicides 70
Burnham, Essex 9, 91–2, 93, 221
Burnham, Somerset 203–4
Burrowes, Francis 83, 138
Burrows, Margaret 174
Burrows, Samuel 138, 139, 222
Burton, Romford 39
Burton, William (churchwarden) 158
Burton, William (Reading preacher) 206
Burton Latimer, Northamptonshire 69, 82,
  86, 167, 199, 211, 219
Burwash, Sussex 188
Bury, Sussex 176
Bussie, Christian 192
'busy controllers': as insult 46, 47, 164, 203,
  217
butchers 94–5, 151
Butleigh, Somerset 49, 154
Butler, Jane 77
Butler, Sarah 46
Butterwicke, Lincolnshire 4
Buttsbury, Essex 118–19
Buttsby, Essex 65
Byckenell, Ralph 169, 225

Cadbury, John 73
Calbourne, Isle of Wight 36, 54
Callion, Philip 167

Calne, Wiltshire 94, 147–8, 154, 170, 213
Calvert, Francis 178
Calvert, George 40, 90–1
Calvinism 4, 25, 26, 30, 209, 219
Campion, Edmund 184, 203
Cane, Thomas 94
Canewdon, Essex 37
Canning, William 150
Canons of 1604 116, 118, 120, 210
Capper, Denise 92
card games 85, 146, 212
Carleton, Northamptonshire 102, 175
Carpenter, Thomas 154
Carrick, John 172, 174
Carrington, Christopher 37
Carswell, John, and wife 150
Carter, Prudence 51
Carter, Thomas 92
Castell, George 80
Castle Cary, Somerset 195
Castle Combe, Wiltshire 157
Castleton, Dorset 167
Castletown, Dorset 131
Catcott, Somerset 93–4
catechism-writing 26–7
catechizing 26–30, 47, 220–1; children 9, 10,
  28, 38, 61, 62–3, 138, 220; godparents
  60; ignorance leads to exclusion from
  communion 60–2; lack of cooperation
  62–3; private 113, 114; public 27–9;
  servants 27–8, 29, 30, 220; use of variant
  versions 63; women 28, 29; youths 29,
  30, 61
Catford, Jane 71
Catholic priests: executions 25
Catholic recusants 6, 8, 11, 81, 102,
  184–201; advice on defence of 186;
  burial 71, 194–6, 197, 198; certificates of
  conformity 191; 'church papists' 184–5;
  co-existence with Protestants 194, 224;
  and communion 185, 186, 188, 189, 190,
  191–2; conscience cited by 186–8;
  converts (to and from Protestantism)
  189–91; difficulties of 193–4; fines 191;
  Gifford's 'Papist' character 13, 40, 183–4,
  200–1, 203, 218; Gifford's (Protestant)
  view of 196, 197, 198, 200–1, 203, 205;
  hostility towards 196–7; linked with fear
  of Spain 198; missionaries 203; numbers
  stabilized after 1606 218; outspoken
  188–9; Recusancy Act (1581) 80;
  reluctance of neighbours to report 197;
  rumours of uprisings by 199–201; ruses
  by 191–3; tolerance of 197–8
Catholicism, nostalgia for 203–4, 205–6
Catlin, Robert 106, 109, 135, 222
Catterall, Robert 115

Caundle Marsh, Dorset 80
Caversham, Berkshire 85–6, 92, 109, 115
Cawdrey, Robert 27
Chacombe, Northamptonshire 31, 157
Chadderton, William, bishop of Lincoln 46, 197
'Chamberlain the sorceror' 64
Chandler, John 118
Chapman, Katherine 88
Chapman, Mary 133, 134
Chapman, Sybil 105
Chapman, Thomas 62
Chappell, Roger 152
Chappell, Walter 82
Chapple, Essex 113–14, 118
Chard, Somerset 96–7, 119, 150
Chardstock, Dorset 195
charity 148, 205
Charlbury, Oxfordshire 69
Charlcombe, Somerset 91
Charles I, king of Great Britain 115, 116, 198, 199, 200, 209, 210, 216, 217, 226; declaration on sports 66, 116, 221
Charlton Mackrell, Somerset 94
Charlton-on-Otmoor, Oxfordshire 39, 69
Charminster, Dorset 28, 65
Cheddar, Somerset 116
Chelmsford, Essex 105, 108, 116, 132
Cheltenham, Gloucestershire 148
Chelvey, Somerset 44
Chelwood, Somerset 118
Cheriton, Hampshire 192
Chesham, Buckinghamshire 160
Chesham Bois, Buckinghamshire 109
Cheshire, John 43
Chesseldyne, Edmund 158
Chesterblade, Somerset 129, 166
Chew Magna, Somerset 18, 226
Chew Stoke, Somerset 213
Chewton, Somerset 119
Chewton Mendip, Somerset 76
Chichester, Sussex 94, 102, 106, 153, 214
Chicke, Benjamin 76
Chigwell, Essex 44, 74
Chilcompton, Somerset 158
Child, Lawrence 147
Child, Robert, wife of 86
childbirth: thanksgiving after 34; *see also* churching
Childerditch, Essex 32, 146
children: catechizing 9, 10, 28, 38, 61, 62–3, 138, 220; disruptive in services 88, 89, 139; fate of unbaptized 225; illegitimate 38, 70, 77, 124, 147–8, 149, 159; predestination doctrine 25; *see also* baptism; childbirth
Childs, Joan 130

Childswickham, Gloucestershire 48
Chilton, Buckinghamshire 72
Chilworth, Hampshire 123–4, 131, 216–17
Chinnock, William 115–16
Chippenham, Wiltshire 108
Chipping Norton, Oxfordshire 70, 88, 93, 172–3, 174
Chipping Ongar, Essex 86, 115, 129, 193
Chipping Warden, Northamptonshire 73
Chithurst, Sussex 212
Christchurch, Dorset 189–90
christening *see* baptism
Christmas 68, 147, 173–4, 223
Church, Thomas 94
church rate 9, 139, 170, 212, 213
churches: animals in 88, 90, 92, 176, 197; Catholic burials in 195; disrespect for and defiling 170–2, 223; needing repair 6, 45, 80–1, 141, 210; removal of images 217; windows smashed 216; *see also* services
Churchhouse, Dorothy 169
churching 34, 39, 40, 69, 79, 106–7, 109–10, 116, 126; of Catholics 194; mock 175; pew set aside for 107, 110, 119, 134; at rail 119, 139; seen as popery 119, 138; wearing veil or kerchief for 107, 109–10
churchwardens: accounts and reports 6–8; and catechizing 62–3; concealment of breaches 9–10; discretion 9; dislike of predestination and election doctrines 25; disputes between 133, 134–5; disrespect for 157–8, 212; duties 5; exclusion from communion 45; excommunication of 211; and expense of changes 212; and games 152–3; influenced by local opinion 10, 11; interrogated by bishops 210; negligence 90; non-attendance by 81; and non-attendance of others 80–2, 84–5, 87; and poor relief 205; private grudges 22; raid alehouses 147; reactions to nonconformist clergy 33–4; and recusants 192, 195, 197, 198; and sexual offenders 149; shortcomings 7–9; support Sibthorpe in Northampton 136; and traditional festivals 66; and wine supply 177–8
churchyards: arguments and discussions in 133–4, 184, 224, 226; burial of Catholics 194, 195; burial of excommunicates 71, 77, 195; burial of suicides 70; dancing in 93; defiling 171, 223; disrespectful behaviour in 22, 44, 46, 85, 87, 90, 120, 128, 132, 137, 156, 175, 176, 178, 189, 213; games in 94, 152; maypoles in 65, 66; not seen as special 223; repairs 154
Cirencester, Gloucestershire 114

Civil War, English 215–17
Clapton, Northamptonshire 93, 221
Clark, Ann 76
Clark, Robert 167
Clark, Thomas 17, 60
Clarke, Dorothy 118–19
Clarke, Henry 9
Clarke, Jane 28
Clarke, Robert 96
Clarke, Samuel 53–4
Clavering, Essex 196
Claydon, Elizabeth 159
Cleare, Robert 81
Cleaver, John 134
Clement, John 187
Clement, Richard 29
Clement, Thomas 109
clergy 36–56, 218–20, 222; adultery 53, 54;
    aggressive behaviour 139, 140; attitudes to
    refusals to kneel for communion 107–8;
    and baptism 30–1, 32, 33, 34; 'black coat'
    as insult 54–5; and catechizing 26–30,
    60–1, 63; conflict of roles as preacher and
    pastor 55–6; courts' jurisdiction over
    5–6; discipline by 42–7; disputes
    between 131–3, 136, 137, 140; disputes
    with parishioners 74–5; disrespect for
    156–7, 166–7; disruptive 39–40;
    drunkenness 38, 166; godly objections to
    109; hard-line 219; harshness 41–2,
    45–7; high turnover of curates 36;
    hypocrisy 38, 40; insults to 50–3, 54–5;
    Laudian 214, 217, 219, 220, 222;
    marriage of 196, 204, 218; mediating role
    48; with medical practice 39; negligence
    38–9, 131; obliged to reject popery 30;
    parish expectations of 36–40; and
    penance cases 161–2; personal malice of
    42–4; praised in biographies 53–4;
    relationships with churchwardens 8;
    reports to bishops 210; Sabbath-breaking
    by 93; sexual immorality 38, 74–5; status
    49–50, 51–6, 218–19; surplice-wearing
    controversy 10, 30–2, 33, 34–5, 110,
    123, 126, 133, 134, 136, 137, 202, 216;
    tact and moderation 47–8; testimonials
    37, 219–20; university education 52;
    violence towards 54, 55; vulnerability to
    ridicule 48–9; *see also* sermons
Clevedon, Somerset 83, 190
Clinton, Northamptonshire 111
Clipsam, Martin 131–3, 222
Clipston, Northamptonshire 70
Clive, Lawrence 124
clothes 75, 83; *see also* hats; surplice
Clovely, Anne 191
Clutton, Somerset 157

Coates, John 187
Cock, William 76
Cocke, William 96
cockfights 171
Cogenhoe, Northamptonshire 192
Coggeshall, Essex 9, 43, 76, 87, 160, 163,
    178, 207
Coke, Mr (minister) 51
Colchester, Essex: archdeaconry court 18, 43,
    69, 153, 190; clergy disliked 139, 156,
    222; communion rails 211, 212;
    disrespect for courts 152, 155;
    excommunication cases 70, 71, 72, 77;
    Holy Trinity 72, 138, 139;
    non-attendance cases 80, 83, 111;
    nonconformity 138–40; radicals 126;
    rumours of Catholic attack 200, 224; St
    Botolph's 95, 138, 139; St Giles 63, 70,
    80, 104, 110, 138; St James's 71, 138,
    139, 140; St Leonard's 107, 138–40; St
    Martin's 69; St Mary Magdalene 139; St
    Mary's 138; St Nicholas 83, 119, 138; St
    Peter's 120, 138, 139, 212; St Runwald's
    110, 138, 139
Cold Norton, Essex 45, 65, 84
Coldwaltham, Sussex 60
Cole, Florence 196
Cole, John 107–8
Cole, Richard (of Romsey), wife of 130
Cole Richard (of Wittering) 156
Coleborne, Thomas 93
Coleman, Frances 157
Coleman, Henry 155–6
Coleman, Thomas 77
Coleorton, Leicestershire 28, 47, 220
Coles, Alice 79–80
Coles, Michael 134
Collard, William 86
Collet, Mr (registrar) 154
Collet, William 103–4
Collimore, Thomas 95
Collin, Richard 91
Collin, Thomas 87
Collins, Mrs 109
Collins, Thomas 97
Colson, Christopher 96
Colston, Anthony 115
Combe, Elizabeth 34, 226
Combe, Oxfordshire 71
Combe Bisset, Wiltshire 62
Comes, William 86
Commandments, Ten: debate about 227;
    kneeling for 120; as part of catechism 60,
    61, 63; scepticism about 168
communion: appropriate dress 75; bread 74,
    107, 175, 176, 178, 185, 188, 196;
    Catholics and 185, 186, 188, 189, 190,

communion: appropriate dress (*cont.*)
191–2; exclusion from 42–6, 48, 60–2,
72–3, 139–40, 219; failure to receive 9,
33, 47, 73–5, 119, 126, 131, 133, 135,
136, 202; importance 71–3, 221;
introduction of rail, and subsequent
refusals 118–20, 136, 138–9, 210, 211,
212, 214, 216, 217, 222; kneeling for
(and refusal to kneel) 34, 107–8, 109,
110, 135, 136, 137, 138, 140, 212, 219,
222; mass exclusions 44–5; mocked and
disrupted 175, 176–7; reasons for missing
73–5; received although forbidden 72–3;
received sitting 9–10, 107, 108, 109;
received standing 110, 134, 137; serious
discussions about 224–5; table 120, 136,
211, 212; wine 74, 107, 177–8, 185, 188
Compton, Somerset 155
Compton, Wiltshire 38
conventicles 113–15, 118, 123, 125, 136,
139, 140, 216, 219
conversations (about religion) 5, 34–5, 115,
224–7
Conygrave, Hugh 68
Cooch, Lawrence 45
Cooke, Alice 88
Cooke, Robert (of Daventry) 109
Cooke, Robert (of Feering) 80
Cooke, Susanna and Anne 171
Cooke, Thomas 167
Cooke, William (of Finchingfield) 188
Cooke, William (of Little Bardfield) 165
Coole, Thomas 171
Cooper, Alice 187
Cooper, Anne 69
Cooper, Master 111
Cooper, Richard 161, 223
Cooper, Thomas and Griselda 147
Copeland, John 178
Coppin, Thomas 162
Corbet, Helen 95
Corbett, Richard, bishop of Oxford 68
Corless, Christian 111
Corner, John 71
Cornish, Alice 149
Corpe, Andrew 173
Corringham, Essex 107, 130, 146, 172, 223
Cosbie, Giles 169, 223
Cosin, Elizabeth 173
Cottell, Richard 189–90, 194
Cotter, Master 115
Cotterstock, Northamptonshire 120
Cottesbrook, Northamptonshire 169
Cottesford, Mr (minister) 33
Cottesmore, Rutland 10, 68, 81, 85, 108
Cottingham, Northamptonshire 88, 156, 175
Cotton, Hugh 85–6

Cotton, Isabel 205
councillors, royal 210
courts, church: accused of greed and
corruption 154–5; apparitors 155–6;
and catechism 60–1, 62; Colchester 18,
43, 69, 152, 153, 155, 190; disputes
between clergy and parishioners 74;
disrespect for 152–4, 155–6; fear of 214;
Gloucester 153, 154–5, 218; jurisdiction
5–6; mock 223; oaths 76; Oxford 69, 76,
153, 154; Peterborough 71, 77, 87, 88,
90, 109, 111–12, 153, 161; records 7–8,
12, 37, 53, 211, 212; volume of use 153;
Wells 32, 112–13, 152, 153, 154, 155,
166, 192; Winchester 47, 60–1, 74, 186
Cousin, Robert 130
covetousness 151
Cowde, Osmond 87
Cowdrell, Emma 190
Cowley, Gloucestershire 33
Cowper, Geoffrey 42
Cowper, Richard 170
Cox, Lawrence 186–7, 191
Cox, Samuel 63
Cox, William 162
Crabb, Mary 189
Crabb, Robert 86
Craddock, John 169
Craddock, Mrs 116
Cranford, Mrs 106
Cransley, Northamptonshire 106, 107
Craven, Christopher 110
Creech, Richard and Robert 94
Creed: as part of catechism 28, 60, 61, 62, 63;
standing for 116–17, 118, 120, 128, 137
Creed, Widow 37
Crewkerne, Somerset 97, 163
Cricke, Thomas and Elizabeth 87
Cricket, William 72
Cricket Malherbie, Somerset 166, 168
crime 64, 86, 207
Crisp, Nicholas 85, 170, 224
Crixeth, Essex 77
Cron, John 95
Crooke, Samuel 32, 53, 165
Croose, John 172
Croscomb, Somerset 90
cross-dressing 150–1, 223
crossing (in baptism) 30–1, 32, 33, 34, 105,
137, 219, 220
Crouch, Abraham 90, 92
Crouch, Samuel 139
Crowe, Richard, and wife 139–40
Cudworth, Ralph 54
Cuffe, John 81
Culliford, William and Jane 191
Culpeck, Elizabeth 77

Culverwell, Ezekiel 1, 53
Culworth, Northamptonshire 191
Cummins, Abraham 128
Curle, Walter, bishop of Bath and Wells 211
Curles, John 92
Currier, George 68
Curry Rivel, Somerset 54, 94
Curtis, Ursula 102
Cutcombe, Somerset 48
Cutfold, John 105–6
Cuthbert, Mr (minister) 91

Dade, Henry 29
Dagenham, Essex 82, 95, 117, 147, 153
Daggle, William 155
Dallington, Northamptonshire 106
Danbury, Essex 2, 4, 122
dancing 45, 47, 65, 66, 84, 92–3, 104, 124, 137–8, 212; Parliament's order against 216
Daniel, Thomas 162
Dansey, Mrs 106
Danvers, Mr (minister) 75
Darby, William 35
Daventry, Northamptonshire 64, 106, 108, 109
Davey, John 43
Davey, Robert 119
Davidge, Mary 20, 160
Davie, Annabella 69
Davies, George 80, 93
Davies, Richard 190
Davis, Thomas 115, 125, 226
Davy, John 123–4
Davy, Nicholas 123
Davy, Richard 123
Dawes, John 153
Dawson, Robert 27
Day, John and Cecily 54
Day, Philip 204
Day, Robert 39
Deacon, William 51
Deane, Hugh 84
Deane, Lucy 196
Dearsley, Robert, wife of 45, 162–3
death: deathbed confessions 70–1, 77, 127–8; disrespect for 70, 178–9; praying for the dead 205–6; visiting the dying 39; *see also* burials
Debden, Essex 163
Declaration of Sports (1618) 47, 136; *see also* Book of Sports
Deddington, Oxfordshire 68, 123
Dee, Mr (minister) 43
defiling 171–2
Delarue, Martin 125

'deliverances' 196
deliveries, Sunday 151
Dell, Henry 160
Demander, John 40
Denbigh, John 38
Denby, William 226
Denham, Richard 130
Denman, Mr (minister) 45
Dennat, Stephen 77
Dennis, Susan 34–5, 104, 226
Dennison, Stephen 74
Dent, Arthur 1–5, 208; death 1, 53; difficulties over surplice-wearing and the cross 30; imitations and influences 1–4; ministries 4, 122; praised 53; style 5; *Opening of Heaven Gates* 26; *Pathway II* (attributed) 1–2; *The Plain Man's Pathway to Heaven* 1–5, 12–13, 206, 207, 210, 218; *The Ruin of Rome* 1; *A Sermon of Repentance* 1; *see also* Antilegon; Asunetus; Philagathus; Theologus
Denton, Northamptonshire 49, 95, 154
Derrick, Francis 153
Deryner, John 169
Desborough, Nicholas 80
Desborough, Northamptonshire 194
Devenish, Master 114
Devereux, Widow 176
devil 41, 55, 105, 124, 138, 155, 169, 183, 226
Dexter, Ralph 147
dialogues 2–4, 47
Dickenson, David 76
Digby, Ambrose 168
Digby, James 189
Digby family 198, 199, 200
Dike, Richard 28
Dinder, Somerset 69
Dinghurst, Widow 154
Dingley, Northamptonshire 88
Disney, William 191
disputes *see* conversations; quarrels
Ditcheat, Somerset 25, 66, 94, 140, 204, 211, 226, 227
Ditchling, Sussex 212
Dix, Anne 167
Dix, Maurice, wife of 17–18, 111
Dix, Richard 123
Dixon, John 90
Dobbs, Thomas 153
Dobson, Widow 77
Dod, John 30–1, 112
Doddinghurst, Essex 33
Doddymeade, Robert 8
Dodford, Northamptonshire 9, 88
Dodson, William, and wife 116–17
Doggett, John 44

Dogmerfield, Hampshire 51
Dolling, Joan 154
Donhead St Mary, Wiltshire 66
Donnington, Sussex 62, 107, 119
Donyatt, Somerset 43, 66, 94, 162
Dorchester, Dorset: libels 126–7, 129
Dorchester, Oxfordshire 146, 190
Dorvall, Arthur 66, 94, 226
Douglas, William 45
Douse, Richard 198
Dove, Mr (minister) 105
Dovercourt, Essex 23
Downe, John (minister) 32, 44
Downe, John (wife-seller) 170
Downham, Essex 150
Downing, Mr (minister) 89
Downing, William 133, 134–5
Dowse, Stephen 86
Dowtie, Mary 119
Dowtie, William 205
Drake, George 124
Drake, John 150
Draper, Matthew 120
Drayton, Somerset 95
Drew, Charles 64
Drewett, William 163
Driffield, Gloucestershire 36
Drinkwater, Thomas 84
drunkenness 97, 112, 130, 145–7, 222, 223;
    associated with Royalists 215; and
    bell-ringing 67, 178; in church 171, 172,
    176; of churchwardens 45;
    churchwardens' reporting of 8, 9, 10, 11,
    157; of clergy 22, 38, 52, 53, 166;
    discipline of 46, 160; at festivals 66;
    personal denunciations in church 21–2,
    23; of registrar 154; repentance for 77;
    sermons against 20–1, 23; *see also*
    alehouses
Duck, Dr 154
Duckett, John 89
Duckett, William 120
Duckwell, Ralph 188
Dudman, John, wife of 107
Dulverton, Somerset 71
Dundry, Somerset 93, 171
Dunkerton, Somerset 22
Dunstead, Richard 86
Dunster, Somerset 71, 76, 127–8, 152
Dyas, Simon 156
Dyer, William 178
Dyght, John 66
Dymock, Gloucestershire 10
Dyrham, Gloucestershire 39
Dythes, William 61

Earls Barton, Northamptonshire 125, 177,
    197
Earl's Colne, Essex 108, 161, 208
East Brent, Somerset 66, 154
East Ham, Essex 83, 125–6, 146, 176
East Hanningfield, Essex 32, 44, 45, 113, 140,
    219
East Hornden, Essex 208
East Mersea, Essex 74
East Pennard, Somerset 167, 173
East Tilbury, Essex 83, 178, 189, 204
Easter: communion 8, 9, 22, 27, 33, 42, 43,
    44, 47, 61, 71–2, 73, 74, 75, 119, 133,
    135, 136, 190, 191; games 84; offering
    44; reconciliation before 48
Eastington, Gloucestershire 61
Eastney, Hampshire 106
Easton, Eleanor 148
Easton, Northamptonshire 91
Easton Maudit, Northamptonshire 45, 151–2
Ecclestone, William 126
Ecton, Northamptonshire 197
Edgeworth, Gloucestershire 61
Edgill, John 119
Edington, Somerset 25, 126, 170
Edlington, Lincolnshire 25, 189
Edmunds, John 83
education: of clergy 52
Edwards, Francis 138
Edwards, John 71
Edwin, Richard 76
Egleton, Rutland 54
Eldridge, Robert 73
election, doctrine of 24–6
Elizabeth I, queen of England 206, 207,
    210–11
Elkins, John 55
Ellington, Huntingdonshire 27, 70
Elmore, Gloucestershire 60
Elmstead, Essex 72, 128–9, 208
Elsemere, Aaron 105
Elsenham, Essex 120
Elsfield, Oxfordshire 175–6
Elton, Northamptonshire 94
Ely, William 147
Emms, John 172, 174
Enewe, Henry 87, 160, 207
England, Thomas 152
English Combe, Somerset 109
Erbury, William 213
Essex: Catholicism in 193–4
Essex, archdeaconry of 43, 153, 154,
    155
Essex, commissary of 153, 155
Estgate, Richard 156

Estmond, Nicholas 195
Estwicke, Thomas 73
Etchingham, Sussex 212
Evans, John 129, 166
Evans, Robert 80
Eve, Henry 60
Eve, Thomas 60
Evenley, Northamptonshire 71–2
Everard, John 159
Everdon, Northamptonshire 8, 34, 126
Everett, John 49
Everley, Wiltshire 83
Everson, Richard 152
Evorey, John 162
Ewens, John 49
Ewes, William 94, 227
excommunication: and baptism 70; and burial 71, 77, 195; church attendance continues after 68–9, 131, 132; and churching 119; of churchwardens 211; and communion 72, 108; excessive use of 45, 47; of recusants 193, 195, 196; repentance 77; as sanction 6, 158, 162; unconcern for 48, 97, 161, 162–3, 225; *see also* absolution
Exford, Somerset 72, 204–5
Exton, Rutland 91, 163, 171

Fabian, John 38
Fage, Edward 33
Fairlight, Sussex 190
Fairsted, Essex 159
Fareham, Hampshire 47, 206
Farington, Somerset 71
Farmer, Anne 116
farming 8, 95–6; cattle 83, 91, 96, 207–8; haymaking 10, 97; ploughing 87, 168; sheep-shearing 95, 167
Farne, Richard 117
Farringdon, Somerset 112–13, 176
Farrington, William 129–30
Farthing, Eleanor 10, 97
Farthingstone, Northamptonshire 31
Farthington, Northamptonshire 61
Faulkbourne, Essex 191
Fawcett, Katherine 147
Fawsley, Northamptonshire 109
Feering, Essex 80
Fering, Sussex 11, 90
festivals, traditional 65–7; *see also* May festivities; Midsummer; Whitsun
Fiddington, Somerset 119
Field, Grace 130
Field, John 204
Filkins, William 73, 109
Finchingfield, Essex 188, 189
Finedon, Northamptonshire 161, 171

fines: for absenteeism 82, 84–5; as commutation of penance 158–9; recusancy 191; unconcern for 153
Fingringhoe, Essex 110
Firmin, Edward, wife of 110, 139
Fisher, Christopher 85, 146
Fisher, Edward 18
Fisher, Elizabeth 191
Fisher, John 71
Fisher, Margaret 87
Fisher, Mary 83
Fisher, William 71
fishing 94, 96, 208
Fleetwood, John 73
Fletcher, Elizabeth 150
Fletcher, William 162
Flint, John 94
Flitwick, Bedfordshire 47
Flore, Northamptonshire 195
Folke, Dorset 39, 41, 51
Folkingham, Lincolnshire 70
football 84–5, 93, 221
Ford, Edward 153
Ford, Robert 146
Ford, William (of Thurleigh) 37
Ford, William (of West Ham) 156
Fordham, Essex 17, 74
Fordington, Dorset 81, 114
Forester, Abraham 41
Forrin, Widow 65
Fortescue, John 191
Fossett, James 18
Foster, Francis 34
Fotheringhay, Northamptonshire 8, 67, 157
Foulkes, Petronella 155
Foulness, Essex 85, 90, 170
Foxcote, Somerset 90
Foxwell, Henry 189, 196, 224
Foxwell, Robert 82
Frank, Mary 159
Fraston, Elizabeth 71
Freele, Anne 197, 224
Freeman, James and Ursula 22
Fretherne, Gloucestershire 61
Frewen, Lewis 9
Friend, John 111
Frith, John 75
Frogg, John 170
Frogmore, Robert 73
Frome, Somerset 85, 151, 163
Fry, John 205
Fry, William 38
Fryer, Robert 151, 208
Fryerning, Essex 158, 171
Fulke, Valentine 65
Fuller, John 161

Fuller, Richard 159
funerals *see* burials
Funtington, Sussex 105–6

gadding 111–13, 129, 215, 221–2, 226
Gainsford, Anne 48
Galloway, Richard, wife of 103–4
gambling 147; *see also* card games
games and sports 42, 65–6, 84–5, 93–4, 136,
    146, 152–3, 171, 227; 1618 declaration
    on 47, 136; 1633 declaration on 66, 116,
    221; Parliament's order against 216
gardening 96, 213
Gardiner, Samuel: *The Way to Heaven* 2
Gardiner, Thomas 157
Gardner, Grisell 208
Gardner, Thomas 71
Garewe, Matthew 102
Garnett, Robert 189
Garrett, Agnes 65
Garrett, Seth 161
Garrett, William (biographer) 53
Garrett, William (of Colchester) 156
Garth, Thomas 69
Gascoigne, Thomas 152
Gawler, John 55, 168
Gawton, Richard 63
Gay, John 146
Gay, Richard 178
Gaye, Richard 187
Gayhurst, Buckinghamshire 199
Gaylett, William 18
Gaylord, Thomas 153
Geldart, Janet 185
Geneva 225
Gent, William 115
George, Goodwife 64
George, John 90
George, Thomas, wife of 71
Gewyn, Margery 173, 175
ghosts 225–6
Gibb, John 75
Gibbs, John 147
Gibson, Thomas (of Little Oakley) 83
Gibson, Thomas (of Ridlington) 109
Gifford, George 6, 12, 78, 208; on arbitrary
    discipline by clergy 42, 43; career 183–4;
    on ignorance of laymen 59, 60;
    prosecuted for nonconformity 202;
    published sermons 26; *A Brief Discourse of
    Certain Points of the Religion which is
    among the Common sort of Christians,
    which may be termed the Country Divinity*
    (Zelotes/Atheos debate) 2, 4, 25–6,
    40–1, 183, 202–3, 204, 206, 210, 219; *A
    Dialogue between a Papist and a Protestant*
    2, 13, 40, 183–4, 196, 197, 198, 200–1,
    203, 205, 218; *A Dialogue Concerning
    Witches and Witchcrafts* 2, 64, 183
Gilbert, James 178
Gilby, John 21
Gilby, Matthew 135
Gilder, George 39
Giles, George 117
Gilkes, Thomas 159
Gillet, Isabel 64
Gilman, Lawrence 132
Gimlett, Margaret 169
Glascock, Henry 194
Glascock, Master 102
Glascock, Thomas 87
Glastonbury, Somerset 25, 87, 96, 102–3, 124
Glessom, Ralph 177
Gloucester: catechizing 61, 62; courts 153,
    154–5, 218; St Nicholas 73; sermon on
    dancing 93
Gloucestershire: petition 214, 215
Glover, William (Burton Latimer, 1613) 86
Glover, William (Burton Latimer, 1617) 82
Glover, William (Burton Latimer, 1634) 69
God: attitudes to 5, 6, 227; centrality of 5,
    180; duty to 76, 78
Godd, Robert 212
Goddard, John 89
Godfrey, Christian 76–7, 226
Goding, Jane 36
godly, the 101–41, 179–80, 206–7, 208–9,
    210–11, 213, 214, 222–3; attitudes to
    Catholics 198; and the Bible 129; and
    Civil War 215–16, 217; and communion
    107–9, 222; conventicles 113–15; dislike
    of ceremony 106–7, 116–20; dislike of
    surplice and crossing (in baptism) 30–5,
    126; importance of sermons to 110–13;
    insulted as 'puritans' 122–5, 126–9;
    nonconformity 104–9; outrage against
    the profane 129–41; and parish disputes
    131–40; refusal to stand for Creed,
    Epistle and Gospel 117–18; Robert
    Bolton on 122; *see also* nonconformity
godparents 60, 105, 148, 172
Godsave, Alice 149
Godshill, Hampshire 102
Goffe, Joan 107
Goldhanger, Essex 18, 96, 170
Goodale, John 120
Goodier, John 172
Gooding, William 70–1
Goodman, Joan (of Burnham) 92
Goodman, Joan (of Fiddington) 119
Goodman, William 133, 134–5
Goodson, Julie 152
Goodwin, Robert 213

Goodwin, Roger 139
Goodwin, William 178
Goodyear, Richard 198
Goodyer, Nicholas 67
Goosen, Thomas 92
Gorway, John 8
Gosney, Joan 169
Gospel: reading 34; standing for 34, 117–18
Gosse, John 175
gossips 11
Gough, Master 108
Gowers, Thomas 118
Graffham, Sussex 22, 37, 68, 84, 167, 197
Granger, Thomas: on anti-clericalism 55; on the ungodly 130; *Paul's Crown of Rejoicing, or, The Manner How to Hear the Word with Profit* (Eulalus/Mataologus debate) 3, 4, 19, 30, 42, 129, 130
Grant, Dr 52
Grantham, Lincolnshire 64
Gray, Henry 84
Gray, Hugh 171
Gray, Robert 68
Grays Thurrock, Essex 150–1
Great Baddow, Essex 211, 219
Great Bardfield, Essex 8, 85, 162, 179, 193
Great Bedwyn, Wiltshire 93, 169, 221
Great Bentley, Essex 9, 117, 128
Great Bromley, Essex 171
Great Burstead, Essex 29, 74, 105–6, 167, 178, 207–8
Great Chesterford, Essex 82
Great Chishall, Essex 119, 222
Great Hallingbury, Essex 85
Great Holland, Essex 51, 87, 168–9
Great Oakley, Essex 156, 172
Great Rissington, Gloucestershire 39
Great Rollright, Oxfordshire 159
Great Saling, Essex 95
Great Sampford, Essex 170
Great Stambridge, Essex 120
Great Tew, Oxfordshire 150
Great Tey, Essex 64, 177
Great Totham, Essex 68
Great Wakering, Essex 116, 156
Great Waltham, Essex 81, 108
Great Warley, Essex 38, 86, 171
Green, Jeremiah 156
Green, Joan 205
Green, Thomas 188
Greene, George 61
Greene, Master 111
Greene, Mrs 195
Greenfield, John 94
Greenfield, Mr (minister) 166
Greenfield, Samuel 29
Greenhall, Thomas 149, 160–1, 162

Greenham, Richard 203
Greens Norton, Northamptonshire 199
Greensted, Essex 45, 162–3
Greenway, Samuel 85
Grendon, Northamptonshire 50
Grey, John 29, 223
Grey, Mary 77
Grey, Robert 208
Grey, Thomas 43
Griffiths, Lawrence 166
Grigg, John 90
Griggs, Thomas 109
Grigson, Thomas 227
Grove, William 104–5
Grover, Eleanor 162
Growte, John 179
Gryce, William 173
Gulliver, Alice 123
Gunpowder Plot 87, 189, 196, 198
Guthrie, William 176

Hacker, John 158–9
Hacket, Thomas 140
Hackett, William 125
Hackwell, Essex 84
Haddock, Bridget 157
Haddon, Dorothy 155
Hadleigh, Essex 106
Hadstock, Essex 61, 96, 110, 212
Haggard, Blaise 87
Hailes, Matthew 106
Hailsham, Sussex 212
Haines, Ralph 66, 211
Halbert, Agnes 93
Hall, Edward 166
Hall, Frances 186
Hall, Humphrey 157
Hall, Richard 108
Halsted, Essex 159
Halstock, Dorset 10, 74
Halton, Oxfordshire 71
Hambledon, Hampshire 106
Hambleton, Rutland 89, 110, 171
Hamer, Bridget 220
Hamon, Robert 102
Hampton Poyle, Oxfordshire 73
Handsworth, Staffordshire 125, 129
Hanneys, Berkshire 157
Hannington, Northamptonshire 117
Hannold, Richard 170
Hanslope, Buckinghamshire 110, 196, 198
Hanwell, Oxfordshire 30–1, 112
Harding, Thomas 96
Harding, William 212
Hardwick, Alice 83
Hardwicke, Gloucestershire 84

Hare, Walter 86
Harmer, Elizabeth 191
Harmer, Thomas 146
Harnhill, Gloucestershire 36
Harrell, William 77
Harrington, Daniel 116
Harris, Anne 9
Harris, James 29
Harris, John, and wife 116
Harris, Mr (minister) 167
Harris, Thomas 151
Harrison, Owen 197−8
Hart, Anne 37
Hart, John: *The Burning Bush Not Consumed* 3
Hartford, Anthony 49−50
Hartford, John, and wife 125−6
Hartpury, Gloucestershire 45, 84
Harvard, Thomas 125
harvests, poor 207
Harwich, Essex 50, 208
Harwood, Henry and Venus 46
Haselbury, Somerset 152
Haselrigg, Mrs 195
Hasper, Master 195
Hasselden, Edward 93
Hatch, Robert 208
Hatfield Peverel, Essex 18, 33, 86
hats: worn in church 10, 89, 90, 120, 138, 139, 170
Hattersley, Joseph 52
Havering, Essex 38, 80
Hawes, William 161
Hawkins, Anthony 81
Hawkins, John 93
Hawkins, Kimberley 161
Hawkwell, Essex 54, 170
Hawsted, Mr (minister) 50
Haydon, Dorset 34
Hayes, Thomas 87
Haynes, Agnes 160
Haynes, Phoebe 111
Haynes, Ralph 226
Haywood, Thomas 139
Hazeleigh, Essex 105
Headbourne Worthy, Hampshire 225
Heale, Thomas 157
Heath, George 176
Heathfield, Somerset 41
Heckford, Elizabeth 128−9
Heckles, Thomas 88
Hedge, Humphrey 156
Hedge, Lawrence 150
Hele, John 156
Hellam, Mr (church absentee) 82
Hellar, John 93
Hellier, Alice 106
Hellier, James 166

Hellier, John 88
Helpston, Northamptonshire 88, 91, 94, 95, 149, 161, 162
Hemingby, Lincolnshire 21, 41
Hempsted, Essex 82, 102
Henley-on-Thames, Berkshire 109−10
Herbert, John 49
Hermitage, Dorset 8, 44−5
Herriard, Hampshire 19−20
Herstmonceux, Sussex 107
Hewes, Thomas, wife of 18
Hewitt, Cecily 123
Hewlett, Mr (minister) 91
Hewson, Daniel 139
Heysham, John 8
Heytesbury, Wiltshire 161
Heywood, Ralph 33, 134
Hibberd, Thomas 88
Hickman, John 134
Hickman, Thomas 33
Hieron, Samuel: *The Preacher's Plea* 1, 3, 4
Hieron, William 21, 41
Higgins, John 172, 174
Higgs, Margery 172
High Commission 139, 214, 220
High Easter, Essex 194
High Littleton, Somerset 104
Highworth, Wiltshire 71, 91
Hildersham, Arthur 107, 140
Hill, John (of Cottesbrooke) 169
Hill, John (of Foxcote) 90
Hill, Mary 193
Hill, Richard 91
Hill, Robert: *The Pathway to Prayer and Piety* 2
Hill, William 114
Hill Farrance, Somerset 147
Hillard, Robert 168
Hillary, John 49−50, 117
Hilliard, John 91
Hills, Elizabeth 61−2
Hilton, Joan 106
Hinde, Henry 133, 134
Hinton Charterhouse, Somerset 94
Hippesley, Henry 193
Hiscox, Richard 170
Hiscox, Toby 149
Hitchcock, George 155
Hix, John (of Dinder) 69
Hix, John (of Moorlinch) 168
Hoard, Samuel 108
Hobbes, Richard 49
Hobbs, William 84
Hoby, Thomas 84
Hockley, Essex 91
Holbrooke, Master 156
Holland, Hugh 204

Holland, Robert 120
Holland, Essex 72
Holloway, Richard 71
Holman, Richard 89, 219
Holton, Oxfordshire 195
hood, academic: failure to wear 137
Hooe, Sussex 116
Hooke, Samuel 51
Hopkins, James 64
Horkstow, Lincolnshire 31
Horn, Agnes 172
Horncastle, Essex 112
Hornchurch, Essex 32, 64, 106, 107, 111, 114, 162, 221
Horndon-on-the-Hill, Essex 155
Horne, Gabriel 122
Horne, Robert, bishop of Winchester 60
Horney, John 190
Horningsham, Wiltshire 206
Horseman, Mistress 71, 195
Horton, Berkshire 168
Horwood, John 106
Hoskins, Thomas 111
Houghton, Master 21
Houghton, Hampshire 107
Houlder, Lewis 129
House, John 157
Howard, John 204, 225
Howard, Richard 83
Howe, Humphrey 172
Howen, Francis, wife of 96
Howlett, John 9
Howse, William 73
Howt, John 171
Hudson, William 162
Huish Episcopi, Somerset 213
Hulatt, Christopher 29
Hullan, William 170
Hullavington, Wiltshire 65
Hulyard, Richard 93
Humphrey, Nicholas 155
Humphrey, Thomas 82
Hunston, Sussex 31
Hunt, Alexander 67
Hunt, Richard 92
Hunt, William 21
hunting 94
Hurman, Marmaduke 94
Hursley, Hampshire 187
Husband, John 220
Hussey, Gilbert 21
Hutton, Somerset 62
Hyndye, Anne 84

Iffley, Oxfordshire 96
ignorance 59–62; discipline of 44

Ilchester, Somerset 81
Ilkeston, Derbyshire 67
illegitimacy 38, 70, 77, 124, 147–8, 149, 159; *see also* mothers, unmarried
Ilminster, Somerset 71
images, religious 217
Inckforby, Dr 48
Incly, Richard 106
Ingatestone, Essex 120
Ingrave, Essex 37, 208
Innes, William 23
insults (to clergy) 50–3, 54–5
Inworth, Essex 27, 44, 63
Ireland, William 187–8
Ireland: military failures in 207
Irthlingborough, Northamptonshire 188–9, 193
Isham, Mrs 116
Isham, Northamptonshire 55, 67, 195
Isley Walton, Leicestershire 154
Islip, Northamptonshire 22
Isodde, Thomas 48
Itchen Abbas, Hampshire 187
Ivy, John 154

Jackson, Andrew 173
Jackson, Mr (curate) 109
Jackson, William 155
James, Dr 32, 154
James, Philip 112
James, Richard 64–5
James, Susan 167, 219
James, Thomas 43
James, Tiffany 71
Jarmyn, Sarah 176
Jarvis, Edward 175
Jarvis, John 225
Jeake, Samuel 197, 224
Jeanes, Christian 71
Jeffery, Richard 84
Jenison, Robert 52, 218
Jenkins, David 38–9
Jenkinson, John 170
Jennings, Christopher 118
Jesuits 203
Jobson, John 178
Johnson, Agnes 76
Johnson, Edward 81
Johnson, John (of East Ham) 146
Johnson, John (of Storrington) 117
Johnson, Mr (curate) 49
Johnson, Robert 45, 109
Johnson, Thomas 45
jokes and laughter 29, 149, 150, 162, 166–7, 172–7, 178–9, 197, 211, 212, 223–4; in church 48–9, 88–9, 136, 137, 167, 172, 175, 176–7, 223

Jones, Henry 151
Jones, Joan 62
Jones, Lewis 84
Jones, Margery 61
Jones, Ralph 67
Jones, Thomas 115
Jones, William 172
Jordan, Richard 23
Joy, Richard 146–7
Joyce, Henry 125
Joyner, Mr (minister) 20

Kaye, William 972
Kayes, Joan 126
Keepe, John 54, 170
Kelmarsh, Northamptonshire 88
Kelvedon, Essex 38, 54, 86, 156
Kendall, Richard 88
Kennell, Dorothy 115
Kent, Susan 47, 124
Kent, Thomas 83, 177
Kese, Richard 169
Kettering, Northamptonshire 4, 53, 68–9,
      103, 122, 199, 200, 213
Kewen, Alice 187
Keynsham, Somerset 66, 187, 188
Keynton, George 80
Keys, Henry 146
Kibbit, John 171
Kidderminster, Worcestershire 215, 217
Killingworth, Henry 91
Kilmersdon, Somerset 68, 161
King, Henry 72–3
King, John 102
King, Matthew 49
King, Nicholas 89
King, Richard 126
King, Susan 138
King, Thomas (of Brightlingsea) 152
King, Thomas (of Witney) 116
King, Thomas (of Wylye) 91
King, William 225
King's Bench, court of 191
King's Cliffe, Northamptonshire 21
King's Sutton, Northamptonshire 63, 64, 92,
      204
King's Worthy, Hampshire 38, 67
Kingscote, Gloucestershire 151
Kingsdon, Somerset 29
Kingsthorpe, Northamptonshire 28
Kingston, Somerset 10, 97
Kirby, Mary 74
Kirby, Mr (minister) 37
Kirby, Philip 70
Kirkham, William 95
Kirkland, Nathaniel 10

Kitchener, John 212
kneeling (and refusals to kneel): for
      churching 119; for Commandments 120;
      for communion 34, 107–8, 109, 110,
      135, 136, 137, 138, 140, 212, 219, 222;
      for Lord's Prayer 137; for prayer at burial
      119
Knight, Alexander 105
Knight, Alice 148
Knightley, Sir Richard 134
Knook, Wiltshire 91
Knott, Everard 91
Knuckles, Rachel 148

Lacy, Sir John 159
Laindon, Essex 39
Lake, Thomas 225
Lamb, Thomas, and wife 70, 138, 139
Lambe, Dr John 136, 137, 152, 153
Lambert, Abigail 130
Lambert, Mr (minister) 111, 221
Lamerton, Richard 127
Lamport, Northamptonshire 65
Lancelot, Humphrey 86–7
Lancing, Sussex 44, 147
Lane, Robert 8, 44–5
Lane, Thomas 83
Langford, Dorothy 168
Langford, Essex 44
Langham, Rutland 64
Langley, Robert 18
Langley, Essex 90
Larking, Mother 152
Lathom, Thomas 111
Laud, William, archbishop of Canterbury 18,
      115, 139, 170–1, 210, 211, 212, 214,
      215, 216, 219, 222
laughter *see* jokes and laughter
Launce, William 126
Launden, Alice 69, 163
Launden, Edward 154
Lavor, John 154
Lavor, Thomas 155
Lawrence, William 126
Layer Breton, Essex 174
Layer Marney, Essex 9, 88–9, 118, 169
Lea, Elizabeth 136
Leach, Henry 109
Leach, John 114
Leave, Matthew 155
Lee, John 47, 91, 124, 177
Lee, Nicholas 51
Lee, Thomas 125
Lee, William 86
Leech, John 162
Leek, Gregory, wife of 134

Legge, John 149
Leghman, William 125
Leicester 10, 64, 154
Leigh, George 96
Leigh, Essex 1, 28, 43, 171
Lent 85
Lenthall, William 192
Leonard Stanley, Gloucestershire 103
Lester, Henry 83
Leverton, Mr (minister) 67
Lewes, Sussex 176
Lewgate, Robert, wife of 105
Lewger, William, and wife 131
Lewis, Christopher, and wife 197
Lewis, John 166
Leyden, William 102
Leyton, Essex 76, 84
Liam, Elizabeth 45
Liddell, Thomas 86
Lilbourne, Northamptonshire 211
Lillingstone Lovell, Berkshire 49
Lincoln, Robert (of South Ockendon) 46
Lincoln, Robert (of Twyford) 187
Lincoln, Thomas 46
Lincoln 189, 197
Lindsell, John 159–60
Lingfield, Surrey 48
Linley, Richard 153
Lister, Brian 31
Litchfield, Henry 169
Little, Thomas (of Great Burstead) 207–8
Little, Thomas (of Littlebury) 195
Little Baddow, Essex 118, 171
Little Bardfield 165
Little Bentley, Essex 118
Little Billing, Northamptonshire 51, 177
Little Braxted, Essex 75
Little Bromley, Essex 120
Little Casterton, Northamptonshire 21, 39
Little Chishall, Essex 80
Little Dunmow, Essex 41
Little Harrowden, Northamptonshire 113
Little Horkesley, Essex 77
Little Houghton, Northamptonshire 48
Little Laver, Essex 109
Little Oakley, Essex 83
Little Oakley, Northamptonshire 197
Little Sampford, Essex 10, 195
Little Sodbury, Gloucestershire 81
Little Somerford, Wiltshire 66
Little Thurrock, Essex 95
Little Totham, Essex 106
Little Wakering, Essex 80
Little Waltham, Essex 61
Little Yeldham, Essex 106
Littlebury, Essex 112, 195
Littlewood, Joseph 139

Littlewood, Winifred 107
Lobley, Alice 185
Lock, Mr (minister) 61
Lock, John (of Edington) 25, 126
Lock, John (of Ilminster) 71
Lock, Peter 168
Locke, William 225–6
Locking, Somerset 38–9, 49
Lockwood, Thomas 81
Loddington, Northamptonshire 178
London, Richard 80
London 64, 74
Long, Alice 114
Long, Robert 204
Long, Simon 62
Long Bennington, Lincolnshire 46
Long Buckby, Northamptonshire 31
Long Load, Somerset 124
Lord of Misrule 38, 173–4
Lord's Prayer: kneeling for 137; as part of
    catechism 60, 61, 62, 63
Lorkin, Thomas 79
lost property 64
Lovell, John 96
Lovell, Richard 124
Lowe, John 54
Lowick, Northamptonshire 197
Lownie, Robert, and wife 80
Lucas, William 157
Lucke, William 95
Luddington, Master 102
Luddington, Northamptonshire 49
Lufton, Somerset 109
Lullington, Somerset 225
Lund, Anne 192
Lund, Maurice 192
Lunes, William 75
Luthy, Wilfrid 74
Lutton, Lincolnshire 36–7
Lutton, Northamptonshire 117
Luxborough, Somerset 166
Lyde, Somerset 196
Lydney, Gloucestershire 49, 81
Lyme, Richard 90
Lyme Regis, Dorset 10, 66, 67, 81, 127, 140,
    213, 222
Lyndon, Rutland 93
Lyne, Mary 196, 224

Mabbott, Thomas 45
Maber, Timothy 8
MacDonnell, Brian 188
Madehurst, Sussex 93, 221
Madye, Meredith 105
Maggs, Edward 149
Maisemore, Gloucestershire 73

Major, Agnes 135–6
Major, Leonard 18, 135–6, 221–2
Makernes, Richard 105
Maldon, Essex 2, 4, 90, 120, 125; All Saints 104–5, 183–4, 202
Malin, William 90
Malson, Thomas 11
Man, Clement 61
Man, Robert 155
Manning, Matthew 95
Manning, Samuel 51
Manningham, John 129
Mannock, William 140
Manton, William 110
Manuden, Essex 29, 93, 96, 223
Maple, William 95
Mapledurham, Oxfordshire 193
Mapperton, Dorset 25, 31, 40, 122–3
Maresfield, Sussex 212
Marholm, Northamptonshire 31, 75
Market Rasen, Lincolnshire 54
Marks, Master 220
marriage 6; and catechism 60; of Catholics 194; of clergy 196, 204, 218; dancing at 84; mock 173–5, 224; recusants at 197; without ring 34
Marston, Somerset 155
Marston Bigot, Somerset 125
Marston Magna, Somerset 152
Marston St Lawrence, Northamptonshire 66, 73
Martin, Christopher 29
Martin, John 155
Martinists 125
Martock, Somerset 71, 155, 168
Martyr Worthy, Hampshire 191
Mary, Virgin 168, 205, 222, 223, 226
Mary I, queen of England 196, 210–11
Mascall, Thomas 156
Massey, Susan 157–8
Masters, John 154
Mathew, Thomas 154
Matthew, Anthony 93
Maule, Richard 92
Maunder, Elizabeth 70
Maxey, Northamptonshire 28
May, Richard 175
May, Roger 51–2
May festivities 65–6, 128, 141, 222, 227; maypoles 66, 140, 211, 226
Mayatt, Walter 80, 88
Mayles, William 148
Meade, Agnes 107
Meadopp, Thomas 119
Meare, Somerset 40, 90–1, 169, 178
Mears Ashby, Northamptonshire 151
meditating 113

Mee, Judith 106
Meeching, Sussex 212
Melksham, Wiltshire 114
Mells, Somerset 8, 151, 155
Mercer, Richard 123
Mercy, George 96
Mere, Wiltshire 10, 146–7
Merriott, Somerset 163
Merstone, Hampshire 60
Merton, Margery 151
Michenor, John 86
Mickleton, Gloucestershire 31
Middlam, Robert 203, 204
Middlezoy, Somerset 20, 76–7, 94, 160, 226, 227
Midhurst, Sussex 197
Midsummer 84, 223
Milborne, Thomas 176
Milcombe, Oxfordshire 113
Miles, Richard and Clare 190
Millard, John 23
Millard, Samuel 23, 24, 103
Millard, Thomas 112
Miller, Elizabeth 60
Miller, Joseph 49
millers 95, 151–2, 167, 191
Mills, Alice 187
Mills, Katherine 81
Mills, Robert 157
Milton, Hampshire 86–7
Milton, Northamptonshire 55, 85
Minehead, Somerset 46, 51–2
Miner, Jane 79
Minstead, Hampshire 204
Minsterworth, Gloucestershire 90
Misson, John 172–3, 174
Mistley, Essex 177
Mitchell, Edward 66, 104
Mitchell, Matthew 113
Monck, Elizabeth 71
Monksilver, Somerset 175
Montacute, Somerset 168
Montagu, Richard, bishop of Chichester 214; *A New Gag for an Old Goose* 209
Moore, John, and wife 70
Moore, William 168
Moorlinch, Somerset 23, 82, 166, 168
Morcott, Rutland 161
More, William 149
Moreton, Essex 108, 205
Moreton Pinkney, Northamptonshire 112
Moreton Valence, Gloucestershire 103, 222
Morgan, John (of Axbridge) 151
Morgan, John (of Wells) 189
Morley, Francis 70
Morris, Mark and Eleanor 149–50
Morris, Thomas 64

morris dancing 66, 84, 92
Morse, Thomas 43
Morton, Thomas (of Axbridge) 80, 225–6
Morton, Thomas (of Axminster) 196
Morton Valence, Gloucestershire 39
mothers, unmarried 44, 47, 69, 130, 147–8, 149, 153; *see also* illegitimacy
Mottershead, Mellior 28
Moulsham, Essex 188
Moulton, Northamptonshire 7–8, 90
Mouncke, John 82
Mount, Richard 75
Mountford, Robert 151
Mountnessing, Essex 81
Mucking, Essex 33, 80, 88, 90
Mudford, Somerset 166
Mudgley, Somerset 82
Mullins, Bartholomew 44–5
Munck, Edward 41
Munden, Essex 82, 148
Mundham, Sussex 60
Munt, Samuel 72
Myles, William 187

Nailsea, Somerset 44, 81, 109
Naishe, John 157
Nash, Anne 81
Nash, George 156
Nassington, Northamptonshire 65
Nation, Robert 213
Navestock, Essex 130, 151
Neale, Thomas 171
Needham, Thomas 52
Negus, William 43
Netherby, Dorset 213
Neverd, John 170
Nevill, Humphrey 22
New Year 171
Newball, John 130
Newbury, Berkshire 107, 157
Newcastle-upon-Tyne 52, 200, 218
Newcomen, Thomas 139, 222
Newent, Gloucestershire 204
Newington Bagpath, Gloucestershire 38
Newman, James and Ellen 148
Newman, John 96
Newman, Mr (minister) 43
Newnham 64
Newport, Essex 31–2
Newton, John 108
Newton, William 159
Nicholl, John 109
Nicholls, John 106
Nicholls, Richard 103, 119
Nichols, Josias 206–7
Nicholson, John 89

Nightingale, William 86
nonconformity 11, 30–5, 37, 104–10, 115–21, 211, 216, 217, 222; and baptism 30–1, 32, 33, 34, 105–6; and bowing and standing 116–18; and ceremony 106–7, 116, 119–20; in Colchester 138–40; and communion 107–9, 118–19; hard-line clergy 219; and parish disputes 131–40; petitions against 214–15; as poor index of godliness 120–1; and Prayer Book 104–5; and surplice 30–2, 33, 34–5; varying reasons for 109–10; visibility and protests 115–16; *see also* godly, the; radicalism
Normanton, Northamptonshire 61, 90
Norrington, Edward 34
Norris, Francis 125, 129
North Leigh, Oxfordshire 192
North Luffenham, Rutland 45, 67, 93, 109, 161, 189
North Ockendon, Essex 102, 155
North Petherton, Somerset 197
North Shoebury, Essex 46
North Stoke, Somerset 41
North Waltham, Hampshire 73
Northampton 70, 103, 153, 213; All Saints 27, 73, 75, 106, 109, 117, 135, 136, 137, 211, 212, 222; disputes in 135–7, 140; preachers 18, 221–2; Robert Bolton's sermon 122, 209; rumours of Catholic uprisings 199; St Giles 63, 80–1, 86, 89, 105, 113, 117, 135–6, 137; St Peter's 119–20; St Sepulchre 37, 89, 106, 135, 136, 137; *see also* Sibthorpe, Robert
Norton, Essex 130
Norton, Somerset 61
Norton Disney, Lincolnshire 191
Norton St Philip, Somerset 96
Norton under Hamdon, Somerset 126
nostalgia 203–4, 205–6
Nowell, Dean 63
Noyes, David 93
Nun, John 83
Nutcomb, Robert 48
Nuthurst, Sussex 156

Oakham, Rutland 109, 167, 171, 175, 177
Oakley, Essex 94
Oakshott, Thomas and Jane 106
Oath of Allegiance 189
oaths 76
Odcombe, Somerset 79
Oddington, Gloucestershire 84
Ogbourne St Andrew, Wiltshire 91
Ogbourne St George, Wiltshire 89
Okeman, Richard 105

Old, Northamptonshire 157
Old Cleeve, Somerset 169
Ongar, Essex 69
Orcheston, Wiltshire 190
organs 115–16, 125, 212, 214, 226
Orlibeare, John 170
Orsett, Essex 8
Orton, Mary 160
Orton, Northamptonshire 172
Osborne, Henry 8
Osborne, John 172
Osborne, William 140
Otterbourne, Hampshire 186, 191
Ottery, Dorset 38
Ottis, John 25
Ottyes, John 102–3
Oundle, Northamptonshire 18, 21, 54, 91,
    94, 102, 106, 107, 120, 140, 157, 167
Over Compton, Dorset 169, 225
Overstone, Northamptonshire 33
Overton, Hampshire 38
Oving, Agnes 48
Owen, David 75, 109, 135, 137, 154, 163,
    222
Oxendon, Northamptonshire 77
Oxenhall, Gloucestershire 204
Oxford 64, 71, 116; Catholics 190, 194, 200;
    courts 69, 76, 153, 154; May celebrations
    66, 128, 141, 222, 227; St Aldates 70; St
    Mary Magdalene 163; St Michael's 194;
    St Peter-le-Bailey 66, 104, 117–18, 128,
    141, 222; Whitsun celebrations 128
Oxfordshire: petition 214
Oxley, Leonard 174
Oxley, Ralph 104

Packington, Leicestershire 220
Page, Francis 72
Page, Henry 17, 110–11
Page, William, and wife 159
Paine, John (of Banwell) 62–3
Paine, John (of Great Oakley) 156
Painter, Gabriel 188
Painter, Widow 186
Palm Sunday 176, 177
Palmer, Matthew 134
Palmer, Richard 114–15
Palmer, Thomas 134
Palmer, William 176
Pamphlin, Mrs 71
Pamplet, Thomas 105
Pannell, Christopher 176
Pannell, Richard 64
papacy: views on 194, 200, 203, 224
Papists *see* Catholic recusants
Parham, Sussex 39

parishes: disputes 131–40; expectations of
    clergy 36–8, 40–7
Parker, John 71
Parker, Richard 112
Parker, Thomas 34–5
Parker, William 55
Parliament 215, 216, 217
Parmeter, Thomas 157
Parnell, George 32
Parr, Ambrose 75
Parratt, Robert 196
Parrot, Jane 73
parsonages, repair of 37–8
Parsons, Atherwyn 226
Parsons, John 176
Parsons, Nicholas 84
Partridge, Simon 166
Partridge, William 131, 132, 133
Passfield, Francis 84
Paston, Northamptonshire 42, 55
Patterick, Mr (minister) 21
Pattinson, Master 106
Paul, Thomas 193
Pavie, John 146
Pawlett, Somerset 226
Payne, Agnes 163
Payne, John 105
Payne, William 129
Peacock, John 27
Peacock, William 150
Peakirk, Northamptonshire 111
Pearce, Mr (minister) 74
Pearson, John 173
Pearson, Mother 64
Pease, Master 29
Peep, Richard 124
penance 6, 9, 11, 48, 70, 125, 151, 153, 154,
    158–62; commutation 158–60; full 148,
    158, 160, 174, 204; learning the
    catechism as 60–1; mocked 160–1;
    refusals to perform 6, 69, 160, 163, 223;
    re-offenders 147, 161; sympathy for
    penitents, and disputes over 161–2
Penfold, Richard 67–8
Penn, Thomas 119
Penn, William 92
Pensford, Somerset 45, 118, 163
Pentall, Goodwife 154
Penton Mewsey, Hampshire 196
perambulations 34
Perke, John 23
Perkins, William 124, 130, 207; *Six Principles*
    63, 113
Perriman, Aaron 111
Perrott, John 124
Perry, Philip 131, 132
Peryn, William 102

Pestell, Thomas 47, 48, 52, 220
Peterborough: burials of excommunicates 71,
    77; cathedral 90, 211; Catholic militancy
    189; diocesan court 71, 77, 87, 88, 90,
    109, 111–12, 153, 161; dislike of David
    Owen 109; gadding 111–12; shopkeepers
    151; standing for the Creed 116–17;
    wizards 64–5
Peters, Richard 176
petitions 214–15
Pettit, Eusby 172
Pettit, John 82
Petworth, Sussex 86
pews: churching 107, 110, 119, 134; disputes
    over 218
Phelps, Mary 193
Philagathus (Arthur Dent's 'honest man') 3, 5,
    12, 50, 54, 59, 92, 122, 141, 221, 222,
    224; character 101; on popery 206
Philbricke, Ralph 85
Phipp, John 48, 167
Picke, Thomas 29
Pickman, John 111, 221
Piddington, Edward 134
Piddington, Elizabeth 134
Piddington, Oxfordshire 38, 74–5
Pierce, Thomas 150
Pierce, William, bishop of Bath and
    Wells 23–4
Piggott, Alexander 113–14
Pike, Joan 155
Pilat, Francis 54
Pink, Mary 47
Pinson, William 54
Pippen, John 86
Pippett, Jeffrey 165–6
Pippin, Matthew 70
Pitminster, Somerset 11, 112, 117
Pitney, Thomas 155
Pitsford, Northamptonshire 154
Pittiver, John 130
Pitto, Elizabeth 173–4
Pitton, Wiltshire 70
Platt, Thomas (of Hampshire) 187
Platt, Thomas (of Wiltshire) 91
Playfere, Thomas: *The Pathway to Perfection* 2
Pledger, Philip 113
Pleshey, Essex 212
Plumer, Thomas, wife of 65
Podimore Milton, Somerset 55
Pole, Roger 175
Poling, Sussex 62, 82
Pollet, Petronella 153
Poole, Robert 106
Poole, Thomas 161
poor relief 137, 205
Poore, William, wife of 155

Pope, John 80
Pope, Samuel and Agnes 75
Pope, Thomas 90
'popery' (as derogatory term) 119
Portbury, Somerset 82, 172
Porte, Ralph 47
Porter, Elizabeth 186
Porter, Isabel 186
Porter, Jeremiah 147
Porter, Robert 190
Portishead, Somerset 84, 149
Potter, Agnes 161
Potterspury, Northamptonshire 49,
    84–5
Powell, John, and wife 178–9
Powell, Thomas 155
Pratt, Robert 18
prayers: considered more important than
    sermons 225; kneeling for 119; new 116;
    see also Lord's Prayer
preaching *see* sermons
predestination 24–6, 123, 126, 145, 189,
    209, 210
Prentice, John 120
Prentice, Richard 178
Presgrave, Mr (apparitor) 152
Presgrave, Silvester and Agnes 126
Presgrave, William 64
Prestbury, Gloucestershire 39
Preston, Northamptonshire 27
Preston Plucknett, Somerset 153
Preston upon Stour, Gloucestershire 157
Price, Lewis 27
prices 205, 207
'priest' (as derogatory term) 51
Prim, William 136, 219
Prince, John 193
Prior, Thomas 168, 169
Priston, Somerset 97, 156
Prittlewell, Essex 80, 103
professors *see* godly, the
Protestantism: blamed for England's
    problems 203–4; Catholic objections to
    185–7, 193–4; converts (to and from
    Catholicism) 189–91; effect on clergy 55;
    rejection of ignorance and superstition 59,
    63–4, 65; *see also* Calvinism; godly, the;
    nonconformity; 'puritans'
psalms 206
Publow, Somerset 149, 176
Puckering, William 50
Pulford, John 206
Pulleston, Toby 158
Pulleston, William 158
punishments: imprisonment 166; whipping
    47, 147–8; *see also* fines; penance
Purdie, William 33

'puritans' (as derogatory term) 46, 47, 102,
    104, 112, 118, 122–5, 126–9, 130, 131,
    164, 165, 205, 208–9; Bishops' War seen
    as rebellion of 213; Bolton's defence of
    209; and Civil War 215–16, 217
Purleigh, Essex 64
Pye, John 178

quarrels, unresolved: as cause of missed
    communions 73–4
Queen Camel, Somerset 34, 191

radicalism 125–6
Raffle, Philip 88–9
Ragdale, Robert 167
Rainham, Essex 75
Ramsey, David 188
Ramsey, Elizabeth 114–15
Ramsey, John 62
Ramsey, Essex 103–4, 175
Rand, Samuel 88–9, 169
Randall, Master 106
Randall, Toby 32
Ratcliffe, Thomasine 20
Rate, Lawrence 156
rate, church 9, 139, 170, 212, 213
Rathbone, Richard 33, 133, 134
Rathbone, Susanna 133–4
Raunds, Northamptonshire 63
Rayleigh, Essex 9, 54, 79, 81, 88, 97, 102,
    152, 153, 162
Reade, William 177
reading 113
Reading, Berkshire 206
recusants *see* Catholic recusants
Redburne, Hertfordshire 63
Redman, William 196, 224
Reeve, Ralph 178
Reeve, William (of Chipping Norton) 172
Reeve, William (of Milcombe) 113
Remington, Thomas 96
repentance 25, 76–8
'repetitions' 113–14, 115
Rettendon, Essex 96, 174
Reynolds, George, and wife 63
Reynolds, John (of Bardfield Saling), wife
    of 175
Reynolds, John (of Hockley) 91
Reynolds, John (of Ingatestone) 120
Reynolds, Mary 159
Reynolds, Nicholas 33
Rich, Sampson 54
Richards, Elizabeth 45
Richards, George 125
Richards, John 173
Richards, Thomas 82

Richman, Thomas 94–5
Ridgewell, Daniel 113
Ridgewell, Essex 21
Ridley, William 154–5
Ridlington, Rutland 109
Ridout, Walter 39, 51
Ridout, William 41
Rimpton, Somerset 10
Ringstead, Northamptonshire 69, 115
Ringwood, Hampshire 4, 123, 125, 222
Rixton, Ralph 29
Roane, Anthony 20
Robbin, William, wife of 72
Robbins, Henry 49
Roberts, Edward 88
Roberts, Hugh 137
Roberts, William 82–3
Robins, Henry 94
Robinson, George 173, 175
Robinson, John 54
Robinson, Mr (minister) 44
Rochford, Essex 95, 107, 118, 119,
    187–8
Rock, Thomas 34–5, 104, 226
Rockingham, Northamptonshire 161
Rodmill, Matthew 64
Rogate, Sussex 158
Rogationtide procession 119, 123, 136
Rogers, John 31
Rogers, Timothy: *The Righteous Man's
    Evidences for Heaven* 3–4
Romford, Essex 44, 61, 106, 111, 112, 114,
    129, 154, 162, 168, 186
Romsey, Hampshire 130
Romsley, Shropshire 31
Roode, Robert 96
Root, William 88–9
Roper, Richard 105
Rose, Humphrey 187
Rothersthorpe, Northamptonshire 88
Rothwell, Northamptonshire 65, 87, 88,
    116–17, 152, 171, 197–8
Roundheads 215–16
Rowdon, John 41
Rowe, Alice 166
Rowles, Richard 103
Rowswell, John 55
Roxton, Bedfordshire 225
Royalists 215–16
Royle, Jacob 169
Rudgwick, Sussex 85
Rumbold, James 73
Rushton, Northamptonshire 204
Russell, Alice 83
Russell, George 60
Rutter, Walter 114
Rye, Sussex 129, 196–7, 200, 224

Ryhall, Rutland 71
Rywell, Ellen 150

Sabbath (failure to observe) 6, 8, 92–7, 138,
    139, 207–8, 210, 217, 221, 227; 1618
    declaration on recreations 47, 136; 1633
    Book of Sports 66, 116, 221; dancing 45,
    47, 66, 92–3; disturbing the peace 10;
    drunkenness 66, 146–7; games and sports
    42, 84–5, 93–4, 136, 146, 152–3, 227;
    working 8, 10, 11, 42, 76, 86–7, 94–7,
    110, 130, 151–2, 207–8, 212–13; *see
    also* absenteeism
Sadler, Jeffrey 156
Sadler, Mr (minister) 54
Sadler, Thomas 156
Saffron Walden, Essex 80
St Albans: abbey church 104
St Ives, Huntingdonshire 42
St Mark's Day 45
St Matthew's Day 153
St Osyth, Essex 90, 119
Saintbury, Gloucestershire 96
saints, praying to 206
Salcott, Essex 118, 204
Salisbury, Mr (minister) 93
Salisbury, Wiltshire 10, 64, 115, 149
Salisbury, dean of 123
Salmon, George 87
Salmon, James 29
Salmon, Robert 84
Salmon, Thomas 150
Salterne, Robert 34
Sammes, Anne 28, 62
Sampford, Elizabeth 7
Sampford Brett, Somerset 167
Samuel, William 87
Sandes, Joan 190
Sandford, George 190, 194
Sandhurst, Berkshire 43
Sandie, Richard 138
Sandon, Essex 20, 118
Sares, Thomas 83
Saunders, George 23
Saunders, Nicholas 49, 212
Savage, Dr Repent 154
Sawkin, Abraham 103
Sawyer, Henry 199
Sawyer, John 199
Saye, Thomas 65
Scaldwell, Northamptonshire 21, 41, 92–3,
    130
Scarlett, Francis 220
Scarpe, Joanna 87
Scarr, Elizabeth 95
scolding 7, 9, 11, 46, 204

Scotland 198, 199, 200, 213, 214, 216
Scott, Elizabeth 76
Scott, William 74
Scudder, Henry 97
Seaman, Edward 50
Searles, Mary 69
Seaton, Beatty 108
Seaton, Rutland 112
Seaward, Thomas 138
Seeley, John 191
Selsey, Northamptonshire 18
Selwood, Henry 96–7
Seredge, William 32, 44, 45, 113, 219,
    220
sermons 9, 17–24, 36; centrality of (to the
    godly) 106, 110–13, 135, 221;
    complaints about 19–20, 21–3, 133;
    dislike of 205; disrespect for 167, 176; on
    election and predestination 24–6; failure
    to provide 131, 133; gadding 111–13,
    129, 215, 221–2, 226; hypocrisy 20, 21;
    Laudian 222; long and boring 90–2;
    mock 165–7; mock theme of 'malt'
    166–7; personal attacks in 21–4; political
    implications of emphasis on 207;
    'repetitions' 113–14, 115; Richard
    Bernard and 18, 20, 23–4; Robert Bolton
    on effects of 19
servants 5, 8, 18, 44, 46, 60, 61, 62, 68, 75,
    81, 159, 190, 193, 204; catechizing
    27–8, 29, 30, 220
services, behaviour during 87–92, 175–7;
    drunkenness 171, 172, 176; hat-wearing
    10, 89, 90, 120, 138, 139, 170; jokes and
    laughter 48–9, 88–9, 136, 137, 167,
    172, 175, 176–7, 211, 212, 223; kissing
    88; noise 175; sleeping 9, 11, 88, 89, 90,
    110, 120, 137, 158, 171; talking 87; *see
    also* absenteeism; communion; Sabbath
Severn, Andrew 72–3, 170
sewing 87, 88
Sexton, John, and wife 72
sexual immorality 6, 8, 20, 22, 38, 46, 47, 76,
    147–51, 223; of clergy 38, 74–5;
    deathbed confessions 70–1; and mock
    weddings 173–5; penance and fines
    158–60; prenuptial 44, 47, 159; at service
    time 86; *see also* adultery; illegitimacy;
    mothers, unmarried
Seymour, John 60
Shapwick, Somerset 178, 193
Sharp, Henry 103
Sharp, John 192
Sharpe, John 33
Sharpe, Richard 169
Sharpe, Thomas 118
Sharpe, William 211

Sharrock, Henry 46
Shaw, Robert 91
sheep-shearing 95, 167
Sheldon, Walter 161
Shelford, John 72
Shelley, Essex 62, 114–15
Shepherd, Dorothy 86
Shepherd, Edward 91
Shepherd, Matthew 153
Shepton Mallet, Somerset 49, 112, 114, 172, 178
Sherborne, William 117–18
Sherborne, Dorset 43, 85, 88, 151, 219–20
Sherfield, Hampshire 39
Sherman, William 220
Sherwood, Mr (minister) 103
Shiplake, Oxfordshire 205
Shipton, Oxfordshire 158–9
Shipton-under-Wychwood, Oxfordshire 73
shoemakers 94, 95, 96, 151
Sholeford, Henry 204–5
Shopland, Essex 111
shops 94–5, 96, 151, 157, 224, 226
Shorthampton, Oxfordshire 73
Shortred, Thomas 88
Shotbolt, John 178
Shrovetide 165, 174
Shuttleworth, Joan 157
Sibthorpe, Robert 89, 105, 117, 135–6, 137, 167, 199, 211, 213, 219, 220
sick, visiting the 131
sidesmen 8, 157, 158
Sidlesham, Sussex 153
Siers, Robert 189
Silvester, Arthur 190–1
Silvester, Samuel 156
Simms, Bridget 88
Simms, Thomasine 150, 223
Simons, John 131
Simons, Margaret 171
Simpkin, Cornelius 198
Simpson, Roger 54
Singleton, Sussex 150
sitting: for communion 9–10, 107, 108, 109
Skeat, John 189
Skington, William 88
Skinner, Thomas 65
Skirbeck, Lincolnshire 189
Slade, Edward 149
sleeping: in church 9, 11, 88, 89, 90, 110, 120, 137, 158, 171
Slindon, Sussex 93, 221
Slinge, Mary 188
Slipton, Northamptonshire 116
Slocombe, John 7
Slowe, Mrs 115
Small, Andrew 8

Small, Simon 70
Smallcombe, Thomas 21
Smart, Katherine 28
Smeaton, John 21
Smith, Anne 22–3
Smith, Clement 171
Smith, Dorothy 189
Smith, Elizabeth (of Abington) 20
Smith, Elizabeth (of Headbourne Worthy) 225
Smith, Henry (of Donyatt) 162
Smith, Henry (of Stadhampton) 75
Smith, Isabel 81
Smith, John (of Colchester) 119, 138
Smith, John (of Hambleton) 171
Smith, John (of Headbourne Worthy) 225
Smith, John (of Lydney) 49
Smith, John (of Marston St Lawrence) 73
Smith, Joshua 152
Smith, Richard 225
Smith, Robert (of East Hornden) 208
Smith, Robert (of Hatfield Peverill) 18
Smith, Robert (of Weeley) 104
Smith, Thomas (of Backwell) 170
Smith, Thomas (at Peterborough court) 161
Smith, William (of Edlington) 25, 189, 194
Smith, William (of Pitton) 70
Smith, William (of Winscombe) 72
Smyth, Edmund 87
Snead, William 83
Snook, Thomas 114
Soane, Elizabeth 212
Soane, Robert 110, 212
Soberton, Hampshire 96
Soden, Geoffrey 44
Some, Zachary 20
Somerset, John 170, 224
Somerton, Oxfordshire 190
Sompting, Sussex 64
Sonning, Berkshire 65
sorcerors 64–5
Sorrell, Rose 8, 193
Sorrell, Thomas 120
Sorrell, William 8
soul-sleeping 226
Souldern, Oxfordshire 76
Sounder, Helen 109
South, Katherine 110
South Benfleet, Essex 105, 106, 116
South Cadbury, Somerset 33, 173
South Cerney, Gloucestershire 90
South Hayling, Hampshire 90
South Luffenham, Rutland 27
South Ockendon, Essex 46, 168
South Petherton, Somerset 24, 49, 55, 149, 168, 212, 220
South Shoebury, Essex 1, 4

South Stoke, Oxfordshire 9
South Stoke, Somerset 44, 109
South Weald, Essex 82, 84, 109
Southam, Northamptonshire 109
Southampton: All Saints 54
Southend, John 171
Spain, fear of 196, 198–9, 207, 224
Spanish Armada 188, 196, 198
Spark, John 54
Sparrow, Barbara 22
Spaxton, Somerset 155
Speck, Arthur 66
Speering, Anthony 152
Spell, Gilbert 37
Spencer, Mr (minister) 74
Spigot, Humphrey 226
Spittle, John 176
Spode, Gilbert 51
Sponge, Joshua 43, 52
Spooner, Nicholas 106, 136
Spooner, Richard 62
sports *see* games and sports
Spratt, Master 117
Spratt, Thomas 112
Spratton, Northamptonshire 175
Springfield, Essex 20, 208
Springthorpe, Thomas 91
Spurgeon, Helen 174
Squeere, Thomas 9
Stadhampton, Oxfordshire 72, 75
Stamford, Lincolnshire 173–4, 175
Stamford Rivers, Essex 82
standing: for communion 110, 134, 137; for
    Creed 116–17, 118, 120, 128, 137; for
    Epistle 117, 118; for Gospel 34, 117–18;
    increased reporting of (from 1620) 222
Standlake, Oxfordshire 48
Stanford-le-Hope, Essex 131–3, 137, 222
Stanierne, Thomas 120
Stanion, Northamptonshire 64, 91
Stanley, Mr (minister) 74
Stansted Mountfichet, Essex 9, 96, 102
Stanton Drew, Somerset 160, 163
Stanton Harcourt, Oxfordshire 173
Stanton Prior, Somerset 45
Stanton St John, Oxfordshire 37
Star Chamber, court of 214, 218
Staughton, John 197
Staverton, Northamptonshire 49
stealing: at service time 86; use of sorcerors to
    find stolen property 64
Steeple, Essex 153
Steeple Ashton, Wiltshire 4
Stephens, Henry 167
Stephens, Robert (of Croscomb) 90
Stephens, Robert (of Wanstead) 192
Stephens, Thomas 75

Stephenson, Adam 50
Stepnoth, William 22
Stevenson, Richard 72
Steyning, Sussex 167
Stibbs, Robert 85
Stifford, Essex 87
Stock, Essex 86, 167–8
Stockland, Somerset 34, 96
Stoddon, Joan 76, 152
Stoford, Somerset 169
Stogumber, Somerset 102
Stogursey, Somerset 126
Stoke, Somerset 126
Stoke Albany, Northamptonshire 68
Stoke Bruern, Northamptonshire 33–4
Stoke Doyle, Northamptonshire 118
Stoke Gifford, Somerset 114
Stoke Lane, Somerset 102
Stoke St Mary, Somerset 111
Stokes, Thomas, Andrew and William 163
Stondon Massey, Essex 40, 189
Stone, Joseph (of Chelwood) 118
Stone, Joseph (of Shepton Mallet) 112
Stone Easton, Somerset 92, 221
Stonehouse, Gloucestershire 146
Stonham, Thomas 158
Stony Stratford, Berkshire 162
stoolball 9, 84–5, 93
Storre, William 54
Storrington, Sussex 55, 117
Stoughton, Thomas 205
Stow Maries, Essex 28, 32, 62
Stowell, Gloucestershire 32
Stowey, Somerset 84
Stradling, Francis 93
Stratford, Essex 84, 173
Stratton, Somerset 112
Street, John 102
Street, Richard 155
Street, Somerset 28, 96
Stretton, Rutland 105
Strickett, Janet 185
Strickland, Joan 27–8
Strickland, Thomas 21
Strode, William 166
Stroud, Gloucestershire 36, 37, 178
Strutt, John 91–2
Stubbing, Francis 163
Stubbington, Hampshire 177
Stubley, Ambrose 10
Stuckey, William 126
Sturgeon, John 9, 43–4
Stutbury, William, and wife 72
Sudborough, Northamptonshire 54
suicide 71
Sulgrave, Northamptonshire 79–80
Summings, Thomas 45

surplice 10, 30–2, 33, 34–5, 110, 123, 126,
    133, 134, 136, 137, 202; soiling of 216
Sutton, John 168–9, 223
Sutton, Thomas 22
Sutton, Essex 9, 43–4
Sutton, Northamptonshire 177
Sutton, Somerset 70
Sutton Scotney, Hampshire 83
Swalcliffe, Oxfordshire 44, 159
swearing 72, 76, 90, 97, 110, 119, 130, 145,
    153, 154, 205
Swinden, Gloucestershire 39
sworn men 134, 136
Sydenham, Mary 166
Sydenham, William 82
Symonds, Thomas 76
Syres, Robert, wife of 195
Syresham, Northamptonshire 88

Tabor, Elizabeth 156
tailors 151, 226
Talman, Alice 65
Tansor, Northamptonshire 54, 93
Taunton, Somerset 111, 115, 125, 226; St
    James's 212; St Mary Magdalene 62, 76,
    115, 163
Taylor, Florence 48
Taylor, Henry 169
Taylor, Joan 151
Taylor, John (of Skirbeck) 189
Taylor, John (of Wylye) 91
Taylor, Richard 170
Taylor, Robert 156, 172
Taylor, Sarah 119
Taylor, William 112
Taynton, Gloucestershire 7, 81
teachers 61, 114
Temple, John 71
Temple, Dr Thomas 218
tennis 84, 94
Terling, Essex 113, 118, 211
Tessimond, Margaret 186
Tetlow, Richard 38, 74–5
Tewkesbury, Gloucestershire 72–3, 107, 170
Thaye, Robert 85
Theologus (Arthur Dent's 'divine') 3, 5, 12,
    17, 218; attitude to Antilegon 145, 163,
    179, 208; attitude to Asunetus 18–19,
    59, 63–4, 78; on attitudes to the godly
    122, 129, 141; on doctrine of election
    24–5; favours confrontation 41; on
    minister as teacher 26, 36; on obstinacy
    and ignorance of men 30, 35, 56;
    relationship with Philagathus 101–2,
    110; on three kinds of reprobates 130–1;
    treated with respect 50; on ungodliness of
    Elizabethan age 207

Theydon Garnon, Essex 63
Thistleton, Rutland 116, 211
Thomas, Evan 44, 109
Thomas, William 160
Thomazine, William 8
Thomson, Thomas 174
Thorington, Essex 87
Thornbury, Gloucestershire 95
Thorne, John (of Barrington) 166
Thorne, John (of Norton) 61
Thornton, John 111
Thornton, Oliver 73
Thornton, Richard 148
Thornton Curtis, Lincolnshire 72
Thorp Achurch, Northamptonshire 51
Thorpe, Northamptonshire 88
Thorrington, Essex 7
Thraske, William 155
Threele, Thomas 200, 224
Thresher, William 167
Thrift, Mary 109
thunder 226
Thurlaston, Leicestershire 103
Thurleigh, Bedfordshire 37
Thurloxton, Somerset 61
Tibbut, William 149
Tichborne, William 44, 112
Tillie, John 116
Timsbury, Hampshire 187
Tinwell, Rutland 66
Tirrell, Thomas 120, 139
Titchmarsh, Northamptonshire 112
Titherington, Gloucestershire 39, 81
tithes 43, 53, 218
Todd, Mr (miller) 167
Tollesbury, Essex 83, 172
Tolleshunt Darcy, Essex 18
Tolleshunt Knights, Essex 111, 148
Tolman, Thomas 71
Tomkins, Lucy, Richard and Mary 148
Topsell, Edmund 207
Tormarton, Gloucestershire 172
Tovie, Margery 38
Towcester, Northamptonshire 8, 67
Towersey, Oxfordshire 178
Towlor, Joan 150
transubstantiation 189
Traske, Anthony 35
Trent, Dorset 166, 178
Tresham, Sir Thomas 197
Trevillian, Ralph 225
Trigge, Francis 204
Trinity 167–8
Trott, Grace 46
Trott, John 104
Trott, Richard 168
Trowbridge, Wiltshire 205

Trumell, Robert 17
Tuck, Anthony 169, 180
Tuck, Emma 169
Tuck, Thomas, 169, 223
Tucker, George, wife of 129
Tucker, Hugh 123
Tucker, Joseph 25
Tucker, Sarah 76
Tucker, Thomas 76
Tuckhill, William 109
Tuckley, Richard 106
Tuggle, Richard, and wife 81
Tuke, Thomas: *The Highway to Heaven* 2
Turland, Richard 72
Turner, George 158
Turner, John 188–9
Turner, William 161
Turvill, Richard 204, 205
Turvill, Thomas 59; *The Poor Man's Pathway to Heaven* (debate of Timothy, Ananias and Aquila) 2, 3, 4, 47, 65, 97, 102, 130
Twiverton, Somerset 21
Twyford, Hampshire 187
Twywell, Northamptonshire 173
Tydder, John 34
Tyse, Mr (minister) 20
Tyzer, Thomas 65

Uffculme, Devon 172
Unwin, Sarah 61
Uppingham, Rutland 50, 67
Upton, Somerset 62
Upton Noble, Somerset 213
Upton Scudamore, Wiltshire 33
urinating 171, 172
usury 166

Vavasour, Dorothy 186
Vere, Anne 109–10
Vere, Francis 168
Vigors, William 172
Vincent, Anne 34, 167
Vincent, William 148–9
Vine, Richard 75
Vinton, Thomas 197
violence 156; against clergy 54, 55, 214; by clergy 39; against communion rails 214; against puritans 217
Virel, Mathew: *Grounds of Religion* 78
Virgin, John 79, 180
visitation records 1, 2, 34, 37, 61, 62, 211

Wadd, Richard 66
Wade, Mr (judge) 154
Wadling, Elizabeth 47
Wadling, Joan 124

Wager, Widow 207
Waite, Thomas 38
Wakeford, Anne 84
Wakeford, Richard 167
Wakeham, Martha 158
Wakerley, Northamptonshire 171–2
Walcot, Somerset 156
Walden, Essex 87, 90, 94–5, 105, 119, 155, 179
Walford, William 65
Walgrave, Northamptonshire 147
Walker, Alice 130
Walker, Anne 61
Walker, Elizabeth 110
Walker, Richard 156
Walker, Roger 86
Walker, William 87
Walkwood, Toby 33
Wallander, Edward 155
Waller, John 75
Walmesley, John 49
Walter, Ralph 172–3
Walters, John 162
Walthamstow, Essex 52, 77, 83, 86, 152, 155, 178–9
Wanstead, Essex 130, 192
Wanstrow, Somerset 67
Wantage, Berkshire 63, 205
Warblington, Hampshire 191
Ward, Andrew 65
Ward, John (of Little Yeldham) 106
Ward, John (of West Ham) 67
Ward, John (of Winwick) 64
Ward, Master 111
Ward, Samuel (Ipswich preacher): 'Woe to Drunkards' sermon 146
Ward, Samuel (master of Sidney Sussex College) 52
Ward, Thomas 64
Ward, William 171
Wardley, Rutland 62
Warkworth, Eusebius 69
Warmington, Northamptonshire 93, 221
Warnham, Sussex 161
Warren, Anthony 161
Warren, Edward 48
Warren, Thomas 86
Warrye, Robert 150
Wartling, Sussex 191
Warwick, Anthony 195
Warwick 92
Wash, William 62
Washington, Sussex 51
Wastell, Simon 135
Waston, Anne 48
Wateridge, Philip 74
Waters, Elizabeth 96

Waters, Francis 35
Waters, John 93, 129, 137
Watlington, Oxfordshire 95, 151
Watnaby, John 43, 52
Watnaby, Lucy 43
Watson, Mr (minister) 52
Watson, Ralph 110
Watson, William, and wife 108
Watton, William 146
Watts, Matthew 139
Watts, William 88
Way, Richard 171
Wayte, Richard 226
Weald, Nicholas 29, 74
weather 95, 168
Webb, Anne 108
Webb, Joan 71
Webb, John 67
Webb, Martin 95
Webb, Mr (of Basingstoke) 44
Webb, Mr (of Cold Norton) 45
weddings *see* marriage
Weedon, Northamptonshire 68
Weedon Beck, Northamptonshire 107–8, 111–12
Weedon Lois, Northamptonshire 76
Week St Lawrence, Somerset 29
Weeke, Hampshire 187
Weekley, Northamptonshire 117
Weeley, Essex 104
Weldon, Northamptonshire 175
Welford, Robert 125
Welford, Northamptonshire 39–40, 88, 153
Wellingborough, Northamptonshire 20, 29, 87, 113, 170, 197, 224
Wellington, Somerset 155–6, 213
Wellocke, Elizabeth 87
Wells, Alice 28
Wells, Charles 111, 138
Wells, George 163
Wells, Somerset: apparitors 155–6; archdeaconry court 112–13; argument about excommunication 225; attitudes to courts 152, 153, 154, 155; Catholics 190, 192; consistory court 32, 166, 192; conventicles 115; diocesan court 23, 32, 96; maypoles 211, 226; St Andrew's 69; St Cuthbert's 8, 71, 81, 189, 192; sexual attitudes 149
Welton, Northamptonshire 64, 205
Wem, Elizabeth 88
Wendlebury, Oxfordshire 190
Wendon Lofts, Essex 60
Wenham, Sir Ferdinand 51
Wennington, Essex 20
Went, John 95, 138
Wentworth, Master 225

West, Jane 186
West, John 109
West, William 21–2
West Bergholt, Essex 37, 159
West Bradley, Somerset 148
West Ham, Essex 48, 67, 84, 86, 148, 156, 167
West Hanningfield, Essex 191
West Lidford, Somerset 115–16
West Mersea, Essex 155
West Pennard, Somerset 149
West Tilbury, Essex 147
West Wittering, Sussex 111
Westbourne, Sussex 17, 110–11, 114
Westbury, Gloucestershire 162
Westerleigh, Gloucestershire 111
Westham, Sussex 197
Westly, Samuel 82
Weston, Dorothy 194
Weston Bampfylde, Somerset 87
Weston Favell, Northamptonshire 27, 122
Weston Zoyland, Somerset 171, 177
Wetherall, John 54
Wexham, Buckinghamshire 156
Whale, John 20
Wharton, Mr (minister) 27
Whateley, William 107, 113, 140
Wheatley, Edmund 77
Wheatley, Edward 86, 130
Wheatley, John 76, 77
Wheatley, George 147
Wheatley, Oxfordshire 71, 195
Whissendine, Rutland 11, 64, 102, 149, 212
Whiston, Mr (minister) 46
Whiston, Northamptonshire 34
White, Alice 76
White, James 171
White, John (of Dorchester) 126–7
White, John (of Soberton) 96
White, Josiah 63
White, Mr (minister) 74
White, Robert 213
White, Sarah 151
White, Thomas 21
White, William (of Charlbury), wife of 69
White, William (of Grendon) 50
White Notley, Essex 113
White Staunton, Somerset 166
White Waltham, Berkshire 37
Whitfield, Thomas 31
Whitfield, Northamptonshire 63
Whitgift, John, archbishop of Canterbury 222
Whithead, Edward 90
Whiting, Joan 189
Whiting, John 90
Whitrip, Joan 107

Whitsun 20, 70, 72, 139, 208; celebrations 65–6, 128, 140, 141, 222, 227
Whittacres, Master 105
Whittington, William 90
Whittle, Richard 109
Wick, Anthony 156
Wickes, Edward 95
Wickham, Essex 75
Widford, Essex 61–2, 156, 157
Wieff, Mary 152
wife-selling 170
Wiffen, Robert, and wife 76
Wiggington, Giles 109
Wiggington, Richard, wife of 106
Wilby, Northamptonshire 113
Wildgoose, John 66, 116, 118, 128, 141
Wilkes, Denby 7
Wilkinson, Gregory 186
Wilkinson, Mary 28–9
Wilks, Dr 41
Williams, John 109
Williams, Thomas 28–9
Willis, Hugh 115, 125, 226
wills 6
Wilmington, Sussex 161
Wilson, Elizabeth 27
Wilson, Richard 187
Wilton, Somerset 152–3
Wincanton, Somerset 124
Winchcombe, Gloucestershire 33
Winchelsea, Sussex 211–12
Winchester: abuse of clergy cases 54; apparitors 155; courts 47, 60–1, 74, 186; recusants 186, 187; St Clement's 187; St Maurice's 187
Windsor, Florence 97
wine, communion 74, 107, 177–8, 185, 188
Winford, Somerset 32, 44
Wing, Rutland 169, 205–6
Wingfield, Roger 17
Winscombe, Somerset 63, 72
Winter, Richard 31
Winterborne Kingston, Dorset 55, 72, 168, 196
Winwick, Northamptonshire 64
Wise, Henry 175–6
witchcraft and wizards 64–5
Witcombe, Gloucestershire 154–5
Witham, Essex 95, 113, 156
Witney, Oxfordshire 116
Wittering, Northamptonshire 156
Wivenhoe, Essex 85, 163
Wix, Essex 76
Wokingham, Berkshire 116
Wolfe, Mary 37, 197
Wolgar, William 206
Wollaston, Northamptonshire 113

Wolvercote, Oxfordshire 198
women: behaving badly 179; bells rung for (when 'speechless') 178–9; catechizing 28, 29; considered outside the law 67; and conventicles 115; linked with witchcraft 183; mock baptisms 173; mockery of male authority 166; outspoken about religion 13; scolding 7, 9, 11, 46, 204; souls 149; *see also* churching; mothers, unmarried
Wonston, Hampshire 74
Wood, Francis 146
Wood, John (of North Petherton) 197
Wood, John (of Stanton Harcourt) 173
Wood, Joseph 81
Wood, William 204
Woodfield, Thomas 160
Woodford, Robert 198, 199, 213
Woodham Ferrers, Essex 38
Woodham Mortimer, Essex 110, 120, 151, 188
Woodham Walter, Essex 188, 207
Woodward, Catherine 167
Woolavington, Somerset 171
Wootton, Northamptonshire 150
Wordall, William 82
work: on Sabbath 8, 10, 11, 42, 76, 86–7, 94–7, 110, 130, 151–2, 207–8, 212–13
Workman, John 93
Worksop, Nottinghamshire 23
Worle, Somerset 39, 167
Wormell, John 178
Worsdell, Robert 94
Worsley, Grace 195
Worth, Sussex 46
Wortley, Henry 64
Wortley, William 149
Wotton, Northamptonshire 67
Wotton Underwood, Buckinghamshire 72
Wren, Matthew, bishop of Norwich 214
Wright, George, and wife 119, 222
Wright, John (of Helpston) 91
Wright, John (of Piddington) 75
Wright, Margery 87
Wright, Mr (minister) 156
Wright, Nicholas 155
Wright, Richard 88
Wright, William 84
Wrington, Somerset 32, 53, 62, 109, 116, 165–6
Wroughton, Wiltshire 84
Wylye, Wiltshire 47, 83, 91, 124, 140, 177
Wyn, Joan 226
Wytcher, William 153

Yapton, Sussex 93, 129, 137–8, 223
Yardley Gobion, Northamptonshire 84

Yardley Hastings, Northamptonshire 151, 163
Yates, Catherine 44
Yatton Keynell, Wiltshire 69
Yeo, Ellen 65
Yeovil, Somerset 34–5, 104, 169, 220, 226

York 185–6, 190, 194, 200
Yorke, George 61
Young, Edward 157
youths: catechizing 29, 30, 61
Yowe, George 226